Trafficking in Slavery's Wake

NEW AFRICAN HISTORIES SERIES

Series editors: Jean Allman and Allen Isaacman

*Books in this series are published with support from the
Ohio University National Resource Center for African Studies.*

David William Cohen and E. S. Atieno Odhiambo, *The Risks of
Knowledge: Investigations into the Death of the Hon. Minister John
Robert Ouko in Kenya, 1990*

Belinda Bozzoli, *Theatres of Struggle and the End of Apartheid*

Gary Kynoch, *We Are Fighting the World: A History of Marashea
Gangs in South Africa, 1947–1999*

Stephanie Newell, *The Forger's Tale: The Search for Odeziaku*

Jacob A. Tropp, *Natures of Colonial Change: Environmental Relations
in the Making of the Transkei*

Jan Bender Shetler, *Imagining Serengeti: A History of Landscape
Memory in Tanzania from Earliest Times to the Present*

Cheikh Anta Babou, *Fighting the Greater Jihad: Amadu Bamba and
the Founding of the Muridiyya in Senegal, 1853–1913*

Marc Epprecht, *Heterosexual Africa? The History of an Idea from the
Age of Exploration to the Age of AIDS*

Marissa J. Moorman, *Intonations: A Social History of Music and
Nation in Luanda, Angola, from 1945 to Recent Times*

Karen E. Flint, *Healing Traditions: African Medicine, Cultural
Exchange, and Competition in South Africa, 1820–1948*

Derek R. Peterson and Giacomo Macola, editors, *Recasting the Past:
History Writing and Political Work in Modern Africa*

Moses Ochonu, *Colonial Meltdown: Northern Nigeria in the Great
Depression*

Emily Burrill, Richard Roberts, and Elizabeth Thornberry, editors,
*Domestic Violence and the Law in Colonial and Postcolonial
Africa*

Daniel R. Magaziner, *The Law and the Prophets: Black Consciousness
in South Africa, 1968–1977*

Emily Lynn Osborn, *Our New Husbands Are Here: Households,
Gender, and Politics in a West African State from the Slave Trade
to Colonial Rule*

Robert Trent Vinson, *The Americans Are Coming! Dreams of African
American Liberation in Segregationist South Africa*

James R. Brennan, *Taifa: Making Nation and Race in Urban Tanzania*

Benjamin N. Lawrance and Richard L. Roberts, editors, *Trafficking in
Slavery's Wake: Law and the Experience of Women and Children*

Trafficking in Slavery's Wake

Law and the Experience of Women and Children

Edited by Benjamin N. Lawrance and
Richard L. Roberts

OHIO UNIVERSITY PRESS ↜ ATHENS

Ohio University Press, Athens, Ohio 45701
ohioswallow.com
© 2012 by Ohio University Press

To obtain permission to quote, reprint, or otherwise reproduce or distribute material
from Ohio University Press publications, please contact our rights and permissions
department at (740) 593-1154 or (740) 593-4536 (fax).

Printed in the United States of America
Ohio University Press books are printed on acid-free paper ⊛ ™

20 19 18 17 16 15 14 13   5 4 3 2

Cover image from PRO FO84/1310 reproduced with permission.

Library of Congress Cataloging-in-Publication Data
Trafficking in slavery's wake : law and the experience of women and children / edited
by Benjamin N. Lawrance and Richard L. Roberts.
    p. cm. — (New African histories)
Includes bibliographical references and index.
ISBN 978-0-8214-2002-7 (pb : alk. paper) — ISBN 978-0-8214-4418-4
1. Human trafficking—Africa. 2. Slave trade—Africa—History. 3. Slavery—Law and
legislation. 4. Slavery—History. 5. Women slaves—Africa. 6. Child slaves—Africa
I. Lawrance, Benjamin N. (Benjamin Nicholas) II. Roberts, Richard L., 1949–
HQ281.T7179 2012
306.3'62096—dc23
                                    2012027776

Contents

Preface

REPORTS AND images of human trafficking are appearing with ever greater regularity on television, magazines, and the Internet. Collectively they suggest that we are in the midst of an epidemic of trafficking. The most recent Trafficking in Persons Report from the U.S. State Department heralds the past decade's advances against the scourge of human trafficking, especially on the international scene. Indeed, the past decade has witnessed significant international advances in the fight against human trafficking, and progress has been made in combating human trafficking in many places throughout the world.

But it would be profoundly misguided to buy into the public and popular rhetoric that portrays human trafficking as a new phenomenon. Contemporary human trafficking is a modern rearticulation of an age-old human story. It emerges from the same deep social inequalities that render people vulnerable, poor, illiterate, and desperate. It occupies the same social and economic space in which reside others who are sufficiently wealthy, powerful, and eager to use and abuse the labor and bodies of others. This relationship, generating a persistent demand for slaves and submissive dependents, has done so for millennia. The sooner we understand the historical antecedents of one of the greatest humanitarian challenges confronting us in the twenty-first century, the greater our chance at combating it.

Our interest in human trafficking grows out of a shared commitment to explore historical and contemporary abuses of human rights and human beings and a shared commitment to promote conversations between those who study the past and those whose are engaged with the contemporary world. We strongly believe that historians, legal scholars, anthropologists, social scientists, prosecutors, criminologists, and human rights activists have a great deal to gain from one another by fostering such a conversation across disciplines and across historical periods.

We place a premium on scholarship that engages with pressing social and humanitarian issues. And this volume originated from precisely such an endeavor. It began as two-day international conference held at Stanford University's Humanities Center in 2009. This conference was the tenth in

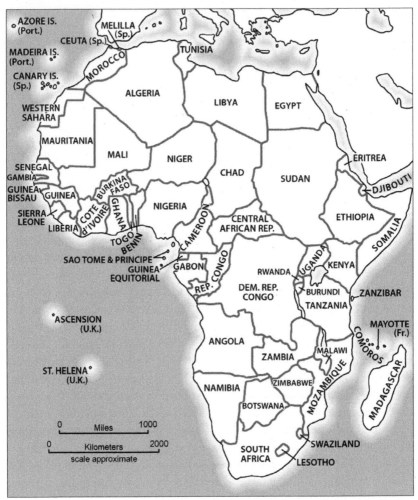

Africa, 2010

an ongoing series called the "Law and Colonialism Symposium." The Law and Colonialism Symposia have encouraged rigorous conversations across disciplines and time periods resulting in volumes addressing contemporary and historical approaches to major legal and human rights issues.

Attending the 2009 conference were scholars from Africa, Europe, and the Americas; they represented various disciplines including history, anthropology, criminology, legal studies, and literary studies. We would like to express our appreciation to all the participants at this conference. As we contemplated the geographical coverage of our volume, we also approached several other scholars and activists. Susan Kreston, Jelmer Vos, Liza Buchbinder, Jody Sarich, and Kevin Bales all agreed to write chapters for this volume that have added considerable depth and breadth to the core of the original participants. We certainly appreciate all their efforts.

We wish to express our appreciation to the Center for African Studies, particularly Diane Jakubowski and Kim Rapp, also the Dean of the School of Humanities and Sciences, the Stanford Humanities Center, and the Stanford University History Department for financial and logistical support for this conference. We also wish to thank various individuals who have provided expertise and support as this conference took the shape of an edited volume, including cartographer Don Pirius, Hugh Alexander at the Images Department at the U.K. National Archives, the anonymous reviewers of the manuscript, series editors Jean Allman and Allen Isaacman for their scholarly guidance, and Editorial Director Gillian Berchowitz and her team at Ohio University Press.

We remain committed to fostering productive conversations among those with different disciplinary orientations but with shared interests in making sense of the complex interplay of social, economic, cultural, and political forces that shape both the past and the present.

Contextualizing Trafficking in Women and Children in Africa

BENJAMIN N. LAWRANCE AND RICHARD L. ROBERTS

THE FALL of the Berlin Wall, in 1989, and the subsequent unraveling of the Soviet Union catapulted the problem of trafficking in women onto the world stage as impoverished Eastern European women were duped by recruiters into the sex trade and trafficked to Western Europe and throughout the world. But trafficking in women and children has a much longer history, and Eastern Europe was only one part of a much bigger and messier worldwide process of the exploitation of women and children. Africa is a central part of this story but one that has not equally captured the world's attention. Trafficking in women and children is linked to the history of Africa's involvement in the global trade in slaves. But it persists because of demand for unfree women and children both in Africa and abroad. Women and children are trafficked for the sex trade but also for a host of other domestic, agricultural, and commercial purposes.

In September 2001 a group of sixty-eight children, between eighteen months and eighteen years old, was rescued from a foundering ship off the coast of Cameroon and returned to Togo.[1] In April of the same year, a larger group of children from several West African countries were rescued from a vessel off the Nigerian coast and brought to the headquarters of the United Nations Children's Fund (UNICEF) in Cotonou, Benin.[2] Scholars and activists can point to numerous incidents involving the trafficking of children almost every year over the past two decades.[3] While various reports by UNICEF and the International Labor Organization (ILO) have previously estimated that as many as two hundred thousand West African children may be bought and sold by professional dealers each year, there is very little reliable data.[4] Trafficking in women and children affects all countries in Africa. Indeed trafficking in Africa has become such big business that vendors often operate hubs in Europe,

North America, and Southeast Asia and feed their human cargo into a much larger international network for trafficking women and children.[5] A 2006 report by the UN Office on Drugs and Crime (UNODC) estimated that "the market for smuggling human beings from Africa to Europe in . . . transfer fees alone could be on the order of $300 million each year."[6] Gail Wannenberg of the South African Institute of International Affairs views human trafficking as the second most lucrative form of organized crime in sub-Saharan Africa, after narcotics.[7] This collection of essays is designed to stimulate a conversation between historians, anthropologists, sociologists, legal scholars, practitioners, and activists, who too often work in relative isolation, and thus to enrich our understandings of this historical and contemporary social justice issue.

Women and children have been bartered, pawned, bought, and sold within and beyond Africa for longer than records have existed.[8] This collection examines the changing modalities of the traffic in women and children in the aftermath of the "end of slavery" in Africa, from the late nineteenth century to the present. The formal end of the slave trade and slavery did not end the demand for servile women and children. Slavery and the many forms of bondage, coercion, and subordination that have operated in Africa in the past are often juxtaposed with the nature of trafficking once slavery and the slave trade were made illegal. Contemporary traffic in women is increasingly conflated with prostitution; and descriptions of child trafficking often merge with critiques of child labor practices. Human trafficking is rapidly emerging as a core human rights issue for the twenty-first century.[9] Scholars, human rights activists, and criminologists need to be mindful of the long history of trafficking in order to better assess and confront its contemporary forms.

In this collection we are interested in the connections between the legacies of colonial conquest, the legal systems that undergirded domination, and the development of international, regional, and domestic legal instruments to address the persistence of trafficking in women and children. Each of the chapters identifies modes of trafficking of subordinate women or children (both boys and girls) and explores how formal and informal legal regimes and weak states contribute to human trafficking in Africa. Collectively the chapters presented here examine governmental and nongovernmental efforts to end trafficking at the local, subregional, and global levels. Several chapters also examine the pressures exerted by international legal conventions on trafficking—dating from the interwar period of the League of Nations and the ILO but continuing in the present day with the United Nations, the US Department of State (USDOS), the US Agency for International Development (USAID), and UNICEF, among others.

The incidents of 2001 narrated above are frequently characterized as part of a broader "humanitarian crisis" gripping sub-Saharan Africa.[10] But they are also part of a set of deeper historical processes throughout Africa. Crafty entrepreneurs have not suddenly turned to trafficking in women and children, but rather, as Beverly Grier has argued, the trade itself is built on antecedents reaching deep into the precolonial and colonial periods that created a dependence on household labor, child labor, and coercion.[11] Our interests reflect a desire to understand the historical context undergirding the structure and currents in the contemporary traffic of women and children in Africa.

Any historical analysis of trafficking in dependent laborers—women and children—into economic conditions not of their choosing must be situated within the wider literature on slavery, the transformations in and decline of slavery, the rise of pawnship and bonding of women and children, and the deeper economic transformations wrought by expanding colonialism and globalization. Indeed, economic transformations during the twentieth century, including the growth of industrial production, actually increased the demand for coerced labor.[12] A number of types of trafficking have been identified in Africa, ranging from abduction, placement for sale, transfers of pawns, forced marriages, and bonded placement, to kidnapping of children to become soldiers and sex slaves for armed conflicts.[13] Yet it is important to distinguish between the traffic in children and women and what has been referred to variously as "cultural placement" (the placement of subordinates with family members in better social and economic standing and marriages).[14] The enslavement of children and women has deep historical roots in and beyond Africa.[15]

TRAFFICKING AND INTERNATIONAL LAW

The early-modern European term *traffick* meant to engage in commerce, to transact, to buy and sell, and to negotiate or bargain for something, whether it was a commodity or a relationship. The term had a derogatory sense insofar as one may participate in a transaction that was either not quite proper or conducted in secret. By the end of the seventeenth century, the derogatory sense of the term was more pronounced. With the establishment of greater controls over the movements of goods and people in the course of the nineteenth century, *traffic* increasingly connoted illegal transactions. In the context of legislative efforts to abolish the slave trade in the eighteenth and nineteenth century, continued trade in slaves became *trafficking*.

Legislative abolition of the slave trade did not stop the trafficking in people. Where demand for coerced people continues, trafficking persists within states and between them. The late-nineteenth-century Scramble for Africa was publicly conducted under the "international" agreements signed by the handful of European nations in Berlin in 1884–85 that pledged to prohibit the export of slaves from Africa. European imperial powers reiterated their commitments to end trafficking in slaves with the General Act of the Brussels Conference, in

1890.[16] Yet few imperial states actively pursued this pledge. In the early twentieth century, antitrafficking efforts reappeared in international law. A twentieth-century innovation in international law was the increased use of the convention, which was an agreement for the regulation of an international affair of common interest that was not considered part of regular commercial transactions. In the realm of human trafficking, the first international convention was the 1904 White Slavery Convention, which sought to suppress the "criminal traffic" of women and girls "compulsively procured for 'immoral purposes.'"[17] While only thirteen European states signed this convention, it signaled the beginning of a concerted, though relatively toothless, international legal regime addressing human trafficking for sexual exploitation. Between 1904 and 1933, four different international conventions addressing trafficking in women and girls were signed.[18] The 1910 convention drew a distinction between trafficking in children, who could not give their consent, and adults, for whom compulsion had to be proved. This distinction remains present in the most recent international conventions regarding trafficking and continues to confound efforts at implementation and enforcement of antitrafficking law. The 1910 convention initiated a twentieth-century revival of humanitarian sensibility regarding egregious labor abuses and trafficking in unfree labor.[19]

With its founding, in 1919, the League of Nations became the crucible for the development of what was to become a dense web of international treaties regarding human trafficking. Rightly criticized for lacking enforcement, the League's requests for periodic reports on state parties' adherence to conventions provided it with the ability to humiliate state signatories, as Richard Roberts describes in chapter 3 of this volume. The League's 1926 Convention to Suppress the Slave Trade and Slavery helped formulate an international legal definition of slavery as "the status or condition of a person over whom any or all of the powers attaching to the right of ownership are exercised." The convention also called on the signatories to bring about "progressively and as soon as possible, the complete abolition of slavery in all its forms."[20] Based on a detailed reading of the voluminous *travaux préparatoires* of the convention, Jean Allain (chapter 7) argues that the intention of those promoting the treaty was not a broad definition of slavery in all its forms, but rather a more limited purview over powers that stemmed from the right of ownership.[21]

In contrast, the 1956 UN Supplementary Convention on the Abolition of Slavery, the Slave Trade, and Institutions and Practices Similar to Slavery purposefully expanded the definition to encompass a broader range of coerced labor conditions, including debt bondage, serfdom, servile forms of marriage, and exploitation of children.[22] In the realm of international human rights law, the 1956 convention extended its mandate to include not just slaves (those owned by others), but those in "slave-like" conditions defined in part by high degrees of direct coercion and compulsion. The 1956 convention was thus congruent with the UN's 1948 Universal Declaration of Human Rights, which prohibited the slave trade and slavery and further prohibited the situation in which a person was held in servitude. To be held in servitude meant also to be held against one's will by violence, threats of violence, or coercion.

The last three decades of the twentieth century witnessed the elaboration of the webs of international treaties that provide the scaffolding for international human rights. The UN played a critical role in this process, but so too did regional conventions and an increasing body of judicial decisions emanating from regional and international human rights courts.[23] Especially important for the purposes of the international law on human trafficking were the Convention on the Elimination of All Forms of Discrimination against Women (1979), the African Charter on Human and Peoples' Rights (1981), and the Convention on the Rights of the Child (1989). Additional protocols clarified protections afforded to children and explained the differences between smuggling and trafficking from the standpoint of organized criminal activity, which we elaborate below.[24] Arguably the most significant changes in the international scene regarding human trafficking occurred in 2000 through a convergence of USDOS and UN activity. The enactment of the US Victims of Trafficking and Violence Protection Act of 2000 (VTVPA) required the department to issue annual TIP (Trafficking in Persons) reports, describing the nature and extent of trafficking in countries throughout the world that had "severe forms of trafficking in persons" and assess those countries' efforts to combat trafficking. A newly aggressive UN promoted the Protocol to Prevent, Suppress, and Punish Trafficking in Persons, Especially Women and Children (the Palermo Protocol), which required signatories to criminalize all acts of trafficking—including forced labor, slavery, and slavery-like practices.[25] TIP reports serve to highlight the global problem of human trafficking and have the capacity to embarrass individual countries into more aggressive action. The 1990s and the first decade of the twenty-first century witnessed the proliferation of international conventions against trafficking, the development of international case law regarding trafficking, and individual countries' efforts to legislate and enforce antitrafficking laws, which are examined in chapters by Margaret Akullo (chapter 9), Allain, Liza Buchbinder (chapter 11), and Susan Kreston (chapter 10).

Current international law on human trafficking appears to agree that three aspects must be present for there to be an *act* constituting trafficking. The first involves some form of the recruitment, transport, transfer, or receipt of a person. The second involves the threat or use of force, often high levels of violence, or other forms of coercion to control the person. And finally, the

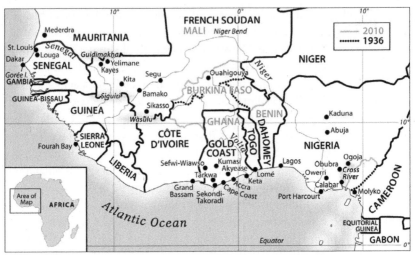

West Africa

subject of these first two aspects must be transported, recruited, or transferred for the purposes of exploitation.[26] Allain's chapter explores the history and status of the concept of exploitation in international human rights law. These three aspects of trafficking are referred to as action, means, and purpose.[27]

Three important issues emerge from this definition. First, a trafficked person need not be a slave, although those held in slavelike conditions were often subjected to trafficking. Second, "illegal," or undocumented, economic migrants are excluded, even though they are transported and often subject to coercion and violence, because the migrant consents to his or her transport. Moreover, the smuggler is not necessarily involved in the migrant's direct exploitation. The smuggler may extort migrants, but unless the smuggler is involved in the direct exploitation of the subject or her body, the purpose aspect of the definition does not apply. This distinction between trafficking and smuggling creates a gray area precisely because the degree of consent on the part of the subject person is often hard to assess, since certain groups are especially vulnerable to coercion. A girl or woman may, for example, consent to be smuggled by way of a variety of promises to find various kinds of work, only to find herself exploited in the sex trade. And third, the criminality of trafficking emerges as paramount by focusing attention on criminal prohibition and prosecution. This third issue points to the tensions between prosecution and protection as responses to trafficking violations. Trafficking is a human rights violation and states are required by international convention to provide protection for the trafficked person. Indeed the tensions between antitrafficking policies that focus on prosecuting criminals and those that protect victims are central to the larger debates about human trafficking and efforts to curtail the practices. Buchbinder's and Kreston's chapters in this volume explore these tensions in their studies of Nigeria, Togo, and South Africa.

MODALITIES OF ENSLAVEMENT AND ANTITRAFFICKING FROM THE ATLANTIC ERA TO THE PRESENT

The relationship between coerced labor and trafficking is embedded in a complex historical nexus that emerged in the context of the transatlantic, trans-Saharan, and Indian Ocean slave trades, and the reshaping of slave systems in sub-Saharan Africa by those regional external trades. Over the course of approximately one hundred and fifty years, the various slave trades and slavery were progressively abolished by statute or decree in different regions of the globe.[28] The many stages of abolition transformed what was previously a legally protected economic activity into an illegal practice. While there was illicit slave trading during the "legal" slave trade to evade taxes and duties, the extension of abolition created a qualitatively different conceptualization of illegality.[29] Western Europe and the United States established naval patrols, freedom courts, and freedom colonies to put substance behind their legislative remedy.

Reconceptualization of the slave *trade* as slave *traffic* represented a key rhetorical intervention reflecting legislative and diplomatic initiatives that progressively outlawed the slave trade and slavery itself.[30] Following its prohibition of the slave trade for its nationals, Britain pursued an aggressive international diplomacy designed to compel or "shame" other slave-trading nations into prohibiting the trade as well.[31] From 1833 to 1838 the British Empire dismantled slavery in its colonies (but not in its protectorates or dependencies), followed by France in 1848. By the 1840s the United States and the United Kingdom joined forces in policing the Atlantic. During the 1850s the slave trade, and indeed slavery, were progressively abolished throughout much of Central and South America. Illegality, established via bilateral and multilateral treaties, continued to fan out across the Atlantic, North and South, over several decades continuing into the 1860s, as ever more regions came under pressure. The final abolition acts of the Western Hemisphere were passed in Cuba and Brazil in 1886 and 1888, respectively.

The transformations in the Atlantic were echoed in the Indian Ocean from the 1870s and 1880s onward. Subsequently, antislavery activities were extended into the African continent. Beginning with the Berlin Declaration of 1885 and the Brussels Act of 1890, European powers with African colonial interests or aspirations regularly and repeatedly agreed to ban the slave trade and end slavery in their colonial possessions. Whereas most colonial powers formally abolished slavery, they often did little to enforce their decrees. Slavery persisted, as did the slave trade, although the scale of enslavement and the trade diminished from its heights during the transatlantic and trans-Saharan trades. Paradoxically, efforts to suppress the slave trade in the Atlantic stimulated the slave trade in the Indian Ocean. The greatest expansion of the slave trade in the Indian Ocean occurred in the nineteenth century.[32] As Bernard Freamon demonstrates (chapter 6), not only were women and children central to the expansion of slavery during the nineteenth and twentieth centuries, but indigenous articulations of Islamic law shielded many communities in the Horn of Africa and the Swahili coast from the Eurocentric legislative paradigms of abolition.

In this context of the expanding illegality of slavery and the slave trade, the conceptual complexity of the identities of trafficked women and children in the modern era is particularly visible. As Freamon, Elisabeth McMahon (chapter 1), and Marie Rodet (chapter 4) suggest, the dependent status of the women and children was partly responsible for the continued trafficking of women and children in Africa.

TRAFFIC IN DEPENDENTS: TYPES OF DEMAND AND FORMS OF SLAVELIKE CONDITIONS

After several decades of scholarship on the modalities of enslavement, we now know that men, women, and children were enslaved in strikingly different contexts. The end of the Atlantic slave trade influenced enslavement in Africa, but its impact was uneven over time and place on the continent. One of the great paradoxes of the abolitionist movement was to encourage the expansion of slavery within Africa as Africans sought to expand domestic production of commodities increasingly in demand for an industrializing world. With the onset of colonialism, preexisting forms of slavery morphed into vehicles for the extension of dependent labor. As described by McMahon and Roberts, small-scale raiding and kidnapping persisted and became central to the supply of unfree labor in the late nineteenth and twentieth centuries.

A crucial component of the history of trafficking of women and children is the persistence of demand, regardless of whether it is for domestic workers, child soldiers, or forced prostitution. Sex trafficking may be among the more visible elements of the worldwide trade in women and children, but it constitutes only one small part of historical and contemporary demands for coerced labor. Unfree women are valued for the full range of domestic services they provide, including sexual services, reproductive capacity, and labor power. Unfree women and girls work in households to augment family labor, as Rodet describes in this volume, but they also perform hard agricultural labor, carry water, and collect firewood over long distances. Various incarnations of patriarchy also feed demand for unfree women, and patriarchs seek to accumulate as many women and children as they can. Demand for trafficked children persists also because of the range of services they, too, provide. Carina Ray (chapter 5) describes the flow of trafficked girls for the sex trade in the Gold Coast, and Kreston examines the demand and supply of girls for the South African organized sex trade. Girls also contribute to domestic labor of all sorts. Boys are in demand for sexual services, but also for domestic work and for agricultural labor.

Pawning was one form of the circulation of coerced labor. Pawning of expendable lineage dependents functioned in a variety of capacities in the early premodern era, but with the arrival of Europeans along Africa's coastal zones, it shifted into a credit mechanism.[33] An unknown number of those sold into the transatlantic trade were pawns.[34] Pawning of women and children seems to have increased with the expansion of legitimate trade and colonialism as demand for credit and the potentialities for debt increased.[35] Pawning and bonding continues into the contemporary period, albeit in markedly different and discrete contexts, as the personal testimonies of children explored by Benjamin Lawrance (chapter 8) underscore.

Girls and women were bonded or pawned in the context of famine, rural distress, and economic depression. Parents or guardians (or both) pawned two of the girls aboard *La Amistad* possibly in response to environmental and economic deprivations.[36] As Audra Diptee has noted, "Not only would these parents be putting newly enslaved children into a circumstance that guaranteed them food and shelter, but the money obtained from the sale of their children also enabled the purchase of provisions for the rest of the family."[37] In addition, women and children could easily be disguised as family and thus evade the relatively feeble colonial suppression efforts. Indeed, as Roberts argues in this volume, on the rare occasion that colonial authorities had the capacity to enforce their decrees prohibiting the slave trade and slavery, they often did not understand how Africans disguised enslavement and the slave trade in African "practices." The kidnapping of women and children, transfers disguised as adoption or marriage, and other forms of peonage proliferated as colonial rule expanded.[38] Women and children constituted a significant share of the disguised slave trade from west-central Africa analyzed by Jelmer Vos (chapter 2).

Perhaps the greatest irony of the decline of adult slavery in Africa during the colonial period is that slavery-dependent communities and economies were forced to expand their use of child labor. In some instances, the expansion of child labor resulted from the acute labor shortage associated with the massive exploitative systems of extractive concession colonialism that demanded immediate results, including wild-rubber collection in the Belgian Congo and French Guinea, palm oil in Togo, and cotton plantation systems in Tanganyika, Chad, and the French Soudan. The excesses of colonial governments attracted the attention of human rights campaigners. Abuses in concession companies ushered in new regulatory roles for international and nongovernmental agencies, as discussed in Lawrance's chapter. As slavery declined, child bondage expanded. Gwyn Campbell, Suzanne Miers, and Joseph Miller argue that "child victims have been central" to the modern development of slavery and coerced labor.[39] Richard L. Roberts and Suzanne Miers argue that children were "more easily kidnapped, controlled, and acculturated."[40] Indeed, the trafficking of girls in northern Nigeria, western Ethiopia, Algeria, and Mauritania surprised and confounded European powers. As Ray describes in this volume, the presence of significant numbers of girls from the Cross River region of Nigeria in the Gold Coast during the 1940s became a major trafficking scandal within the British Empire. Many were trafficked to service the sex trade linked to the large presence of Allied troops in the Gold Coast. As colonialism drew parts of highland Angola closer to the metropole, Ovimbundu turned to child labor to produce the cash crops they sent along the train lines.[41] These are only two examples of the numerous consequences of colonial labor exploitation throughout sub-Saharan Africa.[42]

ACTION AND MEANS: FORMS OF TRAFFICKING

Throughout the colonial period and into the postcolonial period, traffickers of women and children sought to conceal their slaves in more slippery terms such as *pawn* or *bonded person*, or simply as their wives and children, thus disguising trafficking as cultural placement. In the precolonial period, pawns helped individuals and groups raise credit. In the colonial period, it was not uncommon for women and children to be pawned to others to raise money for taxes.[43] A pawn could be held for the length of a loan; the labor of the pawn paid the interest on a loan. Pawns could be redeemed outright, or, as was often the case with girls, they were married to their creditor and the bridewealth paid off the debt. Perpetual servitude could often stem from pawning, such as the contemporary practice of *trokosi* among Ewe in Togo and Ghana.[44]

Because pawnship and related statuses lay "in the vague middle ground" between formal slavery and fluid "African institutions," this was the site of considerable expansion of unfree labor during the colonial period, and it provides the key to understanding the growth in the sub-Saharan African labor trafficking in the colonial and postcolonial periods.[45] Toyin Falola and Paul Lovejoy identify several factors crucial to the operation of pawnship. The first is an ideology among many African communities that viewed pawnship as a form of "constructed kinship" that "functioned as a mechanism for reallocating individuals as a means of acquiring capital or providing security for debt."[46] Pawnship was tied closely to marriage, especially "forced marriage."

While pawnship appears to be a prevailing paradigm whereby children and women entered trafficking networks, the chapters in this volume also point to the persistence of a second avenue of recruitment and one that has proliferated in the context of present-day regional and civil wars.[47] Violent abduction,

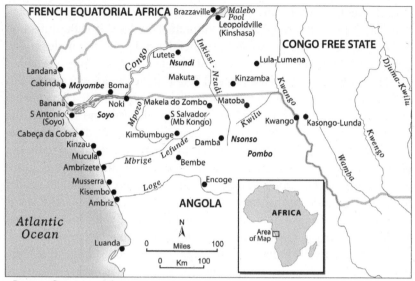

Lower Congo, c. 1890

particularly in contexts of conflict, included capture in wars and targeted kidnapping.[48] Small-scale and opportunistic kidnapping was also a source of trafficked women and children during the colonial and postcolonial periods. Chapters by Freamon, Kreston, McMahon, Roberts, and Vos in this volume all describe cases of violent kidnapping and abduction. McMahon contributes to this debate when she argues in this volume for the concept of social vulnerability; women and children were especially vulnerable to kidnapping when they were alone or in small groups. Recently freed slaves who lived apart from their former masters were also especially vulnerable to opportunistic kidnapping and reenslavement precisely because they were not enmeshed in dense kinship networks that reduced social vulnerabilities. Freamon describes the long history and wide geographical reach of trafficking in women and children in the Islamic parts of the Indian Ocean world. Abductions in the context of violence funneled women and children into trafficking networks throughout the late twentieth and early twenty-first centuries in sites of conflict such as Sierra Leone and Liberia, and more recently the conscripted child armies of Uganda, Sudan, Central African Republic, Democratic Republic of the Congo, Côte d'Ivoire, and Guinea-Bissau.[49]

EXPLOITATION: THE WORK OF
TRAFFICKED WOMEN AND CHILDREN

There are and have been many ways of recruiting dependent women and children. Marriage, adoption, indenture, bonding, slavery, and the free market, among other means, have been used to recruit and coerce dependent labor. From the standpoint of antitrafficking laws, it is the intention of the recruiter or user to exploit his or her dependent's labor under conditions of coercion and use or threats of violence that determines whether an act of trafficking has taken place. There is therefore a vagueness in this definition as exploitation and coercion may exist in the free-labor market and in marriages. Anne Gallagher argues that the Palermo Protocol (the aforementioned 2000 UN trafficking protocol) does not define exploitation, but rather provides a list of contexts in which exploitation of trafficked people occurs: "the exploitation of the prostitution of others, or other forms of sexual exploitation, forced labour or services, slavery or practices similar to slavery, servitude, or the removal of organs."[50] Explaining the legal status of the concept of exploitation as linked to the issues of trafficking is central to Allain's chapter in this volume. Allain traces the convergence of the legal regimes dealing with trafficking and exploitation and explores how these practices were elaborated over the course of the major twentieth-century international conventions.

At the core of the problem of trafficking lies the issue of demand. Those at the end of the chain of acquisition of dependent and exploitable labor are interested in acquiring labor for a whole host of reasons including enhancing patriarchy, power, and financial reward. Chapters in this volume provide case studies of the connections between trafficking and exploitation. Rodet describes how the demand for coercible dependent female and juvenile female labor coincided with the end of slavery in French West Africa. McMahon explores how demand for coercible women and children resulted in kidnapping and trafficking. Roberts explores how the demand for coercible children for both agricultural tasks and for begging within the context of Senegalese traditions of Islamic education resulted in cases of trafficking. Freamon similarly explores how demand for coercible and exploitable women and children in the Islamic Indian Ocean led to a continued supply, even in the face of both Islamic legal restrictions and international legal efforts to prohibit such trade. Vos examines the recruitment and trade in trafficked women and children from west-central Africa. Issues of sexual exploitation of trafficked children are central to Akullo's discussion of Operation Paladin in the UK and lie at the core of Kreston's discussion of trafficking in girls and women in South Africa.

The status of the legal definition of exploitation is central to the late-twentieth- and early-twenty-first-century efforts to prevent and prosecute traffickers and users of trafficked person. It is also central to the debates among human rights advocates about the responsibilities of states toward trafficked people.

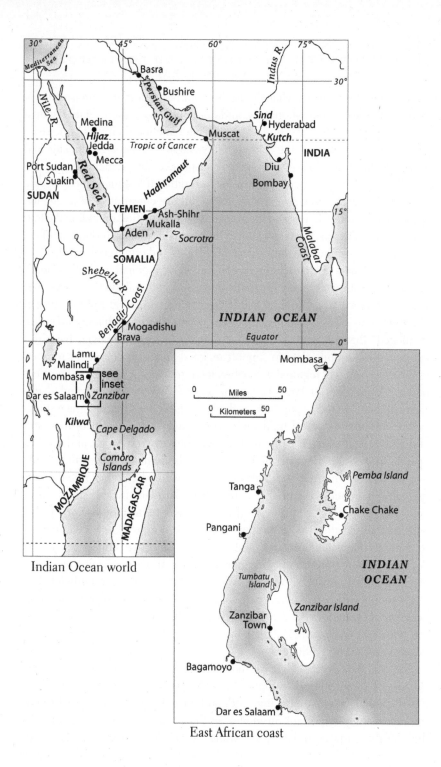

Indian Ocean world

East African coast

Collectively the final five chapters in this volume explore the intersection of humanitarianism, international law and domestic law, and interstate regional policies. Whereas the six historical chapters are anchored around close readings of archival evidence, the contemporary chapters approach trafficking and antitrafficking from diverse disciplinary perspectives but remain deeply empirical. The scale of coerced labor in Africa is difficult to gauge, and the scale of trafficking even more so, because they both are constitutive of a "hidden population."[51] Indeed, new and highly clandestine activities, including the trafficking of children in Africa and abroad for body parts and even ritual sacrifice, are further concealing the dimensions of mobility and criminal networks.[52]

Empirical data on trafficking may be domestic, regional, or Africa-wide.[53] Africa-wide estimates often emanate from international bodies concerned with exploitative labor, such as the ILO, which claimed 80 million African children between ages five and fourteen (or 40 percent of that cohort) were "exploited" through work in 1998.[54] A number of regional bodies have also attempted to compile data to support regional "plans of action" to respond to the emergence of regional and subregional trafficking networks. The Economic Community of West African States (ECOWAS) collects and shares national data "on the means and methods used, on the situation, magnitude, nature, and economics of trafficking in persons, particularly of women and children."[55] Trafficking is particularly big business in West Africa, and vendors operate hubs throughout the globe for which human cargo constitutes only one element of international networks for movement of other illicit goods, including narcotics, diamonds, counterfeit pharmaceuticals, small arms, and toxic waste.[56] The Southern African Development Community, for its part, established the SADC Strategic Plan of Action to Combat Trafficking in Persons, Especially Women and Children, effective August 2009.[57] As domestic and regional trafficking operations in Africa now constitute parts of larger global networks, African trafficking statistics are also embedded in international data sets. As some data sources are "classified," reports may have no references, such as the US Department of Justice's claim that 800,000 to 900,000 victims are trafficked globally each year and 17,500 to 18,500 are trafficked into the United States.[58]

National data on child labor is more accessible than trafficking data partly because of the institutional support the ILO provides in domestic data collection. National data on trafficking, while still uncommon in Africa, are becoming increasingly important for analyzing the contours of trafficking of children for the purposes of labor, but women as victims remain undercounted.

National labor surveys have been commissioned from all sub-Saharan African domestic statistics agencies. Few have been completed. At this time, data on child labor (but not dependent or subordinate women), much of it related to trafficking, is available only from about one quarter of sub-Saharan Africa. At best, these are educated guesses.

Reports investigating child labor tied to trafficking networks are often very detailed, but numbers are complicated by the variety of categorizations, which cannot be mapped neatly from one study onto another. Nigeria, for example, in a 2000 report, identified over 15 million "as working children," of whom 52 percent were male. Among other things it described so-called "new types of child labor," including "young bus conductors, child begging and scavengers and child prostitution."[59] In 2003 the Ghana Child Labour Survey estimated between 1.0 and 1.4 million child laborers, but set this against the specific constraints on child work as proscribed by the 1998 Children's Act.[60] The ILO estimated between ten and fifteen thousand West African children work on cocoa plantations in Côte d'Ivoire, sold by middlemen to farm owners for up to $340 each.[61] In the Tanzanian coffee sector, 60 percent of laboring children were girls and 40 percent boys, while in the country's tobacco sector the percentages were reversed.[62] Among six hundred working children interviewed in Gabon between 1998 and 1999, only seventeen were Gabonese.[63] A Ugandan survey of 16,345 households in 2004 noted that 20 percent had children "working for pay, 34 percent had children working without pay, while 21 percent had children working as a result of armed conflict."[64] Burkina Faso is experiencing an increase in child migration from rural communities to urban areas or abroad. A 2002 study showed that approximately 333,000 rural Burkinabe children between ages six and seventeen (9.5 percent) lived beyond close proximity of their parents.[65] And in South Africa, approximately ten thousand children perform "paid domestic work" wherein they "face conditions that are likely to be detrimental to their health or development."[66] Aderanti Adepoju divides trafficking in Africa into three broad categories: trafficking in children primarily for farm labor and domestic work within and across countries; trafficking in women and young persons for sexual exploitation outside the region (exportation); and trafficking in women from outside the region for the sex industry (importation).[67]

Trafficking of women and children continues to affect all countries in sub-Saharan Africa, and national and regional networks are also part of larger Africa-wide and transcontinental networks, as Akullo's chapter demonstrates.[68] Beginning with an assessment of child trafficking through Heathrow Airport, Akullo brings a criminologist's perspective to the European Union's efforts to curtail trafficking from Africa on Europe's borders and through bilateral agreements with African nations to enhance their capacities to police trafficking.

Kreston's chapter focuses on South Africa, which has emerged as a major regional site of recruitment and destination for human trafficking. Kreston critically evaluates the South African government's response to what is clearly a crisis in human trafficking in the region and far beyond with the perspective of a former child crimes prosecutor.

Women and children continue to be drawn into contemporary trafficking networks in ways that resemble the historical antecedents explored by Rodet and McMahon. Pawnship and kidnapping and various other forms of subterfuge provide a continuous supply of new coerced laboring subjects. Whereas the sources for Roberts and Rodet are colonial court records and administrative memoranda, personal narratives from trafficking victims and perpetrators today appear more often in the reports of a nongovernmental sector eager to attract attention to their respective causes. As Lawrance demonstrates in his chapter, the public relations advocacy adopted by "neo-abolitionist" humanitarian organizations in pursuit of their antitrafficking objectives produces important framing devices, in both the language of the reports and the use of imagery. NGOs may deploy resources on a regional basis. Some, such as Plan International and Save the Children, operate hierarchically and remotely.[69] Some, such as Anti-Slavery International, propose regionwide projects with multinational NGO cooperation led by one local partner.[70] Terre des Hommes deploys regional and subregional directors to oversee the projects of domestic NGOs.[71] Others coordinate networks of domestic researchers and finance the teamwork of local activists through jointly funded grants.[72] Irrespective of their internal operational structure, NGOs deploy the personal testimony of trafficking victims and perpetrators to accentuate the urgency of the humanitarian crisis and consolidate public opinion behind the need for a firm legislative response. In some countries, like Ghana, NGOs played a very direct role in the promulgation of new legislative instruments.[73] As Lawrance argues, the current proliferation of NGO activity on trafficking resonates with a rich vein of historical production originating with the activities of early abolitionists and missionaries.

The 2009 UN Global Report on Trafficking in Persons contains data on thirty-seven sub-Saharan nations. Each individual country summary contained important data. When interpreted collectively they demonstrate significant trends in sub-Saharan African trafficking. Some countries focus exclusively on children as victims and adults as perpetrators. Countries also provide data on traffickers and on prosecutions in which female traffickers account for a significant number of traffickers, ranging from eight percent in Benin to 62 percent in Nigeria.[74]

While child victimization and child labor are preponderant categories in sub-Saharan Africa, several nations also collected data on sexual exploitation and on adults both as perpetrators and victims. As Buchbinder's chapter demonstrates, Nigeria's national antitrafficking strategy is expansive and well financed. Buchbinder provides insight into two very different child antitrafficking approaches employed by Nigeria and Togo. Whereas Nigeria focuses primarily on suppressing criminal trafficking, Togo is more concerned with child "welfare" in their home regions as a means to reduce the incentives for trafficking.

The annual USDOS TIP report has richer comparative data on trafficking but focuses on the criminalization of trafficking and antitrafficking legislative developments. Increasing attention to criminalization and the abandonment of earlier attempts to lessen the demand for dependent labor, characteristic of the 1980s and early 1990s, reminds us of an observation of Jean and John Comaroff to the effect that legal responses only "appear" to offer remedy.[75] Unlike the UN-authored documents, the US report uniquely "ranks" states by their "compliance" with antitrafficking goals articulated in the 2000 US VTVPA and its subsequent reauthorizations. The US ranking of states demanded by the VTVPA has had profound implications for domestic strategies combating trafficking, as Buchbinder indicates.

Under US and international pressure, African nations are increasingly turning to criminalization as a strategy to safeguard the flow of development and aid monies. Ruby Andrew and Benjamin Lawrance's examination of domestic legislative programs suggests the emergence of several paradigms of criminalization and additional tensions as a response to US pressure.[76] As Akullo shows, European regional concerns, specifically with respect to immigration and unaccompanied minors, are also transforming how European nations understand trafficking, in particular when the subjects or victims are African.

╰╮

This book explores the continuities and discontinuities over the long history of the trafficking of African women and children for labor and sexual exploitation. The chapters in this volume provide insights for students of human rights and of trafficking in women and children to understand the complex interplay of history, ideology, globalization, labor demand, poverty, and social vulnerabilities in yielding persistent but changing forms of the demand and supply of coerced women and children in Africa and throughout the world. The conversations in this volume among historians, legal scholars, criminologists, anthropologists, and activists demonstrate that fuller understandings of historical trajectories of change are needed to deal effectively with contemporary global problems.

We believe that there is significant value in putting pressing contemporary issues into historical perspective. A deep, historical view enables us to critique patterns of antitrafficking legislation over time and offers important insights into contemporary debates. Collectively, the chapters analyze why some laws have never been effective and have had unfortunate consequences and why other laws have worked reasonably well. And equally important, the historical and contemporary chapters give a personal voice to the experience of women and children, from Mauwa on the Swahili coast in 1896 to Elsie in postapartheid South Africa.

Given the prominence of human trafficking in the early-twenty-first-century international agenda of human rights, a number of important issues remain unanswered. Core concepts such as slavelike conditions and exploitation remain vague. Common vocabulary as a way toward creating mutually intelligible reports and policies are needed. Greater clarity on the meanings of such core concepts will no doubt emerge in the course of regional and international court decisions regarding trafficking cases. Translating such agreement into concepts available to scholars and practitioners will be needed in order to advance informed policy.

Policymakers need to be mindful of the mutability of slavelike conditions over time and place. As several of our contributors discuss, traffickers during the colonial and postcolonial periods have been adept at disguising trafficked persons as wives and children, thus evading efforts at the international level to make more legible the acts of trafficking. Academic scholars can play important roles in providing policymakers with historical contexts and insights into local practices.

Most efforts to combat human trafficking have occurred at the level of supply, thus criminalizing the traffickers. The long-term success in combating trafficking can only occur if serious efforts to change the demand side of the equation are addressed. Such efforts will have to confront deep-seated cultural practices that exploit women and children. Thus, students of trafficking can contribute to informed policy by making clear the historical foundations and changes to the demand for coerced and coercible dependent labor.

Policymakers and scholars depend on good and accessible data. Despite efforts by the USDOS TIP reports and the requirements to provide information through the Palermo Protocol, good data on the scale of human trafficking are still not available. Part of the problem has been the focus on trafficking for the sex trade, which is a core component of human trafficking, but only the tip of a much more complicated phenomenon. Good data, common vocabulary, and a sensitivity to the mutability of human trafficking will contribute significantly to the efforts by historians, anthropologists, legal scholars, and human rights practitioners to better understand the problem of human trafficking and address its many incarnations. Human trafficking may be a central part of the twenty-first century human rights agenda, but it has long and deep historical roots.

NOTES

1. Suzanne Miers, *Slavery in the Twentieth Century* (Walnut Creek, CA: AltaMira Press, 2003), 427; "Child Slaves Returned to Togo," BBC News, 24 September 2001, http://news.bbc.co.uk/1/hi/world/africa/1560392.stm.

2. "'Slave Ship' Timeline," BBC News, 17 April 2001, http://news.bbc.co.uk/1 /hi/world/africa/1281391.stm.

3. Ticky Monekosso, "West Africa's Child Slave Trade," BBC News, 6 August 1999, http://news.bbc.co.uk/1/hi/world/africa/412628.stm.

4. The estimate of two hundred thousand has been widely circulated in news media and is partly based on D. Verbeet, "Combating the Trafficking in Children for Labour Exploitation in West and Central Africa," synthesis report, ILO/IPEC, Abidjan, July 2000.

5. Ticky Monekosso, "Africa's Trade in Children," BBC News, 18 January 2001, http://news.bbc.co.uk/1/hi/world/africa/1122416.stm.

6. UNODC, "Organized Crime and Irregular Migration from Africa to Europe" (2006), 19, http://www.unodc.org/pdf/research/Migration_Africa.pdf.

7. http://www.saiia.org.za/war-and-organised-crime-opinion/organized-crime-and -corruption-in-africa.html.

8. Suzanne Miers and Richard L. Roberts, eds., *The End of Slavery in Africa* (Madison: University of Wisconsin Press, 1988); see also Gwyn Campbell, Suzanne Miers, and Joseph C. Miller, eds., *Women and Slavery*, 2 vols. (Athens: Ohio University Press, 2007); Campbell, Miers, and Miller, eds., *Children in Slavery through the Ages* (Athens: Ohio University Press, 2009); Campbell, Miers, and Miller, eds., *Child Slaves in the Modern World* (Athens: Ohio University Press, 2011).

9. See Helen M. Stacy, *Human Rights for the Twenty-First Century* (Stanford: Stanford University Press, 2009), chap. 1.

10. See for example, Mahmood Mamdani, "The New Humanitarianism," *Nation*, 10 September 2008; special issue, *Disasters: The Journal of Disaster Studies, Policy and Management* 25 (2001); Liisa Malkki, "Speechless Emissaries: Refugees, Humanitarianism, and Dehistoricization," *Cultural Anthropology* 11, no. 3 (1996): 377–404; Makau Mutua, "The Interaction between Human Rights, Democracy and Governance and the Displacement of Populations," special issue, *International Journal of Refugee Law* (Summer 1995): 37–45.

11. Beverly Grier, "Invisible Hands: The Political Economy of Child Labor in Colonial Zimbabwe, 1890–1930," *Journal of Southern African Studies* 20, no. 1 (1994): 27–52; Grier, *Invisible Hands: Child Labor and the State in Colonial Zimbabwe* (Portsmouth, NH: Heinemann, 2005).

12. Kevin Bales, *Disposable People: New Slavery in the Global Economy* (Berkeley: University of California Press, 1999). See also David Kyle and Rey Koslowski, eds., *Global Human Smuggling* (Baltimore: Johns Hopkins University Press, 2001). For an earlier period, see David Northrup, *Indentured Labor in the Age of Imperialism, 1834–1922* (New York: Cambridge University Press, 1995) and François Renault, *Libération d'esclaves et nouvelle servitude* (Abidjan: Les Nouvelles Éditions Africaines, 1976).

13. For forced "marriage" in the context of war, see Annie Bunting, "Stages of Development: Marriage of Girls and Teens as an International Human Rights Issue," *Social and Legal Studies* 14, no. 1 (2005): 17–38; Jennifer Gong-Gershowitz, "Forced Marriage: A 'New' Crime against Humanity?" *Northwestern University Journal of Human Rights* 8, no. 1 (2009): 53–76; Jenni Millbank and Catherine Dauvergne, "Forced Marriage and the Exoticization of Gender Harms in U.S. Asylum Law," *Columbia Journal of Law and Gender* 19, no. 4 (2011).

14. International Labour Organization, "Stopping Forced Labour: Global Report under the Follow-up to the ILO Declaration on Fundamental Principles and Rights at Work: Report of the Director-General, 2001," 50; Esther Goody, *Parenthood and Social Reproduction* (Cambridge: Cambridge University Press, 1982); Suzanne Lallemand, *La circulation des enfants en sociétés traditionelles* (Paris: L'Harmattan, 1993); Jessaca B. Leinaweaver, *The Circulation of Children: Kinship, Adoption, and Morality in Andean Peru* (Durham, NC: Duke University Press, 2008).

15. Claire Robertson and Martin Klein, eds., *Women and Slavery in Africa* (Madison: University of Wisconsin Press, 1983); Campbell, Miers, and Miller, *Women and Slavery*; Campbell, Miers, and Miller, *Children in Slavery*.

16. Miers, *Slavery in the Twentieth Century*.

17. Anne T. Gallagher, *The International Law of Human Trafficking* (Cambridge: Cambridge University Press, 2010), 13, 55–59.

18. The conventions were signed in 1904, 1910, 1921, and 1933. By 1933, the twenty-six state parties exhibited a much more international character. See Gallagher, *Human Trafficking*, 57n16.

19. See, for example, J. P. Daughton, "Behind the Imperial Curtain: International Humanitarian Efforts and the Critique of French Colonialism in the Interwar Years," *French Historical Studies* 34, no. 3 (2001): 503–28. On the debate over eighteenth and nineteenth humanitarianism see Thomas Bender, ed., *The Antislavery Debate: Capitalism and Abolitionism as a Problem in Historical Interpretation* (Berkeley: University of California Press, 1992).

20. Articles 1 and 2, respectively, of the Convention to Suppress the Slave Trade and Slavery, 1926.

21. Jean Allain, *The Slavery Conventions* (Leiden: Nijhoff, 2008), 207–18; Gallagher, *Human Trafficking*, 181–82.

22. Gallagher argues that had the signatories of the 1926 convention intended a broader mandate over practices similar to slavery, there would have been no need for the 1956 convention to articulate the more expansive definition. Gallagher, *Human Trafficking*, 181.

23. Stacy, *Human Rights*, 141–69.

24. See especially the Optional Protocol to the Convention on the Rights of the Child on the Sale of Children, Child Prostitution, and Child Pornography (2000); the Protocol against the Smuggling of Migrants by Land, Sea, and Air, Supplementing the United Nations Convention against Transnational Organized Crime (2000); the Protocol to Prevent and Punish Trafficking in Persons, Especially

Women and Children, Supplementing the United Nations Convention against Transnational Organized Crime (2000).

25. US Department of State, Office to Monitor and Combat Trafficking in Persons, Trafficking in Persons Report 2010, "Introduction: 10 Years of Fighting Modern Slavery," http://www.state.gov/g/tip/rls/tiprpt/2010/142746.htm.

26. Gallagher, *Human Trafficking*, 78–79.

27. Ibid., 29–42.

28. Hugh Thomas, *The Slave Trade: The Story of the Atlantic Slave Trade, 1440–1870* (New York: Simon and Schuster, 1997).

29. See, for example, David B. Davis, *The Problem of Slavery in the Age of Revolution, 1770–1823* (Ithaca: Cornell University Press, 1975); Davis, *Slavery and Human Progress* (New York: Oxford University Press, 1984); Kenneth J. Banks, "Official Duplicity: The Illicit Slave Trade of Martinique, 1713–1763," in *The Atlantic Economy in the Seventeenth and Eighteenth Centuries*, ed. Peter A. Coclanis (Charleston: University of South Carolina Press, 2005), 229–51.

30. See Joseph C. Dorsey, *Slave Traffic in the Age of Abolition: Puerto Rico, West Africa, and the Non-Hispanic Caribbean* (Gainesville: University Press of Florida, 2003).

31. Keith Hamilton and Patrick Salmon, eds., *Slavery, Diplomacy and Empire: Britain and the Suppression of the Slave Trade, 1807–1975* (Brighton: Sussex Academic Press, 2009); Suzanne Miers, *Britain and the Ending of the Slave Trade* (New York: Africana, 1975).

32. Campbell notes that it is estimated that over two million slaves were exported from East Africa between 1830 and 1873, when slave shipments from Zanzibar were banned. See Gwyn Campbell, "Introduction: Slavery and Other Forms of Unfree Labour in the Indian Ocean World," in *The Structure of Slavery in Indian Ocean Africa and Asia*, ed. Campbell (London: Frank Cass, 2004), ix; Edward A. Alpers, "The African Diaspora in the Northwestern Indian Ocean: Reconsideration of an Old Problem, New Directions for Research," *Comparative Studies of Asia, Africa and the Middle East* 17, no. 2 (1997): 62–82.

33. Paul Lovejoy and David Richardson, "Trust, Pawnship, and Atlantic History: The Institutional Foundations of the Old Calabar Slave Trade," *American Historical Review* 104, no. 2 (1999): 333–55.

34. P. E. H. Hair, "The Enslavement of Koelle's Informants," *Journal of African History* 6, no. 2 (1965): 193–203; Ray Kea, *Settlements, Trade, and Polities in the Seventeenth-Century Gold Coast* (Baltimore: Johns Hopkins University Press, 1982); Joseph C. Miller, "The Significance of Drought, Disease and Famine in the Agriculturally Marginal Zones of West-Central Africa," *Journal of African History* 23, no. 1 (1982): 17–61; Lovejoy and Richardson, "Trust, Pawnship"; Lovejoy and Richardson, "'This Horrid Hole': Royal Authority, Commerce, and Credit at Bonny, 1690–1840," *Journal of African History* 45, no. 3 (2004): 363–92.

35. Paul E. Lovejoy and Toyin Falola, eds., *Pawnship, Slavery, and Colonialism in Africa* (Trenton: Africa World Press, 2003).

36. Benjamin N. Lawrance, "'All We Want Is Make Us Free'—The Voyage of *La Amistad's* Children through the Worlds of the Illegal Slave Trade," in Campbell, Miers, and Miller, *Child Slaves*, 13–36.

37. Audra Diptee, "African Children in the British Slave Trade during the Late Eighteenth Century," *Slavery and Abolition* 27, no. 2 (2006): 187.

38. Don Ohadike, "The Decline of Slavery among the Igbo People," in Miers and Roberts, *End of Slavery*, 437–61; Miers, *Britain*; Martin Klein and Richard L. Roberts, "Pawning in the Depression in French West Africa," *African Economic History* 16 (1987): 23–37.

39. Gwyn Campbell, Suzanne Miers, and Joseph Miller, introduction to Campbell, Miers, and Miller, *Children in Slavery*, 13–14.

40. Miers and Roberts, *End of Slavery*, 40–41.

41. Linda M. Heywood, "Slavery and Forced Labor in the Changing Political Economy of Central Angola, 1850–1949," in Miers and Roberts, *End of Slavery*, 415–36.

42. See Jeanne M. Penvenne, *African Workers and Colonial Racism: Mozambican Strategies and Struggles in Lourenco Marques, 1877–1962* (Portsmouth, NH: Heinemann, 1995).

43. Ohadike, "Decline of Slavery"; Martin Klein and Richard Roberts, "The Resurgence of Pawning in French West Africa during the Depression of the 1930s," *African Economic History*, 16 (1987): 23–37.

44. Robert K. Ameh, "*Trokosi* (Child Slavery) in Ghana: A Policy Approach," *Ghana Studies* 1, no. 1 (1998): 35–62; J. C. Goltzman, "Cultural Relativity or Cultural Intrusion? Female Ritual Slavery in Western Africa and the International Covenant on Civil and Political Rights: Ghana as a Case Study," *New England International and Comparative Law Annual*, 4 (1996): 53–72.

45. Miers and Roberts, *End of Slavery*, 46.

46. Toyin Falola and Paul E. Lovejoy, "Pawnship in Historical Perspective," in Lovejoy and Falola, *Pawnship, Slavery*, 9.

47. See Jerome S. Handler, "Survivors of the Middle Passage: Life Histories of Enslaved Africans in British America," *Slavery and Abolition* 23, no. 1 (2002): 25–56.

48. For sale by family members, see, Charles Piot, "Of Slaves and the Gift: Kabre Sale of Kin during the Era of the Slave Trade," *Journal of African History* 37, no. 1 (1996): 31–49; Joseph C. Miller, *Way of Death: Merchant Capitalism and the Angolan Slave Trade, 1730–1830* (Madison: University of Wisconsin Press, 1988), 380, 668; Miller, "Drought, Disease." For enslavement of children as punishment for parents' actions, see John Thornton, "Sexual Demography: The Impact of the Slave Trade on Family Structure," in Robertson and Klein, *Women and Slavery*, 41, 44.

49. Susan McKay and Dyan Mazurana, *Where Are the Girls? Girls in Fighting Forces in Northern Uganda, Sierra Leone and Mozambique* (Montréal: Rights and Democracy, 2003); A. S. J. Park, "'Other Inhumane Acts': Forced Marriage, Girl Soldiers and the Special Court for Sierra Leone," *Social and Legal Studies* 15, no. 3 (2006): 315–37; Karine Belair, "Unearthing the Customary Law Foundations

of 'Forced Marriages' during Sierra Leone's Civil War: The Possible Impact of International Criminal Law on Customary Marriage and Women's Rights in Post-conflict Sierra Leone," *Columbia Journal of Gender and Law* 15, no. 3 (2006); Jeannie Annan, Chris Blattman, Khristopher Carlson, and Dyan Mazurana, *The State of Female Youth in Northern Uganda* (Medford, MA: Feinstein International Center, Tufts University, 2008);

50. Gallagher, *Human Trafficking*, 34–35, quoting the Trafficking Protocol, art. 3(a).

51. Aderanti Adepoju, "Review of Research and Data on Human Trafficking in Sub-Saharan Africa," *International Migration* 43, nos. 1–2 (2005): 75–98; Guri Tyldum and Anette Brunovskis, "Describing the Unobserved: Methodological Challenges in Empirical Studies on Human Trafficking," *International Migration* 43, nos. 1–2 (2005): 18.

52. "Thames Torso 'Was Human Sacrifice,'" BBC News, 29 January 2002, http://news.bbc.co.uk/2/hi/uk_news/england/1788452.stm. See, for example, Jean Comaroff and John L. Comaroff, "Occult Economies and the Violence of Abstraction: Notes from the South African Postcolony," *American Ethnologist* 26, no. 2 (1999): 279–303; Lesley A. Sharp, "The Commodification of the Body and Its Parts," *Annual Review of Anthropology* 29 (2000): 287–328.

53. Loretta E. Bass, *Child Labor in Sub-Saharan Africa* (Boulder: Lynne Rienner, 2004).

54. International Labour Organization, *Child Labour: Targeting the Intolerable* (Geneva: ILO, 1998).

55. ECOWAS, *ECOWAS Initial Plan of Action against Trafficking in Persons (2002–2003)* (Dakar: ECOWAS Executive Secretariat, 2001).

56. See UN Office on Drugs and Crime, *Transnational Trafficking and the Rule of Law in West Africa: A Threat Assessment* (Vienna: UN Publications, 2009); Monekosso, "Africa's Trade."

57. Record of SADC Ministerial Meeting on Trafficking, Especially Women and Children, Maputo, Mozambique, 28 May 2009.

58. US Department of Justice, Human Smuggling and Trafficking Center, "The Human Smuggling and Trafficking Center: Fact Sheet: Distinctions between Human Smuggling and Human Trafficking," unclassified (2005), 3.

59. Nigeria, Federal Office of Statistics, *Report on National Modular Child Labour Survey Nigeria* (Nigeria: FOS, 2001), 26–27. The study identified 15,027,612 working children: 7,812,756 males and 7,214,856 females.

60. Ghana Statistical Services states, "According to the 1998 Children's Act, children under 15 years are not supposed to be employed. However, by all indications, 22.2 percent of children worked for pay, profit or family gain in the last 7 days preceding the interview. Thus according to the Act, 1,407,770 children under 15 years were estimated to be working in Ghana. Under the same law, however, children can be allowed to do light work if they are 13 years and above. This suggests that all children below 13 years who are in any form of economic activity are in child labour. On the basis of age alone, then, 1,031,220 children in Ghana

could be said to be in child labour." GSS, "Ghana Child Labor Survey" (March 2003), 137.

61. ILO-IPEC, *Lutte contre le trafic des enfants à des fins d'exploitation de leur travail dans les pays d'Afrique Occidentale et Centrale: Problématique du trafic des enfants en Côte d'Ivoire* (Geneva: ILO, 2000).

62. George S. Nchahaga, *Tanzania: Children Working in Commercial Agriculture, Coffee: A Rapid Assessment*, IWFCL no. 13 (Geneva: ILO, 2002), 10; A. Masudi et al., *Tanzania: Child Working in Commercial Agriculture—Tobacco: A Rapid Assessment*, IWFCL, no. 9 (Geneva: ILO, 2002), 14.

63. UNICEF, *Atelier sous-régional sur le trafic des enfants domestiques en particulier les filles domestiques dans la région de l'Afrique de l'Ouest et du Centre* (working paper, Cotonou, 6–8 July; Abidjan: UNICEF, 1998).

64. Uganda, Ministry of Gender, Labour, and Social Development, *Report of the Thematic Study on Child Labour and Armed Conflict in Uganda* (Kampala: ILO, 2004), iv–v.

65. Anne Kielland and Ibrahim Sanogo, *Burkina Faso: Child Labor Migration from Rural Areas* (Washington, DC: World Bank, 2002), 8–10

66. Debbie Budlender and Dawie Bosch, *South Africa Child Domestic Workers: A National Report*, IWFCL no. 39 (Geneva: ILO, 2002), 9.

67. Adepoju, "Human Trafficking," 76–77.

68. In South Africa seventy-nine Nigerian nationals were arrested in 2005 in connection with running a child prostitution ring. See UN Office on Drugs and Crime, *Organized Crime and Irregular Migration from Africa to Europe* (New York: UNODC, 2006), 31n64.

69. Benjamin Lawrance and Wendy Davies, e-mail communication, Plan International, 25 March 2009. See also A. M. J. Van Gaalen, *Review of Initiatives to Combat Child Trafficking by Members of the Save the Children Alliance* (working paper, prepared for the Save the Children Alliance Task Group on Child Trafficking, Montréal, July 2003).

70. Anti-Slavery International, "Projet sous-régional de lutte contre le travail et le trafic des enfants domestiques" (April 2003), inaugurated in Lomé, Togo, 2001.

71. See Inga Nagel, *Kinderhandel in Westafrika: Bericht einer Recherche zum Thema* (Osnabrück, January 2000).

72. For example, Les Associations d'Enfants et Jeunes Travailleurs is coordinated by Enda TM Jeunesse Action and financed by grants from Caritas, Enda Tiers Monde, Save the Children Suède, SKN Hollande, Terre des Hommes Deutschland, Genève, and L'Union Européenne.

73. Benjamin N. Lawrance, "From Child Labor 'Problem' to Human Trafficking 'Crisis': Child Advocacy and Anti-Trafficking Legislation in Ghana," *International Labor and Working Class History* 78, no. 3 (2010): 63–88

74. USDOS, Trafficking in Persons Reports, 2009.

75. Jean Comaroff and John L. Comaroff, "Criminal Obsessions, After Foucault," in *Law and Disorder in the Postcolony*, ed. Comaroff and Comaroff (Chicago: University of Chicago Press, 2006), 32

76. Benjamin N. Lawrance and Ruby P. Andrew, "A 'Neo-Abolitionist Trend' in Sub-Saharan Africa? Regional Anti-Trafficking Patterns and a Preliminary Legislative Taxonomy," *Seattle Journal for Social Justice* 9, no. 2 (2011): 599–678.

PART I

~

Trafficking in Colonial Africa

1 ⌇ Trafficking and Reenslavement

The Social Vulnerability of Women and Children in
Nineteenth-Century East Africa

ELISABETH MCMAHON

IN THE waning years of slavery on Pemba Island in the Zanzibar archipelago, a variety of people, mostly women and children, petitioned the British vice-consul for help because they had recently been kidnapped and trafficked as slaves. Scholars often focus on how the slave trade was suppressed during the abolition era; however, it is clear that slavery survived and was reinvented in new forms by traffickers eager to continue the lucrative process. Trafficking and abolition were not polar opposites in East Africa but rather points on a continuum. As the British cracked down on slave trading, trafficking began on a smaller scale, with individuals kidnapping vulnerable people, especially women and children, and enslaving them. While the British abolished the slave trade along the East African coast in 1873, it took several decades of consistent vigilance before the trafficking of large numbers of individuals began to diminish. Moreover, as Hideaki Suzuki has observed, the increase in kidnapping in the coastal and island regions indicates that as abolition of the slave trade progressed, the areas for "slave hunting" shifted from the large-scale interior caravans into opportunistic captures near coastal shores.[1] Kidnapping had certainly occurred throughout the nineteenth century in East Africa, but the locations and manner of trafficking shifted by the end of the century.

In 1895 a newly appointed vice-consul on Pemba Island attempted to extend British political and economic control to the island. Initially there was little intention that the he would have any interaction with enslaved people; he was there to protect the interests of British citizens and subjects (the island's Indian population). As both Richard Roberts and Jean Allain note (chapters 3 and 7, this volume), European states pushed abolition and antitrafficking policies, and yet they were loathe to enforce them in African colonies. Scholarship on abolition in Africa consistently shows that European colonizers were unwilling to confront the realities of the continuation of enslavement and trafficking in their regions.[2] The cases of women kidnapped into slavery in late-nineteenth-century Pemba are reflected in the developments and problems of trafficking found one hundred years later; in many respects little has changed. While bureaucracies and international agencies have expanded in the intervening years and pushed for expanding legal frameworks, the chapters in this volume show that, absent the will of officials on the ground, legislation alone will not stop trafficking. Moreover, much like the expansion of kidnapping from coastal territories in the nineteenth century, twenty-first-century traffickers continue to adapt their systems and find ways to work around the laws against trafficking. Jody Sarich and Kevin Bales's illuminating exposition on visas, in the afterword of this volume demonstrates that legal systems are continually manipulated to expand the numbers of enslaved people. The cases discussed in this chapter illustrate not only the problems of bureaucracies in dealing with trafficking but also how one official on the ground, willing to make a difference, may enact powerful change.

Most individuals, who complained to the British vice-consul on Pemba that they had been kidnapped, claimed either that they were slaves of someone else already, that they were freed slaves and as such could not be reenslaved, or that they were born free. For the people already slaves, reenslavement meant the unpredictability of new masters, under whom working may or may not have been easier. In general, slaves on Pemba were more likely to work longer hours at agricultural work, thus those captured from Zanzibar or the mainland were likely to resist efforts to sell them to a new master on Pemba. Freed slaves, usually women with no adult male relatives, were especially vulnerable to being reenslaved. For both these groups, reputation significantly impacted the results of their efforts to attain their freedom from the British vice-consul. Women who claimed to have been captured into slavery but never enslaved were less likely to get the vice-consul to believe them than women who either claimed to be slaves of someone else with a good reputation or who had been freed and could prove their community connections. These cases illustrate the vulnerability of women to enslavement. While colonial officials asserted a desire to emancipate slaves, in reality they wanted to emancipate male slaves only, not women. The law that concubines were considered part of the harem, and as such not able to seek emancipation until 1909, highlights the fears associated with allowing female slaves control over their own persons. The British government still viewed all women as dependents and believed a woman should be attached to a man. Women who were successful in contesting their reenslavement via the vice-consul did so because they either placed themselves under the protection of another person, usually male, or had recently lost their male guardian.

During the eighteenth and nineteenth centuries, kidnapping was a major form of enslavement for Africans, especially women and children.[3] The (in)famous narrative of Olaudah Equiano's enslavement began with children being kidnapped. Thus the notion of kidnapping as part of the enslavement process in Africa was commonplace. While scholars often focus on children, adults were also regularly kidnapped in the East African coast during the nineteenth century.[4] The records of Pemba abound with stories of kidnapped children, women, and occasionally men. From the men who were hired as porters but were tied up once on board a ship to the children and women who were kidnapped from the beach and even their homes,[5] the unexpected nature of kidnapping demonstrates the social and physical vulnerability, especially of women and children, in a slave-owning society. Even people born free had to protect themselves from the predations of slave traffickers and also their neighbors. The kidnapping and enslavement of neighbors is less commonly discussed in the literature on slavery. Andrew Hubbell has shown that people in the Niger Bend at times kidnapped their neighbors' children, causing intra-village conflict.[6] As I discuss below, people on Pemba at times turned to the kidnapping of their neighbors in an effort to repay debts or make extra money.

Kidnapping for enslavement, as well as reenslavement, was common in both the interior and coastal regions of nineteenth-century East Africa.[7] From as far north as Lamu to the interior districts and the southern coastal region, opportunistic capture of slaves was a common means of enslavement.[8] A British official stationed in Lamu in 1884 and 1885 complained regularly about the "slave stealers of whom there are plenty in the area."[9] In 1895 the vice-consul on Pemba reported concerns about a disreputable Arab who "was a notorious bad character and stealer of slaves."[10] Katrin Bromber notes that in German-controlled territories "the capture and sale of already freed slave women" was not uncommon.[11] While she argues this was "clearly different from the accepted norm," I would suggest, on the contrary, that it may not have been formally accepted, but nonetheless certainly happened often. Justin Willis argues that around Mombasa, kidnapping happened as early as the 1840s but that it increased by the end of the century.[12] As late as 1920, Harold Ingrams said that people living on Tumbatu Island fled when he arrived because "in the old days slave raiders used suddenly to descend on the island and kidnap any women and children they found."[13]

In the mid-1920s a missionary named Theodore Burtt from the Friends' Industrial Mission on Pemba, wrote down brief "life histories" of twenty-six former slaves living on the mission station.[14] From these records I draw some conclusions about the commonality of kidnapping along the Swahili coast during the late nineteenth century. Of the twenty-six former slaves, four were *mzalia*—people born into slavery on the islands—and the other twenty-two had been kidnapped into slavery. Of those kidnapped into slavery, fourteen were kidnapped as children and eight as adults, although one of the adult men was a dwarf, so he could have been initially mistaken for a child.[15] These data show the emphasis on children as the most vulnerable group to kidnapping and trafficking. Of the eight people kidnapped as adults, five were women. Females made up 66 percent of the overall kidnapped slaves as well, whether as children or adults. Kidnapping occurred with other relatives or friends one-quarter of the time—and these were always among groups of women and children. Females constituted 71 percent of those captured in groups, showing that they were more likely to be kidnapped with family members. Several of the male adults and children mentioned being kidnapped from "the shore," suggesting this was a real place of vulnerability for males. But most interesting is that 14 percent of the former slaves had been reenslaved by new captors and moved to new locations.

This trend of rekidnapping and movement from the kidnapping location was not unheard of. Donald Mackenzie reported in 1895 that "many of the slaves who have been set free by the Consul-General have afterwards been kidnapped and no trace of them has been found."[16] Whether kidnapped in Zanzibar, Tanga, Dar es Salaam, Bagamoyo, or elsewhere, all were taken far enough away that they could not easily seek redress. Even as late as the 1890s, numerous people complained to the vice-consul of being kidnapped in Zanzibar and brought to Pemba for sale.[17] The three kidnapping cases that I discuss in detail here point to a change in a more localized effort by traffickers to avoid the severe penalties they faced if caught selling or trafficking large numbers of slaves. Traffickers were vulnerable too—to new laws that enforced the abolition of the slave trade.[18] The kidnapping cases from Pemba suggest that traffickers began shifting their tactics in response to the new legal infrastructure of the 1890s: from a regional slave trade to a localized selling of slaves. As I argue below, such kidnapping or reenslavement may have been driven by temporary labor needs and not designed as lifetime enslavement.

This chapter explores the cases of three women from Pemba Island (Bahati, Mia, and Mauwa) who were kidnapped or claimed as slaves by neighbors during the 1890s, in a period when slave trading was no longer allowed but slave owning was still legal. While I focus on three women here, orphaned children were also particularly vulnerable to being "claimed" as slaves by neighbors.[19] Illustrating the social vulnerability of these women, in each instance the enslaved woman was either born free or had been living as a free woman for an extended period. Moreover, each was recognized in her community as a free individual. Yet, their other neighbors (and spouse, in the case of Mauwa) did not want to or were unable to defend the women's positions as free to those who enslaved them. All three women approached the vice-consul in the capital of Pemba to clear their names and assert their free identities. Critically, these three cases suggest that the phenomenon Bales describes as the *new* slavery, began well before the beginning of the twentieth century. Bales argues that among the changes from the nineteenth to twentieth centuries is that trafficking became more localized, as people were enslaved "temporarily," and that their enslavement was not based on a racialized identity but rather focused on their vulnerability.[20] These criteria, however, aptly describe the three women discussed here, which suggests that patterns prevalent in the modern era developed earlier than originally thought in response to abolition.

All three women were reenslaved within a two-month period during 1896. Mauwa, who brought her case last on August 25, said she had been taken from her home four months before her arrival at the vice-consulate. That would place her enslavement around early May, just before the June claims made by Bahati and Mia. May and June were still part of the rainy season on Pemba, which was longer than usual in 1896. The clove-picking season usually started in July, and it may be that clove tree owners were calling in debts before the season began in order to prepare for picking. However, the clove harvest for 1896 was particularly low because of the rains, and clove owners worried about profits as the rainy season wore on, knowing that longer rains meant fewer cloves. Regardless, it is particularly telling that all three women were seized during the prelude to clove picking, which suggests that temporarily enslaving people may have been a new practice of labor recruitment.

SOCIAL VULNERABILITY

The social vulnerability of women and children without male "protectors" (husbands, fathers, adult sons, owners) emerges through the variety of cases brought before the vice-consul. From the cases I will discuss, to the many examples of free women and children kidnapped and sold into slavery, it is apparent that women and children were more vulnerable in a slave-owning society, especially at the moment of enslavement.[21] As seen in the data from Burtt, children were more likely to be kidnapped than adults.[22] Suzuki notes that traffickers in the western Indian Ocean region preferred slaves between the ages of ten and twenty and rarely resold slaves over thirty, regardless of gender.[23] Thus children were the most vulnerable group and far less likely than adult women to attempt to attain their freedom. Regardless, the vulnerability of these individuals points to their need to be deeply integrated into their communities as a means of protection. Consular documents mostly record women's complaints, although trafficked children did on occasion seek help.[24] The women who were believed in the consular court had strong communal connections; the vice-consul was quick to dismiss women as untruthful if witnesses disputed their accounts.[25] Moreover, the vulnerability of slaves and kidnapped women is apparent in the refusal of a *kadhi* (Islamic judge) to hear cases brought by "slaves," which explains why so many of the kidnapped women sought help from the British vice-consul. Bernard Freamon argues (chapter 6, this volume) that not only did slaves have a legal right in Muslim communities to use the courts but that these women were clearly enslaved illegally according to the shari'a. Thus women were doubly vulnerable: to enslavement and to ineffective legal recourse.

As Bales notes, social vulnerability is the most important identity for enslavement. This is clearly visible in the preference of traffickers for women and children, people whose identities could be easily subsumed into whatever culture they were sold. Children were more likely to be able to adapt to new languages and cultures, and women who gave birth to children would be incorporated via their children.[26] Even in the cases from the Friends' Mission, one adult man was sold by his brother-in-law possibly because he was an orphan with no family network. As Suzuki notes, most traffickers in the western Indian Ocean were not "professionals" but rather individuals who saw an opportunity to profit.[27] Being vulnerable was the most important identity leading to enslavement.

Marcia Wright has raised the issue of isolation for slaves: "The terrors of cruelty were eclipsed by the terrors of abandonment. Passages [in ex-slave accounts] expressing desperation at being lost in the wilderness, compelled to take the risk of entering a settlement come what may, give evidence of this deep fear of isolation."[28] Thus the fear of isolation forced many escaped slaves into involuntarily reenslaving themselves. In West Africa, Alan Christelow suggests a similar phenomenon, "where slaves, particularly women, tried to escape, if they had no family to escape to, they usually wound up with a new owner."[29] Implicit in his point is that women were socially vulnerable actors in many African societies and most could not escape economic dependence on men or larger family lineages. Abdul Sheriff's work in the Persian Gulf shows that a number of African children and adults who were born free, even in the Persian Gulf, were kidnapped into slavery at some point in their lives.[30] Clearly, kidnapping and reenslavement were widely practiced in the Indian Ocean world. However, often these cases on the coast were isolated rather than systemic. In West Africa, kidnapping raids were regularized and whole populations created structures to protect themselves from outsiders; in the coastal islands of Zanzibar kidnapping was usually done as an opportunity presented itself.[31]

SLAVE-TRADING DECREES AND LEGAL STRUCTURES

The first step in the abolition of the slave trade came with the Moresby Treaty in 1822, which stated that Omani Arabs could not sell slaves to Europeans.

Also, any Omani ships east and south "of a line drawn from Cape Delgado to a point sixty miles East of Socotra and from there to Diu Head" could be searched and confiscated.[32] Only British naval ships, and specifically not the ships of the East India Company could stop them, severely limiting the effect of the treaty, because most ships in the Indian Ocean at that time belonged to the EIC. For the British, the treaty was about keeping African slaves out of India and Mauritius. For the Sultan of Zanzibar, the treaty gave him the support of the British in internal conflicts in Oman, as well as recognition of his rights in East Africa. The actual limitations to Omani trade were very small.

The Hamerton Treaty of 1845 further curbed the traffic in slaves. The treaty agreed that slaves from East Africa could no longer be transported to Arabia, but they could still be shipped between the African coast and the islands. The goal of the British government was to end the African slave trade to Arabia and then eventually shut down the trade within East Africa. Slowly, the British were putting a stranglehold on the East African trade. Enforcement of the treaties was handled by the British consul in Zanzibar; thus during periods where the consul was less inclined to impose the treaties, the slave trade thrived.

After Sultan Majid bin Sa'id's death, in 1870, the British played kingmaker to put his brother Barghash on the Zanzibari throne. Implicit in their support was the understanding that Barghash would help end the slave trade. Although Barghash resisted these efforts, in 1873 he succumbed to economic pressure and signed a treaty to end the slave trade, though not slavery. No longer could slaves be exported from East Africa, nor could slaves be transported from one port to another within the sultanate. Domestic slavery itself was not abolished and owners could take their own slaves with them when they traveled. Even with this treaty, the slave trade continued, albeit in a lesser fashion, and slaves were regularly smuggled into the islands of Zanzibar and Pemba.[33] The price of slaves also jumped tremendously during clove booms, increasing the cost of clove picking. The trade in smuggled slaves was of particular importance in the history of Pemba. With the Zanzibari slave market's closure in 1873, Pemba became a major island port, receiving as many as one thousand slaves per month during 1875.[34] The British navy regularly patrolled the waters around Pemba and skirmishes between naval vessels and Arab dhows often occurred. Until the end of the century, the slave trade continued unabated, although the British continued to patrol the waters of the Indian Ocean and seize slavers.

In 1890 the British government declared a protectorate over the Zanzibari sultan's territories. In August the British had the sultan issue a decree declaring that the "exchange, sale or purchase of slaves—domestic or otherwise is prohibited." While slavery as an institution was allowed to continue, several policies were put into place by the 1890 decree that would force its decline. In addition to the end of selling slaves, only the children of deceased persons could inherit slaves, meaning that other relatives could not inherit slaves, nor could slaves be sold as part of the estate. Another critical element of the decree was the granting of legal rights to slaves. In order to allow slaves to sue their masters for ill treatment, slaves were given access to the courts. Despite Qurʾanic injunctions that slaves should be able to use the courts, in Zanzibar they could not. A number of other rules stemmed from the decree, such as slaves' ability to purchase their freedom, and that all children born to slaves after 1890 were free. The 1890 decree was a major change in the legal rights of slaves and owners on the island. Elite Arab and European businessmen protested the decree, and within a year it was virtually ignored.[35] Thus, when the new vice-consul arrived on Pemba Island and began enforcing the laws of the 1890 decree, many of the slave-owning public were baffled and angered by his intrusions.

On paper, the slaves of the island had legal rights and recourse to the courts after 1890; however, the reality seemingly was very different. The flow of slaves and newly enslaved people to the vice-consul indicates that slaves were either not being heard by the *liwali* (wali, or governor) or in the Islamic courts or were unhappy with the outcomes of their cases. The latter is likely because by 1897 the liwali was unwilling to support slaves in courts. The missionary Theodore Burtt wrote in 1897, "This morning I heard that a woman had been sent by her master to work on another Arab's Shamba [farm]. Having good reason to believe that she was being sold, she ran away and complained to the Wali. He called in both the Arabs, who protested that she was not being sold. The [li]wali accepted their statement and sent the woman off with her new master."[36] This helps explain why none of the women discussed here mentioned going to a local legal representative before petitioning the vice-consul; they knew that local officials would not believe their word against that of those who trafficked them. Instead the women opted to seek out the individual empowered with "consular manumission," a practice of which the vice-consul regularly availed himself in the course of his duties.[37]

THE CASE OF BAHATI

On 10 June 1896 a woman named Bahati came to the vice-consul of Pemba, Dr. Daniel O'Sullivan-Beare. While Bahati had not been kidnapped, she had been forcibly reenslaved, and her case shows both the social vulnerability of women and the importance of having a network of people who could vouch for an individual's identity. Bahati's case also reiterates the jural minor status of women who had to have a male guardian in order to successfully survive, and the shift in legal avenues for women and slaves on the island. Additionally, Bahati's case illuminates the complete lack of enforcement of the 1890 decree, which stated that only children of deceased persons could inherit slaves.

According to Bahati, she was freed in the early 1870s, when still young. Her original Pemban master, Hamedi Cazi, died soon after giving her a freedom paper. Before his death Cazi requested that an Arab named Ali bin Mohena el-Mazrui protect her. Bahati grew up on Mohena's plantation and eventually married a free man. She moved to her husband's shamba and had three children. Bahati's husband died in 1894, and in 1896 Ali bin Mohena died. When Mohena died, his nephew who was charged with settling Mohena's estate claimed Bahati, her three sons, and all their property as his because, he asserted, they were slaves of Mohena. Bahati vehemently denied being a slave of Mohena, but the nephew refused to believe Bahati. The nephew's disbelief at Bahati's statement of her freedom hints at the contestation between slaves and masters.

Other cases from the period indicate that slaves attempted to circumvent the control of masters by refusing to be inherited or by running away.[38] Only a few months after the story of Bahati, another female slave came to O'Sullivan to dispute being inherited by the son of her deceased master. She claimed that she had been given a freedom paper before her master left for Mecca, where he died.[39] After his death, his sons refused to acknowledge her claims, and the vice-consul believed the brothers over the slave woman. In the case of Mauwa, discussed below, the man who kidnapped her claimed that he had inherited her from his father. Thus, both slaves and slave owners were clearly using inheritance in an effort to circumvent the British colonial laws.

In the case of Bahati, by the laws of the 1890 decree, the nephew of Mohena should not have been able to inherit her and her children because they would have been declared free. Clearly, the law was not being enforced, since Mohena's nephew did not think he had to justify his seizure of Bahati and her sons beyond the declaration of them as heritable property. When questioned by O'Sullivan, the nephew responded, "Bahati and her sons were all slaves of his late uncle, as Bahati had formerly resided upon the said uncle's shamba." Because Bahati could not produce freedom papers, the nephew assumed he was within his legal rights to claim her.

O'Sullivan investigated Bahati's case because "she [stated that she was] well known to her neighbors amongst whom she had resided for the past twenty years, that she and her sons were free people."[40] Her neighbors acknowledged that Bahati and her sons were indeed free and that she was considered part of the local community. Her ownership of land—which was uncontested when her husband died—as well as her children born to a free man, were recognized as markers of her own status as a free woman. Bahati convinced the vice-consul that she was a free woman through her integration into the community. In the vice-consul's deliberations, it never arose that the nephew was not legally allowed to inherit Bahati. The decision was based solely on Bahati's reputation as a member of her community and as a freed slave woman.

THE CASE OF MIA

As the story of Bahati attested, individuals could be reenslaved, even after years of freedom, and it was quite common for a person to be reenslaved multiple times.[41] Within a few weeks of Bahati's plea to O'Sullivan for help, another woman, named Mia, came to him for help. Around 1883, Mia had received her freedom from her master, Tippu Tip, one of the most infamous slave traders in nineteenth-century East Africa. Mia does not say how old she was when she originally received her freedom, but she did tell O'Sullivan that she lived in Bagamoyo, along the coast, not far from Pemba. Almost as soon as she regained her freedom, however, Mia was kidnapped, reenslaved, and brought to Pemba for sale to work on a clove plantation.

The 1880s saw an intensified period of the British blockade against the slave trade between the mainland and the coastal islands. Mia had been put on an Arab dhow with several other kidnapped people to be sold in Pemba. As they approached the island, a British navy vessel gave chase. The slave trader hustled his cargo onto the beach near the edge of the water and yelled for them to take shelter in the nearby mangrove forest. However, before the slave trader could get away, he was shot by the British and killed. The kidnapped "cargo" fled in different directions, knowing neither the intentions of the British nor the terrain. Mia does not mention traveling with any of the other enslaved people, suggesting that they likely entered local communities seeking help in order to avoid the devastating isolation described by Marcia Wright. Mia managed to make her way to the town of Chake Chake and threw herself on the mercy of the liwali, Baruk bin Bedwi. The liwali gave Mia her freedom, although he "committed her to the care" of Ibrahim bin Madini. Thus, Mia was still restricted to the charge of a man.

Mia lived on the shamba of Ibrahim for ten years but eventually moved out on her own. She did not give a reason why she decided to live on her own, but in 1893 she rented a small plot of land from a woman named Binti Hamadi. Mia supported herself by making and selling pots and growing vegetables for food. Mia contentedly lived on this plot for three years, regularly hawking her pots in the neighboring area. This gave Mia a public face; people knew her in the community. After about three years living near Binti Hamadi, Mia heard a knock on her door one night. It was Amur bin Suleiman, Binti Hamadi's husband. Amur seized Mia, tied her arms behind her back, and hustled her into a waiting canoe. Amur then took her across the Chake Chake Bay to the shamba of a man named Masood bin Abdullah.

After ten days at the shamba of Masood, Mia was able to escape and came to O'Sullivan for help. Mia's case demonstrates the changed legal atmosphere concerning slaves, because she went to the vice-consul instead of the liwali. The current liwali was the son of the one who had freed her thirteen years earlier, so it would seem likely that she would turn to the liwali for help. However, freeing slaves was no longer simply an easy way of building *baraka*, or blessings, in heaven; slaves were now commodities difficult to replace. If Mia had gone to the liwali, Masood could have argued, as he did to the vice-consul, that she was his runaway slave and since she did not have a freedom paper, he likely would have won his case before the liwali.

When interviewed by the vice-consul, Masood stated that he believed Mia to be a runaway slave of his from six years previous, and he was paying Amur for her return. Amur, on the other hand, completely denied kidnapping Mia. According to Mia, Amur knew she was a free woman because when she wanted to rent the land from his wife, Amur went to inquire about Mia from Ibrahim bin Madini, the man she had lived with for ten years. Amur's research on Mia showed his fear that Mia was a fugitive slave, and he did not want to harbor a runaway slave. His concern about her status when she initially rented the land raises several issues. First, that free individuals worried about angering slave owners by sheltering runaway slaves. Second, that the movement between being free and a slave could be as simple as escaping to a place you were not known. Third, people used their reputations to protect themselves. Fourth, by inquiring about Mia's identity and knowing she was free, he knew that no one (but Mia) would complain about reenslaving her.

Mia took her case to O'Sullivan because she categorized her kidnapping and transfer to Masood as the *sale* of a slave, not returning a runaway slave. Selling slaves was illegal at this point and would be cause for O'Sullivan to become involved. Mia's movement in the wider community selling her pots likely offered her an opportunity to learn more about the new vice-consul and his politics, as well as the 1873 decree against slave trading, which she already knew about from her own earlier experiences.

Mia was not the only slave who showed agency in her dealings with difficult masters and the British colonial state. An earlier case, from 1885, of a slave woman who did not want to be transferred by her master to Pemba from Zanzibar illustrates slaves' understanding of the 1873 decree against slave trading. In that case a slave woman told a friend who worked for the British navy that she was being taken "against her will" to Pemba and on what day and boat she was leaving. After the boat got underway, the British navy stopped it and liberated the female slave.[42] While many rural slaves probably did not know the details of sultanic decrees, those able to move freely in communities and urbanized coastal areas understood how to use the language of the law to protect their interests.

Another case from 1896 suggests that even individuals born on Pemba to free parents could find themselves enslaved. The story of Binti Mauwa illustrates the problems faced in the nineteenth century by individuals, and especially women, who were of the "African" population on the island. Binti Mauwa was an Mpemba woman, born free and married to a free man. While her husband was away, an Arab man named Abedi and his retinue of relatives and slaves came to her house one evening, tied her up, and took her to another Arab man in order to repay a debt. Binti Mauwa protested that she was a free woman, but both men ignored her pleas and Abedi so intimidated her that she eventually told the other Arab man that she was actually Abedi's slave.

After four months of living as a slave, she escaped and came to the viceconsul, who after inquiries declared that she was indeed a free Mpemba woman. Binti Mauwa's story indicates that for the elite population of the island, the local, free population was a de facto labor reserve. Taking a slave from someone was more likely to arouse the ire of another slave owner, whereas taking someone who was already free was far less likely to cause the kidnapper problems, as in the case of Mia. Many men went about the island armed, heavily in some cases, with a retinue of relatives and slaves who could help subdue any resistance to them.[43]

In the case of Mauwa, it is significant to look at the language and ideas that both she and Abedi, her abductor, used in their presentations to the viceconsul. When she arrived at O'Sullivan's office, Mauwa accused Abedi of kidnapping and *selling* her to the other Arab man. Abedi defended his actions in two particular ways that used the language of what he believed was acceptable practice. First, he argued that Mauwa had been his father's slave, and that when his father died, Abedi inherited her. This would have been a legitimate inheritance, if Mauwa were proven to have ever been a slave.[44] It may have been more practical to kidnap a person who was born free because they would not have a freedom paper, such as a former slave may possess. Second, Abedi argued that he had not sold Mauwa, but rather intended to use her labor to repay his debt to the other man. Clearly, Abedi was skirting the law by using the language of transfer of labor rather than of the person.

Just as Bahati and Mia before her, Mauwa was able to convince O'Sullivan to clear her name and remove her from the custody of the slave owner to whom Abedi had given her. A critical element of Mauwa's success in arguing her case was the testimony of her neighbors that she was indeed a free woman and was born on Pemba to free parents. Interestingly, Mauwa's husband never appeared to claim Mauwa or protest her disappearance. He was either gone for a long period, working as a sailor or on an overland caravan, or had left Mauwa but had not officially divorced her. Either way, his absence left her in a vulnerable position.

⌒

The stories of Bahati, Mia, and Mauwa offer insight into a number of aspects of life on Pemba Island during the period between the end of the slave trade and slavery. From the three stories, it appears that kidnapping and reenslavement were commonplace practices, against which individuals had to protect themselves. Their stories also show how reputation, respectability, and relationships in the community and with men were defensive devices for socially vulnerable women. An identity of landowning was not enough to offer individuals a guarantee of freedom; however, having neighbors who would attest to their identity did matter in regaining their liberty. Social vulnerability, rather than a racial identity, was the element that allowed these women to be trafficked.

The traffickers who abducted people followed very specific patterns. If they planned to take people to an entirely different area to sell—for instance, kidnapping them in Bagamoyo, on the mainland, and selling them on Pemba Island—then anyone could be abducted, regardless of their status. The unfortunate trafficker who made the mistake of abducting a slave of the sultan on Zanzibar regretted this pattern when he tried to sell her on Pemba and she told every would-be purchaser that she belonged to the sultan. She was an "unsaleable abductee" because her identity could so easily be traced. If a trafficker intended to sell the abductee locally, then it was much safer to kidnap a free or formerly enslaved person rather than someone who was currently a slave. A free person had a harder time proving they were free than did a person who was known as a slave. Moreover, a local slave owner would report their missing slave as a runaway and would be on the lookout; a free person would be less likely to be missed by neighbors.

Furthermore, when the kidnapped people appealed to the British vice-consul—and when the traffickers were brought before the vice-consular court—they both used the language of the Sultan's decrees in an effort to win their cases. The enslaved women did not bring suit on the grounds of being enslaved, but rather of being sold to another individual, which was illegal. Likewise, those who trafficked in abductees often tried to justify their behavior based on customary understandings of an ongoing patron-client relationship. The vice-consul did not help all the enslaved people who came to him for help, rather he weighed the evidence offered about the past history and relationship between the kidnapper and the abductee. The reputation of the enslaved women was crucial in his decisions.

The last issue these three cases illuminate is the change in attitude among slaveholders on the island after the 1890 decree. While the sultan essentially abandoned the decree and it was not fully enforced, its promulgation put the slaveholders of the island on notice that change was coming. This apprehension of changes related to slavery is one likely reason for the shift in the relationship between court officers and enslaved people who came to the courts looking for help. In the 1880s, when Mia went to the liwali for help, he gave her freedom, although it was decidedly attached to the "protection" of a man. But thirteen years later she turned to the vice-consul, rather than the liwali, for protection and defense of her standing as a free woman, highlighting the changing legal and social dynamics concerning slavery on the island. This change suggests that the trafficking of enslaved people was moving into a new framework for the illegal abduction of people into slave labor, a framework that would become more common in the twentieth century.

NOTES

Abbreviations

FFMA   Friends' Foreign Mission Association, Pemba
FHAL   Friends House Archives, London
ZNA   Zanzibar National Archives

1. Hideaki Suzuki, pers. comm., 14 November 2009.

2. See Kristin Mann, *Slavery and the Birth of an African City: Lagos, 1760–1900* (Bloomington, Indiana University Press, 2007), 5–6, chap.3; Paul E. Lovejoy and Jan S. Hogendorn, *Slow Death for Slavery: The Course of Abolition in Northern Nigeria, 1897–1936* (Cambridge: Cambridge University Press, 1993), chap. 2.

3. Paul Lovejoy, *Transformations in Slavery: A History of Slavery in Africa*, 2nd ed. (Cambridge: Cambridge University Press, 2000), 3–4; Patrick Manning, *Slavery and African Life* (Cambridge: Cambridge University Press, 1990), 88–89.

4. Michael Tuck observed that 36 percent of women were kidnapped. Tuck, "Women's Experiences of Enslavement and Slavery in Late Nineteenth- and Early Twentieth-Century Uganda," in *Slavery in the Great Lakes Region of East Africa*, ed. Henri Médard and Shane Doyle (Athens: Ohio University Press, 2007), 176.

5. Vice-Consul files AC2/24, AC5/1, AC5/4, AC5/5, AC8/5–8/8, AC9/2, ZNA.

6. Andrew Hubbell, "A View of the Slave Trade from the Margin: Souroudougou in the Late Nineteenth-Century Slave Trade of the Niger Bend," *Journal of African History* 42, no. 1, (2001): 39. Also see Suzanne Miers, "Slavery: A Question of Definition," in *The Structure of Slavery in Indian Ocean Africa and Asia*, ed. Gwyn Campbell (London: Frank Cass, 2004), 6.

7. Jan Georg Deutsch and Michael Tuck suggest small-scale opportunistic kidnappings were the *most* common kind. Deutsch, "Notes on the Rise of Slavery and Social Change in Unyamwezi," in Médard and Doyle, *Slavery*, 88; Tuck, "Women's Experiences," 176–77.

8. Patricia W. Romero, *Lamu: History, Society, and Family in an East African Port City* (Princeton: Markus Wiener, 1997), 55–59; Katrin Bromber, "Mjakazi, Mpambe, Mjoli, Suria: Female Slaves in Swahili Sources," in *Women and Slavery*, vol. 1, ed. Gwyn Campbell, Suzanne Miers, and Joseph C. Miller (Athens: Ohio University Press, 2007), 111–28.

9. Romero, *Lamu*, 59.

10. Vice-Consul, Pemba, to Consul General, 31 July 1895, AC5/1, ZNA.

11. Bromber, "Mjakazi," 118–19.

12. Justin Willis, *Mombasa, the Swahili, and the Making of the Mijikenda* (London: Oxford University Press, 1993), 74.

13. William H. Ingrams, *Arabia and the Isles* (London: Kegan Paul International, 1998), 29.

14. Theodore Burtt personal papers, notebook 1923–26, FHAL, FFMA, Pemba.

15. His size may have left him particularly vulnerable, as he was the only person among the twenty-six who was rekidnapped and sold on three separate occasions.

16. Donald Mackenzie, *A Report on Slavery and the Slave Trade in Zanzibar, Pemba, and the Mainland of the British Protectorates of East Africa* (London, 1895), 18.

17. Letters from Vice-Consul to Consul General, 10, 27 July 1896, 18 February 1897, AC9/2, ZNA.

18. Hideaki Suzuki, "Behind the Numbers: The Realities of Slave Trade in the Nineteenth-century Western Indian Ocean Based on Tales of Slaves," paper presented at the *Tales of Slavery* conference, University of Toronto, May 2009, 19.

19. As a young man, Saife bin Ambri said he was born to a free man, but when his father died the neighbor claimed Saife as his slave. For the story of Saife, see FHAL, PZ(F)/3 Pages of Register of Slaves and Case Notes, no. 16 of 1898.

20. Kevin Bales, *Disposable People: New Slavery in the Global Economy*, rev. ed. (Berkeley: University of California Press, 2004), 15.

21. See AC2/24 (7 January 1897), AC5/2 (27 June 1896; 2 July 1896; 27 July 1896; 25 August 1896), AC5/3 (4 May 1895), ZNA; Edward A. Alpers, "The Story of Swema: Female Vulnerability in Nineteenth-Century East Africa," in *Women and Slavery in Africa*, ed. Claire C. Robertson and Martin A. Klein (Portsmouth, NH: Heinemann, 1983), 185–99; Margaret Strobel, *Muslim Women in Mombasa, 1890–1975* (New Haven: Yale University Press, 1979); Marcia Wright, *Strategies of Slaves and Women* (London: James Currey, 1993).

22. Notebook, 1923–26, Theodore Burtt personal papers, FHAL, FFMA, Pemba.

23. Suzuki, "Behind the Numbers," 20.

24. See AC9/2 (18 April 1895; 10 July 1896; 18 February 1897), AC8/5 (9 September 1903), ZNA.

25. See, for example, AC2/24 (7 January 1897), ZNA. Also Susan F. Hirsch, *Pronouncing and Persevering: Gender and the Discourses of Disputing in an African Islamic Court* (Chicago, 1998), 67.

26. Suzuki, "Behind the Numbers," 21.

27. Ibid.

28. Wright, *Strategies*, 2.

29. Alan Christelow, "Slavery in Kano, 1913–1914: Evidence from the Judicial Records," *African Economic History* 14 (1985): 67.

30. Abdul Sheriff, "The Slave Trade and Its Fallout in the Persian Gulf," in *Abolition and Its Aftermath in Indian Ocean Africa and Asia*, ed. Gwyn Campbell (New York: Routledge, 2005), 113.

31. For defensive structures, see Walter Hawthorne, "The Strategies of Small-Scale Societies: Defending Communities from Slave Raiders in Coastal Guinea-Bissau, 1450–1815," in *Fighting the Slave Trade: West African Strategies*, ed. Sylviane A. Diouf (Athens: Ohio University Press, 2003). For example, one day a boy in Zanzibar was on the beach with his family's adult slave. When the slave was offered money for the child, the slave sold his master's son into slavery. J. E. E. Craster, *Pemba: the Spice Island of Zanzibar* (London: Unwin, 1913), 136. Robert N. Lyne comments, "Natives come with the most amazing stories of how they were kidnapped and sold." Lyne, *Zanzibar in Contemporary Times* (London: Hurst and Blackett, 1905), 187–88.

32. Moses Nwulia, *Britain and Slavery in East Africa* (Washington, DC: Three Continents, 1975), 43.

33. For changes in slave movement, see Jonathon Glassman, *Feasts and Riot: Revelry, Rebellion, and Popular Consciousness on the Swahili Coast, 1856-1888* (Portsmouth, NH: Heinemann, 1995).

34. See "Geography and Travels," *American Naturalist* 12, no. 11 (1877): 763; Nwulia, *Britain and Slavery*, 140.

35. Norman R. Bennett, A *History of the Arab State of Zanzibar* (London: Methuen, 1978), 166–67.

36. Theodore Burtt, *Slaves in Zanzibar and Pemba* (London, 1897), 3.

37. Suzanne Miers, "Slavery and the Slave Trade in Saudi Arabia and the Arab States on the Persian Gulf, 1921–63," in Campbell, *Abolition*, 121. Also see Sheriff, "Slave Trade," 115.

38. For Binti Mabrooki, see Elisabeth McMahon, "'A Solitary Tree Builds Not': *Heshima*, Community and Shifting Identity in Post-emancipation Pemba Island," *International Journal of African Historical Studies* 39, no. 2 (2006): 197–219.

39. Letters from Vice-Consul to Consul General, 22 December 1896, 7 January 1897, AC9/2, ZNA.

40. Sullivan-O'Beare, letter, 27 July 1896, AC5/2, ZNA.

41. Stories of Mia and Lasi, 5 July 1896, AC9/2, ZNA.

42. Manipulation of the system was common. See *Correspondence with British representatives and agents abroad, and reports from Naval Officers and the Treasury relative to the slave trade, 1885* (London, 1886), no. 101.

43. Letter, 25 August 1896, AC9/2, ZNA. For discussion of armed Arab men, see case files about Ali bin Abdulla, AC2/19 (1895–96), AB70/3, ZNA.

44. No evidence indicates Mauwa knew Abedi or his father before her abduction.

2 ⧢ "Without the Slave Trade, No Recruitment"

From Slave Trading to "Migrant Recruitment" in the Lower Congo, 1830–90

JELMER VOS

AGAINST A current of anti–slave trade measures adopted by Great Britain and its allies since the early nineteenth century, the slave trade in the lower Congo region of west-central Africa experienced a major revival between 1830 and 1860. Since the Congo River itself had become the heart of the Atlantic slave trade in Africa by mid-century, it also became the focal point of French efforts to recruit African indentured servants for France's West Indian possessions. This chapter examines the development of both the illegal slave trade in the Congo and the French legal migration scheme that was an integral part of it. The analysis concentrates in particular on the age and gender structure of the trade, which was increasingly biased toward male children, the origins of the slaves, and the causes of their enslavement. A final section looks at changes in the patterns of slave trading in the lower Congo after the closing of the export trade in the 1860s. On the eve of colonial rule a regional trade in slaves, driven by African demand and focusing on women and children, still continued. Its multiple directions were determined by the centers of wealth that were emerging throughout the region as a result of the new export trade in commodities.

THE ILLEGAL SLAVE TRADE FROM THE CONGO, 1830–65

From the late sixteenth century to the close of the Atlantic slave trade, in 1866, west-central Africa dominated the supply of slaves to the Americas. Of a total 12.5 million slaves shipped from Africa to the Americas, an estimated 5.7 million left via ports on the long stretch of coast south of Cape Lopez, in modern Gabon.[1] But the importance of the region as a supplier of labor for New World slave societies was never greater than in the nineteenth century, when roughly two million west-central Africans embarked on vessels carrying them to Brazil and Cuba by and large.[2] As Great Britain was relatively successful, by treaty and force, in suppressing the slave trade north of the equator after 1807, slave trading became the domain of Luso-Brazilian and Spanish merchants. Within west-central Africa, however, the regional distribution of slave departures was subject to fluctuations primarily caused by the official abolition of the slave trade by Brazil in 1831, subsequent suppression efforts south of the equator, and the dramatic fall of Cuban slave prices in the 1860s. The trade's core feature throughout this period, as David Eltis notes, was the rise of the Congo River as the main site of slave trading.[3]

Roquinaldo Ferreira has called the Brazilian 1831 law abolishing the slave trade "the threshold to the illegal phase of the Angolan trade," and he claims that it added "momentum to a process of decentralization of shipments away from Luanda and toward northern Angola."[4] Brazilian merchants from Luanda saw their business threatened by potential suppression and sought new outlets in Ambriz and Cabinda, ports previously dominated by French and British slavers.[5] Joined by a growing number of Cubans, they built barracoons, where human cargoes were held until the moment of embarkation. In Ambriz, according to the British vice-consul in Luanda, "so late as the year 1849 there were upwards of twenty factories belonging to parties solely engaged in slave traffic. Many of these factories belonged to [or] were directed by individuals who figured in this city as persons of importance . . . that place might with justice have been termed the slave shipping port of Loanda."[6] He further explained that after the British navy burned many of the coastal factories in 1842, slave dealers avoided storing slaves near "the point," as the Ambriz harbor was known, and moved their depots to villages inland. Moreover, as British and Portuguese efforts to suppress the traffic intensified in the mid-1840s, slavers increasingly sought refuge in the Congo River, which was harder to patrol than the Atlantic seaboard. In the words of Eltis, the Congo could claim "the dubious distinction of being the last major source of African labor for the Americas."[7]

The latest numerical evidence provided by the Voyages Slave Trade Database confirms these trends.[8] The database provides information on 419,506 slaves carried to the Americas from ports in west-central Africa from 1831 to the end of the traffic, which is about 47 percent of the estimated total number of slaves traded in the same region during that period. On the basis of the data, it is possible to calculate the northern ports' share of the total trade from west-central Africa. By projecting these percentages onto the estimated trade, approximates can be obtained for the total number of slaves carried from Ambriz, the Congo River, and the Loango coast (table 2.1).

Table 2.1 shows, first, that initially the largest number of slaves from the Congo region north of Angola embarked in ports on the Loango coast, which

TABLE 2.1

Estimated slave departures from Congo ports, 1831–65

	Ambriz		Congo River		Loango coast		All Congo ports	
	SHARE OF WC AFRICA (%)	SLAVES	SHARE OF WC AFRICA (%)	SLAVES	SHARE OF WC AFRICA (%)	SLAVES	SHARE OF WC AFRICA (%)	SLAVES
1831–35	8.26	8,231	2.61	2,600	17.22	17,166	28.09	27,997
1836–40	4.58	11,165	6.91	16,834	13.65	33,278	25.14	61,282
1841–45	8.58	10,858	1.91	2,416	16.98	21,500	27.47	34,775
1846–50	23.30	60,660	7.06	18,393	18.87	49,124	49.22	128,178
1851–55	10.45	3,839	51.96	19,089	4.72	1,733	67.12	24,661
1856–60	11.16	8,618	55.51	42,844	31.62	24,404	98.29	75,865
1861–65	2.97	1,246	74.77	31,387	20.23	8,490	97.97	41,123
Totals	11.80	104,617	15.07	133,563	17.57	155,695	44.44	393,881

Note: The Loango coast includes the ports of Cabinda, Congo North, Kilongo, Loango, Malembo, and Mayumba. Excluded from my calculations are the "unspecified" ports in West Central Africa; any share the Congo ports may have among these is thus not factored in.

profited from the commercial infrastructure and inland supply networks largely put in place during the eighteenth century.[9] Second, the importance of the Congo ports in the west-central African slave trade increased dramatically after 1845, when the Portuguese began to suppress the trade in Luanda. Slave dealers responded by relocating to ports north of Luanda, in particular Ambriz. After 1850 decline set in as Brazil effectively abolished the slave trade, Portugal occupied Ambriz (in 1855), and Portuguese and British naval forces destroyed many coastal barracoons. But, third, while the slave trade from the Congo region briefly declined after 1850, it became increasingly centered in the Congo River, especially at Boma, which by this time had become the prime location for Cuban slave traders.

Eltis explains the longevity of the slave trade in the Congo region by the late rise of legitimate commerce, which only developed here in the late 1850s, and the ease with which traffickers could move slaves.[10] Trying to negotiate with a group of African brokers about the possibility of developing agriculture on the banks of the river Congo in 1848, a Portuguese officer found that for them supplying slaves was the easiest way of getting access to foreign goods.[11] A French captain exploring the Congo's potential for produce exports in 1847 observed that Ambriz "has little to offer if it is not for trading slaves," although some factories were buying small amounts of ivory, gum copal, and copper. The situation was similar further north, in Cabinda, Loango, Kilongo, and Mayumba.[12] In 1857 a French naval officer commented that "the Congo River is now full of slave traders and all other trade is left aside for [local merchants] to indulge in shipping slaves aboard the numerous vessels that quietly wait for them."[13] Hard to patrol, the river had become the main refuge of slavers evading the British navy. River slaves were also moved along the coast north and south of the estuary, to Cabinda, Ambriz, and Ambrizete. As one officer explained in 1848, "there are no established ports for shipment . . . the slaves are run from point to point . . . nearly all . . . come from Embomma."[14]

Another important characteristic of nineteenth-century exports was the unusually high proportion of children, especially boys.[15] As demonstrated in table 2.2, during the final years of British slaving, children constituted roughly 17 percent of the slaves traded from the Congo region, which was about average for the Atlantic slave trade as a whole in that period. It was, however, a low ratio compared to earlier periods and might be partially explained by the Dolben Act of 1788, which limited the number of slaves carried by British vessels, thus raising transportation costs and diminishing the incentive for slavers to ship low-value slaves such as children.[16] In any event, the proportion of children grew after Britain withdrew and reached especially high levels during the illegal phase of the traffic, when practically one in two slaves sold in the Congo ports was under fifteen.

The preponderance of children in the slave trade after 1830 may be explained by decreasing shipping costs (due in part to the introduction of faster American-built vessels), a reduction in crew size, and perhaps also by fear of abolition on the part of Cuban and Brazilian planters. All these may have been factors stimulating slavers to purchase ever-larger numbers of children, because they cost less, were easier to control, and provided a longer-term investment than adults. But while the export trade victimized ever more children, the preponderance of males was also significant. After 1830, on average just about one in five slaves carried from the Congo ports was female (table 2.2). This exceptionally low female ratio may be explained by the higher domestic value placed on women in this region compared to other parts of Africa.[17]

In short, by the mid-nineteenth century the Atlantic slave trade was strongly focused on the Congo River, which accounted for roughly two-thirds of all slaves leaving Africa after 1850, while the human cargo leaving the river were overwhelmingly male and consisted to an unprecedented degree of children. This was the context in which the Marseille-based trade house of Régis started its business of recruiting indentured servants for the Caribbean islands of Guadeloupe and Martinique.

TABLE 2.2

Proportion of children and male slaves in the Congo slave trade, 1791–1865

Period	Children (%)	Standard deviation	Male (%)	Standard deviation
1791–1810	16.9	16.6	65.5	6.8
1811–30	24.1	17.5	65.4	15.1
1831–50	51.1	15.8	80.4	10.8
1851–65	39.3	21.5	76.4	14.0

Note: Between 1791 and 1865 the Congo ports included Ambriz, Cabinda, Congo River, Rio Zaire, Congo North, Kilongo, Loango, Malembo, Mayumba, and Penido.

Following a contract with the French government to supply twenty thousand African migrant workers to Guadeloupe and Martinique, in 1857 Régis began its recruitment of indentured laborers in the Congo.[18] The Régis contract was part of a wider European effort—that also included Britain, Portugal, and the Netherlands—to recruit indentured labor after abolition. As very few free Africans volunteered to work overseas on long-term contracts, however, more often than not these new recruitment schemes tapped into existing slave supplies. Thus most of the roughly two hundred thousand African migrant workers shipped to European colonies in this era of "free" labor were either slaves redeemed from African dealers or liberated Africans from intercepted slaving vessels.[19]

Régis, with commercial experience in Angola, centered his operations in Boma, the heart of the Atlantic slave trade, knowing there would be no shortage of laborers available.[20] While the recruitment of workers largely took place in Boma, newly constructed factories in Banana and Loango housed the migrants before departure. The legal counterpart of the old slave barracoons, these factories had the capacity to house up to fourteen hundred workers. Over six years, vessels owned by Régis carried 17,262 liberated slaves from west-central Africa, of whom 15,845 arrived at their American destination. Each year Régis shipped an average of 2,877 slaves from the Congo, which, if added to the yearly average of 11,699 slaves for the regular slave trade, amounted to roughly 20 percent of the annual supply in the region.

While Régis centered his operations in the Congo River because it held the largest market for the export of labor, his agents had to compete with Portuguese middlemen purchasing slaves for Cuba. Initially, the French were hopeful that both parties would not poach in each other's territory: the Portuguese were mostly interested in purchasing children, whereas the French concentrated on contracting adults. In practice, however, it was difficult to uphold such a neat market division. As one of the naval officers supervising the migration scheme observed, "we refuse the majority of non-adults that they [the Portuguese] particularly, and justifiably, seek. . . . Meanwhile due to the habits induced by the slave traders in the [African] brokers the number of children from 10 to 14 years offered for purchase is still and will for a long time be very considerable."[21] Children were apparently preferable, as they could be more easily trained to plantation life and better withstood the changes in climate, nutrition, and habitat. This observation is affirmed in recent studies on age differentials, disease, and mortality.[22] Although the French were limited by contract to redeeming adults, market conditions forced them to take substantial numbers of children.

TABLE 2.3

Age and gender distribution of migrants embarked on the *Clara* and *Stella*, 1857

AGE GROUP	Clara (449 migrants)		Stella (797 migrants)		Total (1,246 migrants)		
	MALE	FEMALE	MALE	FEMALE	MALE	FEMALE	%
10–14	29	19	106	78	135	97	18.6
15–19	68	49	32	71	100	120	17.7
20–24	92	31	420	22	512	53	45.3
25–29	143	1	61	–	204	1	16.5
30–34	12	–	5	–	17	–	1.4
35–39	4	–	–	–	4	–	0.3
Unknown	1	–	2	–	3	–	0.2
Total	349	100	626	171	975	271	100.0

Table 2.3 shows the age and gender distribution of the liberated slaves who embarked on the *Clara* and *Stella*, the first vessels to ship African migrant workers from the Congo to Guadeloupe and Martinique, in 1857.[23] Seventy-eight percent of all migrants were male, which was about average for west-central Africa in that period. But contrary to the agreements made with the French government, one in five slaves purchased by Régis was fourteen years or younger, an unpleasant reality even if this ratio was still well below the regional average. Another striking fact is that an overwhelming majority of females (80 percent) was between ten and twenty years and thus had just reached child-bearing age or recently come out of puberty. As often happened in the regular slave trade, a number of women had been recruited with infants. The youngest of these, a Yombe girl named Temba, was fifteen years old.

French agents tried to combat Portuguese competition by offering comparatively higher prices. Subsidized by the French government, at the start of business in 1857, they were able to pay African brokers more than the value of 120 francs paid for slaves by the Portuguese traders. As competition increased, prices in the river peaked at 200 to 280 francs in early 1860. But shortly thereafter, French recruitment benefited from a dramatic price collapse, reflecting a structural decline in the market in Cuba.[24] Over the years Régis established close relations with particular brokers, although success in trade always depended on having an adequate assortment of barter goods.[25] African brokers were sometimes unhappy with the French purchasing strategies, including selecting workers according to age and physical attributes. By contrast, Portuguese middlemen bought "wholesale without worrying too much about waste [*déchet*]."[26] African traders could also not understand why the French paid less for children than for adults, particularly since agents buying for the Cuban market made no distinction.[27]

Although the French often expressed frustration with the Portuguese, the success of their migration scheme ultimately relied on the vitality of the regular slave trade. On several occasions when Portuguese traders were raising prices and buying larger numbers, the French were able to accelerate their enrollments with the increased supply of slaves.[28] One naval officer acknowledged that the French practice of "repurchasing" slaves fed off the illegal trade and that effective abolition of the slave trade would also mean the end of French recruitment. "Our demand would not be sufficient to maintain a trade that is needed for an adequately supplied slave market. We can therefore say without the slave trade, no recruitment."[29] Ultimately, the French were only minor players in Boma's market, which largely depended on price fluctuations in Cuba.

Other factors influencing the recruitment of workers, besides Portuguese competition, were related to seasonality. The market for slaves tightened during the rainy season as the trade routes from the interior were cut off by heavy rainfall (usually in March and April).[30] In the months before the rainy season local demand for agricultural labor increased. During this period slaves were used to clear the fields and plant crops, tasks that involved male labor. Thus in January 1860 a French officer noted that recruitment had slowed because labor was diverted to cultivation, adding that now mostly women, children, and the physically weaker men were offered for sale.[31]

ORIGINS OF SLAVES

The first two vessels of Régis, the *Clara* and *Stella*, arrived in the Congo in April 1857, when the factories to house the migrant workers had not yet been constructed. The embarkation process therefore took longer than planned, disease began to spread among the purchased slaves, and it was decided that both vessels would leave the unhealthy environment of the river and embark the remainder of their recruits in Loango—even if most were purchased in Boma—from where both vessels left in November and December, respectively.[32] The embarkation lists of the *Clara* and *Stella* also indicate the "place of birth" of each individual migrant. It is unclear whether the slaves interviewed by French officials understood a question about their birthplace literally or instead, more flexibly, as one about their origins. The names slaves provided may have alluded to birthplace, residence, or place of enslavement. At the very least they tell about the places where the migrants resided before their embarkation.

Table 2.4 lists the main places of origin (frequency ≥ 1 percent) of the slaves embarked. Using nineteenth-century data on Africans origins obtained through an interview process is evidently problematic. One problem is linguistic distortion: the place names were pronounced by (illiterate) Africans and written down by a French official unfamiliar with the language. Another

TABLE 2.4

Main origins of migrants embarked on the *Clara* and *Stella*, 1857

	Clara (449 migrants)	Stella (797 migrants)	Total (1,246 migrants)	% of all migrants
Boma	25	179	204	16.4
Congo	13	50	63	5.1
Sundi	13	50	63	5.1
Tando/Tandu	–	43	43	3.5
Loango	9	22	31	2.5
Cabinda	2	24	26	2.1
Mayombe	8	9	17	1.4
Kaie	7	9	16	1.3
Kilongo/Chilongo	9	7	16	1.3
Kacongo	1	11	12	1.0
Binda	5	7	12	1.0

difficulty concerns the localization of the places, as many were and are still fairly common in different regions of west-central Africa. Nevertheless, most places listed in the table are familiar to scholars of the region and identifiable with a high degree of reliability.

Boma needs no introduction.[33] Congo referred to an area south of the Congo River with close ties to the old kingdom of Kongo. This Congo group included one slave, thirty-year-old Mialla, who identified himself as "Muchi-congo" and thus likely originated from the kingdom's capital, Mbanza Kongo, or a village in the near vicinity. Sundi was a region between Boma and Malebo Pool (Kinshasa), which used to be the kingdom's northernmost province; the town of Mbanza Sundi was its center. Tandu was located south of Malebo Pool and east of Sundi. Loango, Cabinda, Kilongo (Chilongo), and Kacongo were ports on the Atlantic coast north of the Congo estuary or, alternatively, small polities in the immediate hinterland of these ports. Kaie might have been the coastal town Kayi, which was the birthplace of the Cabindan ex-slave interviewed in 1850 by Sigismund Koelle in Sierra Leone.[34] Mayombe, or Yombe, was a region located deeper inland from the coast, but still west of Boma and Sundi. Last, Binda was a village on the Congo River's north bank not far to the east of Boma.

Thus all the places listed in table 2.4 are located in the lower Congo region, and although the origins of the sixteen thousand migrants Régis subsequently shipped from the Congo would undoubtedly show a different distribution from those embarked on the *Clara* and *Stella*, the preponderance of Boma, Congo, and Sundi slaves would probably remain unaltered. French officials used to argue that roughly 90 percent of the slaves marketed in Boma came from regions in the near or far interior and that no slaves originated from villages on the banks of the Congo River.[35] Table 2.4 indicates, however, that the largest number of slaves came from within the Boma community itself. That the site of slave trading was a major source of slaves traded was repeated in Loango ports. Besides Binda, a number of other riverside villages supplied slaves to the Boma market. Some slaves, for example, indicated they were born in familiar places like Noki, Ponta da Lenha, and Soyo.

Meanwhile many, if not most, of the slaves coming from regions inland originated from places in the lower Congo. Some slaves had been traded from the upper Congo, like those who gave Biangala and Kongolo as their origin. Others, like the few registered Yaka, may have come from regions east of the Kwango River. Furthermore, in 1859 a French officer liberated eighteen children aged eight to ten from a Portuguese trader, who had bought them in Mucula, south of the Congo estuary. Asked about their origins, the children, many looking ill and underfed, stated they had marched for thirty days from a place about a hundred leagues (about five hundred kilometers) inland. This could have been anywhere, but they had possibly been traded from Malebo Pool, a main corridor for the river trade.[36] Cases like these notwithstanding, the data on slave origins first and foremost point to the historical role of the Kongo people of modern Angola and Congo-Kinshasa as effective and significant producers of slaves. In the final decades of the Atlantic slave trade the transmittance of Kongo culture was therefore a defining feature of the African diaspora.[37] On the African side, moreover, the salience of Sundi and Congo identities points to the versatility of long-established regional commercial networks. Trade routes that previously supplied slaves from Malebo Pool to Luanda via Mbanza Sundi and Mbanza Kongo were partly redirected to serve the growing Boma market and coastal ports.[38]

CAUSES OF ENSLAVEMENT

Details were collected on the causes of enslavement of 2,571 Africans, roughly a fifth of all migrants shipped by Régis.[39] Table 2.5 provides a full range of social conflicts that could result in enslavement. Women occasionally opposed the dominance of male elders by refusing to marry; young men sometimes refused orders to work. Various forms of criminal behavior, contempt for religious charms, and improper sexual conduct posed further threats to the established social order. In earlier times not all these misdemeanors might have ended in slavery, but society had changed under the impact of the Atlantic trade in slaves. Norm Schrag has observed that Kongo legal systems were increasingly abused to enslave people and lineage heads began to sell those who were not normally subject to sale, including free men, pawns, clients, and assimilated slaves. Alleged

TABLE 2.5

Causes of enslavement of 2,571 Africans purchased under the French migration scheme

Cause of enslavement	Men	Women	Children	Total
Born into slavery	761	698	70	1,529
Sold by kin, not having committed any crime	244	164	5	413
Kidnapped and sold by neighboring groups	26	11		37
Sold to support others in lineage	9			9
Sold by parents	42	4		46
Sold for refusing to marry		8		8
Sold for refusing to work	2	3		5
Sold by husband for committing adultery		12		12
Enslaved at death of parents	38	25	6	69
Enslaved to pay debts or fines of parents	36	15	2	53
Enslaved for theft	67	46	3	116
Enslaved for theft committed by parent	97	68	12	177
Enslaved for adultery (with another's wife)	34			34
Enslaved for adultery committed by parent	8	9	8	25
Enslaved for crimes committed by themselves (murder, arson, assault, lack of respect for charms, etc.)	16	8		24
Enslaved with family for being party to lost case brought before chiefly tribunal	7	14		21
War captive	3			3
Total	1,390	1,085	106	2,581

troublemakers and people lacking strong kinship connections were often the first victims of judicial corruption, also when households had to sell members for reasons of debt or food shortage.[40] A late nineteenth-century eyewitness observed that chiefly power was regularly manipulated to dupe those lacking sufficient social protection, as chiefs imposed penalties on "the weak and the unwary" for trespassing chiefly taboos that functioned as laws of prohibition.[41]

By far the larger number (60 percent) of slaves recruited by the French were born into slavery. Constituting the most vulnerable group in their home communities, they had, under unspecified circumstances, fallen victim to the forces of the slave trade pervading Kongo society. Another major category comprised individuals who had been sold into slavery by their own families for reasons they themselves did not specify but were unrelated to crime. However, for many young adults and children the cause of their enslavement had been an alleged theft by a parent. Men and women were also frequently enslaved as they themselves were accused of theft. Parents could meet their fines for debts, judgments, and theft by transferring their children. Children were thus often victimized to compensate for the crimes or financial obligations of their parents. Children and young adults would also often end up in slavery upon the death of their parents; without parental protection they might have fallen victim to the greed of their neighbors or they possibly subjected themselves voluntarily to a new guardian, a practice known around Mbanza Kongo as "eating the goat."[42]

Table 2.5 further suggests that by the mid-nineteenth century warfare hardly played a role in the production of slaves in west-central Africa and that even kidnapping had little importance as a mechanism of enslavement. Kidnapping had been the most common cause of enslavement for liberated west-central African slaves interviewed by the German missionary Sigismund Wilhelm Koelle in Sierra Leone around 1850. The majority had been enslaved in the 1830s and had already been living in Sierra Leone for more than a decade by the time of their interview, so they pertained to a generation of slaves prior to those who left the Congo through the French migration scheme. But the brief personal histories collected by Koelle indeed confirm that, notwithstanding the blatantly violent procedure of kidnapping (six cases), most often "peaceful" mechanisms were used to produce slaves in the Angola-Congo region in the middle decades of the nineteenth century. Thus, three slaves had been sold by their relatives for no stated reason, including a Teke slave who had been sold at the age of seventeen and was carried through Mayombe to the Loango coast. Three slaves had been sold because of crimes committed by their relatives. These included the case of Kumbu from Mayombe, who, already a father, was enslaved after his sister was accused of witchcraft, and the case of an Mbete man who was enslaved at age sixteen after his mother had run away from his father; for several years he was traded from one place to another before ending up aboard a slave ship in Loango. Another three individuals had been enslaved on account of adultery, debt, and "bad conduct." Finally, one Kimbundu speaker was originally pawned at the age of twenty-four as compensation for a sexual crime committed by his maternal uncle, but he was sold to Portuguese traders in Luanda before his mother could redeem him.[43]

Scrutinized by Great Britain, in 1862 the French government had to make a decision on whether or not to prolong the migration scheme, whose measure of success was largely evaluated from a humanitarian perspective. The fundamental question posed to the officials in charge was how much the *rachats* (slave ransoms) contributed to the internal African slave trade. The ensuing responses foreshadowed a future academic debate.[44] Souzy, a French officer supervising the Congo scheme, argued that the impact was minimal. In his view European slave purchasing contributed little to the development of slavery in Africa, as "Europeans have only taken advantage of an established state of affairs."[45] Taking a continentwide perspective, he explained, "Slavery is fundamental to the social condition of these people . . . the purchase of several million slaves at a few scattered points along its coast would not have a significant influence on the general state of its populations."[46] But his superior, Didelot, had a more negative view on the business and stated that the European trade stimulated the internal slave trade. Since French recruitment relied on the inland supply mechanisms feeding the Boma market, he claimed France was just as guilty as the "immoral" slave traders of perpetuating the traffic.[47] This second perspective informed the decision of the French emperor to discontinue the migration scheme in July 1862.

BETWEEN ABOLITION AND COLONIAL RULE

The last slaving vessel departing from west-central Africa for Cuba left the Congo River in 1865 with over twelve hundred slaves.[48] The export trade in slaves had come to an end, but internally slave trading continued. The main feature of this new era was that slaves were no longer overwhelmingly traded toward the Atlantic coast, but were now moved in different directions across the lower Congo, generally following newly expanding centers of wealth. Wealth became increasingly concentrated in places connected to the developing trade in commodities, which included coastal zones specializing in the production of vegetable oils, but also places in the interior that were important centers for the burgeoning ivory and rubber trades. In these different locales, including some that had played active roles in supplying the Atlantic slave trade, riches made in commerce were commonly invested in slaves.

Slaves, in particular women and children, were wanted for a number of reasons. Female slaves were valued for their reproductive capacities. In the matrilineal societies of the lower Congo, the offspring of free wives in theory belonged to the mother's clan. Husbands could circumvent this problem by adding female slaves to their households, as their ownership of a slave wife's children was ensured because slaves were in principle kinless.[49] Wealthy persons also kept slaves as a form of security; they were assets their owners could use to cover unexpected debts or fines.[50] Most important, however, women and children were an essential means to broaden a household's economic foundation, especially with regard to agriculture.[51]

Men successful in the sale of export crops would try to expand their agricultural production by investing their newly earned riches in slaves, particularly women as they held both productive and reproductive powers.[52] According to the Swedish missionary Laman, who worked among the Sundi from 1891 to 1919, men would clear woods, cut grass, and prepare the soil, but women planted and harvested. The peanut harvest was the most important of all, and it was considered a women's crop. Although women sold produce on local markets, men were usually in control of the export trade. Laman observed that successful businessmen "were unable to invest their assets in anything but slaves." That they preferred female over male slaves was reflected in the prices for both: in the Pool area, where the Sundi bought many of their slaves, a man was on average worth one hundred fifty pieces of cloth, whereas a young woman might cost up to four hundred pieces. Male slaves were, indeed, also purchased, but they were mainly employed in what were considered manly occupations. As Laman put it, a wealthy person would purchase "a wife in order to get good progeny" and "men to serve as tappers of palm-wine."[53]

Dom Paulo, a middleman who ruled the town of Vumpa, on the south bank of the Congo River, converted his riches into people. Vumpa was home to a number of European trade factories whose business there centered on purchasing palm produce and peanuts from traders like Dom Paulo. The large number of slaves and the thirty-six women who were part of Dom Paulo's household impressed a Portuguese visitor in 1886. His wooden house, with stores attached, was full of firearms, liquor, textiles and other European goods. He would occasionally supply textiles on credit to local merchants in want of merchandise to buy produce. But another destination of such prestige items had, obviously, been their conversion into female and other slave dependants.[54]

The same was happening elsewhere in Kongo. In the 1880s the population of Mbanza Kongo was increasing as the riches that townsmen made in trade-based jobs—as interpreters for the European factories, caravan managers, or porters—and the selling of local produce such as sesame and peanuts were invested in women and slaves. The Christian missions that came to Mbanza Kongo at the same time as the trade factories also played a part in the local economy. They were not only places where refugee slaves could find shelter; they also brought with them their own economy of construction works and transport requirements. The wages to be gained at the European factories and mission stations, paid out in textiles and other prestige goods, were traded for slaves who were integrated in the community. Throughout the lower Congo, towns were expanding and splintering at the same time through the influx of new dependants. Young men turned wealthy in the ivory, rubber, and produce trade and who could afford a number of wives and slaves began to set up their own villages, or did so in company with other newly rich traders, so as to mark their independence from their hometown. Thus along the caravan routes a regular pattern emerged, with large towns breaking up in distinct parts, creating a line of little hamlets. From Tungwa, a town in the wealthy Makuta district, north of Mbanza Kongo, counting some three thousand inhabitants in the 1880s, originated seven new villages in a period of ten years.[55] A Dutchman traveling up to Kinshasa in 1883 was struck by the population densities in this region and noted that children made up a large part of the local village populations.[56]

Ivory and rubber caravans brought many of the slaves purchased by more affluent inhabitants of Mbanza Kongo from the eastern Zombo region.[57] The local Portuguese missionaries, who had adopted a policy of redeeming slave children after other strategies of establishing a Christian nucleus had failed, also tapped into this supply. According to one visitor, the majority of the mission pupils originated from the Makuta and the Zombo regions.[58] Missionaries of the Congrégation du Saint-Esprit, who had been present in the lower Congo since the 1870s, followed a similar policy of slave purchases. Their schools relied on the acquisition of slave girls, since local community elders sought to retain young females within their own households. Slave boys also had to be purchased, since the local young men attending the mission schools were generally free men who would not marry women of slave status, would normally leave the mission after a few years anyway, and also refused to perform any tasks related to agriculture. The Spiritan Fathers usually purchased slave children through local African dealers or European factory agents, some of whom had experience in recruiting slave workers. Occasionally a priest checked out a caravan with slaves for potential recruits. Correspondence from the Spiritans shows that in the 1880s Malebo Pool still functioned as the biggest slave market of the lower Congo. Furthermore, they found Boma to be the easiest place to obtain children. Some of the children purchased by the missionaries were slaves by birth; others had been sold into slavery, as their families were unable to feed them or because of debts, theft, and other minor misdeeds. The children were always in large part paid for in goods, especially textiles, and their prices could range from 50 to 220 francs, often depending on whether they were purchased alone or as part of a group.[59]

Thus on the eve of colonial rule a domestic trade in slaves, carried out through an array of interconnected regional markets, still existed in the lower Congo. This network was founded on trade routes that supplied vessels bound for Brazil, Cuba, and the French West Indies with Kongo slaves. But with the Atlantic outlets practically closed since 1865, slaves were being sold in all directions, as African merchants throughout the expanding commercial network used to invest their wealth in slaves. Incidentally, the trade brought people from different regions together. In the early 1880s, Malebo Pool, itself exporting slaves to the lower Congo, was partly inhabited by Kongo, Zombo, and Makuta slaves who had been sold together with European cloth, rifles, and gunpowder for the ivory brought in from the upper river.[60] The effects of this trade were still discernible in the twentieth century. Among the Sundi, for instance, people of slave descent were commonly known as Kongo, as many of their ancestors had been brought into the region from the south.[61]

According to Father Philippe-Prosper Augouard, by the late 1880s slaves were no longer visibly traded in the lower Congo, as the region was being rapidly integrated in the new colonial order. Augouard began to use his travels on the Ubangi River, in upper Congo, which remained beyond colonial control for another decade, to recruit children for the Spiritan mission in Brazzaville. Slave dealers at the market of Bangui coveted European goods such as guns and beads (but apparently not textiles), which the missionaries were able to supply. The prices for children were considerably lower than those previously paid south of Malebo Pool—Augouard never paid more than 25 francs—although the costs of transporting goods and slaves up and down the Ubangi and Congo Rivers eliminated much of the differential.[62]

Meanwhile, south of the lower Congo a new form of forced labor had emerged under Portuguese colonial rule that, like the earlier French migration system, blurred any distinction between slavery and indentured servitude. Well into the twentieth century old caravan routes that connected Angolan markets to the interior of west-central Africa supplied a significant number of slaves recruited as *serviçaes* (contract workers) for the cocoa plantations of São Tomé and Príncipe.[63] The Kongo region of northern Angola fell largely outside these slave supply networks and very few Kongolese were ever recruited under this colonial labor regime.[64] Occasionally the embarkation ledgers in the Portuguese archives include individuals of Kongo origin, like Cassua, a twenty-year-old man who had been recruited in the hinterland of Novo Redondo in 1876. Cassua was enslaved as a child and raised in Luanda, but after an unsuccessful escape he was conscripted and put on a vessel bound for São Tomé, aptly named *Saudade* (longing).[65] But cases like this were exceptional and Cassua's presence among 177 other *colonos* aboard the *Saudade* was really an offshoot of a domestic trade in slaves between Kongo and Angola. Under colonialism the Congo district of northern Angola never became a center for the export of indentured servants to São Tomé, whose labor supplies were instead dependent on the more extensive slaving networks of central Angola.[66]

⌒

The African slave trade to Cuba and Brazil increasingly concentrated on the Congo River and focused ever more on male children; women made up only a small part of the labor supplies, as Africans were more reluctant to release female slaves. These characteristics also structured French efforts to recruit migrant workers for the West Indies in the lower Congo around 1860. Recruitment of African contract labor was effective only to the extent that it relied on slave supply networks that had been developed over the course of the nineteenth century. The postabolition recruitment of supposedly voluntary labor could thus never be separated from the contemporaneous slave trade and was, in fact, practically impossible without it. Spiritan missionaries who began to ransom slave children in the lower Congo in the 1870s depended on the same commercial infrastructure dating from the illegal phase of the Atlantic slave trade. From the perspective of African dealers, therefore, the "liberation" of slaves was merely a continuation of the old slave trade.

Data from the French recruitment scheme in turn shed light on the origins of slaves purchased in the lower Congo and the causes of their enslavement. Here two conclusions stand out. First, during the final decades of the Atlantic slave trade, most slaves leaving the Congo originated from regions near the main ports of embarkation, in particular Boma. Second, many children were enslaved to pay off legal fines or debts incurred by their parents. In areas close to the coast, judicial systems were increasingly corrupted to produce slaves for the export trade; children were often the victims of this process. The increasing reliance on child slaves in the nineteenth-century slave trade out of Africa foreshadowed the widespread exploitation of child labor by African communities under colonial rule, as attested by several contributions to this volume.[67]

NOTES

Abbreviations

AHU	Arquivo Histórico Ultramarino, Lisbon
ANOM	Archives Nationales d'Outre-Mer
FM	Fonds Ministériel
SG	Série Géographique
TSTD	Trans-Atlantic Slave Trade Database

1. For the early period, see Linda Heywood and John Thornton, *Central Africans, Atlantic Creoles, and the Foundation of the Americas* (New York: Cambridge University Press, 2007).

2. See TSTD, table, Estimates, 1501–1866, http://www.slavevoyages.org/tast/assessment/estimates.faces.

3. David Eltis, *Economic Growth and the Ending of the Transatlantic Slave Trade* (Oxford: Oxford University Press, 1987), 173–77.

4. Roquinaldo Ferreira, "The Suppression of the Slave Trade and Slave Departures from Angola, 1830s–1860s," in *Extending the Frontiers: Essays on the New Transatlantic Slave Trade Database*, ed. David Eltis and David Richardson (New Haven: Yale University Press, 2008), 314–15.

5. Ferreira, "Suppression," 323. See also Susan J. Herlin, "Brazil and the Commercialization of Kongo, 1840–1870," in *Enslaving Connections*, ed. José Curto and Paul Lovejoy (Amherst, NY: Humanity Books, 2004).

6. Governador geral interino to Ministro e Secretário do Estado dos Negócios da Marinha e Ultramar, no. 14, Luanda, 6 April 1853, AHU, SEMU-DGU, Angola, nos. 1111–12, encl. no. 3: Vice-consul Brand to Governo Geral, Luanda, 15 March 1853.

7. Eltis, *Economic Growth*, 165.

8. TSTD. The data can be obtained through the following link: http://slavevoyages.org/tast/database/search.faces?yearFrom=1831&yearTo=1866&mjbyptimp=60700. Subsequently, in Tables, the rows have to be adjusted to five-year periods and the columns to embarkation ports. For the estimated volume of the slave trade from west-central Africa between 1831 and 1865, see http://slavevoyages.org/tast/assessment/estimates.faces?yearFrom=1831&yearTo=1865&embarkation=7.

9. For Loango, see Phyllis Martin, *The External Trade of the Loango Coast, 1576–1870* (Oxford: Clarendon Press, 1972).

10. Eltis, *Economic Growth*, 175–77.

11. António Manoel de Noronha to Barão da Ribeira de Sabrosa, no. 2, Luanda, 21 November 1839, Copia no. 1: João Maria Ferreira do Amaral to António Manoel de Noronha, Luanda, 20 November 1839, AHU, SEMU-DGU, Angola, no. 785, maço 2.

12. Rapport du navire Antilope, ANOM, FM, SG, Afrique IV/23.

13. Rapport sur le rachat des captives dans le Rio Congo et la baie de Loango, 24 September 1857, ANOM, FM/SG, Sénégal XIV/23b, Vallon, no. 12.

14. Commodore Hotham to Palmerston, 29 March 1849, 5 December 1848, encl. in Admiralty, National Archives (Kew), FO84/782, cited in Eltis, *Economic Growth*, 177.

15. Eltis, *Economic Growth*, 175.

16. David Eltis and Stanley Engerman, "Was the Slave Trade Dominated by Men?" *Journal of Interdisciplinary History* 23, no. 2 (1992): 253.

17. Eltis, *Economic Growth*, 69; Herbert Klein, "African Women in the Atlantic Slave Trade," in *Women and Slavery in Africa*, ed. Claire Robertson and Martin Klein (Portsmouth, NH: Heinemann, 1997); Joseph Miller, *Way of Death* (Madison: University of Wisconsin Press, 1988), 159–64, 387–88. See also David Eltis and Stanley L. Engerman, "Fluctuations in Sex and Age Ratios in the Transatlantic Slave Trade, 1663–1864," *Economic History Review* 46, no. 2 (1993): 308–23.

18. The number of migrants agreed upon was later reduced to fourteen thousand.

19. David Northrup, *Indentured Labor in the Age of Imperialism, 1834–1922* (Cambridge: Cambridge University Press, 1995), 44–51.

20. François Souzy, "L'immigration africaine aux Antilles," *Revue maritime et coloniale* 9 (1863): 90–100. After the Portuguese occupation of Ambriz, in 1855, Régis moved to the Congo River. See Ministre de l'Agriculture, Commerce et Travaux Publics to Ministre de la Marine et des Colonies, Paris, 3 August 1857, ANOM, FM/SG, Afrique VI/4.

21. Vallon, "Notes sur l'immigration africaine," Paris, September–October 1859, ANOM, FM, Généralités 124/1086.

22. Eltis and Engerman, "Slave Trade," 238; Eltis and Engerman, "Fluctuations," 318; Simon Hogerzeil and David Richardson, "Slave Purchasing Strategies and Shipboard Mortality: Day-to-Day Evidence from the Dutch African Trade," *Journal of Economic History* 67, no. 1 (2007): 160–90.

23. État signalétique des émigrants embarqués sur la Clara, ANOM, FM/SG, Martinique, 127/1137; État signalétique des émigrants embarqués sur la Stella, encl. in Protet to Ministre de la Marine et des Colonies, Gabon 20 December 1857, Service Historique de la Défense, Départemente de la Marine, BB4/745. I would like to thank Lauren Glaser for her help in transcribing these documents.

24. Souzy to Didelot, 12 October 1862, ANOM, FM/SG, Sénégal XIV/23c, cited in François Renault, *Libération d'esclaves et nouvelle servitude* (Abidjan: Les Nouvelles Éditions Africaines, 1976). For Cuban slave prices, see Laird Bergad, *The Comparative Histories of Slavery in Brazil, Cuba, and the United States* (New York: Cambridge University Press, 2007), 158.

25. Souzy to Didelot, 9 February 1862, ANOM, FM/SG, Sénégal XIV/23c, annex to Didelot to Ministre de la Marine et des Colonies, no. 144–45, Gabon, 17 March 1862, printed in Renault, *Libération*, 184–87.

26. Vallon, no. 12, Rapport sur le rachat des captives dans le Rio Congo et la baie de Loango, 24 September 1857, ANOM, FM/SG, Sénégal XIV/23b.

27. Vallon, Notes sur l'immigration africaine, Paris, September–October 1859, ANOM, FM, Généralités 124/1086.

28. Gillet to Chef de division, no. 15, Congo, 27 February 1860; Bosse to Ministre de l'Algérie et des Colonies, no. 185, Gabon, 23 July 1860, both at ANOM, FM/SG, Sénégal XIX/23c.

29. Didelot to Ministre de la Marine et des Colonies, Fernando Po, 2 March 1862, ANOM, FM/SG, Gabon-Congo I/2a.

30. Gillet to Chef de division, no. 17, Loango, 27 March 1860; no. 19, Congo, 22 April 1860, ANOM, FM/SG, Sénégal XIX/23c.

31. Gillet to Chef de division, no. 13, Congo, 13 January 1960, ANOM, FM/SG, Sénégal XIX/23c. See also Stephen Behrendt, "Markets, Transaction Cycles, and Profits: Merchant Decision Making in the British Slave Trade," *William and Mary Quarterly* 58, no. 1 (2001): 171–204.

32. Souzy, "Immigration."

33. Boma is also the name of a kingdom northeast of Malebo Pool, near the confluence of the Zaire and Kwa-Kasai Rivers, from which slaves were sold into the Atlantic trade. See Philip Curtin and Jan Vansina, "Sources of the Nineteenth Century Atlantic Slave Trade," *Journal of African History* 5, no. 2 (1964): 199, 204; Vansina, *Paths in the Rainforest: Toward a History of Political Tradition in Equatorial Africa* (Madison: University of Wisconsin Press, 1990), 230. Only a study of the personal names of the Boma slaves aboard the *Clara* and *Stella* can determine whether they originated from the Boma port or the Boma kingdom. A first look suggests that many slaves came from the Kikongo language group, thus originating from the Boma port.

34. S. W. Koelle, *Polyglotta Africana*, ed. P. E. H. Hair and David Dalby (1854; Graz: Akademische Druck- und Verlagsanstalt, 1963), 13.

35. Souzy to Didelot, 9 February 1862, annex to Didelot to Ministre de la Marine et des Colonies, nos. 144–45, Gabon, 17 March 1862, ANOM, FM/SG, Sénégal XIV/23c, in Renault, *Libération*, 184–87.

36. Bosse to Ministre de la Marine et des Colonies, Gabon, 24 June 1859, ANOM, FM/SG, Gabon-Congo I/1b.

37. See Oscar Moráguez, "The African Origins of Slaves Arriving in Cuba, 1789–1865," in Eltis and Richardson, *Extending the Frontiers.*

38. Susan H. Broadhead, "Trade and Politics on the Congo Coast, 1770–1870" (PhD diss., Boston University, 1971), 134, 144, 241.

39. Souzy, "Immigration," 100.

40. Norm Schrag, "Mboma and the Lower Zaire: A Socioeconomic Study of a Kongo Trading Community, c. 1785–1885" (PhD diss., Indiana University, 1985), 126–35, 147–52.

41. John H. Weeks, "Notes on Some Customs of the Lower Congo People," *Folk-Lore* 19–20 (1908–9): 309–10.

42. Ibid., 32.

43. Koelle, *Polyglotta*, 13–15. Also see Curtin and Vansina, "Sources"; P. E. H. Hair, "The Enslavement of Koelle's Informants," *Journal of African History* 6, no. 2 (1965): 193–203.

44. See Walter Rodney, "African Slavery and Other Forms of Social Oppression on the Upper Guinea Coast in the Context of the Atlantic Slave-Trade," *Journal of African History* 7, no. 3 (1966): 431–43; J. D. Fage, "Slavery and the Slave Trade in the Context of West African History," *Journal of African History* 10, no. 3 (1969): 393–404; Paul Lovejoy, *Transformations in Slavery: A History of Slavery in Africa*, 2nd ed. (Cambridge: Cambridge University Press, 2000); John K. Thornton, *Africa and Africans in the Making of the Atlantic World, 1400–1800*, 2nd ed. (Cambridge: Cambridge University Press, 1998), 72–125.

45. Souzy to Didelot, 9 February 1862, annex to Didelot to Ministre de la Marine et des Colonies, no. 144–145, Gabon, 17 March 1862, ANOM, FM/SG, Sénégal XIV/23c, in Renault, *Libération*, 184–87.

46. Souzy, "Immigration," 96.

47. Didelot to Ministre de la Marine et des Colonies, no. 121, Fernando Po, 2 Mar 1862, ANOM, FM/SG, Gabon-Congo I/2b. Also see Renault, *Libération*, 116.

48. TSTD, voyage ID 5052.

49. Weeks, "Customs," 414. Also Wyatt MacGaffey, "Economic and Social Dimensions of Kongo Slavery," in *Slavery in Africa*, ed. Suzanne Miers and Igor Kopytoff (Madison: University of Wisconsin Press, 1977), 238, 243.

50. Prosper Augouard, *28 années au Congo*, 2 vols. (Poitiers : Société Française d'Imprimerie et de Librairie, 1905), 1:492.

51. Hendrik Blink, *Het Kongo-Land en zijne bewoners in betrekking tot de Europeesche staatkunde en den handel* (Haarlem, 1891), 137, 139; Augouard, *28 années*, 1:198, 229, 244. For a longer-term perspective, see Susan Broadhead, "Slave Wives, Free Sisters: Bakongo Women and Slavery c. 1700–1850," in Robertson and Klein, *Women and Slavery.*

52. F. de Bas, "Een Nederlandsch reiziger aan den Congo," *Tijdschrift van het Nederlandsch Aardrijkskundig Genootschap*, 2nd series, 1, no. 1 (1884): 145; *Tijdschrift* 4, 2nd series, 4, no. 1 (1887): 172.

53. Karl Laman, *The Kongo*, 4 vols., vol. 1 (Stockholm: Victor Pettersons, 1953), 116, 151; vol. 2 (Uppsala: Almqvist, 1957), 31, 56–57. For Laman's survey of Kongo slavery, see Wyatt MacGaffey, "Kongo Slavery Remembered by Themselves: Texts from 1915," *International Journal of African Historical Studies* 41, no. 1 (2008): 55–76.

54. José Maria Pereira Folga, Relatório, Santo António do Zaire, 20 November 1886, AHU, SEMU-DGU, Angola, 1ª repartição, pasta 7 (no. 791), 1887.

55. António Brásio, *D. António Barroso* (Lisboa: Centro de Estudos Históricos Ultramarinos, 1961), 105, 107–8; W. H. Bentley, *Pioneering on the Congo*, 2 vols. (1900; New York: Johnson Reprint, 1970), 1:42, 137; *Missionary Herald of the Baptist Missionary Society* (1879): 71; (1880): 120; (1888): 453; (1890): 294.

56. F. de Bas, "Een Nederlandsch reiziger aan den Congo," *Tijdschrift van het Nederlandsch aardrijkskundig genootschap*, 2nd series, 3, no. 2 (1887): 361.

57. Thomas Lewis, "Life and Travel among the People of the Congo," *Scottish Geographical Magazine* 18, no. 7 (1902): 361–63.

58. Josef Chavanne, "Reisen im Gebiete der Muschi-congo im portugiesischen Westafrika," *Petermanns Mitteilungen aus Justus Perthes' geographischer Anstalt* 32 (1886): 102.

59. Jelmer Vos, "Child Slaves and Freemen at the Spiritan Mission in Soyo, 1880–1885," *Journal of Family History* 35, no. 1 (2010): 71–90.

60. *Missionary Herald* (1883): 79.

61. Laman, *Kongo*, 2:56–57, 133.

62. Augouard, *28 années*, 1:492; 2:70, 79, 102, 184, 278.

63. William G. Clarence-Smith, "Cocoa Plantations and Coerced Labor in the Gulf of Guinea, 1870–1914," in *Breaking the Chains*, ed. Martin Klein (Madison: University of Wisconsin Press, 1993).

64. Jelmer Vos, "Slavery in Southern Kongo in the Late Nineteenth Century," in *Trabalho forçado africano*, ed. Centro de Estudos Africanos da Universidade do Porto (Porto: Campo das Letras, 2006), 331–33.

65. Relação, 11 December 1876, encl. in Curador geral, no. 3, 3 January 1877, AHU, SEMU-DGU, Angola, 2ª Repartição, pasta 2 (no. 889).

66. Linda Heywood, "Slavery and Forced Labor in the Changing Political Economy of Central Angola, 1850–1949," in *The End of Slavery in Africa*, ed. Suzanne Miers and Richard L. Roberts (Madison: University of Wisconsin Press, 1988).

67. See especially Rodet, chap. 4, and Freamon, chap. 6, in this volume.

3 ⤷ The End of Slavery, "Crises" over Trafficking, and the Colonial State in the French Soudan

RICHARD L. ROBERTS

AMONG THE great paradoxes in the making of the modern world were the unintended consequences of European abolition of the transatlantic slave trade and, later, slavery itself. Far from yielding an industrious and obedient working class, the abolition of the slave trade encouraged freed men and women to become peasants in their efforts to control more of their labor and their time. Formal abolition of the slave trade, first by the Danes, the British, and the Americans, and later by most of the industrializing world, did not end the demand for slave labor. The transatlantic slave trade persisted until Cuba prohibited new slave imports in the 1860s and Brazil abolished slavery in 1888. Even then, the demand for coerced labor led to the trade in indentured labor, sometimes mirroring the conditions of the transatlantic slave trade and at other times reflecting older and regional patterns of debt bondage.[1]

For Africa and Africans, the abolition of the transatlantic slave trade, which led to a gradual reduction in the demand for slaves in the Americas, stimulated demand for slaves in Africa. The nineteenth century witnessed an increased demand for slave labor on the continent as prices declined and as Africans responded to increased opportunities to invest in production to meet growing regional and international demand.[2] Increased demand for slaves within Africa permitted the established warrior states to persist; it increased tensions between peasants and warrior elites, who responded to market stimuli in different ways; and it led to the rise of new warrior states, which expanded slave catchment areas and their state-building enterprises.[3] This was the context in which Europeans conquered Africa in the last quarter of the nineteenth century. European colonial powers used anti–slave trade ideologies to justify colonial conquest.[4] Few colonial powers in Africa, however, had the means and the will to suppress the slave trade.

In thinking about the issue of trafficking in the early colonial period in Africa, we should be mindful of the complex interplay of several mutually reinforcing yet contradictory processes.

Contradictory Policies on Slavery

First among these processes are the often contradictory policies regarding slavery and the slave trade on the colonial, metropolitan, and international levels. France's history of antislavery and anti–slave trade actions is rich and contradictory. Revolutionary France had abolished slavery in 1792 only to see Napoléon I reinstate it in 1802 as part of France's effort to reclaim Saint-Domingue from its rebels, who sought to establish the principles of the revolution. After its defeat in Europe, in 1815, Britain pressured France into abolishing the slave trade by its nationals in 1818, but it was less than enthusiastic about enforcement. Following the July Revolution, in 1830, France criminalized the slave trade, imposed two- to five-year sentences on traders, up to twenty years for captains of slave ships, and actually applied the law in the tiny French outposts in Senegal.[5] How well the law was applied remains an open question. Between 1831 and 1882, only eleven cases of trafficking were heard by the Cour d'Appel of Senegal. Seven led to prison sentences. Three of the seven also led to the forfeiture of the ships carrying the slaves.[6]

The 1848 revolution clarified French policy that French soil liberates all who touch it, but as I argue below, French officials in Senegal sought to limit the impact of this decree by circumscribing what constituted French soil. France was a signatory to all the major international anti–slave trade and antislavery conventions, beginning with Berlin in 1885, Brussels in 1890, Saint-Germain-en-Laye in 1919, the 1926 Slavery Convention of the League of Nations, and the UN General Assembly's 1948 Universal Declaration of Human Rights and 1956 Supplementary Convention on the Abolition of Slavery, the Slave Trade, and Institutions and Practices Similar to Slavery.[7] Yet slavery and the slave trade persisted in French colonies in Africa.

At the colonial level senior French officials implemented laws regarding slavery and the slave trade in response to metropolitan pressure and in response to local events on the ground, where policies and practices often contradicted each other. In explaining the tensions between policy and practice, I am reminded of Bruce Berman and John Lonsdale's insights regarding the contradictory pressures on the colonial state in Africa: "The colonial state indeed straddled not one but two levels of articulation: between the metropole and the colony as a whole as well as within the colony itself. It therefore had a dual character: it was at once a subordinate agent in its restructuring of local production to meet metropolitan demand, yet also the local factor of cohesion over the heterogeneous, fragmented and contradictory social forces jostling within."[8] To explain the tensions between policy and practice, we also need to recognize the capacity of the colonial state to enact policy, no matter at which level it was produced.

The Capacity of Colonial States to Implement Policy

Organizations and institutions on these various levels had limited capacity to implement policy, regardless of its contradictory character. The historiographical debates about whether or not the colonial state in Africa was strong or weak are rich and complex.[9] For our purposes, I am partial to Jeffrey Herbst's concern with the capacity of the state to "broadcast power."[10] According to Herbst, what gives the colonial state (and its legacy in the postcolonial state) its specific quality was its inability to broadcast its power far beyond the central places in the colony, thus the capital and the district headquarters. Thus, no matter what policy was decreed, what it meant in practice was modified by the state's limited capacity to broadcast its power spatially and implement policies widely.

Even where the colonial state was able to broadcast its power, it often did not understand the realities on the ground, which further limited its policies. James Scott's concept of legibility is useful in explaining further the failure of the colonial state in accomplishing what it set out to do. Scott argues that in its effort to make sense out of complex local practices, the state often simplifies realities to fit into its own preconceived categories.[11] When implementing policies designed to change local practices, the results are often unanticipated and contradictory. Such was the case in French colonial efforts to suppress the slave trade and slavery. Slave traders merely moved away from district headquarters and often disguised their slaves as wives and family or hired porters.

Expanding Forms of Documentary Reporting and the Imperial "Crises" of the Interwar Period

The interwar period introduced new pressures into colonial policy that senior colonial administrators and the Ministry of Colonies in Paris could not easily ignore. The establishment of the League of Nations, regardless of how ineffective it was in many areas, nonetheless changed the nature of international scrutiny on conditions in the colonies. Because of diplomatic and journalistic pressure exposing abuses throughout the colonial world, the League established commissions, including the Temporary Commission on Slavery, which called for reports and investigations into claims of alleged persistence of slavery. The International Labor Organization, founded as part of the League's broader mandate, pressured colonial states into explaining policies governing labor practices, including forced labor.[12] The 1920s also witnessed the maturation of new forms of documentary reporting, which further opened colonial practices to wider scrutiny and debate.

The late 1920s also saw the publication of popular travelers' accounts of Africa that illuminated colonial abuses. Especially important were André Gide's *Voyage au Congo* (1927) and his *Le retour du Tchad* (1928), which focused primarily on French Equatorial Africa, and Albert Londres's *Terre d'ébène (la traite des noirs)* (1928), which covered both French West Africa and French Equatorial Africa.[13] Gide's travels were initially framed as part of a novelist's engagement with exotic Africa but quickly turned political as he was confronted with evidence of quotidian abuses of colonial officials and bosses of the concessionary companies. Gide vigorously rebutted challenges to his accounts, further intensifying public attention to colonial issues.[14] In contrast, Londres had a public presence as a reporter and foreign correspondent for several Parisian papers. Londres used his voyage to Senegal and the French Congo in 1928 to expose the corruption and contradictions of French colonialism.[15] Gide and Londres contributed to a sense of imperial crisis in the late 1920s. As Nicholas Dirks has argued, "Scandals point to the underlying tensions and anxieties of an age, even as they work ironically to resolve crises by finding new ways to repress these tensions and anxieties. Scandals require careful management, and they elicit widespread vicarious attention."[16] This flurry of public debate and scrutiny concerning conditions in French West Africa may not have achieved the status of a scandal. It nonetheless made public officials and the colonial ministry vulnerable to humiliation.[17]

The publication of books by Gide, Londres, and others provoked a flurry of public debate about empire and colonialism that coincided with efforts by newly formed international organizations to raise issues about colonialism and what at the time stood for human rights. These international organizations had little enforcement power. What they did have, however, was the power to humiliate imperial powers through "condemnatory reportage."[18] These international organizations, growing groups of domestic nongovernmental organizations, and individuals put pressure on colonial ministries, which in turn put pressure on colonial administrators, to address these practices and abuses.[19] I call these punctuated moments of pressure on colonial administrations crises; and they yielded the evidence we find in the colonial archives.

The Changing Nature of Demand for Coerced and Coercible Labor

No matter how limited the colonial state's capacity to broadcast its power, the elaboration of anti–slave trade and antislavery legislation and policies effectively ended the state's tacit support of slavery. Because the colonial state in French West Africa rarely broadcast its power effectively, it did relatively little to end the slave trade and slavery directly. However, by abolishing the legal category of the slave, which occurred in the 1903 decree establishing a colonial legal system in French West Africa and in the 1905 decree prohibiting the alienation of another person's liberty, it did so indirectly.[20] Masters could no longer turn to the state to seek return of a slave. These two decrees (1903 and 1905) have a complex relationship to the massive exodus of slaves in French West Africa that began in 1905 and more or less ended in 1912. Not all slaves left their masters, but the events of this period led to a profound reorganization of slavery and the slave trade in the region.[21]

These two decrees and the slave exodus led to a gradual change in the composition of slavery in French West Africa and to a change in the strategies of enslavement and the slave trade. Whereas males had composed a significant part of the West African internal slave trade in the second half of the nineteenth century, trafficking after 1905 increasingly consisted of the most vulnerable groups by gender and age: women and children. The elderly were also among the most vulnerable, but they offered little of value to potential buyers. Women, in contrast, provided sexual services, labor power, and reproductive capacity. Free women often experienced "slavelike" conditions through marriage, especially when they were not consulted on their choice of husbands and where bridewealth transfers looked to the outsider as if they were sales.[22] Children often experienced abrupt ruptures from their mothers through custody disputes, pawning, and various forms of fosterage. They often found themselves in slavelike conditions, whether they were purchased or not, and they had even less recourse to kin networks and access to courts than did women.[23] Children were also more easily socialized into dependent and subordinate roles.[24]

The Nature of the Supply of Such Labor

As Suzanne Miers and Kevin Bales make clear, slavery persists to this day because of demand for coerced labor.[25] Demand for child camel jockeys in the Arabian Peninsula continues to stimulate trade in children, often from Africa and over long distances. The *trokosi* system in Ghana continues to be fed by families who seek ritual cleansing from their transgressions by supplying the priests with young girls. Unfree boys and girls work plantations in Côte d'Ivoire; girls and women are recruited into the sex trade and domestic work by unscrupulous recruiters; whole families find themselves working without pay in futile efforts to pay off debts sometimes inherited from a previous generation. Women and children are still valued as slaves in the desert regions of Mauritania and Niger, where aristocratic sensibilities relegate menial forms of herding and domestic work to coerced and dependent people. Girls are coerced into sexual slavery and sold from one trafficker to another in South Africa; African children are trafficked into the United Kingdom and the European Union. The list could go on and on.[26]

Where there is demand for coerced labor, there will be those who supply such labor by kidnapping or by subterfuge. Because of the failures of the colonial state to broadcast its power and its failure to identify the trade in slaves as such, we have only sparse documentation about the trafficking of women and children in the aftermath of the end of slavery. But we do have some (see below).

THE COLONIAL STATE AND ITS EFFORTS TO PROHIBIT THE SLAVE TRADE AND SLAVERY

The effort to curtail slavery and the slave trade in French West Africa has a long and tortuous history. On paper, the French moved aggressively to criminalize the slave trade in 1831 and to abolish slavery altogether in its colonies in 1848. Article 7 of the 1848 law maintained that "the principle that the soil of France liberates the slave who touches it is applied to the colonies and possessions of the Republic."[27] In Saint-Louis and Gorée, slaves were emancipated, although masters often retained slave children under a form of apprenticeship.[28] Elsewhere in colonial Senegal, however, the decrees prohibiting the slave trade and abolishing slavery were often subordinated to the imperatives of colonial rule and the realities of limited capacity to broadcast power.

The abolition law was originally applied to the tiny French towns of Gorée and Saint-Louis, where masters and merchants were fearful that their lives and livelihoods would be disrupted. African merchants of the gum trade, the most important element of Senegalese commerce at this time, cut off shipment to Saint-Louis for fear that once the slave porters and agents entered the town, they would be freed. African merchants of Saint-Louis petitioned the governor for a suspension of the abolition, which he granted. Under consultation with the head of the judiciary of Senegal, Faidherbe further compromised abolition when he made application of article 7 a political tool of colonial expansion. Inhabitants of African villages newly annexed to Senegal were to be considered subjects, not citizens, and therefore not bound by the abolition decree.[29] In contrast, only slaves of Senegal's enemies were to be freed; fugitive slaves of friendly chiefs were considered vagabonds and expelled from French posts.

The legality of returning fugitive slaves and of the slave trade—which fed the expanding demand for labor in the peanut basin and in the towns of the colony as long as commerce kept churning—was unclear. In 1876 and again in 1878, under the energetic direction of a French magistrate, who was less willing than his predecessors to subordinate the rule of law to political expediency, four Africans accused of procuring slaves and selling them in Saint-Louis were tried. In only one instance, the case of N'Jak N'Diaye, a French citizen through his birth in Saint-Louis or Gorée, was a verdict of guilty of contravening the abolition act returned. N'Diaye was, however, sentenced to six months in prison, a relatively mild sentence for what should have been treated far more harshly.[30] By 1883, Victor Schoelcher, a French parliamentarian and abolitionist who had been instrumental in the initial abolition of 1848, helped inflame public opinion in France and thus brought pressure on West African colonial authorities to make the practice of antislavery conform to legislation, especially with respect to tolerating the slave trade on French soil.[31] District officers were instructed to introduce a procedure for liberating fugitive slaves after a three-month waiting period.[32] As the French expanded conquest, they confronted an environment shaped by decades of persistent warfare that led to a significant increase in the trade and acquisition of slaves throughout the western Sudan.[33] As the pace of the Scramble for Africa increased, the primary European powers engaged in the process came to Berlin in 1884 and 1885, to agree on formulas for claiming territory, to avoid conflicts over contested claims, and to promote "free trade." As part of the broader free-trade ideology, participating powers pledged to prohibit the export slave trade from Africa and to suppress operations on land that fed it.[34] As would be the case for so many of these international instruments, little thought was given to implementation and enforcement.

As the Scramble accelerated, so too did pressure, mostly from metropolitan humanitarian and missionary societies, to act more aggressively against the slave trade. The leading African colonial powers thus met again in Brussels in 1890 to decide on ways to suppress the slave trade. The signatories to the Brussels Act of 1890 reiterated the principle that the occupation of Africa was part of broader antislavery measures and they agreed to pass and enforce laws against the capture, transport, and sale of slaves on land and sea. Various bilateral and multilateral agreements reinforced international search and seizure of ships transporting slaves on the Atlantic and Indian Oceans in particular. The signatories also agreed to restrict the sales of firearms and liquor in Africa, believed essential to the trade in slaves.[35]

Despite increasing political rhetoric favoring the suppression of the internal slave trade in the newly conquered regions of West Africa, the French military machine actually encouraged the slave trade. Martin Klein has written extensively on the ways in which the French colonial conquest indirectly and directly fed the slave trade. The French colonial army included a host of African auxiliaries, for whom success in battle translated into the booty of war: captured cattle, stores of grain, and people. French soldiers often kept a slave or two for domestic purposes and rewarded loyal followers with slaves.[36]

Paris grew increasingly frustrated with the military's disregard of its ministerial orders and its disregard for the rule of law. The Ministry of Colonies appointed Alfred Grodet, a civilian with experience in Guyana and the Antilles, as governor of the French Soudan in 1894. Grodet took steps to suppress the slave trade even if the trade indirectly supported conquest and the struggling colonial state.[37] Grodet wrote in 1894, "I cannot admit that on the territory of the Republic at the headquarters of a *cercle*, among the articles of purchase and sale, are representatives of the human species."[38] Grodet's order 273 was to be posted in market centers as well as district headquarters in both French and Arabic. It required village chiefs under threat of punishment to report all slave caravans to the French administrators of the cercle, who then automatically liberated the slaves and fined the traders.[39] Far from having the desired effects, Grodet's decree pushed the slave trade underground. Traffickers continuously devised subterfuges to maintain their supply of slave to markets of French West Africa and the desert. Some relied on the loophole in the decree when they designated their slaves as salaried porters; others claimed that the women in the caravan were actually their wives. Others changed routes to avoid French posts.[40] Given the continuing tensions between Grodet and military leaders eager to pursue conquest, the military disregarded his orders and undermined his authority. After barely a year in office, the minister of the marine and colonies recalled Grodet to Paris.

Colonel Edgard de Trentinian, who succeeded Grodet in 1895, backpedaled on the issues of slavery and the slave trade. In July 1895 he cautioned his administrators to follow a more gradualist course in suppressing the slave trade and slavery. These issues, he wrote require "infinite tact and prudence, if one does not wish to turn the land topsy-turvy and result in its complete economic ruin."[41] This was a crucial period for the military as it prepared for the final push of conquest, and Trentinian did not want to have to deal with massive unrest spurred by energetic antislavery actions. French victory over the kingdom of Sikasso and Samory Touré's state in 1898 gave them hegemony over organized violence in the colony but did not mean the end of enslavement or the slave trade. Enslavement and the slave trade continued, fueled now more by small-scale raids and kidnapping, and it fed growing demand for slaves in the savanna and Sahel as well as deep into the desert.

In 1899, Governor William Ponty oversaw the first sustained period of civilian rule in the French Soudan. In 1901 he laid out a major policy statement that committed the colonial state to end slavery and the slave trade, but gradually so as not to "provoke large scale disorder."[42] Ponty gave no time frame for his policy. Here is yet another example of French colonial efforts to deflect pressure from anti–slave trade public opinion by arguing that the colony was not yet ready for such aggressive intervention in its social and economic order.

A new form of abolitionist pressure emerged from the foundations of the colonial legal system enacted into law on 10 November 1903.[43] In 1903, Secretary General Martial Merlin sent explicit instructions to the newly created native tribunals that "native tribunals cannot be permitted to rule in litigation relative to the state of captivity, which we cannot permit to be juridically recognized. . . . In cases submitted to them, neither native nor French courts can any longer take account of the supposed status of the captive."[44] In effect, the 1903 decree removed the legal underpinnings of slavery and tied the hands of the administration. No longer could masters turn to the administration in an effort to use the power of the state to support the authority of the master over his or her slaves. We shall never know to what extent the slaves were aware of the 1903 decree. But by 1905 slaves of Banamba started a massive exodus from their masters that spread outward in ever-widening circles over the next half dozen years. The Banamba events forced the administration to clarify further its position on slavery and the slave trade. On 12 December 1905, Governor General Ernest Roume formally outlawed enslavement and the sale of slaves. Together with the nonrecognition of the legal status of slavery, the 1905 decree effectively ended slavery by eliminating new enslavement and withdrawing the state's support of the rights of masters over their slaves.[45]

THE PERSISTENCE OF TRAFFICKING

Governor Grodet's 1895 order and Governor General Roume's 1905 decree made trafficking in people a crime.[46] For this chapter, I examine the episodic nature of trafficking "crises" that periodically sent jolts of activity from Paris to Dakar and from Dakar to local administrators and sometimes from Dakar to Paris. What I call trafficking crises were particular events or policies—some colonial, others international—that galvanized the administration into action. Crises are by their nature episodic. They flare brightly for a moment, but then they wane in intensity. These bursts of policy and implementation are rarely sustained over time in the absence of continued pressure from the nongovernmental sector.

Among the earliest evidence we have of trafficking in the French Soudan comes from a set of prison records that were generated in response to the questions regarding proportionality in sentences for crimes. In 1900, Governor General Jean-Baptiste Chaudié railed against district officers who inflicted punishments wholly out of character with the offense; even minor offenses resulted in long prison sentences—in some cases even life imprisonment. Too often, Chaudié wrote, "commandants have a disdain for the life and liberty [of the natives], which I believe must characterize our system of justice in regard to the natives."[47] For Chaudié, the regularization of the native justice was an unambiguous effort to control the French military officers. It was also the foundation of respect for French law and civilization.

Table 3.1 captures the range of sentences for trafficking in 1899. What is not at all clear from the records—and what bothered Chaudié—was what determined whether a trafficker was sentenced to one or ten years imprisonment. But even more worrisome from Chaudié's standpoint was that traffickers were

TABLE 3.1

Prison sentences for crimes including trafficking in 1899, by selected districts in the French Soudan

Prison sentence	Total number	Trafficking (n/% of total)	Bamako (n/% of total)	Kayes	Kita	Segu	Sikasso	Siguiri
1 year	24	9/38%	...	5	...	1	1	2
2 years	42	15/36%	3	2	1	1	8	...
3 years	27	10/37%	...	1	...	1	8	...
5 years	60	9/15%	...	5	...	1	1	2
10 years	10	0	...	...	...	...		...
10–20 years	16	3/19%	...	...	...	...		3
Life sentence	37	9/24%	...	...	...	...		9
Total	216	55/26%	3/5%	13/23%	1/2%	4/7%	18/32%	16/28%

Source: CAOM, Soudan VIII/2.

often sentenced to the same term as those whose crime was of a very different order, thus weakening the status of the crime of trafficking. For example, some traffickers were sentenced to one year in prison, as were thieves accused of stealing jewelry and "millet from an occupied house." Other traffickers were sentenced to three-year prison terms, as were thieves accused of stealing "three silver bracelets." A thief who stole wine and another who stole rice received five-year terms, as did a kidnapper of six "nonfree" people. The latter trafficker, who also murdered one of the captives in the course of kidnapping, received a two-year sentence; so did someone who stole a cow.

The descriptions of the crimes in the records are very sparse, but some further distinctions can be made, as seen in table 3.2. Most often the records refer to the trafficking of "captifs" or "non-libres," as one would expect when describing those involved in the slave trade. The records sometimes qualify this general statement by indicating that the trafficker was accused of kidnapping and transporting "free" individual or kidnapping "refugees," especially those fleeing from Samory or returning to the region he had occupied. Occasionally, the records indicate whether the person trafficked was female or a child. The plural terms *captifs* and *non-libres* are not gender specific; they may include a mix of males and females. The records sometimes describe the crime as the "theft of a child" and sometimes indicate the rape and kidnapping of "captives." As the "crisis" over proportionality of sentence waned, so did the trail of trafficking in the archives. Trafficking reappears in the archives when the next crisis emerged.

Following World War I, the Paris Peace Conference led to the establishment of the League of Nations, the mandate system governing the seized colonies and territories of the defeated powers, the ILO, and a vague commitment

TABLE 3.2

Categories of trafficked people, 1899

Category	Number	Percentage
Slave (*captif, non-libre*), gender not specified	24	43%
Male slave (*captif*)	5	9%
Female slave (*captive*)	8	14%
Free (*libre*)	7	13%
Child	8	14%
Undetermined	4	7%
Total	56	100%

Source: CAOM, Soudan VIII/2.

to "secure fair and humane conditions of labor" at home and in the mandated territories, which also meant dealing with the persistence of slavery.[48] Britain, France, and Belgium met outside Versailles in 1919, at Saint-Germain-en-Laye to renegotiate the Berlin and Brussels conventions, mostly regarding restrictions on the arms and liquor trades. Subsumed within these negotiations was the issue of slavery and the slave trade. The Saint-Germain-en-Laye convention committed these powers to "secure the complete suppression of slavery in all its forms, and of the slave trade by land and sea."[49] But no enforcement mechanisms were defined.

Religious and secular humanitarian groups, as well as international diplomatic posturing over the debate whether to admit Ethiopia into the League, pressured the League to establish a commission on slavery, which was to inquire into the "resurgence" of slavery, especially in Africa.[50] In 1922 the League requested all member states to provide information on slavery. This was only a request, but it nonetheless sent a bolt of activity from the Ministry of Colonies to the colonial administration in Dakar and thence outward to the lieutenant governors of the various colonies. The minister wanted a report that examined the efforts and status of the campaigns against slavery in the various colonies and the measures, including criminal sentences, that were being implemented to suppress slavery.[51] The data for the following chart come from one of these documents.

The report indicated that the administration was pleased with itself: "The curve of judicial statistics signifies above all progress already realized in the struggle against slavery in the territory of French West Africa. . . . The developments recounted in this report demonstrate that for her part, France has largely fulfilled its obligations imposed on state parties to the Brussels Act and

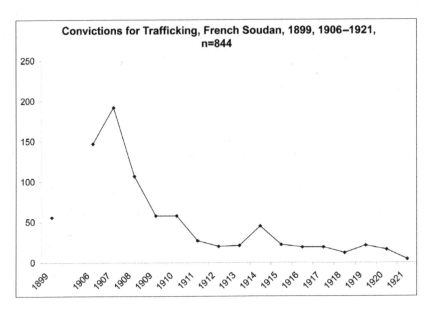

Convictions for Trafficking, French Soudan, 1899, 1906–1921, n=844

that its cooperation in the grand work of liberating the African populations has not been the least active nor least fecund [of its fellow signatories]."[52]

In order to prove its effectiveness in suppressing the slave trade, included in the file is also a transcript of a 1916 criminal trial against N'Diouga Guèye, accused of buying two children kidnapped by a Mauritanian trader, probably near the north bank of the Senegal River. Although Guèye resided in the village of Same, Gandiolais district, the trial was held in Louga, not far from Saint-Louis. What is especially useful for our purposes is that the trial includes the testimony of three kidnapped boys. The first child witness was Guibril Guèye, age ten, born in Mauritania, near Mederdra.

> I was kidnapped[53] at the same time as my brother, several years ago, but I do not know exactly when. It was a Moor named Amir, who one day during the absence of my mother, asked my brother and me to give his camels something to drink. Arriving at a stream, the Moor ordered us to follow him and we could not refuse. We walked for a long time, over many months, and finally we arrived at a village, which I later learned was called Same. There the Moor made us enter the house of Guibril M'Baye, where the three wives of Guibril brought us food, each in turn. The day after our arrival, the Moor returned with a Wolof and ordered my brother to follow that man and to go begging for him. My brother left and I did not see him again for a long time. I stayed for three days in that house and then the Moor took me to N'Diouga Guèye, with whom I've lived since. It was sometime

later that I met my older brother while I was in the fields [working] and heard from his mouth that he lived in the village of Diadj with Amadou Diop.

Momar M'Baye, Guibril Guèye's elder brother, was the next witness.

> I was kidnapped with my younger brother. It must be now about two and a half years ago, but I cannot be sure. We stayed several months with the Moor who stole us, he was called Amar and he was accompanied by Illy Ould Sidy Bayar of the tribe of the Ooumlailen; we stayed in a camp called Riobane. I don't know the name of the village where we stopped and where I was sold. I do not remember the name of the women who brought us food, but I only stayed 24 hours in that house with my brother.

The third child witness was Gora, about four years old, who could not remember his family name. All he said in the trial was, "I remember that I lived with the Moors who then left me with N'Diouga Guèye."[54]

The trial also included testimony from Massouda Fall, mother of Guibril and Momar, two of the three kidnapped boys. She is identified in the transcript as a merchant of wood, aged around thirty-five, and neither a relative nor a "servant" of the accused. She stated at the trial that the kidnapping occurred around Tabaski (December) 1913 near the town of Mederdra, along the border between Senegal and Mauritania. Nearly three years later, completely by chance, she found herself face to face with her youngest son in the district of Tivaouane in Senegal. Guibril told her that he was living with N'Diouga Guèye. Massouda Fall then went to the district headquarters and submitted a complaint.

N'Diouga Guèye was also interrogated. He admitted that he bought the two young children. He claimed that he had bought the first one about seven years ago and the second more recently, only in 1916, and that he paid 160 francs for the first and 150 francs for the second. The president of the tribunal asked if he knew that the sale of a human being was a contravention of the law. N'Diouga Guèye responded, "Yes, I know, but as does everyone in Gandiolais, we buy slaves. I do just like the others." "Do you know others who have bought slaves?" "Yes." "Who are they?" "I know who they are," stated N'Diouga Guèye, "but I will not tell you their names. All of Gandiolais are aware of this trade." "So, you refuse to name the names of the others who have committed the same misdemeanor?" "Yes, I won't say anything. You can kill me [and I won't say anything]." "Where did you get the money with which to buy [these children]?" "It was with the profits from my harvest." Other witnesses testified and much of the rest of the trial sought to implicate the wife of N'Diouga Guèye's brother-in-law, who had fed the kidnapped children, in this case of trafficking.

This trial provides a rare window into the trafficking of children and suggests a complex, multidirectional movement of children back and forth across the Senegal River between Senegal and Mauritania. Most of the literature and the evidence from the files in this collection testify to the continued demand for slave children and women among the desert tribes of Mauritania, where the slaves performed the menial tasks of daily life to support the social hierarchies. The N'Diouga Guèye case suggests that there was considerable demand in the hinterland of Saint-Louis for child labor and that traffickers were not above kidnapping children in Mauritania and transporting them to Senegal. The trafficking in children to Saint-Louis and Gorée had been active since the 1848 abolition of slaves in these two towns. In 1903, Governor General Roume finally clarified what was clearly an ambiguous social category by requiring that those who held minors as apprentices were obliged to register them and to pay into an account a monthly salary that would then be given to the apprentice when she or he became an adult.[55]

Children trafficked into households were vulnerable and exploited. Evidence from early-twentieth-century Gold Coast indicates that trafficked or apprenticed girls were especially liable to sexual abuse. Such vulnerability to sexual abuse and exploitation persists to this day.[56] Furthermore, the case indicated that N'Diouga Guèye used the elder boy to beg in the established tradition, but distorted the process since most mendicancy was linked to Qur'anic education.[57] Guèye used the younger boy to help with the labor in the fields. I am not sure what if anything occurred at the level of policy as a result of the League's 1922–23 inquiry into slavery and trafficking. Nonetheless, in the face of the exposés by Gide and Londres, by 1929 France had signed the Slavery Convention of 1926 and agreed to suppress both slavery and the slave trade in its colonial territories. France also agreed to provide regular reports on its progress in fulfilling the terms of the convention.

Included in the 1922–23 file, the lieutenant governor of Mauritania produced a report that explains the problem of the suppression of the slave trade as due to the state's limited capacity to broadcast power and illuminates some of the theoretical issues raised at the beginning of this chapter.

> Since our effective occupation of Mauritania, events of trafficking have
> come to our attention, thanks to complaints, denunciations, and public
> rumors. They have been regularly repressed. . . . Since our installa-
> tion in Mauritania, no one is ignorant of our efforts to suppress slavery
> and the trade in blacks. However, the criminal sentences for such acts
> have been few. [Between 1908 and 1922, there were only nine cases

of trafficking brought before the native tribunals.] . . . The immensity of the land, often uninhabited and bordered on the east and north by desert, the total absence of a civilizing power between northern Mauritania and southern Morocco, the incursions of pillagers, and the extent of our borders does not always permit us to intercept traffickers. But when we hear of these acts, we always pursue them.[58]

Broadcasting power remained a fundamental challenge in Mauritania.

Article 2 of the 1926 Slavery Convention required that the state parties (referred to as High Contracting Parties) "prevent and suppress the slave trade" and "bring about, progressively and as soon as possible, the complete abolition of slavery in all its forms."[59] The persistence of slavery and trafficking in Mauritania was raised repeatedly at the commission and in reports to the commission. In response to these demands, in 1931 the Ministry of Colonies organized a "committee of experts" to investigate conditions in French West Africa. This "committee of exports" forms the third of our "crises" in the history of trafficking in the aftermath of the end of slavery and reflects on some of the theoretical issues raised at the beginning of this chapter.

The experts' report indicated that trafficking, or at least conviction for trafficking, was indeed declining: in the French Soudan, there were only 10 convictions for trafficking between 1918 and 1923, four between 1923 and 1926, and none between 1926 and 1931. The committee attributed this decline to the thirty-five years of French influence and military service, which has opened the "horizons" of the natives and infused them with ideas of individual progress. The committee did note, however, that a "disguised" trade in women and children persisted. This often took the form of pawning and forced marriage. The report argued that condition of women and children within the African family organization often "restricted the liberty and the human dignity" of women, but was sanctioned by "tradition" and thus "tolerated by us." Change in women's status was a "delicate" task and it would not be possible to "act immediately upon the liberation of women from the yoke of the family." But progress was being made, the report noted; "frequently young girls refuse to marry the man chosen by the head of the family, who is responsible for the group and its property."[60]

In 1931 the slavery commission put renewed pressure on states parties to document their policies to suppress slavery and the slave trade. In a letter to the minister of colonies, interim governor general Auguste Dirat admitted that some areas in Mauritania remained "unadministered" and there were some where residual practices of slavery persisted despite "energetic antislavery efforts."[61] The governor general effectively admitted that the colonial state did not broadcast its power throughout the colony.

The Great Depression deepened, the Popular Front took colonial matters seriously, including the condition of women and their consent in marriage, but war in Europe brought an abrupt end to these efforts to broadcast power and to control the transformations on the ground. Nor was the colonial state able to regularly see realities on the ground, either because they chose not to or because they could not determine the difference between a wife and a slave. Slave trafficking persisted in Mauritania throughout the colonial period.

⌣

French colonial efforts to suppress trafficking in women and children were shaped by the interplay of international humanitarian and governmental forces seeking to force colonial states to live up to their oft-stated commitments to abolish slavery and the slave trade. In many areas of French West Africa, overt slavery and the slave trade disappeared. In other parts of the colonial federation, trafficking in women and children persisted. I have identified five aspects of the persistence of trafficking in women and children that may apply to other regions of Africa and the world where trafficking persists. These are the continued demand for coerced labor; the supply of such coerced and coercible labor; the effects of contradictory policies on the international, national, and local levels; the ability to implement policy; and the pressure exerted on international and national actors by international and nongovernmental organizations. Such pressure, which was at best episodic, caused flurries of activities that targeted trafficking, but only rarely were such activities sustained. As a result trafficking may be been pushed underground, but it was not eliminated.

In this chapter, I have traced how pressure from the League of Nation's Commission on Slavery led to periods of heightened administrative engagement with the issues of trafficking. French colonial administrators often responded quickly to such pressure by claiming at times that the African societies were not yet ready for aggressive social engineering and at other times that they were indeed making significant progress in eradicating trafficking. I also argued that the colonial state's capacity of intervene effectively in the problem of trafficking of women and children was shaped by their failure to broadcast power, especially in the relatively vast spaces of the Sahel and the Sahara, where demand for women and children continued throughout the colonial period. Closely linked to the weakness of the colonial state to broadcast its power was its inability "to see" clearly that trafficking in women and children was often disguised as marriage, adoption, and as family members traveling in distant areas. That trafficking in women and children persists to this day only reflects the sustained demand for servile women and children not only in Africa, but throughout the world.

The story of slavery and trafficking continues. Women and children remain especially vulnerable to declining economic conditions and to being trafficked. The problems of broadcasting power, interpreting local practices, states' willingness to invoke culture as a defense of inaction, and the episodic nature political response to humanitarian crises remain barriers to effective enforcement of global human rights regimes.[62]

NOTES

Abbreviations

ANS   Archives Nationales, République du Sénégal
AOF   Section Afrique Occidentale Française
CAOM   Centre des Archives d'Outre-Mer

1. David Northrup, *Indentured Labor in the Age of Imperialism, 1834–1922* (New York: Cambridge University Press, 1995), chaps. 2, 5.

2. Paul Lovejoy and David Richardson, "The Initial 'Crisis of Adaptation': The Impact of British Abolition on the Atlantic Slave Trade in West Africa, 1808–1820," in *From Slave Trade to "Legitimate" Commerce*, ed. Robin Law (Cambridge: Cambridge University Press, 1995), 46–52; Lovejoy, *Transformations in Slavery: A History of Slavery in Africa*, 2nd ed. (New York: Cambridge University Press, 2000), chap. 8.

3. Martin A. Klein, *Slavery and Colonial Rule in French West Africa* (Cambridge: Cambridge University Press, 1998); Edward A. Alpers, *East Africa and the Indian Ocean* (Princeton: Markus Wiener, 2009).

4. Suzanne Miers, *Britain and the Ending of the Slave Trade* (New York: Africana, 1974).

5. Sue Peabody and Keila Grinberg, eds., *Slavery, Freedom, and the Law in the Atlantic World* (Boston: Bedford/St. Martin's, 2007); Klein, *Slavery and Colonial Rule*, 19–21. See also Trevor R. Getz, *Slavery and Reform in West Africa: Toward Emancipation in Nineteenth-century Senegal and the Gold Coast* (Athens: Ohio University Press, 2004), chap. 4; L. C. Jennings, *French Anti-Slavery: The Movement for the Abolition of Slavery in France, 1802–1848* (New York: Cambridge University Press, 2000).

6. "Relevé des arrêts rendus par la Cour d'Appel du Sénégal pour faits de traits de noirs, de détournement et de sequestration de personnes depuis la loi du 4 Mars 1881," ANS, 2 K 27, Repression de la traite et captivité au Sénégal, 1902–1907. I thank Martin Klein and Paul Lovejoy for making available the Klein microfilm collection.

7. The best description of the international campaign to end slavery is found in Suzanne Miers, *Slavery in the Twentieth Century* (Walnut Creek, CA: AltaMira, 2003).

8. Bruce Berman and John Lonsdale, "Coping with the Contradictions," in *Unhappy Valley: Conflict in Kenya and Africa*, ed. Berman and Lonsdale, 2 vols. (Athens: Ohio University Press, 1992), 80.

9. For a sample of these debates, see John Lonsdale, "States and Social Processes in Africa," *African Studies Review* 24, nos. 2–3 (1981): 139–225; Crawford M.

Young, *African Colonial States in Comparative Perspective* (New Haven: Yale University Press, 1994).

10. Jeffrey Herbst, *States and Power in Africa: Comparative Lessons in Authority and Control* (Princeton: Princeton University Press, 2000).

11. James C. Scott, *Seeing Like a State: How Certain Schemes to Improve the Human Condition Have Failed* (New Haven: Yale University Press, 1998).

12. See G. A. Johnston, *The International Labour Organisation: Its Work for Social and Economic Progress* (London: Europa, 1970); Susan Pedersen, "Back to the League of Nations," *American Historical Review* 112, no. 4 (2007): 1091–1117.

13. André Gide, *Voyage au Congo* (Paris: Gallimard, 1927); Gide, *Le retour du Tchad* (Paris: Gallimard, 1928); Albert Londres, *Terre d'ébène (la traite des noirs)* (Paris: A. Michel, 1929).

14. Daniel Moutote, *André Gide: L'engagement, 1926–1939* (Paris: SEDES, 1991), 76–84; Christopher Bettinson, *Gide: A Study* (London: Heinemann, 1977), 92–93; Walter Putnam, "Writing the Wrongs of French Colonial Africa: *Voyage au Congo* and *Le retour du Tchad*," in *André Gide's Politics: Rebellion and Ambivalence*, ed. Tom Conner (New York: Palgrave, 2000), 97–107.

15. W. D. Redfern, *Writing on the Move: Albert Londres and Investigative Journalism* (New York: P. Lang, 2004). 118–27. Every year, the Albert Londres Prize is given for the best investigative journalism in France.

16. Nicholas B. Dirks, *The Scandal of Empire: India and the Creation of Imperial Britain* (Cambridge, MA: Belknap Press, 2006), 29–30.

17. For a discussion of imperial scandal as a "moment of ideological discontinuity" that contributed to "remaking empire" in the 1920s, see esp. Mrinalini Sinha, *Specters of Mother India: The Global Restructuring of an Empire* (Durham: Duke University Press, 2006).

18. Martin Thomas, *The French Empire between the Wars* (Manchester: Manchester University Press, 2005), 156.

19. J. P. Daughton, "Behind the Imperial Curtain: International Humanitarian Efforts and the Critique of French Colonialism in the Interwar Years," *French Historical Studies* 34, no. 3 (2011): 503–28.

20. Klein, *Slavery and Colonial Rule*, chaps. 8 and 10; see also Richard L. Roberts, *Warriors, Merchants, and Slaves: The State and the Economy in the Middle Niger Valley, 1700–1914* (Stanford: Stanford University Press, 1987), chap. 5.

21. The nature of the end of slavery in French West Africa is subject to intense debate. For a sample, see Richard L. Roberts, "The End of Slavery in the French Soudan, 1905–1914"; Igor Kopytoff, "The Cultural Context of African Abolition," both in *The End of Slavery in Africa*, ed. Suzanne Miers and Richard L. Roberts (Madison: University of Wisconsin Press, 1988). See also Klein, *Slavery and Colonial Rule*, chaps. 10–11; Gregory Mann, *Native Sons: West African Veterans and France in the Twentieth Century* (Durham: Duke University Press, 2006).

22. But it would be profoundly wrong to equate marriage with slavery. Richard L. Roberts, *Litigants and Households: African Disputes and Colonial Courts in the French Soudan, 1895–1912* (Portsmouth, NH: Heinemann, 2005), chap. 5.

23. See Elisabeth McMahon (chap. 1, this volume) and Marie Rodet (chap. 4) for how women and girls became part of the new coerced-labor force in the aftermath of the end of slavery.

24. Gwyn Campbell, Suzanne Miers, and Joseph Miller, eds., *Children in Slavery* (Athens: Ohio University Press, 2009). On pawns, see Cati Coe, "Domestic Violence and Child Circulation in Southeastern Gold Coast, 1905–28," in *Domestic Violence and the Law in Colonial and Postcolonial Africa*, ed. Emily Burrill, Richard L. Roberts, and Elizabeth Thornberry (Athens: Ohio University Press, 2010).

25. Miers, *Slavery*; Kevin Bales, *Disposable People: New Slavery in the Global Economy* (Berkeley: University of California Press, 1999).

26. See Margaret Akullo (chap. 9, this volume) and Susan Kreston (chap. 10).

27. Quoted in François Renault, *L'abolition de l'esclavage en Sénégal* (Paris: Société française d'histoire d'outre-mer, 1972), 7. See also Klein, *Slavery and Colonial Rule*, chap. 2.

28. Mohamed Mbodj, "The Abolition of Slavery in Senegal, 1820–1890: Crisis or the Rise of a New Entrepreneurial Class?" in *Breaking the Chains: Slavery, Bondage, and Emancipation in Modern Africa and Asia*, ed. Martin Klein (Madison: University of Wisconsin Press, 1993), 197–211. For juvenile delinquency and control over children, see Ibrahima Thioub, "Marginalité juvénile et enfermement à l'époque colonial: Les premières écoles pénitentiaires du Sénégal, 1888–1927," in *Enfermement, prison et châtiments en Afrique*, ed. Florence Bernault (Paris: Karthala, 1999), 205–66.

29. Renault, *Abolition*, 10–11.

30. Roger Pasquier, "À propos de l'émancipation des esclaves au Sénégal en 1848," *Revue française d'histoire d'outre-mer* 54, nos. 194–97 (1967): 188–208.

31. For the French Senate debate of 1 March 1880, see Victor Schoelcher, *L'esclavage au Sénégal en 1880* (Paris: Librairie Centrale des Publications Populaires, 1880). For Schoelcher's role in these efforts, see Schoelcher, *Polémique colonial*, 2 vols. (Paris: E. Dentu, 1886), 2:189–91.

32. Denise Bouche, *Les villages de liberté en Afrique noire française, 1887–1910* (The Hague: Mouton, 1968), 102–4.

33. Roberts, *Warriors*, chap. 3; Andrew Hubbell, "A View of the Slave Trade from the Margin: Souroudougou in the Late Nineteenth-Century Slave Trade of the Niger Bend," *Journal of African History* 42, no. 1 (2001): 25–48; Martin Klein, "The Slave Trade and Decentralized Societies," *Journal of African History* 42, no. 1 (2001): 49–65.

34. See Sybil E. Crowe, *The Berlin West African Conference, 1884–1885* (London: Longmans, Greene, 1942).

35. Miers, *Slavery*, 19–22.

36. Klein, *Slavery*, chap. 5; Roberts, *Warriors*, chap. 4.

37. See William D. Irvine, *The Boulanger Affair Reconsidered* (New York: Oxford University Press, 1989).

38. Grodet to commandant, region sud, 12 September 1894, CAOM, Soudan IV, 1.

39. Grodet, circulaire, 17 May 1895, Kayes, ANS-AOF, K 19. Liberated slaves were usually sent to villages de liberté, located strategically along military supply routes, so that freed slaves could be easily impressed into the carrier service. See Bouche, *Villages de liberté*.

40. Rapport sur la captivité, Sokolo, 1905, ANS-AOF, K 19; rapport politique, Segu, Apr. 1904, Archives Nationales, République du Mali, 1 E 71.

41. Letter, no signature [Colonel Trentinian], 16 November 1895, ANS-AOF, K 19.

42. Rapport sur la situation politique des cercles du Haut-Sénégal-Moyen Niger, 1 April 1901, Kayes, ANS-AOF, 2 G 1–14.

43. See esp., Roberts, *Litigants*.

44. Instructions accompanying the decree of 10 November 1903, ANS-AOF, K 16.

45. See Martin A. Klein and Richard Roberts, "The Banamba Slave Exodus and the Decline of Slavery in the Western Sudan," *Journal of African History* 21, no. 3 (1980): 375–94.

46. Students of trafficking should consult the registers of criminal cases heard at the level of the tribunal de cercle. The perspective from this court would provide a fuller sense of the volume of trafficking cases and detail on actual acts.

47. Governor-General Chaudié to Minister of Colonies, with copies to 1ère Direction, 1ère Bureau, and Sec-gen 3ème Bureau, St. Louis, 21 March 1900, CAOM, Soudan VIII, 2.

48. Michael D. Callahan, *Mandates and Empire: The League of Nations and Africa, 1914–1931* (Brighton: Sussex Academic Press, 1999).

49. Convention quoted in Miers, *Slavery*, 61.

50. Miers argues that this interest in the resurgence of slavery was also linked to Ethiopia's admission to the League.

51. Minister of Colonies to Governor-General, AOF, 27 October 1922, Paris, ANS, 2 K 4.

52. Report, no title, no date [probably 1923], ANS, 2 K 4.

53. The term used was *volé*, stolen.

54. Justice indigène, Cercle de Louga, Affaire de traite, 23 August 1916, ANS, 2 K 4. The complete transcript and a fuller discussion of this case appears in Richard Roberts, "A Case of Kidnapping and Child Trafficking in Senegal, 1916," in *African Voices on Slavery and the Slave Trade: The Sources*, ed. Alice Bellagama, Sandra Greene, and Martin Klein (New York: Cambridge University Press, forthcoming). Portions of the trial transcript appear here with permission.

55. Arrête determinant la situation des mineurs délivrés de la condition de captivité, Dakar, 23 November 1903, ANS, 2 K 4. See also Thioub, "Marginalité juvénile."

56. Coe, "Domestic Violence." See also E. Benjamin Skinner, A *Crime So Monstrous: Face-to-Face with Modern-Day Slavery* (New York: Free Press, 2008).

57. For context, see Rudolph T. Ware, "Njàngaan: The Daily Regime of Qur'anic Students in Twentieth-Century Senegal," *International Journal of African Historical Studies* 37, no. 3 (2004): 515–38.

58. Lt. Governor, Mauretania, to Governor-General, Saint-Louis, 22 January 1923, ANS, 2 K 4.

59. Kevin Bales, *New Slavery: A Reference Handbook* (Santa Barbara: ABC-CLIO, 2000), 79.

60. Governor-General, AOF, to Minister of Colonies, Dakar, 15 January 1932, ANS, K 113.

61. Governor-General to Minister of Colonies, confidential letter, Dakar, 30 July 1931, ANS, K 133.

62. See Sally E. Merry, *Human Rights and Gender Violence* (Chicago: University of Chicago Press, 2006).

4 ⮝ "Under the Guise of Guardianship and Marriage"

Mobilizing Juvenile and Female Labor in the Aftermath of Slavery in Kayes, French Soudan, 1900–1939

MARIE RODET

FOLLOWING THE colonial conquest of the French Soudan in the second half of the nineteenth century and with the official ban of slavery decreed in French West Africa in 1905, slaves began to leave their masters. In the region of Kayes, women, who made up the majority of the slave population, were also the majority of those leaving.[1] The departure of female slaves restricted the domestic and agricultural workforce for slave-owning noble families. Noble women were especially concerned by the flight of slaves because their ability to recruit labor was limited. Both men and women increasingly had to turn to their own lineages to recruit dependents in order to augment their workforce. Men, however, always had better access to lineage workforce than women because in patrilineal and patrilocal societies, like those of the region of Kayes, women married into their husbands' lineages and thus had fewer opportunities to recruit clients and lineage labor.[2] Women could count on the help of their daughters to alleviate the daily workload. They also used the labor of children who had been entrusted to them by their families.

With the increasing demand for domestic labor due to the end of slavery, the system of child fosterage seems to have expanded during the first twenty years of the twentieth century. In the region of Kayes, the intensification and expansion of child fosterage allowed women to gain additional labor. They used their own family networks and relied on former forms of bondage, which did not completely disappear but were transformed in the aftermath of the end of slavery in order to acquire and control new labor, which was almost exclusively juvenile and female.

With emancipation, former slaves acquired the right to create their own lineages. Female and male former slaves sought to keep their family units together—whether by staying with their former masters or in leaving them

86

together. For former slaves, gaining control over the family, and therefore over the labor of family members, was one of the major areas of struggle during the emancipation process. Former masters struggled to keep their former slaves on their fields and thus under their control.[3]

The end of slavery in the Kayes region coincided with a series of poor harvests, drought, and food crises.[4] Even as former slaves and former masters struggled over control of former slaves' labor, the food crises contributed to the trafficking of former slave women and children. During times of food crisis, the boundary between guardianship and bondage often blurred. Foster-age and debt bondage were both used socially to control the circulation of an increasingly juvenile and female workforce. Most of the children pawned, sold, or fostered were girls. Trafficking in girls contributed to the persistence of social hierarchies in the aftermath of slavery.

In the aftermath of the end of slavery the boundary between fosterage, child bondage, pawnship, and forced marriage of girls was often vague, and it was in this world that considerable numbers of children and young women moved. Evidence for these processes is found in transcripts of civil-court disputes in the region of Kayes for the first half of the twentieth century. These documents, as well as complaints addressed to the administration and colonial correspondence, testify to the numerous attempts made by the men and women of the region to gain or keep custody of children and therefore to secure access to juvenile labor force in a time of tremendous social and economical change.

MOBILIZING JUVENILE AND FEMALE LABOR IN THE AFTERMATH OF SLAVERY

Given the high degree of social mobility and ecological crises that coincided with the end of slavery, it should not be surprising that the issue of guardianship of children became prominent in the jurisprudence of the courts of the region of Kayes. These issues emerged most often when divorce occurred or when the father died; mothers tried to keep their children when the father or the father's kin claimed them. Brothers, sisters, and even mothers of the deceased husband were often in court to assert their rights of guardianship over the children. The payment of bridewealth by the family of the groom to the family of the bride officially transferred to the husband and his kin custody rights over the children he had with his wife. In July 1907, Penda, the grandmother of Alkasoum on the father's side, who had lost his father and whose mother had just remarried, claimed her rights over the child.[5] The court granted guardianship to the grandmother. In January 1908, Mohamadou K. came to the provincial court of Kayes to claim the guardianship of his younger sister, who had been entrusted to a neighbor, Coly D., when their father died.[6] The court gave Mohamadou custody of his sister.

In May 1910, Téné and Coumba D. came to the court of Kayes to claim custody of Ouarata, their deceased brother's twelve-year-old daughter, who lived with her mother.[7] The court dismissed their case, as according to Maliki Islamic law the custody of girl children belonged to the child's mother until marriage or the remarriage of the mother.[8]

When divorce occurred, women sought to keep their daughters with them to augment their labor. In most cases and as the customs permitted, divorced spouses reached a compromise in which the daughters stayed with their mother up to their marriage. Divorced husbands usually agreed. They asserted rights over their daughters only when they were ready to be married, in order to claim the bridewealth.

From 1907 to 1910, custody disputes in the provincial court of Kayes were relatively stable, forming 6 to 10 percent of the overall caseload.[9] By 1911 and 1912, when the impact of the end of slavery was being felt throughout the region, custody cases shot up to 16 and 23.5 percent of the caseload, respectively.[10] Even more significantly, the percentage of cases dealing directly with custody issues of former slave children increased in 1911 to 26 percent of all custody cases and in 1912 to 43 percent.[11] Under slavery, children of slaves belonged to the master of the mother. In 1911 and 1912, former slaves sued their former masters for control over their children, and divorced men and women of slave origin were in court to fight over the custody of their children. This trend demonstrates that men and women, former slaves and former masters, as well as husbands and wives struggled to define and often redefine rights over children in order to increase the number of their dependents.[12]

Custody cases also reveal complex transactions in the value of child labor and in cost of subsistence during fosterage. In the cases of disputes between former slaves and former masters over children, the masters claimed compensation for the food and maintenance provided for several years for the child. Even if in most cases we do not know the exact circumstances of the fosterage of the child, it is reasonable to imagine that the reimbursement of the expenses for the child was a way for the former masters to seek compensation for the loss of workforce. It was thus a kind of ransom. In May 1910, Brahima T. came to the court of Yélimané reclaiming his wife and his child. Fourteen years earlier, while Brahima T. was working in a farming village some distance from Yélimané, his master had given his wife and child to Waly G. Waly G. told him that his wife was deceased and that he could have his child back but only if he paid compensation for the expenses he spent on their food. The court ordered Brahima T. to pay 90 francs, an amount equivalent to the price of a slave child in 1904, when slavery was still legal.[13]

In the first years of the existence of the provincial courts, many former slaves—women and men—turned to the colonial administration and the colonial courts in order to secure their rights over their children. Nioumou S., a former slave from the cercle of Kayes, tried to see the commandant of Kayes in order to secure his help in liberating her still-enslaved family. The commandant's interpreter, who also served as a gatekeeper of access to the commandant, refused her request. In 1905 she traveled to Saint-Louis in order to present her grievances directly to the governor general.[14] With the end of slavery, both female and male former slaves attempted to gain control over their families. Even if war, sale, and purchase had scattered kin across different regions and households, freed slaves attempted to trace their still-enslaved family members and secure their freedom. In 1907, Makan C., who in 1900 had acquired her own freedom after having worked in Senegal and returned to Kayes, asked the prosecutor's office in Kayes for the court's help in regaining custody of her children who, she claimed, were still enslaved in the cercle.[15] These examples support Martin Klein's assertion that the struggle for the control over family life was one of the most important issues of emancipation.[16]

In the patrilineal world of the region of Kayes, slave and free women alike usually had little claim on their own children. This situation prevailed especially when bridewealth transfers had occurred, which automatically transferred custody rights over the children to the husband and his family. Men therefore could usually invoke custom to maintain control over children. In order to challenge men's control over children, some women of slave descent turned to the colonial administration and the courts to claim their rights over their own children. During the first years of the operation of the colonial courts, the judges were favorably inclined to grant a former slave woman divorce and custody of her children if no bridewealth had been given for her. Slave marriages or marriages between master and slave were rarely formalized by the payment of a bridewealth, or if so, the latter was likely to be merely a token.[17] With the introduction of a new legal system in French West Africa in 1903 and the prohibition of new enslavement in 1905, the colonial administration urged the courts to no longer acknowledge any slave status in their judgments. In April 1910, Diamou D. came to the court of Yélimané to ask for his child. He explained that he and Awa D. were slaves of the same master. They married. He then left for Yélimané-refuge, the liberty village of the region, where runaway slaves and slaves freed from France's enemies were housed. The pregnant Awa refused to follow him. Diamou was in court to claim his child. Awa declared to the court that she had never received any bridewealth, and witnesses confirmed this. The court decided that the child would stay with the mother.[18]

A significant change in the colonial court's jurisprudence occurred in the early 1910s. Whereas earlier the courts were inclined to accept women's suits for divorce, increasingly after the middle of the 1910s, colonial courts ordered them—regardless of their former status—to return to their husbands.[19] As wives and daughters, they had to remain under the control of male guardians. Divorce cases linked to the issue of slavery increasingly followed the general pattern of the court's ruling that children belonged to their father. After the early 1910s, the courts therefore reaffirmed men's exclusive control of the family workforce. In response to their diminished control over their own children, women of slave descent, who had separated from their husbands, increasingly demanded compensation for the expenses they had incurred as a result of maintaining their children when claimed by their husbands. In April 1907, Boubakar T., who divorced Assa one year earlier, claimed their two children since Assa was about to remarry.[20] In compensation Assa asked for reimbursement of the cost of their food for one year. The court awarded custody of the children to the father but ordered him to reimburse Assa for the food expenses for the children for one year.

Mobilizing juvenile labor by securing rights over children and by controlling their circulation became a major issue of the end of slavery. The circulation of juvenile labor through the system of fosterage was a well-established practice, but it seems to have expanded with the increasing need for domestic labor following abolition. The expansion of fosterage through family networks of migration helped alleviate labor shortages. Women increasingly turned therefore to their family network in order to gain new labor force, especially through the migration of young girls, referred to as young maids. Studies on the migration of women from the region of Kayes in the recent past have shown that these young girls were mostly from poor and low-status families, mostly likely of slave origin.[21] Traditionally, brides of noble status were accompanied to the family of the groom by young female slaves they received as presents from their parents and who would help them out in their new household.[22] Following the prohibition of new enslavement of 1905, this practice was likely transformed so that "young maids" of former servile status became substitutes for the young female slaves who helped the new bride with her household chores.[23]

In times of tremendous social and economical changes, as in the first twenty years of the twentieth century, the boundary between fostered children, maids, and pawned children, especially for young girls of slave origin, became blurred.[24] In the 1920s, Kani C., a young Soninke of slave descent from Guidimakha, had to leave her family to go further north to a small village of the colony of Mauritania to work for a noble woman for two or three years because of the hardship her family suffered.[25] In her account, it is unclear whether she was entrusted or pawned to this woman or if she simply went to work freely in this village to help her family. It is probably not a coincidence that Kani C. was of servile status and her new guardian a woman of noble status. This last example underlines the complex and blurred transition experienced by categories such as unfree and free labor in the aftermath of the end of slavery. This case also raised questions about the distinction often made between slavery and pawnship. The local population of former slave status probably understood pawnship as slavery.[26] But colonial justice and anti–slave trade policy made a distinction between slavery and pawning when confronted with cases of forced bondage following the promulgation of the decree of 1905, prohibiting enslavement in French West Africa. The colonial courts should have considered pawnship a criminal offense, like trading in slaves; but when it involved members of the same family, it was not considered trafficking and was a less serious offense. When confronted with colonial justice, the persons involved in the transaction attempted to claim that trafficked or pawned girls were members of their family and destined to get married. As most of the pawned children were girls, many ended up marrying creditors. In reality, most were girls of former slave status. Some of them were lured into accompanying the trafficker with promises of marriage and higher social status.[27] Most were simply further trafficked as concubines and domestic workers. While girls and young women continued to be trafficked under the guise of marriage, the trafficking of children also continued under the guise of guardianship and fosterage. Trafficking increasingly targeted the most vulnerable groups: women and children, who were to become central to the development of modern-day slavery.[28]

TRAFFICKING IN WOMEN AND CHILDREN IN POSTABOLITIONIST FRENCH SOUDAN

With the abolition of enslavement, in 1905, trafficking of women and children was transformed and reorganized in order to adapt to the new circumstances. In some cases, the colonial administration closed its eyes to the persistence of trafficking because it did not fully understand the blurred boundary between trafficking and forced marriage, fosterage, and pawnship. Under the guise of marriage, pawning persisted, especially in times of economic crisis. In the midst of the Great Depression, the persistence of the slavery-like condition of pawning caused a scandal in France.

The colonial administration was sometimes actively implicated in the trafficking of children. The administrators often "entrusted" freed slave children to craft workers or tradesmen as apprentices. In reality, many were considered slaves and simply exploited as before. Young girls were given jobs as maids in families of tradesmen or entrusted to the chiefs of the liberty villages.[29] The official end of slavery often simply transformed forced bondage into legal guardianship. Trafficked children were referred to as fostered or adopted, while young slave women were presented as young brides. A petition of 1904, written one year before abolition, seems to be symptomatic of the new discourse that slaveholders used when confronting colonial emancipatory politics. In her letter to the colonial administrator, Caba C. claimed that Captain Barret, the former commandant of the cercle of Kita, had given her a nine-year-old captive named Tébaré following the capture of the city of Sikasso in 1898.[30] The thrust of her petition was that while Tébaré was becoming helpful in the household, "bad people" had advised Tébaré to accuse her of poor treatment and to escape to the liberty village in Kita. She had been to the administrator of Kita, who told her to pursue the issue with the chief of the liberty village. The chief refused to return Tébaré. She then had to come to Kayes to claim the girl, whom she considered her daughter. Unfortunately, the file does not contain the outcome of the case but we can suspect that her complaint was dismissed by the colonial administration because by 1901 slaves residing in the liberty villages could no longer be returned to their former masters.[31] Young former slaves continued to be entrusted by the administration to local notables or colonial agents, even after 1905. In 1907 the commandant of the cercle of Kayes wrote to the governor of the colony of Upper-Senegal and Niger that he authorized two young former slaves, Bilali and Barka, who had been entrusted to Oumar A., a policeman, to go back to their village of origin, Makhana-Liberté. The commandant requested that Oumar A. receive compensation for the maintenance he had provided to Bilali and Barka for four months.[32]

The system of fosterage or of performing domestic labor outside the family home (or both) in order to reduce the economic burden on the family actually has some similarities with pawnship.[33] A debtor, often from a poor family, with a low social status or of servile origin, gave to his or her creditor a member of his or her family as collateral for a loan. The pawn—very often a girl—worked for the creditor until the debtor paid the creditor in full. In some regions of the French Soudan, the labor of the pawn was equivalent to the interest charged, leaving the original loan still to be repaid. Young girls were the most likely people to be pawned because they had significant "material" value. The creditor or somebody of his or her family could marry her if the debtor was unable to repay the original loan, which would be extinguished by its equivalence to bridewealth. Because creditors were very often the wealthiest people of the region, pawnship relations tended therefore to perpetuate the social divisions of the society, leaving pawned girls in conditions akin to slave status. This issue of pawnship is therefore closely linked to the issues of controlling the workforce and gender relations, of maintaining social divisions, and of perpetuating clientelism.[34] Normally, pawnship differed clearly from slavery insofar as it was temporary.[35] It was the contract of pawnship and not the person as such that was the direct property of the creditor.[36] Furthermore, in the case of pawnship, the person remained in the lineage of origin and the reimbursement of the debt allowed the "liberation" of the pawned person at any time.[37]

The work performed by the pawn represented interest on the debt and covered the maintenance costs but did not diminish the debt. This system could lead to numerous contestations, as creditors could take inflation into account, especially in times of hardship, and also seek reimbursement of the maintenance costs of the pawn. Parents often tried to reclaim their pawned children, but they were not always able to make the creditor agree. In 1907, Mady C. came to the court of Bafoulabé to claim his sister who lived with Fallahi C. He explained to the court that his mother, being unable to pay the head tax, had in the past asked Fallahi for help and had therefore pawned her daughter. Since then, the child had remained in Fallahi's care. The court decided that the girl should be given back to her family and that Mady would have to pay two pieces of cotton fabric (*guinée*), a rifle, and 100 francs to Fallahi for the six years of maintenance of the girl.[38]

During this period, young girls were also trafficked under the guise of marriage. This is especially clear in two cases of trafficking heard by the court of Kita in 1906 and 1907. In 1906, Foulanténé N. and Singou T. were accused of the trafficking of a woman called Sakan K. Sakan explained to the court of Kayes, "I was a servant of Foulanténé N. Five months ago, he sent me to Singou T. without telling me anything. When I arrived at his place, Singou T. told me that I henceforth belonged to him, that it had been settled with my former master. I protested against this situation but Singou T. told me that he would marry me; I believed him and I did not register a complaint against him at that time. But as Singou T. never kept his word, I now seek redress against him and against Foulanténé N."[39] However, Foulanténé N. refused to admit that he had sold the woman. He said that he had given her in marriage to Singou T. in exchange for four oxen, but that Singou T. had not formally married her. The court declared that Foulanténé N. and Singou T. were to be found guilty of the sale of a woman. However, the court recognized that even if the "marriage" was a sham, it admitted that Singou T.'s goal was to make Sakan K. his mistress, and therefore it reduced the sentence to six months imprisonment for Foulanténé N. and three for Singou T. Sakan K. was declared free and the four oxen were to be sold for the benefit of the colonial state.

In 1907, Kaba K. M. and Doua D. were tried by the court of Kayes for the sale of a young servant, Kouraba S., for six cows and one donkey.[40] The two accused argued in court that the alleged transaction was actually a marriage. Witnesses at the trial affirmed that a sale had actually taken place. Doua D. and Kaba K. M. were sentenced to a 50-franc fine and five years' imprisonment.

These cases call into question the categories of "wife" and "slave woman," especially when applied to women of slave descent. They also highlight the "shifting" border between the two statuses during the period when the colonial government was implementing antitrafficking measures. In 1907, Moriba S. came to the court of Nioro to complain about his wife: "I bought this woman thirteen years ago, but since our marriage she always refused to work. I ask for divorce."[41] The court granted the divorce.

Despite the abolition of slavery, trafficking cases heard by the courts of the region of Kayes between 1905 and 1907 highlight the persistent labeling of females of slave descent as concubines, workers, and commodities.[42] This situation did not fit into existing French abolitionist categories. In the eyes of the colonial administration, a woman could only be the wife (and therefore a free wife) of a free man. Confronted by cases such as those of Foulanténé N. and Singou T., in which the distinction between slave and wife was blurred, the French administration was reluctant to implement the reality of their abolitionist policies for fear that liberating women would challenge domestic and social stability in the newly conquered territories.

The colonial administration was, however, aware of the limits of its emancipatory policy, especially toward women and children. In a circular of 1906 concerning the decree of 1905 prohibiting new enslavement, the attorney general invited his colleagues to "demand from the defendants written proof and documents issued by the administrative or council authorities testifying to the exactness of their declarations [regarding the status of their "wives" and "children"]. Otherwise you would risk perpetuating under the cover of guardianship and above all marriage real sales of persons, and if the law was implemented this way, the repression of these acts would become, if not impossible, at least difficult."[43]

The provisions of the decree of 1905 should have normally implied the banning and curbing of pawnship in the same terms as slave trafficking. However, confronted with cases of pawnship, the colonial administration was also reluctant to adjudicate them as trafficking when they concerned members of the same family. In the jurisprudence, the distinction was therefore made between trafficking (or slavery) and pawnship, with the latter being considered a relatively minor crime.[44] In 1906, Mamady K. was tried by the court of Kita for the sale of his two nieces.[45] During the trial, Mamady K. testified that he did not intend to sell his nieces, but pawned them against 300 francs in order to settle a debt. He also declared that he did not know that this custom had been abolished. The court sentenced him, according to mitigating circumstances, to six months' imprisonment and the loss of his custody rights. In the same year, the court of Kita also tried Setigui D. for the sale of a young woman.[46] The accusation of trafficking was dismissed, as the court recognized that he had pawned her for a debt and had not sold the young woman, who was a member of his family and for whom he had custody rights. Nonetheless, Setigui D. was sentenced to one year's imprisonment and the loss of his custody rights.

The administration, on the pretext that they did not wish to interfere in local customs, limited whenever possible their intervention in pawnship cases. As most of the people concerned were women, direct intervention from the administration would have meant dealing with issues such as family authority and the structures of customary law concerning marriage.[47] In 1932, Governor General Joseph Brévié, dealing with the issue of women's condition, wrote in a chapter of a report on servile work entitled "Disguised Sale of Women and Children," "But in this field more than in any others, the task that the administration has to undertake proves to be delicate. At the beginning of the occupation, even with a clear vision of the problem to solve, it would have not been possible to undertake any action to completely liberate native women from the family yoke. Any coercion, any brutal attempts at 'detribalization' would have been doomed to immediate and tumultuous failure."[48] It is only by the mid-1930s that the colonial administration, under the pressure of metropolitan opinion and confronted with pawnship cases in which a colonial administrator was involved, clearly stated that pawnship was slavery and implemented specific measures to repress it.[49] And because so many pawns were women, the colonial administration also started to prohibit forced marriages in the late 1930s. At a time of great hardship in the region of Nioro, a father entrusted his young girl to a tradeswoman from Nioro.[50] During the investigation of 1936 conducted by the local authorities, this woman showed a "paper from the commandant." Dated August 1930 and signed by the commandant of the cercle, the paper was a declaration of marriage between the young girl, who was no more than four at the time, and the nephew of the woman, who was about fifty. The inquiry concluded that the commandant had probably signed the paper without verifying the age of the "spouses." The administration entrusted the young girl, whose parents had died in the meantime, to a local notable, where she probably continued to work as a maid. This inquiry was launched following a growing scandal in France regarding the resurgence of pawning in Nioro, apparently with the help of the administration.[51] The Nioro case underlines some of the analogies that could exist between the system of fosterage, forced marriage, and pawnship in times of hardship.

As the pressure of metropolitan public opinion became overwhelming, the administration had to deal simultaneously with the issue of pawnship and forced marriage; Msgr. Joanny Thévenoud raised these two issues with the support in France of Senator Gautherot in the case of a "sale of women" in the cercle of Ouahigouya.[52] From this date, the colonial administration began implementing a series of measures to ban forced marriage, which was increasingly being condemned by the international public opinion as a new form of slavery.[53]

〜

Following the official end of slavery and under the guise of marriage and fosterage, illegal trafficking contributed to the circulation of a juvenile, especially feminine, workforce, thereby upholding the prevailing social hierarchies in post-abolition Mali. Public pressure in France and by international humanitarian groups ultimately forced the colonial administration to implement specific measures to regulate marriage and guardianship.[54] These new regulations did not, however, question the circumstances under which women entered into marriage or whether they had freely consented. This lack of attention to women's situations and women's choices was not surprising because the colonial administration always failed to enforce any law regarding the circulation of women's and children's labor and in some cases implicitly supported forms of unfreedom by reinforcing men's guardianship over women and children in postabolition Soudan and independent Mali.[55]

Although the Modibo Keïta's government formally tried to end slavery-like practices in the 1960s, after independence, by promoting a citizenship rights ideology, modern Mali still has no law formally forbidding slavery. Officially the practice was never criminalized, even if the country has signed the major international conventions banning slavery, including the UN's Universal Declaration on Human Rights. Women and girls in Mali are still trafficked primarily for domestic servitude. The issue of "young maids" in cities such as Bamako has been widely debated for the past twenty years.[56] Legislating about women's and children's trafficking in modern-day Mali would force the state to confront women's and children's status and rights in a society in which forced and arranged underage marriages and child labor are still common practices. A new family code in Mali—under consideration for ten years—set the legal minimum age for marriage at eighteen and mandated women's consent to marriage, as well as equality between men and women with respect to parental rights. In August 2009, Amadou Toumani Touré, the president of Mali, refused to sign the bill in the name of national unity, because of vociferous protests by some Muslim groups and sent the legislation back to parliament. A revised family code has eventually been promulgated by the president of Mali in January 2012. This new code has been regarded by women's rights organizations as violating Mali's international obligations to guarantee women's human rights and nondiscrimination. According to the new code, "a woman must obey her husband" and men are considered "head of family." The legal age for marriage is eighteen years for males and sixteen for females. Religious marriages are henceforth legally recognized.

NOTES

Abbreviations

ANM   Archives Nationales, République du Mali
ANS   Archives Nationales, République du Sénégal

CAOM   Centre des Archives d'Outre-Mer
FA   Fonds Ancien
FM   Fonds Moderne

1. Marie Rodet, *Les migrantes ignorées du Haut-Sénégal, 1900–1946* (Paris: Karthala, 2009), 58–69.

2. Claire C. Robertson and Martin A. Klein, "Women's Importance in African Slave Systems," in *Women and Slavery in Africa*, ed. Robertson and Klein (Madison: University of Wisconsin Press, 1983), 13.

3. For the western Sudan slave exodus, see Martin Klein, *Slavery and Colonial Rule in French West Africa* (Cambridge: Cambridge University Press, 1998).

4. Rodet, *Migrantes*, 87–100.

5. "État des jugements rendus en matière civile et commerciale par le tribunal de province de Kayes," 3rd trimester 1907, Archives Nationales, République du Mali (hereafter ANM), Koulouba (FA), 2/M/123. Due to privacy concerns raised by the regulation issued by the Republic of Mali in 2002 restricting the use of any records held by the National Archives of Mali that might "implicate the private lives of citizens," I use only first names and the first initial of surnames.

6. "État des jugements rendus en matière civile et commerciale par le tribunal de province de Kayes," 1st trimester 1908, ANM, Koulouba (FA), 2/M/123.

7. "État des jugements rendus en matière civile et commerciale par le tribunal de province de Kayes," 2nd trimester 1910, ANM, Koulouba (FA), 2/M/123.

8. "Registre des jugements du tribunal de province de Kayes (December–August 1910)," Archives of the cercle of Kayes, incomplete and unclassified. The courts of the French Soudan recognized different "personal status" within the same legal system, which led regularly to legal and political contention. Up to the decree of 1924, the principal distinction was made between Islamic and customary law. It was finally abandoned with the decree of 1924, which asked the courts to specify precisely the law used for each case.

9. According to the court records held in Bamako, the court of Kayes heard 167 civil cases in 1907, 100 in 1908, 83 in 1909, and 127 in 1910. ANM, Koulouba (FA), 2/M/123. Some records appear to be incomplete.

10. In 1911 and 1912, the court of Kayes heard 143 and 128 civil cases, respectively. ANM, Koulouba (FA), 2/M/123.

11. "État des jugements rendus en matière civile et commerciale par le tribunal de province de Kayes," 3rd trimester 1911, 1st trimester 1912, ANM, Koulouba (FA), 2/M/123.

12. Igor Kopytoff and Suzanne Miers, "African 'Slavery' as an Institution of Marginality," in *Slavery in Africa*, ed. Miers and Kopytoff (Madison: University of Wisconsin Press, 1977), 9.

13. "État des jugements rendus en matière civile par le tribunal de province de Yélimané," 2nd trimester 1910, ANM, Koulouba (FA), 2/M/135.

14. "Justice indigène: Réclamations et requêtes," cercle de Kayes, 1905–20, ANM, Koulouba (FA), 2/M/279.

15. Ibid.

16. Klein, *Slavery and Colonial Rule*, 207.

17. Richard L. Roberts, "The End of Slavery, Colonial Courts, and Social Conflicts in Gumbu, 1908–1911," *Canadian Journal of African Studies* 34, no. 3 (2000): 702.

18. "État des jugements rendus en matière civile par le tribunal de province de Yélimané," 2nd trimester 1910, ANM, Koulouba (FA), 2/M/135.

19. Marie Rodet, "Continuum of Gendered Violence: The Colonial Invention of Female Desertion as a Customary Criminal Offense, French Soudan, 1900–1949," in *Domestic Violence and the Law in Colonial and Postcolonial Africa*, ed. Emily S. Burrill, Richard L. Roberts, and Elizabeth Thornberry (Athens: Ohio University Press, 2010), 74–93.

20. "État des jugements rendus en matière civile et commerciale par le tribunal de province de Nioro," 2nd trimester 1907, ANM, 2/M/135.

21. Sally E. Findley and Assitan Diallo, "Foster Children: Links between Urban and Rural Families?" *Proceedings of the African Population Conference*, 2 vols. (Liège: IUSSP, 1988), 2:282–83.

22. Adietou Siby, interview by the author, Diombougou Marena, Mali, 16 February 2010.

23. For social hierarchies and domesticity, see Lotte Pelckmans, "Mobility and Hierarchy of 'Related' Domestic Workers in Noble Fulbe Families," paper presented at the Sixth International Conference on Forced African Labour, "Slavery, Migration, and Contemporary Bondage in Africa," Wilberforce Institute, 23–25 September 2009.

24. For fosterage and pawnship, see Cati Coe, "Domestic Violence and Child Circulation in Southeastern Gold Coast, 1905–1928," in Burrill, Roberts, and Thornberry, *Domestic Violence*. For fosterage and domesticity, see Mary H. Moran, "Civilized Servants: Child Fosterage and Training for Status among the Glebo of Liberia," in *African Encounters with Domesticity*, ed. Karen T. Hansen (New Brunswick, NJ: Rutgers University Press, 1992), 98–115.

25. Kani C., interview by the author, Bokédiamby, Mali, 25 January 2009.

26. The majority of the pawned were slaves; pawnship was simply another form of slave trafficking. ANM, Koulouba (FA), 2/M/44.

27. Women of slave status could always hope to enhance their status by marrying a noble. Their children would then be considered noble. The lives of women of slave status was largely determined by the status of their "husbands" and the protection of a more powerful patron.

28. Gwyn Campbell, Suzanne Miers, and Joseph Miller, introduction to *Children in Slavery* (Athens: Ohio University Press, 2009), 13–14. In this volume, see the introduction and Richard Roberts (chap. 3).

29. Letter 1841, AP/2, 5 September 1938, CAOM, mf/GGAOF, FM, 17/G/160.

30. Petition of Caba C., 22 March 1904, ANM, Koulouba (FA), 2/M/1.

31. Until 1901 slaves were systematically returned to their masters if the masters claimed them within three months of the date of entry into the liberty village.

32. Commandant, cercle de Kayes, to Lieutenant-Governor, Upper-Senegal and Niger, letter 255, 1907, ANM, Koulouska (FA), 2/M/1.

33. For recent economic and political crises and the risks of exploitation of fostered children and juvenile domestic workforce, see Nicolas Argenti, "Things That Don't Come by the Road: Folktales, Fosterage, and Memories of Slavery in the Cameroon Grassfields," *Comparative Studies in Society and History* 52, no. 2 (2010): 224–54; Mélanie Jacquemin, "Migrations juvéniles féminines de travail en Côte-d'Ivoire: Petites domestiques d'Abidjan originaires de Bondoukou," in "Enfance et migration," special issue, *Journal des africanistes* 1, no. 1 (2011): 61–86.

34. Toyin Falola and Paul E. Lovejoy, "Pawnship in Historical Perspective," in *Pawnship in Africa: Debt Bondage in Historical Perspective*, ed. Falola and Lovejoy (Boulder: Westview, 1994), 6–7.

35. Andrew F. Clark, "'The Ties that Bind': Servility and Dependency among the Fulbe of Bundu (Senegambia), c. 1930s to 1980s," in *Slavery and Colonial Rule*, ed. Suzanne Miers and Martin Klein (London: Frank Cass, 1999), 95.

36. In some cases, however, pawnship ended up in slavery, particularly when the debtor was unable to reimburse the creditor. See Falola and Lovejoy, "Pawnship," 4–6.

37. Martin A. Klein and Richard L. Roberts, "The Resurgence of Pawning in French West Africa during the Depression of the 1930s," in Falola and Lovejoy, *Pawnship*, 306.

38. "État des jugements rendus en matière civile et commerciale par le tribunal de province de Bafoulabé," 1st trimester 1907, ANM, Koulouba (FA), 2/M/103.

39. "État des condamnations prononcées par le tribunal du cercle de Kita sur la répression des faits de traite (du 11 décembre 1905 à ce jour)," 22 March 1906, ANM, Koulouba (FA), 2/M/44.

40. "État des jugements rendus en matière de traite par le tribunal du cercle de Nioro depuis l'application du décret du 12 décembre 1905," 4 June 1907, ANM, Koulouba (FA), 2/M/44.

41. "État des jugements rendus en matière civile et commerciale par le tribunal de province de Nioro," 2nd trimester 1907, ANM, Koulouba (FA), 2/M/135.

42. See especially ANM, Koulouba (FA), 2/M/44, concerned with trafficking cases heard by the courts of the French Soudan (1905–7). See also Emily S. Burrill, "'Wives of Circumstance': Gender and Slave Emancipation in Late Nineteenth-Century Senegal," *Slavery and Abolition* 29, no. 1 (2008): 52.

43. Circular, 7 February 1906, CAOM, mf/GGAOF (FA), K/24.

44. The attitude of the colonial administration in the French Soudan toward this issue kept being ambiguous up to the 1930s. In 1932 some governors still claimed that pawnship was simply a kind of "primitive contract" between consenting people. Letter 36, AP/2, 15 January 1932, ANS, GGAOF (FM), K 113(26). In 1935, Governor General Brévié tried to issue a circular inviting the governors "to substitute to this custom which is incompatible with the spirit of our institutions, work contracts adapted to the indigenous mentality, but presenting especially socially all the desirable guarantees." ANS, GGAOF (FM), 2/K/9(26).

45. "État des condamnations prononcées par le tribunal du cercle de Kita sur la répression des faits de traite," 10 February 1906, ANM, Koulouba (FA), 2/M/44.

46. "État des condamnations prononcées par le tribunal du cercle de Kita sur la répression des faits de traite," 16 March 1906, ANM, Koulouba (FA), 2/M/44.

47. Klein and Roberts, "Resurgence," 306. See also letter 16, AP/2, 22 January 1936, CAOM, Fonds ministériels, AffPol/541.

48. Letter 36 AP/2, 15 January 1932, CAOM, Fonds ministériels, AffPol/541.

49. See ANS, GGAOF (FM), 2/K/9(26), 2/K/11(26), 2/K/12(26).

50. Inspection of the cercle of Nioro, French Soudan, December 1936, CAOM, mf/GGAOF (FM), 15/G/34.

51. "Tortures au Soudan," *La flèche Outre-Mer and L'AOF*, 26 September, 12 November 1936, CAOM, mf/GGAOF (FM), 15/G/34.

52. On this issue, see CAOM, AffPol/541, ANS, GGAOF (FM) 2/K/11(26), 2/K/12(26).

53. Marie Rodet, "Genre, coutumes et droit colonial au Soudan français (1918–1939)," in "Les femmes, le droit et la justice," special issue, *Cahiers d'études africaines*, nos. 187–88 (2007): 583–602. In French West Africa, forced and prenubile marriages were banned by the 1939 Mandel Decree, but the decree rapidly became a dead letter, lacking the means of application. This situation led to the promulgation of a new decree in 1953 (Jacquinot Decree), which was, again, never really applied. Suzanne Miers, "Contemporary Forms of Slavery," *Canadian Journal of African Studies* 34, no. 3 (2000): 716.

54. Rodet, "Genre, coutumes"; Rodet, "Continuum."

55. Rodet, *Migrantes*, 195–205, 207–62; Rodet, "Continuum."

56. The first report to be released on this issue in Mali was written in 1991: Tiéman Diarra and Yaouaga F. Koné, *Les migrations féminines au Mali, la main d'œuvre domestique* (Bamako: Institut des Sciences Humaines, 1991).

5 ⤳ Sex Trafficking, Prostitution, and the Law in Colonial British West Africa, 1911–43

CARINA RAY

IN 1939, Bessey Assor, a Nigerian living in the Gold Coast, traveled back to Nigeria to purchase a young girl. After paying the girl's parents an unspecified amount in cash, Assor brought her to the Gold Coast under the pretense of marrying her to John Nuji. Nuji was later discovered to be a nine-year-old boy and no marriage took place. Rather, according to the Criminal Investigation Division (CID) of the Gold Coast police, "Bessey Assor kept the girl in her room and prostitution was actually practiced by the girl in Assor's house."[1] The CID further reported that the girl would "sit at the doorway of Assor's room and customers were encouraged by her or by Assor to enter the place for the purpose of prostitution." The unnamed girl later testified that Assor had forced her to have sex with many men. Assor's prostituting of the girl was discovered by the president of the Gold Coast branch of the Nigerian Youth Movement (NYM), which had become increasingly active in raising awareness about the traffic of women and girls into the Gold Coast from Nigeria for the purpose of prostitution. The NYM was particularly concerned that the growing traffic was causing "Gold Coast men and women who have not traveled further than their area [to] believe that all the Nigerian women are harlots."[2]

The CID's annual report on traffic in women and children not only documented Bessey Assor's case and her subsequent arrest for procurement, it also warned that the trafficking of women and girls from Nigeria for sex work was on the increase. Noting that the Gold Coast had an unusually lax set of antiprostitution laws for a British colony, the police commissioner, E. C. Nottingham, used the occasion to ask for tougher legislation.[3]

What the report did not say, but would later become evident, was that the spike in sex trafficking was a direct result of the increasing demand for commercial sex occasioned by the influx of thousands of European and American male military personnel into the Gold Coast during World War II. Widespread prostitution led to high rates of venereal disease among military personnel. Growing concerns about this epidemic and its negative impact on the war effort, combined with press scrutiny of the sex trade, ultimately culminated in the adoption of stricter antiprostitution laws in 1942 and 1943, including legislation designed to curb the traffic in women and girls. Concerns about prostitution and venereal disease, however, were not new. Local chiefs had unsuccessfully petitioned the colonial government in 1911 and 1925 to address the unsatisfactory state of the law regarding prostitution; both appeals were made in relation to the harmful effects venereal diseases were having on the health of local populations. The sex workers accused of spreading venereal diseases in 1911 and 1925 were identified as coming from Togoland and Nigeria, respectively.

Their movements underscore what other studies on prostitution have already demonstrated: most women involved in prostitution did not work in their immediate area of origin. They either migrated to another part of their home colony or to a different colony altogether.[4] Precisely because prostitution often involved migration, distinguishing between prostitution as a form of voluntary migrant labor undertaken by individual women and sex trafficking involving a third party in colonial West Africa is difficult and often requires speculation in lieu of definitive evidence. This was especially so in British West Africa before the late 1930s.

Another key difficulty in documenting the history of sex trafficking in the region is defining what constitutes trafficking. Treaties in force at the time defined trafficking in accordance with the 1910 International Convention for the Suppression of the White Slave Traffic.[5] Accordingly, this chapter utilizes the guidelines of the 1910 convention as follows: Article 1 defined trafficking as the procurement, enticement, or leading away of *a woman or girl under age, even with her consent,* by a third party for immoral purposes in order to gratify another person's passions within and across national borders. Whereas Article 1 focused on underage girls and did not require force to be involved, Article 2 focused on nonconsensual trafficking involving *fraud, violence, threats, abuse of authority, or any other method of compulsion* in order to procure, entice, or lead away *a woman or girl over age* for immoral purposes in order to gratify another person's passions within and across national borders. A subsequent convention in 1921 expanded the protocol to include boys, and in 1933 the scope was further widened to include women of full age who were recruited consensually and trafficked across international borders.[6] These treaties, then, defined trafficking without regard to consent. Although the evidence that I examine often gives the impression that women willingly entered the sex trade, even in cases where this was true, it does not mean that they were not trafficked.

Equally challenging is the problem of identifying sex workers in the muddled context of male authorities, both African and European, who were predisposed to thinking that single, mobile, and entrepreneurial African women were prostitutes. There was some genuine cause for confusion: women involved in legitimate long-distance trade across West Africa often plied the same routes between colonies as women engaged in sex work, and they typically lived in the same *zongos* (residential quarters for strangers). Some women likely combined licit and illicit forms of income generation. Incidences of mistaken identity, however, do not explain the overwhelming tendency on the part of authorities to conflate traders with prostitutes. Rather, racist colonial ideologies about African female sexuality played a decisive role in categorizing these women as inherently sexually deviant.

While colonial records offer a window into the prejudices of the time, they provide little insight into the social, economic, and political factors that led some women into prostitution. This chapter combines a regional history of prostitution and trafficking with an analysis of how racial ideologies shaped and in many instances forestalled the development of colonial laws aimed at addressing the sex trade. In doing so it provides a deeper historical context for understanding one of the most pressing problems facing the West African subregion today: the intensely lucrative traffic in human beings within West Africa and, increasingly so, beyond the region's borders to destinations in Europe, North Africa, the Middle East, as well as Latin America and the United States.[7]

BORDER CROSSING, PROSTITUTION, AND VENEREAL DISEASE, CA. 1911–25

In 1911 local chiefs from various parts of the Eastern Province's Keta District complained to the provincial commissioner that prostitutes from neighboring Togoland were crossing into the area and spreading venereal diseases. Rather than being trafficked, the movement of these sex workers into the Gold Coast appears to have been a spontaneous response to the periodic crackdowns on prostitution by Togoland's German colonial authorities, who were concerned with the growing threat sexually transmitted diseases posed to public health.[8] These concerns were linked to German authorities' fears that lower birth rates caused by venereal diseases would reduce future labor supplies.[9] While sex workers were not criminally punished, they were subject to compulsory medical examination. If infected, they were forced to undergo treatment and were often confined during its duration.[10] This limited their ability to work and explains why sex workers responded to these periodic crackdowns by entering the Gold Coast. Given the Keta District's close proximity to the colonial capital, Lomé, where prostitution was most rampant, the quickest route of escape for sex workers based there was to cross the border.[11] Once in the Gold

Coast, their activities quickly alarmed local chiefs, who complained that the women's presence was having deleterious moral and physical consequences on their constituents. John Maxwell, the Eastern Province's commissioner, could not offer much help to the chiefs because, as he explained, prostitution "can only be dealt with at present if the female is under thirteen years of age; if over thirteen, if she is detained against her will, or if she is not a native of West Africa." Readily admitting that there was an "unsatisfactory state of the law as regards prostitution," yet unaware that Togoland regulated prostitution through mandatory health screenings rather than through antiprostitution legislation, he recommended that the Gold Coast government adopt a similar set of laws and further urged "that the keeping of brothels be prohibited."[12]

In rejecting Maxwell's recommendations, Governor James Thorburn justified his decision by arguing that such measures were fundamentally incompatible with the "customs of the [colony's] natives . . . such that it would be practically impossible to so frame laws as to prevent prostitution and yet safeguard the liberty of the subject in giving reach to his natural—even though excessive possibly—inclinations in this regard."[13] In short, Thorburn contended that preventing prostitution and ensuring that Africans were able to satisfy their "natural" sexual "inclinations," were mutually exclusive goals. He concluded that, "much as one may deplore immorality," it was not possible "to render people moral by virtue of passing ordinances." Thorburn placed African sexuality[14] outside the boundaries of legal regulation and opted instead for a non-interventionist policy. He recommended against the introduction of stricter antiprostitution laws in favor of lending "support" to the concerned chiefs should "they take action themselves for the removal of these undesirable visitors."[15] And with that the archives went silent until fourteen years later, when another chief petitioned the administration about the movement of women into the Gold Coast for prostitution and the rise in venereal disease.

In 1925, Chief Kadri English, the self-described "tribal ruler of Hausas in Accra and its environs," complained to the district commissioner of Accra that Hausa women from Nigeria were entering into prostitution and compromising their own piety and the health of their communities:

> Chastity is essential in Mohammadanism especially among women; prostitution is a thing outside our creed—good Hausa women who were living good lives in Northern Nigeria change for the worst on arrival on the Gold Coast Colony in which evil influences are somewhat paramount. . . . At present the women are daily divorcing their husbands without cause in order to carry on immoral practices and the result is sickness and untimely death.[16]

Unfortunately his petition does not indicate the circumstances under which these women were entering the Gold Coast.

English's suggestion that "good Hausa women . . . change for the worst on arrival" by divorcing their husbands and entering into prostitution opens up several not mutually exclusive possible explanations. Some of these women may have entered into prostitution after failing to gain sufficient support from their husbands or finding themselves barred from other forms of income generation. Given the tendency among some male traditional leaders at the time to conflate single or unaccompanied women, especially traders, with prostitutes, Hausa women engaged in legitimate trade may have been wrongly placed into English's category of "good Hausa women" gone bad.[17] Others may have come specifically to engage in sex work and may have been trafficked for that purpose.

Trafficked or otherwise, English held this class of Hausa women responsible for the escalating rate of sexually transmitted diseases and premature deaths. He warned, "Venereal disease is too common among my people and unless a Law is enacted by you or the authorities enforcing the repatriation of all Hausa women without Husbands to their Homes, immorality will be on the ascendant and indubitably defy the praise-worthy endeavours of the Health Officers."[18] In his study of sexuality and prostitution among the Akan, Emmanuel Akyeampong notes that English "wisely linked his petition to colonial concerns about health and finances" because these issues typically gained traction with the colonial state.[19] Administrators who were aware of the negative effect venereal diseases were having on local populations did indeed share these concerns. The colony's attorney general and governor did not.

The secretary for native affairs, H. S. Newlands, succinctly described the split in opinion:

> The position now is that Chiefs, Political Officers and Medical Officers are united in agreeing that steps should be taken to combat prostitution and that the latter is locally an important and growing problem. The A.G. [attorney general] on the other hand is of the opinion that although the subject has been made a punishable offense in Sierra Leone and Nigeria no special legislation in regard to it is at present either necessary or expedient in this Colony; nor, so far as after due enquiry he can gather, is the evil referred to at all so prevalent or serious in this country as it is in many other parts of the world.[20]

Like the colony's chiefs and political and medical officers, Newlands believed that the situation was becoming increasingly serious and needed to be addressed by the Criminal Code:

> Prostitution is a very serious matter to the native communities here and it is ever becoming more serious because the prostitutes are

largely natives of Togoland and Nigeria and therefore in no way under the control of either the native authorities or their families. Every chief with whom I have discussed this matter has welcomed the possibility of action being taken to put a check on prostitution and I would suggest that the addition of a suitable section to the Criminal Code is overdue.[21]

Despite considerable evidence that prostitution was indeed causing the proliferation of venereal diseases, the Executive Council rejected Newland's suggestion. The colonial administration instead decided to abide by the policy established in 1911. It continued to support the efforts of local chiefs to take "action themselves for the removal of [prostitutes], and to prevent others with similar disqualifications from entering their division." This policy had adverse consequences for women who were deemed prostitutes by male traditional authorities in areas such as Akyease, Sefwi Wiawso, and numerous Asante towns. These women, most of whom were single and consequently assumed to be prostitutes, were often subjected to wrongful arrest and detention.[22]

The steadily increasing rate of venereal disease among the colony's African population was not regarded as a significant enough problem to warrant new legislation. As of 1925 the legal system still only had provisions for prosecuting prostitution involving females who were either under the age of thirteen, held against their will, or not natives of West Africa. Subsequent amendments to the colony's legal code did little to address concerns such as those raised by Kadri English and the Keta chiefs. For instance, while the Immigration Restriction Ordinance was amended in 1926 to include prostitutes on the list of prohibited immigrants, it was ineffective in curbing the influx of regional sex workers because West Africans were exempt.[23] In 1936 the Criminal Code was amended to include measures narrowly aimed at procurement. Even though the amendment sought to curb the ability of pimps and brothel owners to procure for their clients, it still allowed sex workers to ply their trade freely.[24] Thus the Gold Coast's antiprostitution laws were anemic in comparison to those in force elsewhere in British West Africa.[25] Given the comparatively lax laws on prostitution and the spike in demand for commercial sex that accompanied the arrival of thousands of male military personnel, the flow of sex workers from Nigeria increased sharply with the onset of World War II. Whereas the evidence for 1911 and 1925 sheds little light on the question of trafficking, archival sources for the late 1930s and early 1940s point to the existence of elaborate networks for trafficking women and girls from Nigeria into the Gold Coast.

In the months preceding the summer of 1941, Accra and Takoradi witnessed an influx of thousands of Europeans belonging to the British military and Royal Air Force (RAF).[26] Takoradi's small airport was transformed into a major base for the RAF and later became home to a sizeable American operation.[27] Accra had the largest presence of Americans, with a total of just over five thousand troops.[28] Although police authorities had noticed an increase in the number of women and girls trafficked into the Gold Coast from Nigeria in 1940, it was not until the following year that Police Commissioner E. C. Nottingham declared that the sudden rise in the number of foreign military men in the colony was causing an "increase in the number of women who earn their living by prostitution with Europeans."[29] Commensurate with the increase in prostitution was an escalation in the number of European military personnel infected with venereal diseases, which alarmed medical authorities. In Nottingham's view this was "an additional reason why these women who are a danger to health should be removed from the immediate vicinity of the large camps housing European personnel." Not surprisingly, he singled out Accra and Takoradi, where the largest populations of military men were to be found, as the towns in which "the conduct of these women is causing embarrassment."[30] Typical of contemporaneous gendered discourses on prostitution, johns were never identified as factors in the prostitution epidemic; nor were their actions considered punishable offenses, constitutive of a public health threat, or cause for embarrassment.

In explaining why the situation had spiraled out of control, Nottingham drew attention to the unsatisfactory state of the law, which tied police hands:

> In the Gold Coast, Police have no power to control these women or to proceed against prostitutes—not being Europeans—who behave in such manner and I urge that legislation similar to that which exists in Nigeria may be enacted whereby some measure of control can be obtained over the movements of this class of person. I particularly invite attention to the fact that the Gold Coast Laws (See Section 435(1) of the Criminal Code) provide that any female *not being a native of West Africa* who follows a calling of a common prostitute is liable to imprisonment without hard labour for six months. From the wording of the section it seems that in the Gold Coast the calling of a common prostitute, provided she is a native of West Africa, is recognized and it is remarkable that the words, "brothel," "keeping," "soliciting," "loitering," "importuning" and etc. do not exist in the Gold Coast Laws.[31]

In short, Nottingham contended that the wartime prostitution problem was the result of both the increased demand for commercial sex and the absence of legal deterrents, which made it a prime destination for sex workers, trafficked or otherwise.

Despite the negative effect that venereal diseases were having on troops, Governor Arnold Hodson and Attorney General H. W. D. Blackall remained impervious to internal calls for greater police powers. Racist notions about African sexuality were again invoked to forestall legislative reform. Echoing the same sentiment expressed by Governor Thorburn in 1911, Blackall argued that "the remedy of making people good by act of parliament is not as easy as he [Commissioner Nottingham] thinks."[32] Hodson and Blackall were equally resistant to external calls for developing strategies to effectively stem the traffic of women and children from Nigeria.

In March 1941, Lord Moyne, the secretary of state for the colonies, asked Hodson for a report on possible measures to combat the traffic.[33] Keen to avoid public criticism, Moyne's request followed the appearance two weeks earlier of an exposé entitled "The Social Question: A Startling Disclosure" on the traffic in the widely read *West Africa* magazine. The exposé's author, Henry Ormston, cited an investigation into the traffic undertaken by Mr. R. K. Floyer, of the Local Authority of Port Harcourt, which found eighty young girls from Owerri Province practicing prostitution in the Gold Coast, allegedly with the consent of their parents.[34]

Aside from the trade itself, Ormston's "startling disclosure" was that it was attributable to "two non-African sub-communities" in the Gold Coast. While he never directly named the two groups, his descriptions suggest that he held Lebanese responsible for orchestrating the sex trade and Europeans responsible for hiring prostitutes.[35] While Lebanese owned many of the colony's dancehalls, which were reportedly popular wartime hangouts for sex workers, and evidence suggests that some Lebanese were involved in supplying prostitutes to Europeans, there is insufficient evidence to judge the extent of their role in the transregional sex trade in colonial West Africa.[36] Evidence does, however, indicate that large numbers of recently deployed European troops were hiring West African sex workers. So, too, were Gold Coast men. Indeed, observers linked the low number of Gold Coast recruits to the sex trade's role in spreading venereal diseases.[37] While Ormston acknowledged that African men were engaging in sexual activity with sex workers, he rejected the idea that Africans organized the traffic. He contended, "Nobody who has any acquaintance with African ways of life will for a moment believe that this is a business between Africans and Africans." To be sure, many Nigerians and Gold Coasters were deeply disturbed by the trade and its deleterious effects. They too wrote to local newspapers to voice their grave concerns.[38] Yet some Nigerian communities not only sanctioned the sex trade, they also actively orchestrated it.

BEHIND THE TRAFFIC IN WOMEN AND CHILDREN: THE NIGERIA–GOLD COAST NEXUS

Returning to the story of Bessey Assor: after Gold Coast police were made aware of her activities by the NYM, she was arrested, tried, and convicted for procurement under Chapter 9 of the Criminal Code, and sentenced to eighteen months in prison with hard labor.[39] Assor's conviction was the only one listed in the CID's 1939–40 annual report, "Traffic in Women and Children."[40] No convictions were reported for 1938. The report, however, warned that the trafficking of women and girls from Nigeria into the Gold Coast was on the increase and cited the recent arrival in Accra and Takoradi of a boatload of women and girls from Nigeria.[41] While the phrase "Traffic in Women and Children" was used, available evidence indicates that the trafficking of children was gender specific to girls.[42]

Concerned by the arrival of the women and girls in the colony, the police launched a wider investigation into the status of Nigerian females in the Gold Coast, estimated to be one thousand in number.[43] While most of the women and girls concerned described themselves as "petty traders," the CID identified them as prostitutes. In explaining how they entered the colony, the CID's report claimed that "while a number of adult girls had come to the Gold Coast alone, a large number had been brought here by elder women on the pretext of marriage or to learn trading and domestic work and had been taught to be prostitutes."[44]

Thus, the circumstances of the nameless young girl purchased from her parents by Assor under the false pretense of marrying her were by no means unique, except that her trafficker was prosecuted. The involvement of the girl's parents, even if unwitting, raises the important question of parental consent or coercion, or both, as factors in British West Africa's flourishing sex trade. As we shall shortly see, some families were involved in organizing the sex trade into which their daughters entered; what is less clear is the extent to which coercion was used to extract their participation. Further complicating this question is the lack of available data on the age of the girls and women involved. Indeed, the term *adult girls* is suggestive of the murky identities of those being trafficked. As Ruby Andrew and Benjamin Lawrance observe, parental coercion remains one of the most difficult elements of child trafficking to track and prosecute, despite the frequency with which it occurs.[45] While the extent of coercion is unclear, the police authorities' admission that most of the girls were misled into the traffic indicates that deception was a widely used strategy.[46] This, in and of itself, raises doubts about the CID's assertion that fear played a negligible role in explaining why trafficked women and girls were "reluctant to give evidence against the women [who brought them to the Gold Coast]." The report claimed, instead, that the joint efforts of the Nigerian and Gold Coast police forces to combat the traffic were made difficult because "in the large majority of cases . . . they enjoy the life."[47] The CID, however, provided no evidence to substantiate this claim.

Like studies on prostitution elsewhere in Africa, the evidence for Nigeria demonstrates that some women succeeded in turning it into a lucrative entrepreneurial enterprise, regardless of how they initially entered the activity.[48] In the case of Nigeria it is possible to discern how many women entered prostitution: they were trafficked by members of the families and communities from which they hailed. According to Nigeria's Governor Bernard Bourdillon, it had become "abundantly clear that migration of women from Nigeria to the Gold Coast for the purposes of prostitution is a profitable and well-organised trade, supported and maintained by the very communities to which the women themselves belong."[49] Citing Obubra Division, in Ogoja Province of the Cross River basin, he noted that investigators had found that "there is hardly a family that has not an interest in it, and Elders openly admit that they receive a fee, amounting to some pounds, from every woman who practices this calling." Bourdillon described the elaborate and closely regulated nature of the trade and its profitability:

> The communities principally concerned maintain Societies, which are responsible for the management of the trade. These Societies have representatives in the Gold Coast who receive and establish the women on their arrival, and it is even claimed that the fees extracted from the latter have rendered the Societies so affluent that they are able to build houses and provide legal assistance for their clients . . . there can be no doubt that the profits from this traffic are considerable, and the case is quoted of one of these harlots who returned recently from the Gold Coast with no less than eighty pounds in her possession.[50]

So great was the revenue generated by women engaged in sex work from Obubra Division that in 1942 their verifiable remittances, alone, totaled nearly £7,000, which was almost twice the division's estimated public revenue for the last tallied fiscal year, 1937–38.[51] While this amount also included remittances from sex workers inside Nigeria, it is one indication of how profitable the enterprise had become during the war.

With specific reference to why such large numbers of Cross River basin women were entering into prostitution as a profession, Benedict Naanen argues that Cross River was economically marginal and underdeveloped in comparison to other areas of Nigeria that had been more centrally integrated into global economic and social networks through colonialism. As a result, many

Cross River women found sex work to be "more profitable than the locally available peasant occupations." Naanen also observes that it was less physically exacting than agricultural labor, the primary peasant occupation available to women; that it offered remuneration in cash, which was significant given the ongoing monetization of the indigenous economy; and that it in turn provided women with the ability to acquire material wealth, property, and other status symbols hitherto unavailable to them in the local economy. These push factors were exacerbated by the fact that the colonial state "eroded the power of indigenous institutions of social control . . . or abolished them altogether" and "provided large territorial space, the demand for commercial sex (through urbanization), and security," which in turn "enabled women to travel freely and far away from their indigenous communities to places where they could profitably escape rural patriarchy and commercialize their sexual freedom."[52]

Yet the existence of community-based systems to regulate the sex trade suggests that colonialism did not necessarily erode indigenous institutions of social control altogether, but either created new ones or forced preexisting ones to adapt to changing circumstances. While it is clear that some community members were aggrieved at the trade, others developed regulatory systems in order to achieve the intended purpose of generating financial revenue while minimizing the trade's negative impact on sex workers.[53]

Given that economic factors played the largest role in pushing women into prostitution, the worldwide economic depression's negative impact on African economies during the 1930s, followed by the economic turmoil occasioned by World War II, helps explain why even centrally located towns and more fully integrated areas, like Calabar, were also hard hit by the sex trade. One of the striking aspects of Nigeria's wartime sex traffic was that it was largely directed toward the Gold Coast. While internal migration within Nigeria was also a pronounced phenomenon of the sex trade, where external migration was concerned, the Gold Coast greatly surpassed other destinations such as Cameroon and Fernando Po.[54] Nottingham identified two factors to explain why this was so. First, the laxity of antiprostitution laws safeguarded sex workers from surveillance and criminal prosecution. Second, during the war sex work became incredibly lucrative as the demand for commercial sex rose dramatically. Profitability and possibility combined to make prostitution a viable means of capital accumulation during a period when other possibilities were either far less lucrative, unattractive, or unavailable.

CONTESTATION, PASSAGE, AND IMPLEMENTATION OF THE LAW

As indicated earlier, the Colonial Office responded to press scrutiny of British West Africa's sex trade by asking Governor Hodson for a report on possible measures to combat the traffic. In his role as adviser to Hodson, Blackall once again resorted to racist rhetoric about African sexuality to argue against enacting antitrafficking legislation. Blackall insisted that even if the Gold Coast was willing to institute a passport system for West Africans and force them to comply with immigration restriction regulations, these measures would prove ineffective. In his view, Nigerian women, especially those coming from Calabar, simultaneously inhabited licit and illicit social worlds, rendering it nearly impossible for authorities to distinguish between women desiring to enter the colony for legitimate purposes, such as traders, and those entering for illicit purposes, such as prostitutes.

> If a Calabar woman makes up her mind to engage in this vocation [prostitution] in the Gold Coast, she will probably put on her passport that she is a petty trader and possibly add that she is a married woman . . . many of the Calabar prostitutes are in fact married women who come here with the consent of their husbands, and it would also seem that the young Calabar girls who come here for this purpose do so with the full knowledge and consent of their parents. . . . I do not see how this will enable the Police to prove that she is a prostitute and as such a prohibited immigrant.[55]

In contrast, it was possible to keep foreign prostitutes from entering the United Kingdom, not only because it already had a passport system, argued Blackall, but also because it was visibly possible to distinguish between immoral and moral European women in a way that was not possible with African women.

Making his point, he gibed, "It does not take a Sherlock Holmes to spot a French lady of easy virtue when she arrives at Dover. But I doubt whether even the eagle eye of Capt. Nottingham could discern the difference between a Calabar petty trader and a Calabar prostitute." Blackall's remark reveals more about its author's racist attitudes and assumptions than it does about the women about whom he presumed to speak so authoritatively. While prostitution certainly increased during the war, substantial evidence also points to the sustained and widespread economic activity of Nigerian female traders in the Gold Coast.[56] Notwithstanding the probability that some women supplemented their income as petty traders with sex work, the idea that all traders were prostitutes and all prostitutes were traders was racist rhetoric. It was precisely the persistence of such racial thinking that forestalled the introduction of stricter antiprostitution and antitrafficking legislation.

The Nigerian government responded to Moyne's request for information on the subject by acknowledging that "more active measures for control of this traffic would now seem to be necessary." Recent investigations had shown that the government's initial approach to solving the problem at its "source" by using antiprostitution education and propaganda was not "likely to prove effective." Governor Bourdillon instead proposed a two-pronged course of action. The first involved refusing "exit permits to women who cannot show good reason for wishing to travel to the Gold Coast." The second relied on the "rigorous prosecution for procuration, prostitution, keeping of brothels, living on immoral earnings, and on any other charges that it may be possible to lay against persons connected with the trade." Bourdillon was convinced, though, that the traffic could not be controlled by Nigeria alone. He urged Hodson to "consider the matter afresh . . . with a view to rendering such active assistance by the Government of the Gold Coast as may be possible." Specifically he asked Hodson to consider refusing admittance to women from Nigeria when "no good reason" was "adduced," and repatriating known "prostitutes and any other persons connected with the profession."[57]

Colonial officials in the Gold Coast remained deeply polarized over the proposed trafficking legislation. While the governor and the attorney general continued to dismiss the need for action, Commissioner Nottingham argued that the colony's inaction was "the underlying reason for this extensive traffic." He criticized the absence of laws dealing with brothel keeping, soliciting, loitering, and importuning, as well as the lack of provisions for expelling prostitutes. He also juxtaposed the concern expressed by Nigeria and the Colonial Office with the Gold Coast's laissez-faire attitude and warned the colonial secretary that "however much Government may feel inclined to permit things to remain as they are some action will have to be taken."[58] He repeated his call for the implementation of stricter antiprostitution laws and requested that Nigeria establish a system of exit permits for all native women. That the proposed system was gender specific to women further indicates the way in which Nigerian women were perceived as requiring special vetting despite evidence that male Nigerian ponces were active in the Gold Coast.

The police commissioner was not only concerned with curbing the influx of sex workers, he also highlighted the importance of granting the police the power of expulsion so that they could "rid Takoradi, Sekondi, Tarkwa, and Accra of a vast number of these women." He asserted that the women, "on finding that they had to reside in places where they had no opportunity for practicing their calling, would, it is believed, automatically of their own free-will return to Nigeria." In addition to the coastal towns, Nottingham highlighted the heavily male populated mining town of Tarkwa as a prime destination to which Nigerian ponces were reportedly trafficking women because even greater profits could be made there.[59]

Nottingham again referenced the colony's unique status within the empire. "In the Gold Coast at present Police cannot prosecute for prostitution, keeping brothels, living on immoral earnings, and similar offences. I believe the Gold Coast must be unique in the British Colonial Empire in not providing Police powers to deal with such offences."[60] Before the Executive Council was asked to consider the proposed recommendations, the colonial secretary's office had already maligned Nottingham's proposals as tangential to the question of trafficking, and unconvincing.[61] When the Executive Council met, their only concessions were agreeing to the Nigerian government's request to refuse entry to Nigerian women who were not in possession of exit permits and to deport, at the expense of Nigeria, any woman found to be a prostitute within eighteen months of her entry into the Gold Coast.[62]

Major legislative reform would have to wait until Alan Burns and Raymond Browne replaced Hodson and Blackall. Headway was finally made in the summer of 1942 when the Executive Council met and approved the implementation of legislation to "prevent the entry and provide for the deportation of Nigerian prostitutes and other persons connected with prostitution."[63] Governor Burns concurred and ordered Attorney General Browne to draft the legislation.[64] Browne successfully introduced a more comprehensive set of amendments to the Criminal Code in order to effectively suppress the traffic in women and children for what he described as "immoral purposes." His proposed legislation—designed to stamp out brothel keeping, defilement of young females, young persons in brothels, seduction of young females, trading in prostitution, and procuration—was complemented by an expansion of the Immigration Restriction Ordinance to prohibit the entry of not only prostitutes but also others associated with prostitution and trafficking.[65] On 20 May 1943, Ordinance no. 7/43 officially came into force, making it an offense to: "(a) Loiter and solicit passengers [passersby] for the purpose of prostitution; (b) Encourage prostitution of girls under 13 years; (c) Allow persons under 13 years to be in brothels; (d) Trade in prostitution or live on the earnings of prostitutes; (e) Keep brothels."[66] Penalties for these offenses ranged from pecuniary fines to imprisonment for two years; all but the first offence were further punishable by deportation for offenders who were "non-natives" of the Gold Coast.

One anomaly in the Immigration Ordinance remained, however. Natives of West Africa were still exempt. Browne's amendments did not address this point and so the letter of the law still technically excluded Nigerians involved in prostitution and trafficking from being defined as "prohibitive immigrants." However, as of July 1943 natives of Nigeria traveling to the Gold Coast were required to hold a national travel document. Subsequently, the Gold Coast requested that Nigeria refuse to issue travel documents to persons who would come under any of the categories specified in the new amendments. While it is unclear how successful these measures were in stemming the flow of persons involved in prostitution and trafficking, the amendments to the Criminal

Code quickly proved effective in allowing police to crack down on prostitution. The police carried out a series of raids throughout the colony between March and July 1943. The raids resulted in the arrest, prosecution, and conviction of 263 people.

The descriptions of those convicted provide a window into the traffic. Seventeen women were convicted for soliciting passersby; six women were convicted for allowing persons under the age of thirteen into brothels (two were jailed for two years and four were fined £30 each); one man was convicted for living on the earnings of a prostitute; 239 women were convicted of keeping brothels. Of the 262 women convicted, slightly over half were Nigerian; the police processed 94 deportation orders against them. The acting commissioner of police remarked in concluding his report on the raids that "police action so far taken has had a good effect. Most of the women are settling down as married women. Those who still cling to this mode of life are now very circumspective. The annoying flagrant loitering and soliciting in the streets in the large towns have now disappeared."[67] The foregoing comments and the statistics underscore how women rather than men were held responsible for the proliferation of prostitution. While it might very well be true that the sex trade in the Gold Coast was largely controlled by women, the fact that only one out of 263 people convicted for prostitution-related crimes was a man says more about gender-based profiling among the police than it does about the nature of the sex trade. Earlier police reports pointed to Nigerian ponces redirecting the sex traffic to mining towns, yet their numbers are not reflected in the aforementioned conviction statistics.

↩

Before 1942–43 the colonial administration's resistance to introducing tougher antiprostitution and antitrafficking legislation was underpinned by a set of racial ideologies that espoused the idea that African sexuality could not be regulated. The entrenched and persistent nature of this belief is evident in the nearly identical statements made by Thorburn in 1911 and Blackall some thirty years later. The strategically racialized and monolithic construction of African sexualities as uncontrollable, and by extension impossible to legally regulate, became the basis of a series of justifications for maintaining the colony's lax laws and forestalling the introduction of antitrafficking measures. Thus, it must be borne in mind that while prostitution and sex trafficking were clearly *growing* problems in British West Africa, colonial authorities in the Gold Coast were particularly invested in painting them as *uncontrollable* problems in order to justify their legislative inaction. This resonates with Richard Roberts's observation that French colonial administrators in the French Soudan often rationalized their unwillingness to respond diligently to international pressure to suppress the traffic in women and children, by claiming that "African societies were not yet ready for aggressive social engineering" (see chapter 3). In both cases Africans were simultaneously constructed as the source of the problem and as an obstacle in the way of solving it.

In their introduction to this volume, Lawrance and Roberts argue for the urgent need to bring together scholars and practitioners to combat the proliferation of sophisticated global networks that have turned human trafficking into an incredibly lucrative transcontinental industry that victimizes millions of people every year. The historical roots of today's human trafficking networks are often far deeper than many policymakers are aware. By way of example, an otherwise comprehensive and well-documented 2006 UNESCO policy paper framed Nigeria's extensive trafficking problem as a postcolonial phenomenon.[68] Yet many of the root causes identified in the report extend further back, into the precolonial and colonial periods. Strikingly, the modes of operation and strategies employed by human traffickers in the colonial period continue to be used today. These include preying on the economic vulnerability of women and girls; deceiving victims into believing that they are being transported for legitimate purposes, such as education, job training, employment, or marriage; the predominance of "madams" who use their connections with the families and communities from which trafficked persons hail to garner their consent; and the role of familial consent or coercion (or both) in pushing women and girls into the sex trade. A survey of the UNESCO paper's bibliography quickly answers why none of this emerged in the report: no historical literature was consulted in its preparation. The report's failure to recognize the historicity of human trafficking in Nigeria signals the need not only for further research but also for greater cooperation between policymakers and scholars of trafficking.

NOTES

Abbreviations

ACC Accra
CS   Colonial Secretary
CSO Colonial Secretary's Office

1. E. C. Nottingham, Commissioner, Gold Coast Police, Criminal Investigation Division, to CS, "Traffic In Women and Children," 18 July 1940, Public Records and Archives Administration Department, Ghana, ACC, CSO 15/1/222. All records are from the Accra branch unless otherwise noted.

2. Benedict Naanen, "'Itinerant Gold Mines': Prostitution in the Cross River Basin of Nigeria, 1930–1950," *African Studies Review* 34, no. 2 (1991): 61.

3. Nottingham to CS, "Traffic in Women and Children," 18 July 1940, CSO 15/1/222.

4. Naanen, "'Itinerant Gold Mines,'" 57–79; Luise White, *The Comforts of Home: Prostitution in Colonial Nairobi* (Chicago: University of Chicago Press, 1990); Emmanuel Akyeampong, "Sexuality and Prostitution among the Akan of the Gold Coast c. 1650–1950," *Past and Present* 156 (August 1997): 158.

5. International Convention for the Suppression of the "White Slave Traffic," 4 May 1910, 211 Consol. TS 45, 1912 Gr. Brit., TS 20. For more on early antitrafficking treaties, see Nora V. Demleitner, "Forced Prostitution: Naming an International Offense," *Fordham International Law Journal* 18, no. 1 (1994–95): 163–97.

6. Demleitner, "Forced Prostitution," 169–71, emphasis added.

7. UNESCO, "Human Trafficking in Nigeria: Root Causes and Recommendations," *Policy Paper Poverty Series*, no. 14.2(E) (Paris: UNESCO, 2006), 11–12. For a recent Togolese trafficking case, see US Attorney, District of New Jersey, "Togolese Woman Sentenced to 27 Years in Prison," 20 September 2010. www.ice.gov/news/releases/1009/100920newark.htm.

8. John Maxwell, Commissioner, Eastern Province, to Acting CS, "Prostitution — Unsatisfactory State of the Law Respecting," 26 April 1911, ADM, 11/1/922, case 86/1911.

9. Daniel Walther, "Sex and Control in Germany's Overseas Possessions: Venereal Disease, Prostitution, and Indigenous Agency," paper presented at the annual meeting of the African Studies Association, Chicago, 14 November 2008). I thank Daniel Walther for sharing this paper with me.

10. Ibid., 6.

11. See ibid., 8.

12. Maxwell to Acting CS, "Prostitution," 26 April 1911, ADM, 11/1/922, case 86/1911.

13. Acting Governor Thorburn to Acting CS, "Prostitution," 8 May 1911, ADM, 11/1/922, case 86/1911.

14. I intentionally use *sexuality* in the singular because colonial ideologies, such as Thorburn's, typically presented a monolithic view of African sexualities as hyperlicentious. Recent scholarship documents the past and present of African sexualities. For an overview, see Marc Epprecht, "Sexuality, Africa, History," *American Historical Review* 114, no. 5 (2009): 1258–72.

15. Acting Governor Thorburn, "Prostitution," 19 May 1911, ADM, 11/1/922, case 86/1911.

16. Kadri English, Hausa Tribal Ruler, to District Commissioner, Accra, "Prostitution," 13 May 1925, ADM, 11/1/922, case 25/1925.

17. On the misidentification of traders as prostitutes, see Penelope A. Roberts, "The State and the Regulation of Marriage: Sefwi Wiawso (Ghana), 1900–1940," in *Women, State and Ideology*, ed. Haleh Afshar (Albany: SUNY Press, 1987), 57.

18. English to Accra District Commissioner, "Prostitution," 13 May 1925, ADM, 11/1/922, case 25/1925.

19. Akyeampong, "Sexuality and Prostitution."

20. H. S. Newlands, Secretary for Native Affairs, to CS, "Prostitution," 1 September 1925, ADM, 11/1/922, case 25/1925.

21. H. S. Newlands, "Prostitution," 1 September 1925, ADM, 11/1/922, case 25/1925.

22. For Akyease, see Nana Ofori Atta, Omanhene of Akyem Abuakwa, to Takwahene Kwabena Amo of Akyease, "Prostitutes—Suggested Measures as to Suppression of Venereal Disease," 21 January 1927, PRAAD Cape Coast, ADM, 23/1/590. For events in Sefwi Wiawso, see Roberts, "State." For Asante, see Jean Allman, "Rounding Up Spinsters: Gender Chaos and Unmarried Women in Colonial Asante," *Journal of African History* 37, no. 2 (1996): 195–214.

23. "Immigration Restriction Ordinance," 1926, ADM, 4/1/124.

24. Criminal Code, 1936, "Drunken, Riotous, and Disorderly Conduct," "Kidnapping, Abduction, and Similar Offences," chap. 9, ADM, 4/1/131.

25. For Nigeria, see T. S. Thomas, Acting Chief Secretary, Nigeria, to A. A. C. Finlay, Acting CS, 14 July 1925, "Prostitution," ADM, 11/1/922, case 25/1925. For Sierra Leone, see Acting CS, CSO, Sierra Leone, to Acting CS, "Prostitution," 21 July 1925, ADM, 11/1/922.

26. Elsewhere I focus more fully on World War II as a watershed moment in the social and legislative history of the sex trade in West Africa. Carina Ray, "The Racial Politics of Anti-Prostitution Legislation: World War II and the Sex Trade in British West Africa" in *Re-Centering Africa in the History of the Second World War,* ed. Carolyn Brown and Judith Byfield (forthcoming).

27. Nancy E. Lawler, *Soldiers, Airmen, Spies, and Whisperers: The Gold Coast in World War II* (Athens: Ohio University Press, 2001), 54–55.

28. James Tobias, e-mail message from US Army Center of Military History, 19 May 2006.

29. E. C. Nottingham to CS, "Prostitutes–Control of by Police," memorandum, Accra, "Traffic in Women and Children," 30 May 1941, CSO, 15/1/222. To date my archival sources have yielded extensive information only about interracial prostitution between European military personnel, who were overwhelming British, and West African sex workers. High rates of venereal diseases among American troops stationed in the Gold Coast suggest that they, too, were involved in prostitution. See Charles M. Wiltse, *The Medical Department: Medical Service in the Mediterranean and Minor Theaters,* United States Army in World War II: The Technical Services (Washington, DC: Department of the Army, 1965), 67.

30. E.C. Nottingham, "Prostitutes–Control of by Police," 30 May 1941, CSO, 15/1/222.

31. Ibid.; emphasis in original.

32. Attorney General to Clerk of Executive Council, "Traffic In Women and Children," 19 September 1941, CSO, 15/1/222.

33. Moyne to Hodson, "Traffic In Women and Children," 29 March 1941, CSO, 15/1/222.

34. H. Ormston, "The Social Question: A Startling Disclosure," *West Africa,* 15 March 1941, 250.

35. Ibid.

36. R. Bayly Winder, "The Lebanese in West Africa," *Comparative Studies in Society and History* 4, no. 3 (1962): 312. See also George Brewer, Director of

Criminal Investigation Department, to Inspector General of Police, Accra, 12 March 1927, in Guggisberg to Amery, "Removal from Service, 1927," 6 April 1927, ADM, 12/5/173, enc. 3.

37. Ormston, "Social Question," 250. See also, M. Chorlton, "Nigerian 'Social Question': Pertinent Posers That Demand Official Enquiry," *West Africa*, 13 September 1941, 887.

38. Ormston noted that Gold Coast newspapers were awash with public commentary by Africans upset by the trade and its affect on wartime recruitment. Chorlton quotes articles in *The Nigerian Eastern Mail* that express similar concerns on the part of Nigerians. Ormston, "Social Question," 250; Chorlton, "Nigerian 'Social Question,'" 887.

39. Nottingham to CS, "Traffic in Women and Children," 18 July 1940, CSO, 15/1/222.

40. As a result of the 1921 and 1923 League of Nations conventions, members issued annual reports on the traffic of women and children. For further information, see Allain (chap. 7, this volume). Colonial Office to Officer Administering the Gold Coast Government, "Traffic in Women and Children," in Confidential Circular Dispatch, "Conventions on Traffic in Women and Children and Obscene Publications," 21 February 1948, CSO, 15/1/222.

41. Nottingham to CS, "Traffic in Women and Children," 18 July 1940, CSO, 15/1/222.

42. Ibid., emphasis added. For more on the gendered nature of trafficking, see McMahon (chap. 1, this volume), Roberts (chap. 3), and Rodet (chap. 4).

43. Nottingham to CS, "Traffic in Women and Children," 18 July 1940, CSO, 15/1/222.

44. Ibid.

45. Benjamin N. Lawrance and Ruby P. Andrew, "A 'Neo-Abolitionist Trend' in Sub-Saharan Africa? Regional Anti-Trafficking Patterns and a Preliminary Legislative Taxonomy," *Seattle Journal for Social Justice* 9, no. 2 (2011): 599–678.

46. On the false promises of marriage as a strategy commonly used by traffickers to lure women and girls, see Rodet (chap. 4, this volume).

47. Nottingham to CS, "Traffic in Women and Children," 18 July 1940, CSO, 15/1/222.

48. For Kenya, see Janet Bujra, "Production, Property and Prostitution: 'Sexual Politics' in Atu," *Cahiers d'études africaines* 65, no. 17 (1977); Bujra, "Women 'Entrepreneurs' of Early Nairobi," *Canadian Journal of African Studies* 9, no. 2 (1975): 213–34; White, *Comforts of Home*. For a cautionary note on overemphasizing women's agency, see Linda Bryder, "Sex, Race, and Colonialism: An Historiographical Review," *International History Review* 20, no. 4 (1998): 811–12.

49. Bourdillon to Hodson, "Traffic in Women and Children," 29 July 1941, CSO, 15/1/222.

50. Ibid.

51. Naanen, "'Itinerant Gold Mines,'" 61.

52. Ibid., 61–66.

53. Chorlton, "Nigerian 'Social Question,'" 887.

54. Naanen, "'Itinerant Gold Mines,'" 60.

55. Blackall to the CS, "Traffic in Women and Children," 26 July 1941, CSO, 15/1/222.

56. Niara Sudarkasa, "Women and Migration in Contemporary West Africa," *Signs* 3, no. 1 (1977): 182–83. See also Gloria I. Chuku, "From Petty Traders to International Merchants: A Historical Account of Three Igbo Women of Nigeria in Trade and Commerce, 1886 to 1970," *African Economic History* 27 (1999): 1–22.

57. Bourdillon to Hodson, "Traffic in Women and Children," 29 July 1941, CSO, 15/1/222.

58. Nottingham to CS, "Traffic in Women and Children," 15 September 1941, CSO, 15/1/222.

59. Ibid.

60. Ibid.

61. L. W. W., Office of the CS, to the CS, "Traffic in Women and Children," 1 September 1941, CSO, 15/1/222.

62. File minute by the Clerk of the Executive Council, "Traffic in Women and Children," 30 September 1941, CSO, 15/1/222. Also Hodson to Bourdillon, "Traffic in Women and Children," 17 October 1941, CSO, 15/1/222.

63. Executive Council Memorandum, Clerk of the Executive Council, "Traffic in Women and Children," 10 August 1942, CSO, 15/1/222.

64. Nottingham to CS, "Traffic in Women and Children," 10 August 1942, CSO, 15/1/222.

65. Browne to CS, "Traffic in Women and Children," 8 September 1942, CSO, 15/1/222. For amendments to the Criminal Code and the Immigration Ordinance, see Burns to Bourdillon, "Traffic in Women and Children," 11 October 1942.

66. Acting Commissioner of Police to CS, "Traffic in Women and Children," 1 October 1943, CSO, 15/1/222.

67. Acting Commissioner of Police to CS, "Traffic in Women and Children," 1 October 1943, CSO, 15/1/222.

68. UNESCO, "Human Trafficking in Nigeria: Root Causes and Recommendations," (2006). Also, Bisi Olateru-Olagbegi, "Brief Overview of the Situational Analysis of Human Trafficking in West Africa," paper presented at the Seventh African Regional Conference on Women, Addis Ababa, 6–10 October 2004.

6 ↶ Islamic Law and Trafficking in Women and Children in the Indian Ocean World

BERNARD K. FREAMON

HISTORIANS MAKE much of the impact that the transatlantic slave trade and New World slavery have had on contemporary understandings of world history and particularly the history of Africa in relation to the Euro-American world. The history of the transatlantic slave trade is thus a central feature in the construction of the West's view of itself.[1] The legacy of African slavery also significantly shapes self-definitions in the Americas, particularly in the United States, the Caribbean, and Brazil.[2]

Another, somewhat less chronicled legacy of African slavery is its foundation as a historical building block in the development of social, political, economic, and religious self-understandings and interactions between and among the peoples living in the Indian Ocean world.[3] The Indian Ocean slave trades and slave systems, as well as the societies they helped create, were highly complex human arrangements, producing elaborate and highly stratified social and labor relationships, military and naval slavery unlike anything seen in the West, debt bondage, predial slavery, quasi-emancipatory statuses in society, and concubinal relationships that sometimes brutally oppressed women and children and at the same time often produced heads of state and other important personages who greatly influenced attitudes and events in those societies.[4] Indeed the entrenched role of slavery in the Indian Ocean provoked Martin Klein to observe, "Those who wished to end slavery in the world faced a more difficult agenda in the Indian Ocean than they did in the Atlantic."[5]

Whereas the face of Atlantic slavery has frequently been described as male, the face of Indian Ocean slavery was predominantly female.[6] In the Atlantic, Africans were confronted and enslaved by Christians; in the Indian Ocean world, Muslims largely conducted the slave trade, and the destinations reached by Africans at the end of their passages were almost always Muslim communities.[7] Indeed, the enslavement and trafficking of women and children, many of whom are sub-Saharan Africans, is still a problem in the Islamic world.[8]

Edward Alpers has observed that Islam did not necessarily provide a unifying dimension for the Indian Ocean slave trade, unlike in the Atlantic, where there was a "uniform domination of Euro-American, Christian culture."[9] Although Muslim actors were ever present, there were tremendous cultural, ethnic, and linguistic variations within circumstances encountered by the slaves as they were transported from locales as varied as the Swahili coast, the Benadir coast in Somalia, Ethiopia, the upper Nile valley and the Sudan, Mozambique, northwestern Madagascar, and the Comoros Islands and transported to places like the Hijaz, Egypt, Yemen, Hadhramaut, the Persian Gulf, the Cape of Good Hope, and the western coast of India.[10] This broad disparity in circumstances makes it more difficult to isolate variables that can assist in understanding self-conceptions and attitudes among those who were involved, either as enslavers or as enslaved. It is my contention that these anomalies likely occurred, in part, because of the presence of Islam. Imam al-Ghazali, a venerated medieval scholar of Islamic law and religion, in discussing relationships of masters and slaves, advised the believers, "Fear God in the matter of your slaves. Feed them with what you eat and clothe them with what you wear and do not give them work beyond their capacity. Those whom you like, retain, and those whom you dislike, sell. Do not cause pain to God's creation. He caused you to own them and had He so wished He would have caused them to own you."[11] Often, as a result of this attitude, recognition of social distinctions between enslaved and free was quite blurred or even unrecognizable.

The American George William Curtis observed that often in nineteenth-century Egypt it seemed only an "accident" that some people were masters while others were enslaved.[12] Islam, therefore, operated as a leveling and often emancipatory influence in relations between masters and slaves and, simultaneously, albeit paradoxically, an entrenching influence in maintaining the structure of the Indian Ocean system.[13] These paradoxical rules and influences were particularly important in the ordering of lives of enslaved women and children and in the development of self-understandings among Africans, both free and enslaved, in the Indian Ocean world. Islam preached the theological equality of all human beings, whether enslaved or free, while still enforcing the legal maintenance of a system of chattel slavery. These paradoxical roles of Islam, and Islamic law, in ordering the lives and relationships of people in the region, are still important today. Therefore, anyone seeking to understand and address human trafficking issues in the Indian Ocean world today must take account of the roles of Islam and Islamic law and their histories in relation to slavery and the slave trades in the region.

The earliest written records demonstrate that an ancient trading bond existed between the peoples of East Africa and the peoples of the Middle East and the Indian subcontinent. Traders seeking to procure slaves and other marketable commodities from East Africa established this bond so that they might trade and barter in the commercial markets along the Indian Ocean coasts to the north and east. Trading routes were therefore developed along at least three axes between the coastal regions, and traders using large oceangoing dhows driven by very reliable Indian Ocean monsoon winds regularly plied these routes.[14] The route of the three axes ran from the East African coast north through the Red Sea to Arabia, Egypt, and the Mediterranean; northeast across the ocean to Muscat and other ports on the southern Arabian Peninsula as well as in the Persian Gulf; and east-northeast to the west coast of India and to ports in east Asia.[15] Slavery was a customary and recognized practice in East African life and many East Africans participated in this lucrative trade, supplying the human commodity to traders who visited their villages and ports.[16]

With the advent of Islam, Arab Muslim seafarers, led by the Omanis as well as by sailors from Yemen, the Hijaz, and the Persian Gulf, largely assumed control of these trading routes. With the rise of the Arab trade, Zanzibar, an island off the coast of East Africa and an Omani colonial outpost, became the most important East African port for the export of slaves across the ocean. The monsoons were so powerful that an oceangoing dhow could make the trip between Zanzibar and Muscat in as little as twenty-five days.[17] The trade in goods and the concomitant slave trade that arose alongside it were dominated by seafaring trading families from Hadhramaut, Muscat, and the Persian Gulf. Although there is sparse documentation of this trade, there is no doubt that it flourished.[18] An American consul in the late nineteenth century in Muscat described the Omani seafarers as "bedouins of the sea."[19] During the monsoon season as many as one hundred dhows came into Zanzibar harbor from India and Arabia carrying cloth, iron, sugar, salted fish, earthenware, and dates. In March and April they returned to their home ports carrying slaves, ivory, tortoiseshell, coconuts, and rice.[20] Estimates vary, but it appears that a typical dhow could hold anywhere from ten or twelve to as many as four hundred souls, exclusive of the crew, all sitting up and packed tightly in rows from stem to stern.[21]

Under the influence of Islamic law and European mercantilism and colonial law, the East African slave trade became a taut sinew connecting Arab, Indian, and European imperialisms.[22] Women generally played an important role in the development of these bonds, both as subjects of the slave trade and as instrumental actors working to further the aims of these commercial and maritime networks. This is consistent with other imperial histories showing the importance of the contributions of women to the imperial enterprise. As

Benjamin Lawrance and Richard Roberts observe in their introduction to this volume, trafficking in women and children is linked to the history of Africa's involvement in the global trade in slaves. I shall examine the influence of the Islamic law of slavery and emancipation on the lives of women in this trade, giving particular attention to the intersection between British abolitionist initiatives and Islamic law and legal culture.

THE BOND OF ISLAMIC LEGAL DISCOURSE

As these empires and subempires flourished, centers of Islamic legal discourse sprung up all over the Indian Ocean world, particularly in Hadhramaut and in Yemen; in Zanzibar and the Comoros, off the East African coast; and on the Indian subcontinent. Scholars in these places, assisted by teachings from major academic institutions in Cairo, Damascus, Baghdad, Mecca, and Medina, developed approaches to Islamic law that often dealt with problems associated with what was a burgeoning and lucrative slave trade. The development of these approaches formed part of a larger effort by jurists and judges to construct a cohesive legal system based on the message of the Qur'an and the teachings of the Prophet. The substantive corpus of this system came to be known as the *shari'a*, which literally means "way," "path," or "road." The term eventually took on a technical meaning, describing laws derived from four sources: the Qur'an, the Sunnah (the example of the Prophet), unanimous consensus of scholars on points of law (*ijmā'*), and analogical reasoning (*qiyās*). The first two sources are primary and the second two are secondary. These are the four sources of Islamic law in the Sunni jurisprudence. The Shi'a use somewhat different definitions of the two secondary sources but follow the same hierarchical approach and methodology.

As is well known, the law did not countenance the activities of the slave traders. Islamic law permits a human being to enter into a state of slavery in only two ways: capture by Muslims in a lawful jihad conducted by a Muslim army against a non-Muslim enemy or birth to two lawfully enslaved parents.[23] The hadith, or normative examples from the Prophet Muhammad's life, the second most important source of Islamic law after the Qur'an, make it clear that the indiscriminate capture and enslavement of free persons not at war with the Muslims is illegal under the shari'a. The Prophet condemned such behavior in no uncertain terms. Although Islamic jurists developed an elaborate and detailed set of rules on slavery emerging out of the capture of persons after military conquest, the jurisprudence also established three important principles designed to guide jurists in handling problems presented by the enslavement of non-Muslims. First, Islamic jurisprudence recognized a presumption of freedom in all cases involving human beings, whether Muslim or non-Muslim; and if there was any doubt about the servile status of a human being, that doubt was to be resolved in favor of a determination of freedom.[24] Second, the jurists determined that no Muslim could lawfully be enslaved.[25] Although conversion to Islam after enslavement did not result in automatic emancipation, it did in many cases make the path to emancipation an easier one. Third, the jurists decreed that children of unions between free men and their enslaved concubines were free by operation of law and were the juridical equal of children born of lawful marriages. A corollary to this rule provided that the concubine-mother, known in Arabic as *umm al-walad* (mother of the child), could not be sold or separated from her free children under normal circumstances and that she, again by operation of law, must be freed at the death of her owner.[26]

Although the Islamic law of slavery was actually quite liberal in comparison to other systems of slave law, the time-honored principles I have described were very often ignored, particularly in matters that involved women and children, and slave traders and slave dealers frequently acted with impunity, causing great suffering, harm, and injustice. In some cases, the purveyors of this suffering and harm were other women, often other African women. Although scholars and judges knew that the conduct of slave traders and their treatment of slaves were illegal under the shariʿa, they most often took no action. There were undoubtedly cases and situations where the shariʿa was invoked in aid of women and children involved in the slave trade but these instances seem to be the exception rather than the rule. As Bernard Lewis and others have observed, this is one of the great paradoxes in the history of Islamic jurisprudence. It will be useful to observe when the Islamic law intervened on behalf of enslaved women and when it did not. I shall now turn to specific examinations of several instances of encounters between women and children and the slave-trading milieu, drawn from a variety of sources. Where appropriate, I shall comment on the relevance of the encounter in terms of the so-called "end of slavery" at the end of the nineteenth century and modern instances of trafficking and slavery in the region today. I will conclude by evaluating these encounters through the prism of Islamic law.

WOMEN AND CHILDREN IN SLAVERY

The town of Barawa, on the Benadir coast of Somalia, is the site of a rich archive of late-nineteenth-century Islamic legal materials drawn from the *qadi*'s (Islamic judge's) court in that town.[27] This archive, recently accessible in English translation, provides us with a window through which we can view the administration of Islamic law on the coast of Somalia at the turn of the century and the roles of women in that milieu. The cases decided by the qadis involved property, marriage, divorce, contracts, gifts, and transactions concerning slaves. The qadi were sometimes assisted in their decision by Italian consular officials working for the colonial administration.

Slavery existed in precolonial, colonial, and postcolonial Somalia. Beginning in the mid-nineteenth century, a robust slave trade developed that supplied human beings to Somalis for domestic service, naval service, agricultural labor, and urban industry. Many of the slaves were non-Somali and were transported into the Benadir area from the south. They were often of Bantu ethnicity. Many worked on farms and plantations in southern Somalia and it was estimated that as many twenty-five thousand slaves, fully one-third of the population, lived on farms along the lower course of the Shebelle River at the turn of the century.[28] As in much of East Africa and the Arab world, slaves were considered a source of wealth and a mark of status. Many slaves lived in urban settlements and were active participants in the economic and social life of Barawa and the other smaller cities on the Benadir coast. The Benadir coast was within the dominion of the sultan of Zanzibar. He appointed the governor of the area as well as the local qadis, although judges often took office on the recommendation of a local grandee or other prominent person. The sultan eventually ceded the territory to the Italians.

The archives of the qadis' court make it clear that women in the Benadir region were not "nebulous figures" in the background of events but rather appear "as an exceptionally active part of the population, very vocal in claiming their rights and participating fully in the town's economic life." Over half the stone buildings mentioned in the archives were, or had been at some time, owned by women. Women were also owners of a wide variety of forms of personal property, including livestock, gold, jewelry, and slaves. The archives record the fact that there were many marriages between the enslaved and free persons, particularly between free men and enslaved women. The compilers of the archive note that women would often come to the aid of men who were in economic distress. Some attained "enviable" economic positions, being able to lend considerable sums of money or owning boats or other valuable pieces of property.[29] In one case a manumitted slave woman recovered a judgment for money lent to a man, perhaps during the time she was enslaved.[30]

Despite these circumstances, the archives also underscore that the experience of the typical female slave could very often be quite unpleasant. Islamic law would, however, be used to protect the interests of the enslaved. For example, the qadi recorded a set of facts involving the kidnapping of a female slave name Zeinab who escaped after being sold by her kidnappers to another. She voluntarily returned to the quarters of her original owner and this generated litigation in the qadi's court between the owner and the alleged bona fide purchaser. The purchaser lost, although the consul ordered the return of his purchase money.[31] The compilers of the archive note that the documents indirectly confirm that the slaves in Barawa were "comparatively well treated," with light punishments for transgressions and very few cases of violence.[32] During this time, the sultans of Oman and Zanzibar negotiated several anti–slave trade treaties with the British government. These treaties generally permitted the citizens of the sultan's dominions to continue trading in slaves along the East African coast, including Somalia, and between East Africa and the Arabian Peninsula. Beginning in 1839 the treaties recognized the fact that Somalis, as Muslims, could not be subjects of the slave trade and were to be freed if discovered on board a slave-trading vessel.[33]

In recent times, by contrast, Somali women and children have been particularly vulnerable to trafficking. They are trafficked to destinations outside the country, specifically to the Middle East, Europe, and destinations in Africa as well as domestically.[34] Women and young girls in Somalia are frequent victims of rape, beatings, and coerced female genital mutilation, and unaccompanied Somali children are often sent abroad, falling prey to traffickers who take advantage of these situations.[35] The increase in piracy off the coast of Somalia brings with it an increase in trafficking in human beings across the Arabian Sea that is reminiscent of the days of the slave trade in those same waters. Somali women and children, like most of the others trafficked in the region, are also transported to other African countries for sexual exploitation and forced labor. Prior to September 2001, up to 250 children were trafficked out of Somalia each month and many still end up in these circumstances.[36] With respect to unmarried women, these reports suggest that conditions for such women and children in Somalia may be worse today than they were at the close of the nineteenth century.

If we move south and examine events occurring in the nineteenth-century heartlands of the dominions of the sultan of Zanzibar, a somewhat different picture emerges. There is a rather old but reliable description of the sale of slaves in Zanzibar, quoting an unpublished account in the Bombay government records and providing us with a "graphic description of the manner in which slaves were exposed for sale in the open markets in Zanzibar, where merchants from Cutch, Sind, Seinee, and other parts of India flocked in great numbers to purchase and carry on a regular traffic in human beings."[38]

> Slaves are brought to the market place early in the day. . . . They are ranged in a line composed of both sexes and all ages, beginning with the least and increasing to the rear, according to their sizes. . . . Children of six years are sold for five or six dollars. The value of a prime slave was about 50, and that of a young girl about 60 dollars. Women with infants did not fetch so high a price as those without them. . . . The various tribes of slaves, . . . brought annually to Zanzibar for sale, and of which 10,000 are supposed to be sent annually to India, could not be accurately described.[39]

From the time of the rise of the importance of Zanzibar in the regional oceanic economy, coinciding with Sultan Saʿid's accession to the sultanate of Muscat in 1804, his subsequent transfer of the sultanate to Zanzibar in 1840, and the concomitant designation of Zanzibar as his imperial capital, slave traders carried on the trade in Africans with relative impunity.

The British navy's efforts during this period were at best a hit-and-miss affair. Gwyn Campbell notes that it is estimated that over two million slaves were exported from East Africa between 1830 and 1873, when slave shipments from Zanzibar were banned.[40] Even after the trade was banned, illegal transport of slaves across the ocean to destinations on the Arabian Peninsula and in India continued for many years.[41] As Jelmer Vos has noted in this volume (chapter 2), abolition in the Indian Ocean world, by the British and by their Muslim vassals, gave tremendous fuel to the illegal oceanic slave trade, especially the trade in women and children. There were never enough naval ships to completely interdict the trade that was now illegal under international rules as well as under Islamic rules and the sultan's edicts.[42] The travails of HMS *Philomel*, a British ship of the line, provide a poignant example. The *Philomel* was an eighty-horsepower steam- and sail-powered gun vessel, or gun brig, built in 1860. She was assigned to the Indian Ocean sometime after 1870.[43]

The *Philomel* had several encounters with slave-carrying dhows during this time.[44] In October 1884 her crew captured a dhow with 154 slaves (128 males, 20 females; archival source does not explain discrepancy involving 6 uncounted slaves) off Ras al-Hadd, and proceedings were instituted against the "nakhoda" (captain) of the dhow and its owner in the vice admiralty court in Muscat.[45] The proceedings contain considerable information about the methods of the dealers and the condition of their cargo, as well as data concerning slave prices and how slaves were disposed of after liberation. Many of the passengers on board the dhow were children, and the evidence showed that they were "mere skeletons," as provisions and water had run short and for two days nothing had been given to the slaves. After disposing of the dhow, the captain of the *Philomel* transported those slaves who were fit enough to travel to Aden, where they were dispersed. Another capture involved a dhow named *Fateh al-Khair*, carrying 51 slaves (30 males, 21 females). Proceedings to condemn the dhow, and cash and goods found on board, were taken at the vice admiralty court in Aden.[46] In both cases the vice admiralty judges had no difficulty condemning the dhow and liberating the slaves. A subsequent report from the political resident at Aden to the secretary of the Bombay government reports that, of 196 liberated slaves brought into the port of Aden by the *Philomel* during that period, 55 boys, one woman, and 22 girls were returned to Zanzibar "for disposal"; 96 men and boys remained in Aden as laborers; three women were given to the Good Shepherd Convent; two women and one girl took up residence with friends in Aden; one freed person remained sick in the hospital; one died; and fourteen women were married off to local suitors.[47]

In an earlier vice admiralty court proceeding involving the *Philomel* and occurring in waters near Zanzibar, there were more difficulties. One night in February 1877, the *Philomel* was anchored off the coast of Tanganyika, near Pangani. As part of its routine, the ship launched one of its skiffs, in the charge of the ship's boatswain, which approached the shore. The archive notes, "It appears that the four slaves (three women and one man) were taken from the shore" on the night of 27 February 1877, and placed on board. "Shortly afterwards, they were carried to Zanzibar, where, on the 9th of March, last [1877], both the boatswain who had received them and the slaves themselves were examined by Dr. Kirk at the British Consulate. Their owner also appeared to claim restitution, on the ground that they had been illegally taken away."[48]

The boatswain testified that the slaves claimed that they were fugitives. It was further stated by the three women that they had been in chains for two years. According to Kirk, the British consular officer (acting as vice admiralty judge), this statement appeared to be inconsistent with the appearance of their bodies, and it was further reported that the boat's interpreter may have been instructing the women on what answers to give during the proceeding. Kirk found that he had systematically taught them what to say, and that explained why they all adhered to a story that was "on the face of it in many particulars evidently false." The owner admitted that he had put the two female slaves, who were his concubines, in chains for forty days as punishment for going out at night. But otherwise, he argued, they were well treated. "The owner further expressed his hope that suitable redress would be given to him against the Commander of the *Philomel* who had, he contended, wrongfully deprived him of his property, when he was transgressing no law, and was not engaged in the Slave Trade either by land or sea."[49]

Kirk sought advice from the commander of a sister vessel of the *Philomel*, the *London*, which happened to be in Zanzibar harbor at that time. The commander, Captain Sullivan, advised that there might very well be a case for a claim of compensation on the part of the owner of the slaves, but he was not sure. In any event, the slaves could not be returned because Sullivan had been involved in arranging for their transportation to Natal, as "liberated Africans," some of whom became indentured workers.[50] Kirk then wrote to the Admiralty in London, seeking directions. It was Kirk's opinion that the slaves could only have been taken on the grounds of humanity, and that the boatswain and, by implication, the captain perhaps should be held blameless for their actions.

H. C. Rothery, a treasury official seconded as a legal adviser to the Admiralty, replied, after having his opinion confirmed by the lords commissioners of the treasury. He agreed with Kirk that there may have been a humanitarian ground for taking the slaves into the boat but, once it was determined that their claim of fugitive status was false, the commanding officer should have arranged either to return the slaves to their owner or to pay him compensation. Rothery then directed that Kirk should entertain the owner's claim for compensation against the commander of the *Philomel.* A separate proceeding would determine whether the commander should be indemnified.[51] The case illustrates to what extent, in some instances, the British were inclined to respect and enforce Muslim claims of slave ownership, particularly of women, under Islamic law.

The activities of Indian residents and commercial traders in East Africa were also particularly troublesome for the British. Sometimes the efforts of the British were of no avail or, in the cases of women and children, may have actually made their situations worse. In 1876, Frederick Holmwood, British assistant political agent in Zanzibar, was instructed to travel to the region around Malindi, Lamu, and as far north as Barawa, on the East African coast, to determine to what extent British instructions to their Indian subjects in the region to cease slaveholding were being followed. Holmwood reported that, in a few cases, slaves that had been manumitted were actually reenslaved by their Indian masters.[52] As Elisabeth McMahon has noted (chapter 1, this volume), reenslavement of vulnerable women was very common in East Africa. Such was the case for two concubines held by Indian Bohra businessmen in 1876.[53] The first case involved a young "Galla" girl who had been tied up for months in ropes by the wife of her owner and beaten, leaving severe wounds.[54] In the second case, a girl of twelve was compelled to marry a man against her will. She escaped and found refuge with Holmwood after learning that he had arrived to investigate cases of enslavement. The two owners were fined and sentenced to short periods of imprisonment by Holmwood, under the authority of the sultan of Zanzibar, and the girls were then handed by Holmwood over to a Khoja Muslim official "with instructions to promote their early marriage with steady single men who intended settling in the country, the money [from the fines] being sufficient to procure their wedding clothes and a decent cottage as a dowry." Here we again see that the British deferred to and incorporated perceptions of Islamic customs and law into their decision making, particularly when it appeared to suit their own ends. These marriages, while purporting to be acts of rescue, were in reality forced marriages that actually tested the limits of Islamic law.

At least one of the women in these accounts was a black African. Others were Indian. Kirk tells the story of Fatima, an Indian slave girl. Fatima came to his attention because she was being offered for sale by a local slave auctioneer in the houses of wealthy Arabs in Zanzibar. It seems that Fatima had been sold into slavery as a very young girl in India by her father, a *jemadar* (low-ranking commissioned officer) in the service of the Bombay government.[55] She was first taken to Hyderabad, in the Deccan plateau of India.[56] She remained in

Hyderabad for some time until her owner took her to Mukalla, in Hadhramaut, on the southern coast of the Arabian Peninsula. She was then sold to an East African man. She eventually found her way to Lamu, Kenya, where she fell into the hands of Saeed Auter, a notorious slave dealer and a Sheheri Arab.[57] Fatima was then sold to a local qadi and she eventually was passed to a young Persian, who put her up for sale in Zanzibar in order to make a profit. When Kirk intervened the bids for Fatima were running as high as $250, a considerable sum at that time. The consular report also indicates that she was exhibited to the wealthy Arabs with a group of Georgian slave women, who were also being offered for sale.[58] Although this account requires more corroboration, it shows that some of the women who found themselves enslaved in Africa were not black Africans.[59] The milieu created was instead a cosmopolitan one, with significant ethnic diversity on both sides of the divide.

The suffering of enslaved women and children did not cease with the formal abolition of slavery in the region. The records of the British consul in Aden before World War II demonstrate that many of the behaviors considered characteristic of nineteenth-century East African slave trade continued into the twentieth century. Aden, on the southern shore of the Arabian Peninsula, lay near the mouth of the entrance to the Red Sea, an area notorious for slave trafficking. Slavers smuggled Ethiopian captives onto the Arabian Peninsula, through well-documented routes, including Yemen and Hadhramaut. Although the slave trade across the sea was acknowledged by everyone to be illegal, once an illegal slave was landed in Yemen or Oman or Saudi Arabia, she or he could be resold because slavery had not been declared illegal by the respective governments of those territories.[60]

Consular reports record many cases of twentieth-century slavery in Hadhramaut, often involving the selling and reselling of kidnapped Ethiopians.[61] These sources show that kidnapping and capture of human beings by deceit or artifice were common methods used by traders in the mid-twentieth century around the Red Sea, particularly with respect to Ethiopian victims. Into the present, Ethiopia and Somalia remain a major source for trafficking in persons, particularly girls and women. Ethiopian women in the Middle East "face severe abuses, indicative of forced labor, including physical and sexual assault, denial of salary, sleep deprivation, and confinement."[62] Thousands of women and girls are trafficked every year to the Middle East, specifically Lebanon, Saudi Arabia, and the United Arab Emirates.[63] One recent estimate suggested that one thousand Ethiopian girls were being trafficked into Beirut, each month.[64] There is also much domestic and regional trafficking within Ethiopia and around the Horn of Africa. These facts are reminiscent of the stark realities of the East African slave trade of the nineteenth and early twentieth centuries. Ethiopian women, particularly Oromo women, were greatly sought after by slave traders because they brought high prices in the slave markets and were highly prized by purchasers for their compliant personalities.[65] The archives show that throughout the twentieth century the British and, later, Arab governments and courts in the region had very little success in preventing the large-scale illegal transport of Ethiopian girls, women, and boys across the Red Sea for sale in the cosmopolitan centers of the Persian Gulf, in India, and on the Arabian Peninsula. If these victims were not the subjects of outright kidnappings, they were often tricked into a life of prostitution or concubinage in the Indian Ocean world or in Europe.

SLAVERY, THE SLAVE TRADE, AND ISLAMIC LAW

The attitude of those learned in Islamic law to these horrific events, particularly events involving the cruel and sometimes life-threatening enslavement of women and children, was often one of silence or quiet acquiescence. We have found, however, that the ʿulamāʾ (religio-legal scholars and jurists) in at least three locations around the Indian Ocean world shared and expressed the opinion that the slave trade and slavery practiced by the Muslims in these locations were patently illegal under the shariʿa. Although some of these opinions were encouraged by British interpreters of Islamic law, they remain important in assessing Muslims' changing attitudes toward slavery.

The following statement appears in a confidential dispatch from the governor's office in Aden to the British colonial secretary on 30 June 1937.

> Qadhis and others "learned in the law" in the Hadhramut towns have informed me that they are of the opinion that there is not one legally held slave in the Hadhramut, and say that the Sharia law does not help those who claim that it would be an interference with religion to abolish them, and the Sharia only allows the enslavement of persons taken in holy wars with infidels and there are no such wars these days.

The diplomat then reports that he asked a "learned (an honest) Qadi of Mukalla" for his opinion on the topic. He quotes the qadi:

> As regards the infidels not at war with the Moslems, the enslavement of them is unlawful. . . . The children of the infidel who have been taken away by the Moslems and sold as a slave are slaves, but if they get married to a free woman, the children should be free and not slaves. . . . As to the present people held in slavery, who are generally be [sic] procured from Abyssinia etc., is it adjudged that they are not legally slaves because their origin cannot really be proved to be from legal [sic] source of enslavement.[66]

Similarly, in 1808, Muslim muftis, "who were accredited Mahomedan law-officers in the service of the British Judicial courts," stated that "only capture in a holy war, or descent from captives taken in a holy war constitutes legal slavery according to Mahomedan Law."[67] This fatwa acknowledges that the ʿulamāʾ of India knew that the capture and forced enslavement of Africans from Zanzibar, Ethiopia, Nubia, and other such places was illegal under Islamic law.

Finally, my own investigation into the attitude of the contemporary ʿulamāʾ on the question of the abolition of slavery in Zanzibar adds a modern perspective to the historical context. I learned of an example of this contemporary attitude in an interview with Sheikh Habib ʿAli Kombo, the former chief qadi (qādī al-qudāt) of Zanzibar and Pemba. In the early 1950s, Sheikh ʿAli Kombo worked as an assistant to a local Islamic scholar, Saʿid bin ʿAli, who taught a variety of Islamic subjects. He remembers that one day a student, Bakr bin Hassan (now deceased), complained bitterly to Saʿid bin ʿAli about attitudes that some Zanzibaris took toward him because of his servile heritage.[68] Apparently Bakr bin Hassan's parents had both been slaves in Zanzibar during the precolonial era and some people had told him that he therefore could be reenslaved. This caused Bakr bin Hassan a great deal of anxiety and torment.

Sheikh ʿAli Kombo remembers that Saʿid bin ʿAli became quite incensed and then determined that he would give a series of lectures to the class on the status of slavery under Islamic law in Zanzibar.[69] Sheikh ʿAli Kombo indicated that the lectures were memorable and that Saʿid bin ʿAli vehemently asserted that the slavery practiced in Zanzibar was not the slavery contemplated by the shariʿa and that those who practiced that form of slavery were transgressors and nothing more than avaricious businessmen engaged in an entrepreneurial enterprise that was itself a transgression. According to Sheikh ʿAli Kombo, Saʿid bin ʿAli, citing all four sources of the shariʿa—Qurʾan, Sunnah, ijmāʾ, and qiyās—established that Bakr bin Hassan was not a slave, that his parents had not lawfully been held in slavery, and that there had never been lawful slavery in Zanzibar, Pemba, or Tanganyika. Sheikh ʿAli Kombo said that this lecture made a big impression on him and that he never forgot it. The lecture took place in the Ngwachani Mosque in Pemba sometime in the mid- to late 1950s.

Saʿid bin ʿAli then subsequently began repeating the lecture as part of his khutba (sermon) usually delivered at marriage ceremonies.[70] Some schools of Islamic law consider recent servile heritage of the male spouse to be a disqualifying fact authorizing the guardian of the bride to refuse to agree to the marriage, and this practice was apparently of some prevalence in Zanzibar. Saʿid bin ʿAli argued in his sermons that such disqualifiers should not be recognized in Zanzibar because the slavery practiced by the Muslims during the precolonial era was patently illegal under the shariʿa. According to Sheikh ʿAli Kombo, Saʿid bin ʿAli's pronouncements caused a great deal of consternation among the ʿulamāʾ

in Zanzibar, particularly the Ibadhi ʿulamāʾ, and eventually a conference of the judges and ʿulamāʾ was called to settle the question.[71] After much discussion, the ʿulamāʾ and judges agreed that Saʿid bin ʿAli was right, and servile heritage was eliminated as a basis for disqualification of a putative spouse in Zanzibar.[72]

These events suggest that the senior Islamic ʿulamāʾ across the Indian Ocean world and across three centuries knew that the capture and enslavement of innocents by Muslim slave traders and slave raiders in Africa was illegal under the shariʿa. This would certainly include the capture and enslavement of innocent women and girls.

These observations are confirmed by the well-known writings of several reform-minded Islamic scholars who emerged out of the Indian colonial experience and took important positions on the question of slavery. Probably the more important, and certainly the most strident, of these scholars was Saiyid Ahmad Khan, a British-educated lawyer, activist, and educator.[73] In 1870, Khan published a monograph, in English, entitled "A Series of Essays on the Life of Mohammed, and Subjects Subsidiary Thereto," that was designed to refute the depiction of Muslim society as rife with slavery, injustice, and bigotry.[74] He argued that only prisoners of war could be enslaved under Islamic law and further that it was Muhammad's successors who were unfaithful to the message of the Qurʾan. As Avril Powell has observed, Khan's publications were probably the first of a genre that has been broadly categorized as modernist, rejecting, inter alia, the legitimacy of slavery in Islam; they had begun to influence thinking "far beyond the boundaries of Indian Islam."[75] Khan also wrote on other subjects, including jihad.[76] These writings preceded by a generation similar modernist writings that were to come out of Egypt at the end of the nineteenth century. It is reasonable to conclude that Khan's discourse may have influenced Muhammad ʿAbduh, the preeminent Egyptian modernist reformer, and his student and biographer, Muhammad Rashid Rida, as well.

The second of the Indian reformers was a Shiʿa Muslim named Sayyid Amir (Ameer) ʿAli. A Cambridge-trained lawyer, he became chief justice of the Calcutta supreme court in the 1890s.[77] His most famous book, *The Spirit of Islam*, was widely read throughout the English-speaking world and translated into several languages.[78] He staked out a more moderate position on slavery, arguing that the Qurʾan and Muhammad intended that the institution would gradually disappear and that abolition was the natural result of any intelligent understanding of Islam and Islamic law.[79]

Both scholars taught a number of others who became influential in Indian ulamaic circles. Perhaps the most important was Chirágh ʿAli, a close associate of Khan and administrator in the princely state of Hyderabad.[80] He published several important treatments of slavery in the 1880s, including one dedicated to the Ottoman sultan ʿAbd al-Hamid II.[81]

In spite of the vigorous arguments of these three scholars and others, slavery and slave trading, with sometimes an active but more often passive connivance of the British mercantilist and oriental imperium, would continue in the British dominions in the Indian Ocean world for many years to come. Be that as it may, it does appear that there was some interest in Egypt in the opinions of the Zanzibari ʿulamāʾ, and that interest may have also extended to inward-looking inquiries on the question of slavery.[82] Professor Amal Ghazal has shown that a member of the Egyptian ʿulamāʾ, ʿAbd al-Rahman al-Kawakibi, actually traveled to Zanzibar in the early twentieth century in an effort to investigate the circumstances of East African slavery, concluding that it should be abolished. These events make it clear that even the Egyptian scholars (acknowledged by many modern scholars to be the leading thinkers in the Islamic world at that time), were concerned about the implications of the slave trade and slavery for Islamic law.[83] This fact is made graphically plain in the writings of Rashid Rida, the most important Islamic scholar writing at the turn of the twentieth century and a student of the great Egyptian reformer Muhammad ʿAbduh. Rida published the views of al-Kawakibi on slavery in 1905, and in his book *The Muhammadan Revelation* Rida considers the question of the legality of slavery and the slave trade under Islamic law, concluding that the elimination of slavery is one of the central purposes of the revelation of the Qurʾan, obligating Muslims everywhere to establish slavery-free societies.[84] Although Rida later modified his views, his initial opinions are jurisprudentially significant.

One might wonder why these opinions did not gain greater currency among members of the population and among imams and lesser religious and legal officials likely more closely involved with questions involving slavery and the slave trade. Recall that the qadis in Barawa routinely adjudicated claims involving slaves, often young women or girls, who may have been the subject of ill treatment or abuse or may have had claims concerning property. No thought seems to be given to the fact that for most of these litigants slavery was illegal. Yet, from the beginning of the twentieth century, a number of ʿulamāʾ, including ʿAbduh and Rida, and later lesser religious and legal figures, did not hesitate to condemn the practice as illegal under the shariʿa. This line of thinking may again become useful now, as activists battle the scourge of human trafficking and forced labor in the Middle East and Africa.

NOTES

Abbreviations

FO	Foreign Office
UKNA	United Kingdom National Archives
UNODC	United Nations Office on Drugs and Crime
USDOS, *TIP*	United States Department of State, Trafficking in Persons Report

Much of the research for this chapter was conducted during a fellowship at the Gilder Lehrman Center for the Study of Slavery, Resistance, and Abolition, Yale University (GLC). Parts were presented in the Legal History Colloquium at New York University School of Law, at Stanford University, and at Yale. I am grateful to participants in these venues for their helpful comments and for the support of the GLC. Thanks also to Brian Baker, Rebecca Fink, Dawn A. Pepin, Jesse D. Rodgers, Desiree Sedehi, and Joseph Stefanelli, all students at Seton Hall University School of Law, for their excellent research assistance.

1. Robin Blackburn, *The American Crucible: Slavery, Emancipation, and Human Rights* (London: Verso, 2012); David Brion Davis, *Inhuman Bondage: The Rise and Fall of Slavery in the New World* (New York: Oxford University Press, 2006).

2. See Joseph E. Inikori and Stanley L. Engerman, eds., *The Atlantic Slave Trade: Effects on Economies, Societies, and Peoples in Africa, the Americas, and Europe* (Durham: Duke University Press, 1992).

3. The Indian Ocean world includes communities with shorelines on the Indian Ocean, the Red Sea, the Persian Gulf, and other saltwater inlets flowing into the Indian Ocean, as well as communities under the economic, political, religious, or social sway of these shoreline communities. See Sugata Bose, *A Hundred Horizons: The Indian Ocean in the Age of Global Empire* (Cambridge, MA: Harvard University Press 2006), 272–82; Shihan Jayasuriya and Richard Pankhurst, eds., *The African Diaspora in the Indian Ocean* (Trenton: Africa World Press, 2003); Joseph E. Harris, *The African Presence in Asia: Consequences of the East African Slave Trade* (Evanston: Northwestern University Press, 1971).

4. Gwyn Campbell, "Introduction," and Martin A. Klein, "The Emancipation of Slaves in the Indian Ocean World," both in *Abolition and Its Aftermath in Indian Ocean Africa and Asia*, ed. Campbell (London: Routledge, 2005), xi, 198.

5. Klein, "Emancipation," 198.

6. Paul E. Lovejoy, *Transformations in Slavery: A History of Slavery in Africa* (New York: Cambridge University Press, 2012), 27, 36.

7. The major exceptions were the largely non-Muslim Madagascar, Mascarene, and Mozambique slave trades. See Richard B. Allen, "The Mascarene Slave-Trade and Labour Migration in the Indian Ocean during the Eighteenth and Nineteenth Centuries," in *The Structure of Slavery in Indian Ocean Africa and Asia*, ed. Gwyn Campbell (London: Frank Cass, 2004), 33–50; Pedro Machado, "A Forgotten Corner of the Indian Ocean: Gujarati Merchants, Portuguese India and the Mozambique Slave Trade, c. 1730–1830," in Campbell, *Structure*, 17–32.

8. Mohamed Mattar, "Trafficking in Persons, Especially Women and Children, in Countries of the Middle East: The Scope of the Problem and the Appropriate Legislative Responses," *Fordham International Law Journal* 26, no. 3 (2003): 756; Khaled Ali Beydoun, "The Trafficking of Ethiopian Domestic Workers into Lebanon: Navigating through a Novel Passage of the International Maid Trade," *Berkeley Journal of International Law* 24, no. 3 (2006): 1016; Dina Kraft, "Bedouin Smugglers Abuse Africans Held for Ransom, Israel Group Says," *New York Times*, 16 February 2011.

9. Edward A. Alpers, "Recollecting Africa: Diasporic Memory in the Indian Ocean World," *African Studies Review* 43, no. 1 (2000): 86.

10. Ibid.

11. Cited and quoted in John O. Hunwick, "Black Africans in the Mediterranean World: Introduction to a Neglected Aspect of the African Diaspora," in *The Human Commodity*, ed. Elizabeth Savage (London: Frank Cass, 1992), 7n10.

12. George W. Curtis, *Nile Notes of a Howadji* (New York: Harper and Brothers, 1851), 56.

13. Bose, *Hundred Horizons*, 4–15; K. N. Chaudhuri, *Trade and Civilization in the Indian Ocean: An Economic History from the Rise of Islam to 1750* (Cambridge: Cambridge University Press, 1985); Edward A. Alpers, "African Diaspora in the Northwest Indian Ocean: Reconsideration of an Old Problem, New Directions for Research," *Comparative Studies of South Asia, Africa and the Middle East* 17, no. 2 (1997): 62–82; Harris, *African Presence*; Esmond B. Martin and Chryssee P. Martin, *Cargoes of the East: The Ports, Trade, and Culture of the Arabian Seas and Western Indian Ocean* (London: Elm Tree Books, 1978).

14. See Alpers, "African Diaspora."

15. Harris, *African Presence*, 28–29 (map 2). Also see Paul Finkelman and Joseph C. Miller, *Macmillan Encyclopedia of World Slavery*, 2 vols. (New York: Macmillan Reference, 1998) 2:xv.

16. Martin, *Cargoes*, 23–25, 31; Harris, *African Presence*, 23–25.

17. C. S. Nicholls, *The Swahili Coast: Politics, Diplomacy and Trade on the East African Littoral, 1798–1856* (London: Allen and Unwin, 1971), 74n1.

18. Reginald Coupland, *East Africa and Its Invaders, from the Earliest Times to the Death of Seyyid Said in 1856* (New York: Russell and Russell, 1965), 17–20; Esmond B. Martin and T. C. I. Ryan, "A Quantitative Assessment of the Arab Slave Trade of East Africa, 1770–1896," *Kenya Historical Review* 5, no. 1 (1977): 73n13.

19. US National Archives, Annual Commercial Reports, Louis L. Maguire, US Consul, Muscat, to Department of State, 21 August 1881, AE1.119:T638; Dispatches from United States consuls in Muscat, 1880–1906 [microfilm], 16.

20. Esmond B. Martin, *Zanzibar: Tradition and Revolution* (London: Hamilton, 1978), 28.

21. Abdul Sheriff, *Slaves, Spices and Ivory in Zanzibar* (London: James Currey, 1987), 224; Christopher Lloyd, *The Navy and the Slave Trade: The Suppression of the African Slave Trade in the Nineteenth Century* (London: Frank Cass, 1968), 194–97.

22. See Thomas R. Metcalf, *Imperial Connections: India in the Indian Ocean Arena, 1860–1920* (Berkeley: University of California Press, 2007).

23. R. Brunschvig, "'Abd," *Encyclopaedia of Islam*, new ed., ed. H. A. R. Gibb, 13 vols. (Leiden: Brill, 1960), 1:36–38. Also see Hunwick, "Black Africans."

24. Bernard K. Freamon, "Slavery, Freedom, and the Doctrine of Consensus in Islamic Jurisprudence," *Harvard Human Rights Journal* 11, no. 1 (1998): 35n135.

25. Brunschvig, "'Abd," 1:26.

26. *Encyclopedia of Islam*, S.U. "unn al-walad," accessed 24 May 2012, http://referenceworks.brillonline.com/entries/encyclopedia_of_Islam2/um-al-walad-com_1290.

27. Alessandra Vianello and Mohamed M. Kassim, eds., *Servants of the Sharia*, 2 vols. (Leiden: Brill, 2006).

28. Vianello and Kassim, "Introduction," *Servants of the Sharia*, 1:39.

29. Ibid., 1:38–44.

30. Ibid., qadi's record 16.1.

31. Ibid., qadi's record 419.1.

32. Ibid., 1:43.

33. "Translation of Additional Articles regarding the Suppression of the Foreign Slave-trade entered into by His Highness Saeed Syud bin Sultan, the Imam of Muscat—1839," in *A Collection of Documents on the Slave Trade of Eastern Africa*, ed. R. W. Beachey (London: Collings, 1976), 107–8. Taken from C. U. Aitchison, *A Collection of Treaties, Engagements and Sanads relating to India and Neighboring Countries*, Delhi, 1933, vol. XI, 299–300 (originally published by Office of Superintendent of Government Printing, Calcutta, 1892).

34. Deepak Adhikari, "Somali Refugees in Nepal: Stuck in the Waiting Room," *Time*, 10 November 2009, http://www.time.com/time/world/article /0,8599,1936578,00.html. See also Mohamed Adow, "Somalia's Trafficking Boom Town," *BBC News*, 28 April 2004, http://news.bbc.co.uk/2/hi/africa/3664633.stm; Jude Kafuuma, "AU Boss Cautions Uganda on Human Trafficking," *New Vision*, 16 October 2009, http://allafrica.com/stones/200910190242.html. Somalis Rescued after Being Abandoned at Sea," *Agence France-Presse*, 5 November 2009.

35. "A Gap in Their Hearts: The Experience of Separated Somali Children," *IRIN*, 6 January 2003, http://www.irinnews.org/webspecials/Somalichildren/default .asp. See also UNODC, *Situational Assessment of Human Trafficking: A 2005 Situational Assessment of Human Trafficking in the SADC Region* (Pretoria, 2007), 28–29, 40–41, http://www.unodc.org/documents/human-trafficking/2005%20UNODC %20Situational%20Assessment.pdf.

36. USDOS, *Trafficking in Persons Report* (2009), "Special Cases," http://www.state .gov/g/tip/rls/tiprpt/2009/123140.htm. UNODC, *Situational Assessment*, 28–29, 40–41.

37. USDOS, *TIP* (2009), "Special Cases."

38. Dady R. Banaji, *Slavery in British India* (Bombay: Taraporevala, 1933), 24. Cutch is the marshlands area of western Gujarat. It was traditionally a maritime center and an independent kingdom ruled by the Jadeja Rajputs. I have not been able to identify the place associated with the reference "Seinee."

39. Ibid., 24–25.

40. Campbell, "Introduction," 5.

41. Raymond C. Howell, *The Royal Navy and the Slave Trade* (New York: St. Martin's, 1987), 181–91.

42. Howell observes that in 1868 there were only six vessels and one thousand men assigned to the East Indies. Only three vessels were assigned slave trade duties, while three were left other duties in the Bay of Bengal, the Arabian Gulf, and the Red Sea. Howell, *Royal Navy*, 67, citing Foreign Office records.

43. UKNA, Admiralty Files, ADM, 135/360.

44. See Jerome A. Saldanha's eight-volume compilation of archival materials on the slave trade and naval matters in the Persian Gulf. Saldanha, ed., *The Persian Gulf Précis, 1903–1908* (1906; Gerards Cross, Buckinghamshire: Archive Editions, 1986).

45. Ras al-Hadd is a coastal village in Oman, southeast of Muscat and the easternmost point on the Arabian Peninsula. The British established vice admiralty courts, well-known European instruments of colonial domination of the seas, in Calcutta, Madras, and Bombay in India and in Muscat, Bushire, Aden, and Zanzibar. Pursuant to treaties and the admiralty law, these courts had primary jurisdiction over the adjudication and condemnation of slaving vessels captured by the British in the Indian Ocean world. The account of the capture of the 154 slaves is contained in a diplomatic despatch entitled "Capture of slave dhows by the 'Philomel' 1885," despatch no. 298 issued from Muscat and dated 31 October 1884, from Lt.-Col. S. B. Miles to Lt.-Col. E. C. Ross, and found in the "Précis on Slave Trade in the Gulf of Oman and the Persian Gulf 1873–1905 with a Retrospective into previous history from 1852," found in vol. 3 of *The Persian Gulf Précis*, 75–79.

46. *Persian Gulf Précis*, 3:76–78.

47. Ibid., 3:75–79.

48. All Zanzibar proceedings from UKNA, FO 881/3254.

49. Ibid.

50. Ibid.

51. Ibid.

52. House of Commons, Parliamentary Papers, 1876 [c. 1588] Slave Trade, no. 4 (1876), 18.

53. Bohras, Shi'a Muslims belonging to the Musta'lian Isma'ili sect, were among the earliest Asian immigrants to East Africa. Hatim Amiji, "The Bohras of East Africa," *Journal of Religion in Africa* 7, no. 1 (1975): 27.

54. Galla is a pejorative term for the pastoral Oromo. See, Mohammed Hassen, *The Oromo of Ethiopia: A History, 1570–1860* (Cambridge: Cambridge University Press, 1990). Alice Werner, "The Galla of the East Africa Protectorate," pt. 1, *Journal of the Royal African Society* 13, no. 50 (1914): 125.

55. Parliamentary Papers, 1872 [c. 657], Class B. East coast of Africa. Correspondence respecting slave trade and other matters. Document no. 38 (Kirk to Earl Granville) and enclosure dated April 8, 1871 (Kirk to Wedderburn), 44–45.

56. Hyderabad has been described as "an Islamic bastion in the Deccan," although other historians have been more guarded with this description. Munis D. Faruqui, "At Empire's End: The Nizam, Hyderabad and Eighteenth-Century India," *Modern Asian Studies* 43 (2009): 5–43.

57. These events occurred in 1871. See Parliamentary Papers, 1872 [c. 657].

58. Parliamentary Papers, 1872 [c. 657].

59. Gwyn Campbell, "Slave Trade and Slavery in the Indian Ocean—A Survey," unpublished paper presented at conference entitled "Dialogue between Civilizations: International Conference on the Indian Ocean, the Largest Cultural Continuum." Zanzibar, Tanzania, 15–17 August 2009.

60. R. W. Beachey, *The Slave Trade of Eastern Africa* (New York: Barnes & Noble, 1976), 157, 159, 160–61.

61. Memorandum, undated, addenda to cases of slavery previously reported (in Hadhramaut) [CO/732/78/1] in Anita L. P. Burdett, ed., *The Slave Trade into*

Arabia 1820–1973, 9 vols. (Chippenham: Archive Editions, 2006), 7:234. These incidents occurred in the early 1930s.

62. USDOS, *TIP* (2011), "Ethiopia."

63. USDOS, *TIP* (2011), "Lebanon," "Saudi Arabia," "United Arab Emirates."

64. This figure was determined in a study conducted in 1999. Beydoun, "Trafficking," 1016; Emebet Kebede, "Ethiopia: An Assessment of the International Labour Migration Situation, the Case of Female Labour Migrants," International Labour Office, http://www.oit.org/wcmsp5/groups/public/———ed_emp/documents/publication/wcms_117931.pdf page 3 (page 11 of .pdf).

65. Beachey, *Slave Trade*, 154.

66. Confidential Dispatch no. 40/79080/36 from Governor's Office, Aden, to Colonial Secretary, 30 June 1937, regarding slavery in the Aden Protectorate and Hadhramaut, app. 4, Burdett, *Slave Trade*, 7:204.

67. Banaji, *Slavery*, 43.

68. Sheikh Habib ʿAli Kombo, interview by author, Zanzibar, 16 October 1999.

69. Ibid.

70. Ibid.

71. The Ibadhi school of Islamic law is that practiced in Oman and in many places in East Africa where Omani religious scholars settled. See John C. Wilkinson, *The Imamate Tradition of Oman* (New York: Cambridge University Press, 1987); Ahmed H. al-Maamiry, *Oman and Ibadhism* (New Delhi: Lancers, 1989); al-Maamiry, *Oman and East Africa* (New Delhi: Lancers, 1979).

72. Kombo, interview, 16 October 1999, at Sheikh Habib ʿAli Kombo's home, near the Muslim Academy, Zanzibar, Tanzania.

73. Khan later became a *sadr amin* (a native trial judge) in the British civil courts and the founder of the Anglo-Mohamedan College at Aligarh. Avril A. Powell, "Indian Muslim Modernists and the Issue of Slavery in Islam," *Slavery and South Asian History*, ed. I. Chatterjee and R. M. Eaton (Indianapolis: Indiana University Press, 2006), 263.

74. Ibid., 265–69.

75. Ibid., 262, quoting H. A. R. Gibb, *Mohammedanism* (Oxford: Oxford University Press, 1970) 124.

76. Rudolph Peters, *Jihad in Classical and Modern Islam* (Princeton: Markus Wiener, 1996), 6.

77. Powell, "Indian Muslim Modernists," 263.

78. William G. Clarence-Smith, *Islam and the Abolition of Slavery* (London: Hurst, 2006), 200.

79. Powell, "Indian Muslim Modernists," 268–69.

80. Ibid., 263.

81. Ibid., 276–77.

82. Lloyd William Matthew, First Minister and Treasurer of Zanzibar Government to A. H. Hardinge, Diplomatic Agent and Consul General to Zanzibar, 22 January 1898, Zanzibar Archives, AC 3/10.

83. Clarence-Smith, *Islam*, 202–6; Amal Ghazal, "Debating Slavery in the Arab Middle East: Abolition between Muslim Reformers and Conservatives," in *Islam*,

Slavery and Diaspora, ed. Behnaz A. Mirzai, Ismael Montana, and Paul E. Lovejoy (Trenton: Africa World Press, 2009), 146–50.

84. Muhammad R. Rida, *The Muhammadan Revelation*, trans. Yusuf T. DeLorenzo (Alexandria, VA: al-Sadaawi, 1996), 142–48.

PART II

∽

Contemporary Antitrafficking in Africa and Beyond

7 ⮑ Trafficking and Human Exploitation in International Law, with Special Reference to Women and Children in Africa

JEAN ALLAIN

IT MAY seem counterintuitive but the issue of the trafficking of women and children in Africa has yet to be addressed in legal terms, at the continental level. This is made easier by the understanding that trafficking is not synonymous with the slave trade and, in fact, gains legal traction in the twenty-first century with the introduction of the 2000 United Nations Palermo Protocol. The genealogy of trafficking is not bound up in the African slave trade at all, but with the "white slave trade," a regime—not surprisingly—having little to do with Africa. Where there exists any discussion on the issue, it is prompted by regard to trafficking not *in* Africa, but *out* of Africa. That impetus is manifest in the Ouagadougou Action Plan, which emerges from the bulwarks of Fortress Europe so as to counter the fears of African migration toward the European Union.

This chapter examines the legal genealogies of trafficking and human exploitation and demonstrates their convergence as "exploitation" comes to form part of the definition of the term "trafficking in persons" as defined by the Palermo Protocol:

> Trafficking in persons shall mean the recruitment, transportation, transfer, harbouring or receipt of persons, by means of the threat or use of force or other forms of coercion, of abduction, of fraud, of deception, of the abuse of power or of a position of vulnerability or of the giving or receiving of payments or benefits to achieve the consent of a person having control over another person, for the purpose of exploitation. *Exploitation shall include, at a minimum, the exploitation*

*of the prostitution of others or other forms of sexual exploitation, forced
labour or services, slavery or practices similar to slavery, servitude or the
removal of organs.*[1]

In turning its attention to the issue of trafficking in Africa, this chapter demonstrates that Europe has led that process. As a result, the continent-wide approach in Africa shows little sign of moving toward establishing a legal basis for suppressing the trafficking. Indeed, the African approach is hardly worth speaking about in print, as money and resources currently allocated to the task demonstrate that African states prefer to simply speak about trafficking in human beings rather than seek to prevent it.

THE GENESIS OF TRAFFICKING AND OF HUMAN EXPLOITATION

The legal regimes of trafficking and human exploitation emerge from different sources, with paternalism in general leading the former and imperialism the latter. These origins are a product of their time and place: late-nineteenth- and early-twentieth-century Europe, which witnessed the Suffragist movements as the early manifestation of female political emancipation; and a Europe at the height of its colonial expansion.

Trafficking

In her 2000 report to the now-defunct United Nations Commission on Human Rights, the special rapporteur on violence against women, Radhika Coomaraswamy, states, "Historically, anti-trafficking movements have been driven by perceived threats to the 'purity' or chastity of certain populations of women, notably white women."[2] In the latter half of the nineteenth century, the backdrop to what would come to be known as the white slave trade was the use of the term by those who sought to end the state licensing of prostitutes. A transnational movement emerged at the turn of the century as a result of an attempt by the International Medical Congress to end the licensing of prostitution so as "to better regulate venereal disease."[3] Such diseases were wreaking havoc with European expansionist ambitions "where mass prostitution was being organized to serve the needs of colonial troops."[4] Like the abolition of the slave trade before it, attempts to suppress the white slave trade originally came from a grassroots movement. Led primarily by what Ethan Nadelmann calls "transnational moral entrepreneurs," the movement was given a statist imprimatur with 1904 International Agreement for the Suppression of the White Slave Traffic.[5]

That agreement sought to provide effective protection for "women of full age who have suffered abuse or compulsion" as well as "women and girls under age." However, the protection forthcoming was hardly effective, as it amounted to little more than monitoring the situation in the states that would become party to the agreement. This included, for instance, an undertaking to "to have a watch kept, especially in railway stations, ports of embarkation, and *en route*, for persons in charge of women and girls destined for an immoral life."[6] The 1904 agreement was followed in 1910 by the International Convention for the Suppression of the White Traffic, which sought to criminalizing the dealing in "whores" ("Whoever, in order to gratify the passions of another person, has procured, enticed, or led away, even with her consent, a woman or girl under age, for immoral purposes, shall be punished"); and the trafficking in "madonnas" ("Whoever, in order to gratify the passions of another person, has, by fraud, or by means of violence, threats, abuse of authority, or any other method of compulsion, procured, enticed, or led away a woman or girl over age, for immoral purposes, shall also be punished").[7] As with the 1904 agreement, the 1910 convention dealt with the transborder issues of trafficking in prostitutes, but it did not address the issue of licensing of brothels in states, this being considered an issue of domestic jurisdiction, within the power of each state party to legislate and thus apparently beyond the powers of an international agreement.

The issue of trafficking was given added emphasis with the establishment of the League of Nations, whose covenant entrusted to the League "the general supervision over the execution of agreements with regard to the traffic in women and children."[8] That supervision was followed by two further conventions during the League of Nations era, the 1921 International Convention for the Suppression of the Traffic in Women and Children and the 1933 International Convention for the Suppression of the Traffic in Women of Full Age. It is here that we see the first emphasis emerging in international law on children and women as vulnerable groups. The first of these instruments, the 1921 convention, was in essence a protocol to the 1904 agreement and 1910 conventions, which extended their scope to allow for the prosecution of "persons who are engaged in the traffic in children of both sexes."[9] The 1933 convention made plain that the traffic in prostitution was punishable "notwithstanding that the various acts constituting the offence may have been committed in different countries"; *countries* being recognized for the purposes of this treaty as including colonies.[10] In 1937 the League sought to consolidate the legal regime related to trafficking into one instrument, but ultimately this work had to be taken up by the United Nations, which replaced the League of Nations after World War II.

The 1950 Convention for the Suppression of the Traffic in Persons and of the Exploitation of the Prostitution of Others consolidates the first four instruments and embodies the substance of the 1937 draft convention. Beyond seeking to punish those who led women and children into prostitution or exploited the prostitution of another, the 1950 convention also ventured into what had previously been considered the domestic jurisdiction of states, requiring the punishment of those who kept or managed a brothel.[11] Not surprisingly, the era of state licensing of prostitution was over. Despite the establishment of five legal instruments during the first half of the twentieth century, Nadelmann notes that the "creation of a global regime against the white slave trade accomplished, in the final analysis, relatively little towards its objective."[12] Instead, what changed was the "social, economic, and demographic conditions" of the late nineteenth century, which had seen "millions of male immigrants in North and South America with scant chance of female companionship apart from prostitutes." Nadelmann argues that much has changed and that, by contemporary standards, there is very little prostitution: "the supply of sex by women other than prostitutes has increased as the development of effective contraception and the onset of the 'sexual revolution' have greatly reduced the inhibitions of female sexual activity."[13] And yet the issue of trafficking has not gone away, having reemerged onto the international agenda with the recognition that trafficking of persons beyond prostitutes is an issue that requires international cooperation. This has resulted in the establishment of the 2000 Palermo Protocol, an instrument that will be returned to having first considered the international legal regime related to human exploitation. The link between the legal regime of human exploitation and the regime of trafficking in persons transpires only in the year 2000 with the introduction of various types of human exploitation into the definition of "trafficking in persons" as set out in the protocol.

Human Exploitation

The regime of human exploitation covers slavery and lesser servitudes and has its genesis in the abolitionist movement of the late eighteenth and the nineteenth centuries, personified by the likes of Thomas Clarkson, Olaudah Equiano, Abraham Lincoln, Victor Schoelcher, Granville Sharp, and William Wilberforce. While the powers seeking to settle the Napoleonic Wars at the 1814–15 Congress of Vienna expressed their wish to "bring to an end a scourge which has for a long time desolated Africa, degraded Europe, and afflicted humanity," and declared that the "universal abolition of the trade in Negroes to be particularly worthy of their attention"; no universal legal agreement was forthcoming for seventy-five years.[14] It was only in 1890, with the final act of the Brussels Conference relative to the African slave trade, that an international regime was established that outlawed the slave trade and established a maritime zone where states could visit ships so as to suppress the trade.[15] That is not to say that nothing had transpired in the intervening years; in fact, through a web of bilateral treaties the United Kingdom had effectively ended the Atlantic slave trade with the focus of the Brussels Conference seeking to suppress the final vestiges of the trade in the Indian Ocean, the Red Sea, and the Persian Gulf.[16]

The 1890 Brussels Conference also called for the suppression of the slave trade on land and set the framework for what would come to be known as the Scramble for Africa by European powers.[17] Suzanne Miers notes, "Hundreds of small wars of conquest were fought and the suppression of the slave trade was a heaven-sent excuse for campaigns."[18] It was the final holdout in Africa, Ethiopia—which had itself joined in the Scramble for Africa—that prompted the League to turn its attention not to the slave trade but to slavery itself.[19] Despite this, and as a result of Ethiopia joining the League in 1923, the focus on slavery turned to establishing a general treaty on the subject; something that was achieved with the coming into force of the 1926 Slavery Convention.[20] The 1926 convention defines both the slave trade and slavery; while most of the other provisions of the convention have fallen into abeyance, its definitions of *slave trade* and *slavery* still hold in international law. According to the convention,

> The slave trade includes all acts involved in the capture, acquisition or disposal of a person with intent to reduce him to slavery; all acts involved in the acquisition of a slave with a view to selling or exchanging him; all acts of disposal by sale or exchange of a slave acquired with a view to being sold or exchanged, and, in general, every act of trade or transport in slaves.

Here then we see that while the *white slave trade* was in fact about the trafficking of prostitutes, the *slave trade* is about the trafficking of slaves.

Slavery itself is defined in the convention as the "status or condition of a person over whom any or all of the powers attaching to the right of ownership are exercised." Both these definitions are repeated verbatim in the 1956 Supplementary Convention; and, where "slavery" is concerned, its definition gains further contemporary importance as it is repeated in substance as the definition of "enslavement" as a crime against humanity within the jurisdiction of the 1998 Statute of the International Criminal Court.

In the same manner, it may be said that little else remains of the 1930 Forced Labour Convention but for the definition of forced labor that also holds today. It reads: "forced or compulsory labour shall mean all work or service which is exacted from any person under the menace of any penalty and for which the said person has not offered himself voluntarily."[21] The United Nations also saw fit to deal, in its early years, with other servitudes by establishing the 1956 Supplementary Convention on the Abolition of Slavery, the Slave Trade and Institutions and Practices Similar to Slavery.[22] Although it introduces them as "practices similar to slavery," this convention in fact defines four types of servitude: debt bondage, serfdom, servile marriage, and child trafficking.[23]

Like all other types of human exploitation mentioned thus far, the conventional servitudes defined in the 1956 Supplementary Convention are in essence all that remains of that instrument in legal terms. This is so, as the legal regime of human exploitation thus far noted had attached to it a requirement to put an end to such exploitation gradually. That gradualist approach, however, has been eclipsed by international human rights law, which requires that the types of human exploitation mentioned thus far (and defined in law) be abolished forthwith. This is made most evident in Article 8 of the UN's 1966 International Covenant of Civil and Political Rights:

1. No one shall be held in slavery; slavery and the slave-trade in all their forms shall be prohibited.
2. No one shall be held in servitude.
3. (a) No one shall be required to perform forced or compulsory labour.[24]

The covenant requires that such obligations be put into effect immediately. Note that while the terms *slavery, slave trade, servitude,* and *forced labor* appear in the covenant, they are not defined. Instead, there is consensus among states that these instances of human exploitation gain their understanding from the original instruments that defined them, that is: the 1926 and 1956 slavery conventions and the 1930 forced labor convention.

THE CONVERGENCE OF THE REGIMES OF TRAFFICKING AND HUMAN EXPLOITATION

The twentieth century witnessed the convergence of the regimes of trafficking and human exploitation within the Palermo Protocol. The instances of human exploitation highlighted in the various instruments just considered find their way into the definition of *trafficking in persons.* It bears reproducing that definition here once more for the sake of convenience:

"Trafficking in persons" shall mean the recruitment, transportation, transfer, harbouring or receipt of persons, by means of the threat or use of force or other forms of coercion, of abduction, of fraud, of deception, of the abuse of power or of a position of vulnerability or of the giving or receiving of payments or benefits to achieve the consent of a person having control over another person, for the purpose of exploitation. *Exploitation shall include, at a minimum, the exploitation of the prostitution of others or other forms of sexual exploitation, forced labour or services, slavery or practices similar to slavery, servitude or the removal of organs.*

The term *protocol* might be explained here as well. Typically it is a term given to a treaty that is negotiated at a later date to supplement an established instrument. In this case the Protocol to Prevent, Suppress and Punish Trafficking in Persons was negotiated at the same time as the mother instrument, the United Nations Convention against Transnational Organized Crime. However, negotiators agreed that the trafficking protocol and a further protocol—the Protocol against the Smuggling of Migrants by Land, Sea and Air—should be distinct from the convention to allow states to decide to which protocol(s) they would give consent.

Three requirements need to be met before an individual can legally be considered to have trafficked in persons. First, they need to have been involved in moving somebody from one location to another (e.g., recruitment, transportation, transfer, harboring, or receipt of persons). Second, that movement must have taken place through various methods (e.g.: "the threat or use of force or other forms of coercion, of abduction, of fraud, of deception, of the abuse of power or of a position of vulnerability or of the giving or receiving of payments or benefits to achieve the consent of a person having control over another person"). Finally, such movement must have been for the purpose of exploiting the individual. It should be noted that the various examples of exploitation laid down by the Palermo Protocol are "at minimum" the types of exploitation to be considered; and thus other types of exploitation than those set out in the definition can also be deemed to be an element of which, if the other two elements are present (the method of trafficking and the means of that trafficking), constitutes trafficking in persons.

Exploitation as a Continuum of Coercion

We now consider the term *exploitation* as an element of the definition of trafficking in persons. The best way to conceptualize exploitation is through a continuum of coercion—a continuum that moves from a situation of free labor to instances where the law seeks to regulate activities as being exploitive, as servile situations that move, ultimately, toward the most extreme type of exploitation: slavery. Such a continuum is recognized in international law through authoritative pronouncements wherein, for instance, the International Criminal Tribunal for the former Yugoslavia, like the European Court of Human Rights, sees exploitation as being hierarchical, the Yugoslav tribunal speaking of "degrees."[25] The European Court of Human Rights, for its part, in the case of *Siliadin v. France*, found that once forced labor has been established, it must then be determined "whether the applicant was also held in servitude or slavery" and that the latter two concepts are indeed "link[ed]."[26] For its part, the Council of Europe, in the explanatory note accompanying its trafficking convention, states that, for instance, servitude is "to be regarded as a particular form of slavery, differing from it less in character . . . than in degree."[27] Likewise, in a number of instances beyond the Palermo Protocol, various types of human exploitation are also grouped together.[28] The continuum of coercion, forces a person to decide between disagreeable alternatives—for instance, between working for less than minimum wage or not working at all—while international law seeks to legislate (through labor law, then human rights law, and ultimately criminal law) so as to ensure that workers need not choose, under duress, the lesser of two evils.

During much of the twentieth century, the international legal regime of exploitation sought to address exploitation by states; yet today it is recognized that exploitation takes place primarily at the hands of nonstate actors such as corporations or businesses. International law is well placed to deal with such transgressions through its own continuum—from labor law, through human rights law, to criminal law. Labor law deals in large part through administrative sanction with reference to the International Labour Organization's international labor standards. International labor standards seek to ensure a decent work environment and have, at their core, the principles established in eight fundamental conventions, which were highlighted in the ILO's 1998 Declaration on Fundamental Principles and Rights at Work.[29] These instruments touch on the following areas of labor relations: freedom of association and the effective recognition of the right to collective bargaining, the elimination of all forms of forced or compulsory labor, the effective abolition of child labor, and the elimination of discrimination with respect to employment and occupation. Beyond this core, international labor standards include ILO conventions and recommendations that deal with labor inspection and administration, wages, working hours, occupational safety and health promotion, employment security, social security, employment policy, social policy, vocational guidance and training, maternity protection, as well as protection to specific categories of workers, including seafarers, fishers, dockworkers, migrant workers, and indigenous peoples. These instruments "aim to guarantee a minimal universal threshold of protection for workers."[30] They do so by acknowledging that states are at various levels of economic development and seek to establish frameworks or regimes to be incorporated into domestic law as a baseline for ensuring the protection of workers, decent work, and adequate standards in the workplace. Thus, international labor standards are the benchmark for determining whether or not a practice is exploitative.

Where such exploitation becomes more severe, whether by degrees or cumulatively, it then moves along the continuum of coercion to those instances deemed exploitation by the Palermo Protocol. Where exploitation meets this threshold, international legal remedies are prescribed where violations are manifest. International human rights law has progressed to the point where today, states recognize that they have an obligation to ensure that rights are protected; in other words, not only is the state itself not to violation human rights, but it also has an obligation—a positive obligation—not to allow private persons or companies to violate a person's human rights.[31] A prime example of this is *Mani v. Niger*, a 2008 case before the ECOWAS Community Court of Justice, which determined that the failure of national judges to denounce the slavery status of Hadijatou Mani Koraou when she appeared before them was "a form of acceptance, or at least, tolerance of this crime or offence" and, as such—although it was an individual who had enslaved Mani Koraou—it was Niger that was "responsible under international law . . . because of its tolerance, passivity, inaction and abstention with regard to this practice."[32]

Such positive obligations of international human rights law create downward pressure, requiring states to have in place a system of protection of workers that seeks to *prevent* exploitive labor practices from reaching the threshold of a human rights violation, to *punish* those who are committing such violations of human rights, to *investigate* with a view to ensuring that such violations do not take place again, and to *redress* the harm caused. In this manner, international human rights law leaves it to states to address the issue but acts as overseer should the state fail to abide by its obligations.

Failure to protect a worker's human rights is ultimately backed by criminal sanctions when exploitation reaches the threshold of enslavement. In such an extreme case, a national policymaker has two options, either to address the exploitive behavior to ensure it does not recur or to face the possibility of standing in the dock for failing to take adequate positive steps to suppress such exploitation. What then is being witnessed in international law is the growth of top-down pressure to conform to legal obligations to end exploitative practices: failure to deal with violations of international labor standards, which by their severity or cumulative effect might rise to the level of a violation of international human rights law, thus forcing the state to act or be held in violation of human rights law. Failure adequately to address violations of international human rights law will then move from being an issue of state responsibility to one of individual criminal responsibility, where exploitation is seen to transpire on a systemwide basis and exploitation increases once more in severity, this time sufficiently to manifest the powers ordinarily attached to ownership.

Where human exploitation is concerned, it may be said that a true hierarchy does exist and though a practice may be tantamount to forced labor, to serfdom, or to debt bondage, if it meets a certain threshold it will also be deemed slavery in law. In law, this hierarchy is recognized as, for instance, the 1926 Slavery Convention speaks of preventing "compulsory or forced labour from developing into conditions analogous to slavery,"[33] while the 1956 Supplementary Convention dealing with practices similar to slavery moves to abolish servitudes "where they still exist and whether or not they are covered by the definition of slavery contained in article 1 of the Slavery Convention."[34] How is this established hierarchy, with slavery at the pinnacle of human exploitation, to be determined in law?

The definition of slavery as established by the 1926 Slavery Convention is "the status or condition of a person over whom any or all of the powers attaching to the right of ownership are exercised."[35] That definition was considered by the High Court of Australia in its 2008 decision in *The Queen v. Tang*. The court established that while the 1926 definition applied to de jure slavery—where one could, in law, own another person—it also applied in situations of de facto slavery—where one had control over another as though they owned them, though not in legal terms. This de facto ownership was understood in terms of the definition as the exercise of a power attaching to the right of ownership, as opposed to de jure ownership, which would entail the exercise of a right of ownership. The contemporary relevance is plain: legal slavery is today all but consigned to history;[36] instances of de facto slavery persist.

In coming to this determination regarding de facto slavery, the High Court made three observations regarding the text and context of the 1926 Slavery Convention: first, as early as 1926 the legal status of slavery no longer existed for many states. Second, the aim of the convention was to bring about the same situation universally. Third, the phrase "status or condition" found within the 1926 definition makes the distinction between de jure ("status is a legal concept") whereas "the evident purpose of the reference to "condition" was to cover slavery *de facto*."[37] In considering what constituted the powers attaching to the right of ownership, the High Court looked to a 1953 report by the UN secretary general, who presented the following as characteristics of such powers:

1. the individual of servile status may be made the object of a purchase;
2. the master may use the individual of servile status, and in particular his capacity to work, in an absolute manner, without any restriction other than that which might be expressly provided by law;
3. the products of labour of the individual of servile status become the property of the master without any compensation commensurate to the value of the labour;
4. the ownership of the individual of servile status can be transferred to another person;
5. the servile status is permanent, that is to say, it cannot be terminated by the will of the individual subject to it;
6. the servile status is transmitted *ipso facto* to descendants of the individual having such status.[38]

This contemporary understanding of slavery as defined by the 1926 Slavery Convention breathes new life into the Palermo Protocol, as for instance one does not have to demonstrate beyond moving a person, say by the use of force, that you intended to legally enslave that person. Instead, if it can be shown that you moved the person through force and then sold them (though you were not legally entitled to), that would constitute trafficking in persons. This contemporary reading is also important as, in international criminal law there exists the crime against humanity of "enslavement" within the Rome Statute of the International Criminal Court (1998), which entails holding individuals criminally liable if they know or had reason to know that enslavement was taking place in a systematic manner in situations under their authority.

If one considers human exploitation from the perspective of a continuum of coercion, what is manifest is the growing magnitude of three items: control, lack of consent, and benefit accrued. The types of exploitation included in the Palermo Protocol speak to various levels of *control*. At its most extreme, control over the person or their labor will be complete and exhibit the powers that would normally be attached to ownership. Having lost autonomy, the enslaved is now treated as an object to be used at the complete discretion of another. Where control is present, so too is *lack of consent*, wherein there is a shift from personal autonomy to being compelled to do something against one's will. For the Yugoslav tribunal, like the Palermo Protocol, this lack of consent results from coercion, deception, or the abuse of power or of a position of vulnerability. These means inducing consent and maintaining control appear to be central to understanding the common characteristics of human exploitation. While they are constituted within the protocol as the means of placing somebody in a position to be trafficked, it must also be recognized that through coercion—as manifest in most of the means outlined in these conventions—individuals are often maintained in exploitative situations. The final commonality to be found in the different forms of exploitation enumerated in the trafficking conventions is the benefit to be gained by some at the expense of others. For the most part, that gain is commercial or financial: work undertaken with the financial or material rewards going to those who exploit. Where it is not, it tends to be sexual or commensurate with perceived "marital duties."

TRAFFICKING IN AFRICA, WITH SPECIAL REFERENCE TO WOMEN AND CHILDREN

In 2000, African states established the African Union as the regional inter-governmental organization for Africa. The African Union, which succeeds the Organization of African Unity, is in large part modeled on the European Union. Still binding within the context of the African Union is the 1990 African

Charter on the Rights and Welfare of the Child, which requires preventative action be taken with regard to the trafficking in children, as well as the 2003 Protocol to the African Charter on the Rights of Women in Africa, which calls for the condemnation and prevention of trafficking in women.[39]

With regard to a move to actualize these obligations, in June 2006 the Executive Council of the African Union endorsed an African Common Position on Migration and Development. While recognizing that "migratory movements occur essentially within the continent," that document acknowledged that there was a need to set out "Africa's role in migration management and development." In setting out its common position, African states sought to give emphasis to issues of trafficking in women and children. Where women are concerned the common position notes:

> Migrant women's vulnerabilities to exploitation are highlighted by the frequently abusive conditions under which they work, especially in the context of domestic service and sex industries in which migrant trafficking is heavily implicated. It is therefore important to give particular attention to safeguarding the rights (labour, human rights, *inter alia*) of migrant women in the context of migration management.

As for children, the position states:

> In many parts of the world, including certain regions in Africa, child trafficking is a critical challenge that must be addressed from different angles including targeted prevention campaigns, protection and assistance to victims of trafficking, training of relevant authorities on how to address trafficking challenges and prosecution of traffickers and their accomplices. Children born as migrants should receive special attention.[40]

No further substantive provisions pertaining to trafficking are found in the common position. Trafficking is mentioned, however, with regard to recommendations that are put forward as to action that should be taken. That action points toward a move to establish a legal framework for dealing with trafficking within the African context. At the national level, these recommendations for action entail strengthening "the mechanisms to combat smuggling and trafficking in human beings including the elaboration of legal instruments"; at the continental level, the "introduc[tion] due process measures including legal frameworks to fight illegal migration and punish those guilty of smuggling or trafficking"; and finally, at the international level, a call for "the easing of the movement of persons through more flexible visa procedures; in order to reduce illegal and irregular migration, and thereby also the role of syndicates dealing in the trafficking of human beings."[41]

The African Common Position on Migration and Development does not appear to have been precipitated by any homegrown desire. Instead, as its preamble notes, it was desirable to adopt "this African Common Position on Migration and Development to enable Africa to ensure that its concerns are properly reflected at the Africa/Europe dialogue and other international fora."[42] Such a dialogue was foremost in the minds of those drafting the common position, as four months later African and European ministers of foreign affairs, and those responsible for migration along with African Union and European Union commissioners, met, resulting in the Joint Africa-EU Declaration on Migration and Development. The declaration is quite frank in noting that "the fundamental causes of migration within and from Africa are poverty and underdevelopment, aggravated by demographic and economic imbalances, unequal terms of global trade, conflicts, environmental factors, poor governance, uneven impact of globalisation and humanitarian disasters." That said, the declaration is less frank in speaking about European Union migration policies with regard to economic migrants seeking to make their way to Europe for a better life. The restrictive immigration policies of Fortress Europe have resulted in the deaths of thousands of African migrants.[43]

Although the term *illegal migration* was mentioned but once in the African common position, and this was only with regard to establishing regional measures specific to the African continent, "including legal frameworks to fight illegal migration," it constitutes one of nine headings set out in the November 2006 Joint Africa-EU Declaration on Migration and Development. African states and the European Union agreed to start taking action as part of a common effort to combat African migration to Europe by "extending support for building institutional capacity and developing projects in countries of origin and transit to combat illegal migration, migrant smuggling and trafficking in human beings" via the implementation of the Joint Africa-EU Action Plan to Combat Trafficking in Human Beings, Especially Women and Children, which was adopted at the same November 2006 meeting.[44]

That plan, commonly referred as the Ouagadougou Action Plan, has a general principle that, in seeking to deal with trafficking, states' approaches "should be based on respect for human rights including protection of victims, and should not adversely affect the rights of victims of trafficking."[45] Mirroring the Congress of Vienna, the action plan notes that "trafficking in human beings, within and between states, is a scourge which states are determined to address." The pathways to addressing this scourge are through prevention and awareness raising; victim protection and assistance; legislation, law enforcement, and policy development; and cooperation and coordination among states. The Ouagadougou Action Plan resulted in the launch in June 2009 of the AU.COMMIT Campaign, the African Union Commission Initiative against Trafficking, and the publication of its Strategy Document 2009–2012.[46]

That strategy document sets out the means by which the Ouagadougou Action Plan can be popularized and implemented. It does this by way of a three-pronged strategy, which deals first with the prevention of trafficking, followed by the protection of victims of trafficking, and finally with the prosecution of those involved in the crime of trafficking. Activities in these areas are meant to take place in successive years; the four-year budget is a mere $600,000. The budget reflects a lack of true commitment by all involved with the issue of trafficking in human beings in Africa. The strategy document is meant to set trafficking in human beings "as a priority on the development agenda of the continent" through a consolidation of existing initiatives found primarily at the level of regional economic communities (RECs). This, the document notes, is a move toward "a more synergized and coordinated" means of approaching the issue of trafficking on the African continent.[47]

↩

The devil is in the details. The Ouagadougou Action Plan—the Joint Africa-EU Action Plan to Combat Trafficking in Human Beings, especially Women and Children—the vanguard of which is a strategy with an annual budget of $150,000 for four years seems hardly worth writing about. The issues of trafficking within the African context remain a low priority; they have been foisted on African states by the European Union, which is most concerned with northward migration. The one-sided nature of the Ouagadougou Action Plan is made most evident in one of its three general principles:

> Poverty and vulnerability, an unbalanced distribution of wealth, unemployment, armed conflicts, poor law enforcement system, degraded environment, poor governance, societies under stress as well as non-inclusive societies, corruption, lack of education and human rights violations including discrimination, increased demand for sex trade and sex tourism are among the root causes of trafficking in human beings and must be addressed.

This humiliating provision is obviously not meant to speak about conditions in Europe but sets the tone for a relationship that objectifies the African continent. It is a measure of the African-European relationship that such a provision can find its way into an official document, and a further measure that African leaders are willing to sign on to such a document.

One would be forgiven for thinking that the issue of trafficking emerges from attempts to abolish the slave trade; yet as the genealogies of the slave trade and the "white slave trade" presented here have made plain, they emerged from very different sources. It is only at the turn of the twenty-first century, with the establishment of the Palermo Protocol, that we see convergence. Attempts to suppress the slave trade are in essence subsumed within the regime of trafficking—the successor to the white slave trade, which now moves beyond prostitution to deal with any type of human exploitation. Beyond prostitution and slavery, the protocol flags the movement of people for the purposes of forced labor, of various types of servitudes, and with regard to the removal of organs.

Trafficking in human beings at the regional level, within the African context, has yet to be addressed in legal terms; it remains at the level of platitudes not action. The campaign and strategic plan attached to the Ouagadougou Action Plan does not bode well for a legal instrument seeing the light of day for some time. Instead the Ouagadougou plan, which is undertaken jointly with the European Union, is most concerned with stopping African migration to Europe. Despite placing emphasis on women and children, trafficking in human beings within the African context has yet to be demonstrated to be an issue of enough traction to attract more than its current $150,000 annual budget—or in other terms, to be considered worthy of employing more than what is, in effect, one senior manager to cover the issue on a continent that boasts a population of over one billion people.

NOTES

Abbreviations

AU   African Union
CoE Council of Europe

1. Article 3(a), Protocol to Prevent, Suppress and Punish Trafficking in Persons, Especially Women and Children, Supplementing the United Nations Convention against Transnational Organized Crime, 2000, emphasis added. Note that the same definition is repeated as "Trafficking in persons" at Article 4(a) of the 2005 CoE Convention on Action against Trafficking in Human Beings.

2. United Nations, Economic and Social Council, Commission on Human Rights, *Report of the Special Rapporteur on Violence against Women, Its Causes and Consequences, Ms. Radhika Coomaraswamy, on Trafficking in Women, Women's Migration and Violence against Women, Submitted in Accordance with Commission on Human Rights Resolution 1997/44*, 29 February 2000, UN Doc. E/CN.4/2000/68, 10.

3. Ethan A. Nadelmann, "Global Prohibition Regimes: The Evolution of Norms in International Society," *International Organization* 44, no. 4 (1990): 514.

4. Laura Reanda, "Prostitution as a Human Rights Question: Problems and Prospects of United Nations Action," *Human Rights Quarterly* 13, no. 2 (1991): 207; Nora Demleitner, "Forced Prostitution; Naming an International Offense," *Fordham International Law Journal* 18 (1994–95): 163–97. In this volume, see Carina Ray (chap. 5) and Susan Kreston (chap. 10).

5. Nadelmann, "Global Prohibition," 514.

6. International Agreement for the Suppression of the White Slave Traffic, 18 May 1904, Article 2.

7. International Convention for the Suppression of the White Slave Traffic, 4 May 1910, Articles 1, 2.

8. Article 23(c), League of Nations, Covenant of the League of Nations, 28 April 1919.

9. International Convention for the Suppression of the Traffic in Women and Children, 30 September 1921, Article 1.

10. International Convention for the Suppression of the Traffic in Women of Full Age, 11 October 1933, Article 1.

11. Convention for the Suppression of the Traffic in Persons and of the Exploitation of the Prostitution of Others, 21 March 1950, Articles 1–2.

12. Nadelmann, "Global Prohibition," 515.

13. Ibid., 516.

14. *Déclaration des 8 Cours, relative à l'Abolition Universelle de la Traite des Nègres*, 8 February 1815, 3 British Foreign and State Papers 972. Note that this series reproduces official documents of the British Foreign Office including international instruments and correspondence.

15. See General Act of the Brussels Conference Relative to the African Slave Trade, 2 July 1890.

16. See Jean Allain, "Nineteenth Century Law of the Sea and the British Abolition of the Slave Trade," *British Yearbook of International Law 2007* 78 (2008): 342–88.

17. See H. L. Wesseling, *Divide and Rule: The Partition of Africa, 1880–1914* (Westport, CT: Praeger, 1996).

18. Suzanne Miers, *Slavery in the Twentieth Century* (Walnut Creek, CA: AltaMira, 2003), 23.

19. See Jean Allain, "Slavery and the League of Nations: Ethiopia as a Civilised Nation," *Journal of the History of International Law* 8, no. 2 (2006): 213–44.

20. See League of Nations, Slavery Convention, 25 September 1926.

21. See ILO, Forced Labour Convention, ILO Convention no. 29, 10 June 1930.

22. See United Nations, *UN Conference of Plenipotentiaries on a Supplementary Convention on the Abolition of Slavery, the Slave Trade and Institutions and Practices Similar to Slavery, Final Act and Supplementary Convention* (New York: UN, 4 September 1956), UN Doc E/CONF.24/23.

23. See Jean Allain, "On the Curious Disappearance of Human Servitude from General International Law," *Journal of the History of International Law* 11, no. 2 (2009): 303–32.

24. International Covenant of Civil and Political Rights, 16 December 1966, Article 8. The provisions of Article 8 that have not been omitted include items such as prison labor, military conscription, emergency assistance, and civic obligations, all of which are deemed to be excluded from the definition of forced or compulsory labor. Note also that the regional human rights systems of Africa, the Americas, and Europe each have treaty provisions dealing with human exploitation.

25. UN, Security Council, International Criminal Tribunal for the former Yugoslavia, *Kunarac et al.* (IT-96-23, IT-96-23/1-A), judgment, 12 June 2002, 36.

26. See CoE, European Court of Human Rights, *Siliadin v. France* (Application 73316/01), 26 July 2005, 37–38.

27. CoE, CoE Convention on Action against Trafficking in Human Beings and Its Explanatory Report, CoE Treaty Series, no.197, 16 May, 2005, 40: "Il ressort que la servitude est une forme particulière d'esclavage, qui s'en distingue moins par la nature que par le dégrée."

28. This includes the Universal Declaration of Human Rights, the Covenant on Civil and Political Rights, and the African, European, and Inter-American human rights instruments.

29. The eight conventions are the Freedom of Association and Protection of the Right to Organise Convention, 1948 (no. 87); Right to Organise and Collective Bargaining Convention, 1949 (no. 98); Forced Labour Convention, 1930 (no. 29); Abolition of Forced Labour Convention, 1957 (no. 105); Minimum Age Convention, 1973 (no. 138); Worst Forms of Child Labour Convention, 1999 (no. 182); Equal Remuneration Convention, 1951 (no. 100); Discrimination (Employment and Occupation) Convention, 1958 (no. 111).

30. International Labour Conference, *Labour Inspection*, General Survey of the reports concerning the Labour Inspection Convention, 1947 (no. 81), and the Protocol of 1995 to the Labour Inspection Convention, 1947, and the Labour Inspection Recommendation, 1947 (no. 81), the Labour Inspection (Mining and Transport) Recommendation, 1947 (no. 82), the Labour Inspection (Agriculture) Convention, 1969 (no. 129), and the Labour Inspection (Agriculture) Recommendation, 1969 (no. 133), Report III (part 1B), Report of the Committee of Experts on the Application of Conventions and Recommendations, Ninety-Fifth Session, 2006, 3.

31. See generally, Sandra Fredman, *Human Rights Transformed* (Oxford: Oxford University Press, 2008); Alastair Mowbray, *The Development of Positive Obligations under the European Convention on Human Rights by the European Court of Human Rights* (Oxford: Hart, 2004).

32. *Hadijatou Mani Koraou v. Republic of Niger*, Economic Community of West Africa States Community Court of Justice, Judgment no. ECW/CCJ/JUD/06/08, 27 October 2008, §86.

33. See League of Nations, Slavery Convention, 25 September 1926, C.586.M.223.1926.VI.

34. See *UN Conference of Plenipotentiaries* (cited in note 22, above).

35. See League of Nations, Slavery Convention, 25 September 1926.

36. In *Mani v. Niger* the finding was of de jure slavery. See note 37, below.

37. *The Queen v. Tang* [2008] HCA39, 28 August 2008, 12.

38. See United Nations Economic and Social Council, Slavery, the Slave Trade, and other forms of Servitude (Report of the Secretary-General), UN Doc.E/2357, 27 January 1953, 28. See also Jean Allain, *The Slavery Conventions: The Travaux Préparatoires of the 1926 League of Nations Convention and the 1956 United Nations Convention* (Leiden: Martinus Nijhoff, 2008).

39. Organisation of African Unity, *African Charter on the Rights and Welfare of the Child*, 1990, Article 29; OAU, *Protocol to the African Charter on Human and Peoples' Rights on the Rights of Women in Africa*, 2003, Article 4(g).

40. AU, Executive Council, *African Common Position on Migration and Development*, Ninth Ordinary Session, EX.CL/277(IX), 25–29 June 2006, items 3.8, 3.9.

41. AU, EX.CL/277(IX), items 5.1(e), 5.2(c), 5.3(g).

42. Ibid.

43. "The Red Cross estimates between 2,000 and 3,000 people die trying to reach Spain every year." See Graham Keeley and John Hooper, "Grim toll of African refugees mounts on Spanish beaches," *Observer*, 13 July 2008, http://www.guardian.co.uk/world/2008/jul/13/spain.

44. See AU, *Ouagadougou Action Plan to Combat Trafficking in Human Beings, Especially Women and Children, the Ministerial Conference on Migration and Development*, 22–23 November 2006, EX.Cl/313 (X), annex IV. Note also the *Decision on Strengthening the Cooperation between the United Nations and the African Union in Combating Trafficking in Human Beings*, adopted by the Assembly of the African Union, 11th Ordinary Session, 30 June–1 July 2008, AU Doc. Assembly/AU/Dec.207 (XI).

45. AU, Ouagadougou Preamble.

46. See AU, Commission, Division of Communication and Information, Media Advisory: Launch of the AU Commission Initiative against Trafficking (AU.COMMIT Campaign), 16 June 2009. Also see AU, Commission, Department of Social Affairs, African Union Commission Initiative against Trafficking AU.COMMIT Campaign, Strategy Document 2009–2012.

47. AU, Commission, AU.COMMIT, 2.

8 ⹌ Documenting Child Slavery with Personal Testimony

The Origins of Antitrafficking NGOs and Contemporary Neo-abolitionism

BENJAMIN N. LAWRANCE

IN 2003, Human Rights Watch (HRW) reported that West African child-trafficking networks involved "thousands of children." The report documented "the trafficking of girls into domestic and market work and the trafficking of boys into agricultural work."[1] The organization made specific recommendations with respect to prosecution and border controls and urged the enactment of new laws to abolish child trafficking and punish traffickers. Among the more interesting aspects of *Togo: Borderline Slavery* was the deployment of real child narratives. Based on several months' fieldwork in Togo, including interviews with approximately two hundred allegedly trafficked children and with state and nonstate actors, the report detailed the presence of trafficking networks in Togo and the subregion.

HRW's foregrounding of personal narratives of "rescued" children constitutes an important dimension of what I interpret as neo-abolitionism, an increasingly significant aspect of humanitarian advocacy. In recent years antitrafficking nongovernmental organizations (NGOs) operating in West Africa are turning to "emotive" children's narratives to reinforce the urgency of the current "crisis" in child trafficking.[2] The use of children's personal life stories has a rich history in Africa and beyond. The resurgence of the "rescued" child narrative in the present demonstrates an important shift in the modality of contemporary global humanitarian advocacy, and marks a return to the emotional and moralizing rhetoric associated with "highly effective" goal-driven consciousness-raising and donor-oriented fundraising of the nineteenth and early twentieth centuries.[3]

The term *neo-abolitionist* first appeared in historical scholarship in the 1960s to describe the focus of US civil rights advocates' on legislative remedy.[4]

Subsequently, neo-abolitionism described revisionist scholarship reevaluating abolitionism and postbellum Reconstruction.[5] I adapt the term to describe the rhetorical interventions and advocacy operations of contemporary anti–child trafficking advocacy. Just as civil rights advocates believed fundamental change flowed from legislative and judicial action, today's neo-abolitionists focus on new antitrafficking laws.[6] And just as Frederick Douglass, W. E. B. DuBois, and others viewed slavery as the primary cause of the Civil War and affirmed the nation's moral obligation to abolish slavery and realize equal rights for all, neo-abolitionism harnesses the moral outrage erupting after each new exposé of child enslavement.[7] Contemporary neo-abolitionists embrace macro trends and transnational analysis and employ a discourse of crisis to amplify the "urgency" of action.[8] And importantly, like nineteenth-century abolitionists, contemporary neo-abolitionists establish effective relationships with the media.

This chapter historicizes the use of personal testimony from contemporary West African child slaves in neo-abolitionist child-trafficking advocacy. For the purpose of my argument I define *advocacy* as a form of communicative action adopted by a civil-society organization to provoke an audience to adopt a position vis-à-vis a particular issue or dynamic.[9] Neo-abolitionist advocacy comprises research reports and campaign literature primarily from NGOs, but also from intergovernmental organizations, focused on mobilizing public interest, shifting political debates, and leveraging resources. Contemporary neo-abolitionism, which draws on the personal accounts of child victims to stimulate interest and enjoin patronage, is part of a rich historical process. Just as child narratives published in nineteenth-century missionary newsletters have been reevaluated by historians as evidence of child enslavement in the early decades of the European-African colonial encounter, contemporary child narratives are emotional mechanisms deployed according to particular thematic tropes that connect with a receptive audience. Child testimony is introduced almost as if it were a drama or dialogue. The contents constitute an important source for the oral history of neo-abolitionism, the internal dynamics of West African child trafficking, and the familial and social origins of today's child slaves.[10]

I begin with an outline of the role children, children's issues, and child narratives have played in the expansion of the humanitarian agenda, from Atlantic abolition to global child abuse and welfare programs. Subsequently, I explore two neo-abolitionist advocacy techniques—namely framing the issue as a crisis and the reproduction of child testimony—which encourage supporters to embrace the urgency of legislative remedy for trafficking. An interrogation of the use of personal child testimony reveals the existence of important thematic tropes. By way of conclusion, I contextualize the contemporary dynamics of child advocacy and the ascendancy of neo-abolitionism and antitrafficking.

Children's life stories and children's welfare have featured prominently in the global dimensions of humanitarian agendas over several centuries. Children's narratives advanced the cause of early abolitionism in the Americas and Europe. The expanding antislavery struggle subsequently highlighted child narratives of enslavement in North American propaganda. In the postabolition United States, the well-being and education of former slave children became a rallying cry for social reformers, whereas on the West African coast missionary activities expanded opportunities for Westernized education as part of a larger project to extend antislavery into the continent and "rescue" child slaves. Simultaneously, child exploitation during the Industrial Revolution thrust poverty and child welfare into the lives of the growing middle classes. By the mid-nineteenth century the currents of child "rescue" had begun to take shape and rescue programs became a benchmark of the new social interventionism. Heroic and romantic stories of child rescue contributed to what Shurlee Swain identifies as an "innately pious" image of the child as a "creature of nature and simplicity."[11] Children's personal stories were a central rhetorical device in the emotional paraphernalia of humanitarianism, which also included the production of melodramatic poems, prayers, songs, and epitaphs.[12] As imperialism and paternalism expanded globally, metropolitan and colonial ideologies of childhood and child welfare profoundly influenced the twentieth-century humanitarian agenda.

The foregrounding of children's life stories in the cause of humanitarianism begins in the late eighteenth and early nineteenth centuries. Abolitionist propaganda in Europe and North America regularly highlighted the processes of child enslavement because it appealed to antislavery sentimentalists as especially brutal and traumatic.[13] Among the most famous child enslavement narratives is that of Olaudah Equiano.[14] Equiano's personal (albeit adult) testimony appeals to the reader precisely because it contextualizes the vulnerability of African children.[15]

As the expanding humanitarian struggle challenged slavery throughout the Western Hemisphere, parallels were drawn between enslavement and child labor. In some instances, a master's authority over a slave was subordinated to "the natural power of a father over his children." In this formulation the "right of northern interference" in slavery in the American South was predicated on the idea that slavery was "*not* a domestic affair."[16] In other contexts, however, as emancipation gained momentum in the West Indies, metropolitan abolitionists began to hypothesize about legislative constraints on children's laboring hours in British mills.[17] One African child, Ka-le, provided an important perspective about the mutiny of the slaves aboard *La Amistad*.[18] His presence grounded the victims' quest for freedom and his emotional appeals highlighted their West African origins and freeborn identity.[19] Antislavery sentiment featured in popular children's novels.[20] Fiction and children's schoolbooks were important avenues for the dissemination of humanitarian antislavery ideology.[21]

In addition to their role in early antislavery propaganda, children and child welfare were at the center of early West African missionary and colonization activities.[22] Sierra Leone's early administrators also stressed the role of children and actually purchased child slaves.[23] As missionary activities expanded along the West African coast, the centrality of child testimony to the evangelical project deepened. Missionaries from Germany and Switzerland prioritized the role of children in the Ewe-speaking Volta River region (the future Gold Coast and Togoland).[24] By the early 1860s the Basel Mission was schooling between five and six thousand children. The mission's *Monatsblatt* positioned freed or "redeemed" slave children at the center of its missionary activities.[25] The "the mass" of the mission schools were comprised of "children we had bought free from enslavement."[26] Clergy were acutely aware of the role that rescued children's narratives played in the Protestant-donation-funded mission activity.[27] It was precisely the stories of "rescued," newly baptized (i.e., doubly saved) children that garnered the interests of parishioners in Europe, so missionaries highlighted their life stories.[28] Just as the freed former child slave became a template upon which US abolitionists and other liberal communities projected their hopes and fears for a newly liberated people, according to Mary Niall Mitchell, fundraising for "rescuing" West African slave children was a means to very moral ends for paternal European colonists.[29] The published personal testimonies of rescued trafficked children are important windows into the context of child enslavement.

Throughout the modern industrializing world, from Europe to Latin America, dramatic exposés of child exploitation thrust poverty and child welfare into the lives of the burgeoning middle class. Dr. Thomas John Bernardo and his contemporaries drew shamelessly on pitiful tales of street children to draw "attention to their cause."[30] Thomas Mayhew's research on child poverty in London transformed sentiment about the consequences of industrialization. Scandalous public revelations of child abuse made headlines throughout the modernizing and industrializing world.[31] The early modern model of state "wardship" for foundlings, orphans, and delinquents in Europe and the colonies was displaced by an imagined social contract that impelled families and households to take a deeper interest in safeguarding the welfare of children.[32]

A firm belief in the "plasticity of childhood" fueled the ideologies of child rescuers.[33] Political and social developments in Europe, the Americas, and

Africa, coupled with a very public narration of destitute children's lives, contributed to the emergence of the idea of childhood as "distinct stage of life" that required action to safeguard.[34] Scholarly consensus appears to be, in Ellen Boucher's words, that childhood by the late nineteenth century was constitutive, in the minds of the growing middle classes, of "innocence, vulnerability, and dependence."[35] Boucher observes that by about 1900 to 1910 "the basic tenets of child saving were firmly established."[36] The "redemption" of children consisted of two key elements: "first, separation from their former lives and, second, a closely regulated upbringing in more 'wholesome,' domestic spaces, preferably in rural environments."[37] This helps explain a transition in child "rescue," from independent mission-raised rescued children of the mid-nineteenth century to the massive expansion of rescue at the inception of formal colonial rule throughout Africa, from about 1885 to 1910. Encouraged by a newly abolitionist mantra emboldening colonization from 1890 onward, missions schools throughout African colonies filled their benches with redeemed former slaves and child pawns.[38] The crudely philanthropic philosophy of the mission school–colonial state partnership attempted to maximize the potential of the natally alienated former child slaves, "transforming them from budding delinquents and ne'er-do-wells" into "honest" and "self-reliant" laborers and servants for the colonial state.[39]

By the turn of the century the relationship between industrialization in the metropole and excess in the colonies could no longer be ignored. The "blood rubber" from the Congo Free State and Brazil's Putumayo River, as well as Cadbury's dependence on slave-produced cocoa, brought the realities of the link between industrial production and bourgeois consumption to the Anglo-American middle-class dinner table with a force and urgency of which the antislave "blood sugar" campaigners a century earlier could only have dreamed.[40] Whereas child laborers had been central to European and American industrial enterprises, by the fin de siècle the increasing regulation of the workplace gave rise to humanitarian models focused on education and social control.[41] As diversification and specialization steadily diminished, the need for Anglo-European children, neglected and impoverished working-class children were reclassified as "special cases" in need of protection.[42] But as the conceptual length of what constituted metropolitan childhood grew during the nineteenth century, the well-being of colonial children deteriorated.[43] The propaganda of humanitarian rescue compelled the bourgeoisie to reflect on the colonial origins of their metropolitan commodities and luxuries.

Enslavement, rescue, and redemption remain important themes throughout the colonial period and into independence, but the personal testimonies of European and African children begin to part ways in the early twentieth century for three reasons. First, as Swain has observed, whiteness becomes "a central organizing category" in rescue.[44] Paternalistic British and American child rescue paradigms became increasingly institutionalized as formal child protection gained legislative support, whereas ideas of childhood and child protection foundered in the colonies. In Southern Rhodesia, exploited child agricultural workers fled to the city, and their stories caused headaches for settler farmers.[45] By the mature colonial period, personal testimonies of children less frequently serve as engines of humanitarian change, but more often than not they surface as indices of delinquency, trouble, and anxieties on the part of European colonizers and colonized African men alike.[46] African children and girls in particular were held to highly racialized and gendered ideals of adolescence.[47]

Second, investigations of scandalous labor exploitation moved away from the domestic sphere of parliaments and became the responsibilities of the International Labor Organization from 1919 and League of Nations' Temporary Slavery Commission from 1924.[48] After the international outcry over brutality in the Congo and the Amazon, colonial states were increasingly sensitive to comparisons between colonialism and slavery.[49] These new international bodies exposed European powers to additional criticism in the 1930s but also redirected anger at private capital, such as Firestone's excesses in Liberia, or the persistence of indigenous slave systems, like Abyssinia.

A third dimension to the deployment of personal testimony concerns the well-documented shift in the historiography of Africa mainstreaming the use of oral histories. As oral historians drew increasingly on elderly informants, the use of child testimony declined. Whereas African historical research on children is just beginning to gain converts, children's narratives have remained important to sociological and anthropological research. With the growth of research on exploitative child labor and the impact of social and civil violence on children, scholarship has found a new interest in the value of child testimony.[50] For increasing numbers of researchers, children's testimonies are an opportunity to situate their work at the nexus of scholarship and advocacy.[51] Areas for the intersection of scholarship and advocacy include cocoa farming, child soldiers, and child prostitution. In collaboration with NGOs and research institutes, the International Initiative to End Child Labor explored the prevalence of younger children on cocoa farms and the impact on their physical health.[52] Cocoa offered a neat, manageable, homogeneous research area, with opportunities for comparing and contrasting national labor systems.[53] This research was seemingly motivated by a generalized desire to improve "empirical understanding" and "facilitate more nuanced debate" about child labor as a way of improving "the living conditions of working children in the short term and the eradication of child labor in the long-term."[54] Similarly, research on child soldiers' experiences of recruitment and fighting is often guided by humanitarian questions, such as how to undo the traumatic experiences of kidnapping, abuse, and warfare.[55]

Collaborations between researchers and advocates employing children's testimony have contributed to international and domestic legislative and industrywide changes. The role of scholarly research and expert testimony in the promulgation of conventions and protocols—such as the inclusion of child soldiering in the 2000 Palermo Protocol, the 2001 passage of the US Harkin-Engel Protocol, and the creation in 2002 of the International Cocoa Initiative—may blur the line between scholarship and advocacy.[56] And with this context in mind, let us examine the discourse of today's neo-abolitionists.

NEO-ABOLITIONIST ADVOCACY AND PERSONAL TESTIMONY

West African neo-abolitionist advocacy from the 1990s to the mid-2000s directed its fire at formal and informal economies (cocoa, mining, street hawking) and at illicit activities (child soldiers, prostitution). The material production of neo-abolitionist activism resonates with the aforementioned modalities of abolition and anti–child abuse campaigns. As a form of "communicative action," the public relations advocacy of neo-abolitionists provokes its audience to enjoin a position vis-à-vis the need for new antitrafficking legislation and to engage donor support. Antitrafficking NGOs employ two important techniques.[57] The first is the metaphor of crisis.[58] But whereas this metaphor permeates the prose and frames the entire content of many NGOs' reports, here I am concerned with documenting the second technique, the use of personal testimony.

An interrogative framework structures the deployment of personal testimony, whereby the information conveyed appears to answer questions or concerns the public has about the nature of trafficking. The interrogative framework has empirical and conceptual dimensions. The testimonies used by neo-abolitionists are generally the product of an earlier interrogative context: more often than not, a post-"rescue" debriefing. This is important because it underscores the intrinsic truth of the data; validity thereby resides in the representation of children as historical witnesses.[59] From a conceptual perspective, the information is conveyed in a manner that appears to respond to questions, although the implied questions rarely appear. This structuring device moves the reader swiftly through the account in a manner that mirrors the coherence of dialog or drama. In my reading of more than sixty published reports available in paper or online, a highly stylized dialogic structure enjoins the lay audience to feel empowered insofar as they become embodied with personal knowledge about a complex human(itarian) drama.

The content of personal testimony covers many themes and ideas, and social scientific data often accompany testimonies. Certain themes are more prevalent than others, including, but not limited to, dislocation, abandonment, abuse, suffering, and helplessness. While there is unanimity about urgency and crisis, and agreement about the common goal of legislative remedy, NGOs are competing for attention and resources. They may pursue niche issues with which they can be distinguished from other NGOs. Photographs are one particularly effective way NGOs differentiate their perspectives, but it is beyond the scope of this chapter to examine them. And finally, the relevance, factuality, and historicity of narratives are underscored by recourse to conventions of the social sciences, including maps, graphs, data sets and statistics, footnotes, and bibliographic citations. The information thus revealed constitutes an important contemporary oral historical record of the experiences of today's slaves.

Before the deployment of children's testimonies, neo-abolitionist reports about antitrafficking routinely frame the activity as a scandal, tragedy, or crisis, onto which the reader (audience) has just stumbled.[60] Neo-abolitionists then observe that the practices attendant to trafficking have reached epidemic proportions, rhetoric that demands urgency and immediate remedy. These revelations are accompanied by concrete, often legislative, solutions.[61] Epidemiological metaphors are particularly effective, as they enable grant writers, such as Romauld Djivoessoun, the executive director of Benin's NGO Autre Vie, to situate trafficking within a spectrum of other "maladies" such as "analphabétisme," "la pauvreté, la violence," and "malnutrition," of which children become "de plus en plus victimes des pratiques inhumaines."[62] Illness and debts associated with incapacity are often reasons for trafficking.[63]

After these initial framing devices, neo-abolitionist production connects with its readership through key themes. One such theme highlights consumer goods exchanged for illicit labor. This trope interrogates why children go with strangers. The motivation of children is a constant thread in trafficking reports, even though children cannot consent to their own bondage. Child narratives often invoke a family context and the collective family welfare, like the explanation of fifteen-year-old "P": "My parents decided to send me because my brother came back with many things: a radio, a motorbike and clothes. The motorbike is now used as a *Zemidjan* [motorbike-taxi] and my mother uses it."[64] Others add the complicating dimension of peer pressure in the pursuit of conspicuous consumption, amplifying the treachery and trickery. Hada's story, from the rather sensationally titled Plan International publication, "For the Price of a Bike," is one such tale: "I was 16 when I said to an older friend that I wanted a bike. He told me that for this I would have to go to Benin to work. I knew him well and I trusted him. . . . [Later] he made other promises. . . . I told my younger brothers that I would go to Benin but did not tell them it was for the bike."[65] Another report describes how young Burkinabe boys leave their villages to work on cotton plantations.

After a year, they return home with a bicycle, a reward unlikely were they to remain on familial farmlands.[66]

A second theme is dislocation, whereby children are bundled about in constantly shifting contexts that diminishes their agency. This trope attempts to answer questions about physical conditions of trafficking. The trope of dislocation emphasizes anonymity and confusion, such as this rather unsurprisingly anonymous excerpt:

> One day, a man . . . came to pick me up at night after he had talked to my godmother. That same night, I travelled with him and nine other children that I didn't know. We travelled by car and the next morning we walked through the forest until we reached the border of a river. With a pirogue we arrived at Molyko. There were people waiting for us. They gave me to one of them and he took me to . . . Tiko where I worked as a domestic.[67]

Dislocation is a multifaceted trope that is often accompanied by children's narratives of helplessness and incomprehension.

Abandonment is a third theme, wherein the child is slowly or quickly coming to terms with the realities of his or her predicament. This trope answers a series of interrelated questions about how children survive, what their daily lives are like, and so forth. Whereas previously, in the domestic setting, there was always someone to run to, narratives emphasizing abandonment depict anomie. Hada, for example, recalled her family life: "I was sad and felt very lonely. I was thinking about my situation and about Papa. I used to cry, and wondered what to do to get back home."[68] Excerpts of child interviews amplify the sense that children are overwhelmed by circumstance, such as the following instance, in which "R" a twelve-year-old child was "discovered" with others working in Nigerian quarries and subsequently "arrested": "[After our arrest] Baba Y came to tell us we would be freed. But I don't understand why we weren't. Sometimes he lets some go, sometimes he hands us over to the police."[69] There is no one to turn to, no shoulder to cry on, and, most important, no home. According to "A," aged twelve, "We never went home. We would always sleep at the gravel pit." The hostile work environment is all-encompassing; there is no safe place.[70]

Abuse and suffering is the fourth theme. This trope highlights the inhumane conditions in which children find themselves and from which they cannot extricate themselves without help. It continues earlier lines of questioning but amplifies the drama by emphasizing survival and desperation. Physical abuse, including sexual assault, is a common experience of trafficked children, and personal testimony of rape, such as Christelle's story, fits within this trope.

"When she was absent, her husband would come to the shop. He would squeeze my breast and my behind. One day as I was tidying up the sitting room, he came and held me tightly to his body. I struggled free and in the process fell in the stairway. . . . Despite my threats, he persisted. Finally, one night, he succeeded in raping me."[71] Overwork, including excessive hours, dangerous tasks, and no remuneration, feature prominently. Descriptions of working conditions often include experiences of violence or punishment, such as this account from "Afi A" and "Ama D": "We sold bread in the market, going around from 6:00 or 7:00 in the morning until night . . . when we got home, our aunt's daughter gave us the flour for the next day's bread. . . . She was not nice to us. If we didn't sell all the bread in one day, she would beat us with a stick."[72] Physical suffering and abuse are often grounded in narratives of fear and desperation. When reflecting on the suffering experience in Côte d'Ivoire, Kofi also remembered his fear of snakes, his inability to communicate in the local language, and a general fear of violence.[73]

A fifth theme of neo-abolitionism is that of hopelessness and helplessness. This testimony trope represents an indirect appeal to the readership for assistance, and it responds to the universal question, what can I do to help? In one example, the audience learns that even after a violent attack, other children do not offer to help. Assoupi's story pares away at any vestigial audience beliefs that someone may empathize with and protect her: "One night my auntie's husband came home from work and asked me if I had prepared food for him and the children. I said no. He said, 'Your aunt gave you money, why didn't you make the food?' I tried to explain, but he jumped on me and started beating me. He dragged me out of the house and told me to go away. . . . Nobody would speak to me after that, so I felt I had to leave."[74]

Even when children have been "rescued" and returned home, the hopelessness pervades their narratives and the trauma of trafficking is relived constantly. Issa, for example, stated, "Today I have difficulty talking about it. I have suffered a lot. I can only see a little way ahead of me."[75] Issa was trafficked at fifteen. After being initially taken to Nigeria, she was forced to board a boat bound for Gabon. Like many such vessels, her boat was unfit for the high seas and sank off the coast of Cameroon. She managed to swim until she was rescued, but she witnessed many others drowning.

TENSIONS AMONG THE
NEO-ABOLITIONIST CONSTITUENCY

So as not to overstate the coherence of neo-abolitionist advocacy, I will briefly examine two areas of tension—the relationship with the news media and the responsibility or culpability of parents and intermediaries. Building on the organizing tropes identified above, individual neo-abolitionist reports make specific claims that both reinforce the normative framework in which they operate as NGOs seeking external support, while simultaneously distinguishing themselves from one another. The title of the report, for example, is very important. While titles must be eye-catching, since the dawn of the Internet, stock phrases and jargon are essential to maximize the utility of search engines. Titles may resonate with news headlines, but the sensationalism of the aforementioned Plan International report is less common.

NGOs, and to a lesser extent IGOs (intergovernmental organizations), compete for media attention. Control of and dissemination of the message is paramount in neo-abolitionism. Many organizations maintain close ties with media outlets, and funnel stories and information as preludes to reports in progress, and these relationships contribute to the rapid circulation of a developing story.[76] Sensationalism contributes to neo-abolitionist reporting. Nigerian and Beninese media spread rumors about the numbers of children working in quarries in Abeokuta, Nigeria.[77] The proliferation of news reports about child slavery around 2000 in West African cocoa plantations resulted in real legislative change. Neo-abolitionists also seek to connect the plight of trafficked children directly and indirectly with the transatlantic slave trade.[78] Human Rights Watch blurred the line between investigative journalism and advocacy in an attempt to connect readers to slave ships from an earlier era.[79] Western media played a large role in the "discoveries" of Nigerian ships loaded with cargoes of child slaves.[80] Cases such as the infamous Nigerian MV *Etireno* offer neo-abolitionists opportunities to draw attention to conflicting approaches by West African governments and entrench the public perception that the slave trade continues.[81] Indeed, a fluid media-NGO relationship with respect to the circulation of knowledge appears to be a defining characteristic of neo-abolitionism.[82]

Difference of opinion about issues, such as parental responsibility for trafficking, is also a vehicle whereby NGOs can engage target donor audiences and distinguish their approaches from those of their humanitarian competitors. Just as children are routinely portrayed as victims, parents are unwilling accomplices and the deployment of parental testimony underscores that. While there are countless reasons for parents to release custodianship of their children to family members or nonkin, NGOs and ILOs are frequently reluctant to cast judgment on parental motivations that detract from the overall goal of a legislative outcome, and adults are rarely, if ever, named. Consider, for example, the simplicity with which Carole's mother's explanation is conveyed: "I gave my daughter to her father's cousin so that she could have a better future. I was divorced and felt overwhelmed. . . . She has come back to me as empty-handed as the day she left. I acknowledge that I have wronged my daughter."[83] This explanation is hardly exceptional, but neo-abolitionists handle such complexity in a variety of ways. Indeed, evidence from the field about parental responsibility tests some of the central assumptions of NGOs.[84]

Since conventions and tropes with regard to parents and intermediaries are more difficult to gauge, reports may whitewash subtle and complex issues, such as the relationship between school fees and work, in turn shifting agency and responsibility.[85] Adult informants, such as one father interviewed by HRW, explicitly address such connections and admit responsibility.[86] When adult informants explicitly admit that money changed hands between "intermediaries" and a parent in the solicitation of child, the interview may also include the parent's excuse or explanation. An ILO report noted that one Togolese woman admitted that a trafficker "gave me 25,000 FCFA ($50) to take care of my child. She promised to find my son a job and said I would receive some money every month." But the mother then commented, "I had no idea what she really had in mind for my child!"[87] Rather than embrace the complex motivations, the neo-abolitionists reinforce the idea that the "overriding cause of child trafficking" is an ongoing economic crisis that forces parents to relinquish their children.[88] One informant observed, "A child is wealth. Once you have a child it means that you have something to exploit, you will no longer die from hunger."[89] This general framework is situated within the prevailing view that an economic crisis has gripped West Africa for decades, a crisis resulting in the corruption of traditions.[90]

Grounding the thematic tropes in most reports is the deployment of social scientific conventions, including data sets, graphs, maps, notes, and bibliography. Elements of most, if not all of these, appear in each of the more than sixty locally and internationally produced reports. Statistics and data sets may be based on information collected by NGOs themselves or constitute assemblages of previous data. Sometimes they are deployed for dramatic effect, but some are of dubious scholarly value, such as the UNICEF claim that two hundred thousand West African children are bought and sold each year (see the introduction to this volume). The Global March against Child Labour publishes fact sheets on several West African countries.[91] The bulletins published by Terre des Hommes are based on limited reception data from rescue and rehabilitation centers.[92] The International Organization for Migration produces data more attendant to scholarly norms, but it has very limited resources in West Africa.[93] More often than not, however, the sources for many statistics deployed are simply impossible to substantiate.

Maps appear frequently in neo-abolitionist reports. IGOs and NGOs highlight transnational, subregional, rural-urban movements in order to emphasize the need for a supranational solution.[94] They may include a broad spectrum of information, from simple national boundaries to mapping internal movements, "trafficking routes," "places of destination," "cross-border trafficking routes," and the "flux de traite en Afrique de l'Ouest."[95] HRW, for example, discerned "four routes of child trafficking into, out of, or within Togo."[96] International leadership, such as that of Anti-Slavery International, provides important guidance to domestic NGOs interested in grant writing, as they negotiate the language distinguishing projects on trafficking from projects on labor.[97] Bilateral and multilateral research projects, such as those supported by ASI, Free the Slaves, or TdH, reinforce the sense that trafficking is subregional, requiring a coordinated solution.[98] Regionwide programs also provide the empirical data to establish regional dynamics, thus reifying the value of multilateral, externally funded projects.[99]

Finally, because neo-abolitionist production is competitive insofar as NGOs are targeting a common audience and seek to stimulate donor interest, many pay careful attention to the design of such documents. The excerpts of testimony are often centered on the page, or placed in a separate highlighted box, in a style that resonates with secondary school and college-level social studies textbooks. Less frequently, the testimony of children (and adults) is interpolated into the body of the report, in a manner that befits social anthropological conventions of participant observation.

CONTEXTUALIZING THE RISE OF CONTEMPORARY NEO-ABOLITIONISM IN WEST AFRICA

Child advocacy agencies operating in West Africa in the contemporary period focused on a spectrum of issues that resonate with the concerns of previous centuries, including, but not limited to, enslavement and trafficking. International, subregional, and domestic agencies operate in all West African countries. Because of the humanitarian mission undergirding child welfare, many NGOs situate their programmatic activities at the delicate intersection of research and advocacy and draw equally from scholarship and activist literature.[100] Exploitative child labor was the central interest of West African child advocacy activity from the mid-1980s until approximately 2000, when it appears to be eclipsed by the subject of trafficking.[101] Whereas child labor advocacy foregrounded social scientific research methods, the approach of neo-abolitionists embraced techniques that enabled an effective interface with the public, including the language of crisis and urgency and emotional children's stories.[102]

Accounting for the discursive shift among child advocacy agencies operating in West Africa—from a labor focus to an antitrafficking agenda, by the late 1990s—directs attention to the discourse and frameworks employed by both communities of activists, as well as the international dynamics accompanying this continentwide transformation.[103] A central factor facilitating the expansion of child labor advocacy was the growing international consensus concerning the rights of the child.[104] Whereas statist apprehensions about children's rights had gained traction in the communitarian principles under-girding the African Charter on Human and Peoples' Rights in 1981, regimes put aside disagreements with NGOs about parental rights over children and ratified the 1989 UN Convention on the Rights of the Child.[105] Emboldened by this development, from 1990 advocacy agencies in Africa turned their at-tention to realizing the rights of children in developing economies.[106] Their subsequent uncovering of the extent of child labor in African economies shat-tered the 1989 truce between the conflicting ideologies of humanitarianism centered on children.[107] African governments and modernization theorists responded to the charge of pervasive and widespread child exploitation with narrowly framed economic arguments.[108] The 1990s thus witnessed a decade-long debate on the relative exploitation and permissibility of various forms of child labor, as "virtually everyone" wanted "to draw the line in a different place, despite the efforts to build a consensus."[109]

The establishment of international standards for identifying the worst forms of child labor created a central tension that shifted the direction of child ad-vocacy toward trafficking. The reconceptualization of child labor into worst forms—and by implication its division into intolerable and more tolerable forms—has been interpreted as reflecting a division between moralism and socialization.[110] The first is rooted in the moral belief that the welfare of all children should be preserved, resonates with the nineteenth-century Euro-pean model of the "sacralization" of the child, and prevailed to 1990.[111] The second, by contrast, does not view child labor as intrinsically bad but rather traditional, and it rejects the rigid Western division between childhood and adulthood.[112] It adopts a relativist and anti-imperialist rhetoric and opens the door to a normative or derivative binary with regard to culturally legitimate (i.e., traditional) practices. The latter model paved the way for the formulation of narrower, goal-oriented campaigns (such as antitrafficking) that left intact newly and much more widespread forms of legitimated (and culturally norma-tive) child labor. Thus while many agencies have worked in the contemporary period to ameliorate the conditions of Africa's children and expand access to their internationally recognized rights, it is within this central tension that the expansive attention of nonstate agencies to child trafficking ought to be considered. Child advocacy agencies operated in an increasingly sympathetic context, but it was also one where neoliberal rights-focused rhetoric coupled with goal-driven approaches garnered greater attention.[113]

Neo-abolitionists in West Africa operate under the precise definitions of the Palermo Protocol of 2000. This precision helps explain the relatively co-herent and complementary messages although many compete for resources. Messages in the form of detailed recommendations, "calls for action," and especially demands for legislation resonate with shared audiences. But in spite of their organizational differences, all neo-abolitionists deploy personal child testimony as part of a sophisticated rhetorical framework, with both a rich and a deeply rewarding history.

NOTES

Abbreviations

ASI   Anti-Slavery International
HRW   Human Rights Watch
TdH   Terre des Hommes

1. HRW, *Borderline Slavery: Child Trafficking in Togo* 15, no. 8(A) (April 2003): 1.

2. Shurlee Swain, "Sweet Childhood Lost: Idealized Images of Childhood in the British Child Rescue Literature," *Journal of the History of Childhood and Youth* 2, no. 2 (2009): 199.

3. Swain, "Sweet Childhood," 199–200.

4. See, for example, Howard Zinn, *SNCC: The New Abolitionists* (Boston: Beacon, 1964).

5. See, for example, D. E. Fehrenbacher, review of *Strange Enthusiasm: A Life of Thomas Wentworth Higginson* by Tilden G. Edelstein and *Means and Ends in American Abolitionism: Garrison and His Critics on Strategy and Tactic, 1834–1850* by Aileen S. Kraditor, *American Historical Review* 75, no. 1 (1969): 212–13.

6. Hugh Davis Graham, *The Civil Rights Era: Origins and Development of National Policy, 1960-1972* (New York: Oxford University Press, 1990).

7. W. E. B. DuBois, *Black Reconstruction in America* (New York: Free Press, 1998); Frederick Douglass, *Life and Times of Frederick Douglass* (1881).

8. Swain, "Sweet Childhood," 201.

9. Jürgen Habermas, *The Theory of Communicative Action* (Boston: Beacon, 1984).

10. Marcia Wright, *Strategies of Slaves and Women: Life-Stories from East/Central Africa* (New York: Lilian Barber, 1993). Sandra Greene, *West African Narratives of Slavery: Texts from Late Nineteenth- and Early Twentieth-Century Ghana* (Bloomington: Indiana University Press, 2011).

11. Swain, "Sweet Childhood," 200.

12. Ibid., 198–214.

13. See, Benjamin N. Lawrance, "'All We Want Is Make Us Free'—The Voyage of *La Amistad*'s Children through the Worlds of the Illegal Slave Trade," in *Child Slaves in the Modern World*, ed. Gwyn Campbell, Suzanne Miers, and Joseph Miller (Athens: Ohio University Press, 2011). See also, Christopher L. Brown, *Moral Capital: Foundations of British Abolitionism* (Chapel Hill: University of North Carolina Press, 2006); Shane White, *Stories of Freedom in Black New York* (Cambridge, MA: Harvard University Press, 2002), 26.

14. Vincent Carretta, "Olaudah Equiano or Gustavus Vassa? New Light on an Eighteenth-Century Question of Identity," *Slavery and Abolition* 20, no. 3 (1999): 96–105.

15. Mike Kaye, *1807–2007: Over 200 Years of Campaigning against Slavery* (London: Anti-Slavery International, 2007), 11; Olaudah Equiano, *The Interesting Narrative of the Life of Olaudah Equiano* (London, 1789); Jerome S. Handler, "Survivors of the Middle Passage: Life Histories of Enslaved Africans in British America," *Slavery and Abolition* 23, no. 1 (2002): 32–36.

16. *Anti-Slavery Record* 3 (1837): 37, emphasis in original.

17. *Anti-Slavery Reporter* 4 (1832): 48.

18. Lawrance, "'All We Want.'"

19. See Horatio Strother, *The Underground Railroad in Connecticut* (Middletown, CT: Wesleyan University Press, 1962), 74–76.

20. J. R. Oldfield, "Anti-Slavery Sentiment in Children's Literature, 1750–1850," *Slavery and Abolition* 10, no. 1 (1989): 45–59.

21. Ruth M. Elson, *Guardians of Tradition: American Schoolbooks of the Nineteenth Century* (Lincoln: University of Nebraska Press, 1964).

22. A. F. Walls, "A Christian Experiment: The Early Sierra Leone Colony," in *The Mission of the Church and the Propagation of the Faith*, ed. Geoffrey J. Cuming (London: Cambridge University Press, 1970), 107.

23. Macaulay to Campbell, 20 June 1798, John Campbell Papers, 1795–1814, Duke University Library Manuscript Collection.

24. See Birgit Meyer, *Translating the Devil: Religion and Modernity among the Ewe in Ghana* (Edinburgh: Edinburgh University Press, 1999); Sandra E. Greene *Sacred Sites and the Colonial Encounter: A History of Meaning and Memory in Ghana* (Bloomington: Indiana University Press, 2002); Seth Quartey, *Missionary Practices on the Gold Coast, 1832–1895* (Youngstown, NY: Cambria, 2007).

25. *Monatsblatt der Norddeutschen Missionsgesellschaft* 13, no. 149 (May 1863): 645; trans. A. Parkinson. Thanks to Sandra Greene for sharing this.

26. Ibid., 646.

27. Ibid., 645.

28. Ibid., 646–47

29. Mary N. Mitchell, *Raising Freedom's Child: Black Children and Visions of the Future after Slavery* (New York: NYU Press, 2008).

30. Swain, "Sweet Childhood," 200–201.

31. Eric A. Shelman and Stephen Lazoritz, *The Mary Ellen Wilson Child Abuse Case* (Jefferson, NC: McFarland, 2005); Alison Rattle and Allison Vale, *Amelia Dyer, Angel Maker: The Woman Who Murdered Babies for Money* (New York, 2007); Nara Milanich, *Children of Fate: Childhood, Class, and the State in Chile, 1850-1930* (Durham: Duke University Press, 2009).

32. See John Boswell, *The Kindness of Strangers: The Abandonment of Children in Western Europe from Late Antiquity to the Renaissance* (New York: Pantheon, 1988); Thomas M. Safley, *Charity and Economy in the Orphanages of Early Modern Augsburg* (Atlantic Highlands, NJ: Highlands Press, 1997); Joel F. Harrington, *The Unwanted Child: The Fate of Foundlings, Orphans, and Juvenile Criminals in Early Modern Germany* (Chicago: University of Chicago Press, 2009). For Latin America, see Bianca Premo, *Children of the Father King: Youth, Authority, and Legal Minority in Colonial Lima* (Chapel Hill: University of North Carolina Press, 2005).

33. Swain, "Sweet Childhood," 200–201.

34. Ellen Boucher, "The Limits of Potential: Race, Welfare, and the Interwar Extension of Child Emigration to Southern Rhodesia," *Journal of British Studies* 48, no. 4 (2009): 917.

35. Boucher, "Limits," 917. She cites Viviana Zelizer, *Pricing the Priceless Child: The Changing Social Value of Children* (New York: Basic Books, 1985); Hugh Cunningham, *The Children of the Poor: Representations of Childhood since the Seventeenth Century* (Oxford: Blackwell, 1992); Carolyn Steedman, *Strange Dislocations: Childhood and the Idea of Human Interiority, 1780-1930* (Cambridge, MA: Harvard University Press, 1995); Harry Hendrick, "Constructions and Reconstructions of British Childhood: An Interpretative Survey, 1800 to the Present," in *Constructing and Reconstructing Childhood*, ed. Allison James and Alan Prout (London: Falmer, 1997), 34–62.

36. Boucher, "Limits," 920. For tropes of rescue, see Shurlee Swain, "Child Rescue: The Emigration of an Idea," in *Child Welfare and Social Action in the Nineteenth and Twentieth Centuries*, ed. Jon Lawrence and Pat Starkey (Chicago: University of Chicago Press, 1991), 101–20; Swain, "The Value of the Vignette in the Writing of Welfare History," *Australian Historical Studies* 39, no. 2 (2008): 199–212.

37. Boucher, "Limits," 920.

38. See, Benjamin N. Lawrance, "Most Obedient Servants: The Politics of Language in German Colonial Togo," *Cahiers d'études africaines* 40, no. 159 (2000): 489–524.

39. Boucher, "Limits," 920. For "natal alienation," see Orlando Patterson, *Slavery and Social Death* (Cambridge, MA: Harvard University Press, 1982). See also Pier Larson, "Horrid Journeying: Narratives of Enslavement and the Global African Diaspora," *Journal of World History* 19, no. 4 (2008): 431–64.

40. Richard Collier, *The River That God Forgot: The Story of the Amazon Rubber Boom* (London: Collins, 1968), 54–58; Lowell J. Satre, *Chocolate on Trial: Slavery, Politics, and the Ethics of Business* (Athens: Ohio University Press, 2005); James Duffy, *A Question of Slavery* (Oxford: Clarendon Press, 1967).

41. Peter Kirby, *Child Labour in Britain, 1750–1870* (New York: Palgrave Macmillan, 2003), 93–130.

42. Pamela Horn, *Children's Work and Welfare, 1780–1890* (Cambridge: Cambridge University Press, 1994).

43. Thomas E. Jordan, *Victorian Childhood* (Albany: SUNY Press, 1987).

44. Swain, "Sweet Childhood," 205.

45. Beverly C. Grier, *Invisible Hands: Child Labor and the State in Colonial Zimbabwe* (Portsmouth, NH: Heinemann, 2006).

46. Lynn Thomas, *Politics of the Womb: Women, Reproduction, and the State in Kenya* (Berkeley: University Of California Press, 2003); Brett Shadle, *Girl Cases: Marriage and Colonialism in Gusiiland, Kenya, 1890–1970* (Portsmouth, NH: Heinemann, 2006).

47. Lynn Thomas, "The Modern Girl and Racial Respectability in 1930s South Africa," *Journal of African History* 47, no. 3 (2006): 461–90.

48. Suzanne Miers, *Slavery in the Twentieth Century* (Walnut Creek, CA: AltaMira, 2003).

49. Frederick Cooper, "Conditions Analogous to Slavery: Imperialism and Free Labor Ideology in Africa," in *Beyond Slavery*, ed. Cooper, Thomas C. Holt, and Rebecca J. Scott (Chapel Hill: University of North Carolina Press, 2000), 108.

50. Anne Kielland and Maurizia Tovo, *Children at Work: Child Labor Practices in Africa* (Boulder: Lynne Rienner, 2006).

51. Bernard Schlemmer, ed., *The Exploited Child* (London: Zed Books, 2000); Susan Levine, "'Picannin' Wages and Child Labor in the South African Agriculture, Mining, and Domestic Service Industries: 1658 to the Present," *Anthropology of Work Review* 17, no. 1 (1996): 42–50.

52. L. Diane Mull and Steven R. Kirkhorn, "Child Labor in Ghana Cocoa Production: Focus upon Agricultural Tasks, Ergonomic Exposures, and Associated Injuries and Illnesses," *Public Health Reports* 120, no. 6 (November–December 2005): 650.

53. International Institute of Tropical Agriculture, "Child Labour in the Cocoa Sector of West Africa: A Synthesis of Findings in Cameroon, Côte d'Ivoire, Ghana, and Nigeria" (Accra, 2002); Carol Off, *Bitter Chocolate: The Dark Side of the World's Most Seductive Sweet* (New York: New Press, 2006); Morten Bøås and Anne Huser, *Child Labour and Cocoa Production in West Africa: The Case of Côte d'Ivoire and Ghana* (Oslo: Fafo Institute for Applied Social Science, 2006).

54. Bøås and Huser, *Child Labor*, 7.

55. See, for example, Ilene Cohn and Guy S. Goodwin-Gill, *Child Soldiers* (Oxford: Oxford University Press, 1994); Alcinda Honwana, *Child Soldiers in Africa* (Philadelphia: University of Pennsylvania Press, 2006).

56. Kevin Bales, *Understanding Global Slavery* (Berkeley: University of California Press, 2005), 81–4; Bales, *Ending Slavery* (Berkeley: University of California Press, 2007), 196.

57. See Maureen Taylor, "Civil Society as a Rhetorical Public Relations Process," in *Rhetorical and Critical Approaches to Public Relations*, ed. Robert L. Heath, Elizabeth Toth, and Damion Waymer (New York: Routledge, 2009), 76–91.

58. Frank E. Millar and Debra B. Beck, "Metaphors of Crisis," in *Responding to Crisis*, ed. Millar and Robert L. Heath (Mahwah, NJ: Lawrence Erlbaum, 2004), 153–66.

59. See Lucy S. McGough, *Child Witnesses: Fragile Voices in the American Legal System* (New Haven: Yale University Press, 1994).

60. For trafficking as "tragedy," see Plan Togo, *For the Price of a Bike: Child Trafficking in Togo* (Dakar, Senegal: Plan International, 2005), 5; HRW, *Borderline Slavery*. For trafficking as "scandal," see Associations d'Enfants et Jeunes Travailleurs, *Migrations, confiage et trafic d'enfants en Afrique de l'Ouest* (n.d.).

61. A report by TdH speaks of "La 'crise' de septembre 2003." TdH, Olivier Feneyrol, *Les petites mains des carrières de pierre: Enquête sur un trafic d'enfant entre le Bénin et le Nigéria* (Cotonou, Benin: T&H, December 2005).

62. Romuald F. Djivoessoun, *Le trafic d'enfants: Une lutte multi-sectorielle* (Benin: Autre Vie, 2001[?]).

63. TdH, *Petites mains*, 22.

64. Ibid., 18.

65. Plan Togo, *For the Price*, 18.

66. Albertine de Lange, *Going to Kompienga: A Study on Child Labor Migration and Trafficking in Burkina Faso's South-Eastern Cotton Sector* (Amsterdam: IREWOC, 2006).

67. International Labour Office, *Unbearable to the Human Heart: Child Trafficking and Action to Eliminate It* (Geneva: ILO, 2002), 21.

68. Plan Togo, *For the Price*, 18.

69. TdH, *Petites mains*, 14.

70. Ibid., 14.

71. Plan Togo, *For the Price*, 17.

72. HRW, *Borderline Slavery*, 22.

73. Plan Togo, *For the Price*, 21.

74. HRW, *Borderline Slavery*, 23.

75. Plan Togo, *For the Price*, 33.

76. See, for example, Basile Groult, "Enlèvement et trafic d'enfants," *Actualités en Afrique* 93 (20 December 2005), www.vidome.com/date/2005/12.

77. TdH, *Petites mains*, 11.

78. See, for example, Sumana Chatterjee and Sudarsan Raghavan, "A Taste of Slavery: How Your Chocolate May be Tainted," *Knight-Ridder Washington*, 24 June 2001.

79. HRW, *Borderline Slavery*, 20 (including references).

80. See, for example, http://news.bbc.co.uk/1/hi/world/africa/1560392.stm.

81. UNICEF, *La traite d'enfants en Afrique de l'Ouest: Réponses politiques* (Florence: UNICEF, 2002), 5.

82. IRIN's account of trafficking in Zakpota, Benin, while drawing on interviews, is anchored around the TdH perspectives. Agence Press IRIN, "Benin: When a community is dirt poor everyone finds child trafficking acceptable," IRIN, 28 February 2005, http://www.irinnews.org/Report/53193.

83. Plan Togo, *For the Price*, 9.

84. Roger Ouensavi and Anne Kielland, *Child Labor Migration from Benin: Magnitude and Determinants* (World Bank, 2001), 31.

85. TdH, *Petites mains*, 22.

86. HRW, *Borderline Slavery*, 14.

87. ILO/IPEC, *Combating Trafficking in Children for Labour Exploitation in West and Central Africa* (Geneva: ILO/IPEC, 2001), 3.

88. Plan Togo, *For the Price*, 20.

89. TdH, *Petites mains*, 19.

90. Bonayi Dabiré, "Le confiage des enfants, alternative à une transition de crise?" in *Les transitions démographiques des pays du sud*, ed. Francis Gendreau (Paris: AUPELF-UREF, 2001): 407–21; Abade Messan, "Le placement des enfants dans un contexte de crise au Togo" (working paper, Lomé, Togo, 2002), 1.

91. See, for example, Global March against Child Labor, "Report on the Worst Forms of Child Labor: Ghana" (2004).

92. TdH, Délégation générale Bénin-Togo, "Trafic d'enfants: L'expérience de Tdh au Bénin et au Togo" (May 2001); TdH, "Info Bénin: Le trafic d'enfants, un phénomène massif!" (2005).

93. International Organization for Migration, "New IOM Figures on the Global Scale of Trafficking," *Trafficking in Migrants* 23 (April 2001).

94. Ibrahim Sanogo and Anne Kielland, Terre des Hommes, *Burkina Faso: Child Labor Migration from Rural Areas* (Washington, DC: World Bank, 2002), 8–10; E. Beauchemin, *The Exodus: The Growing Migration of Children from Ghana's Rural Areas to the Urban Centres* (Accra: Catholic Action for Street Children/UNICEF, 1999).

95. ASI, *Projet sous-régional contre la lutte contre le travail et le trafic des enfants domestiques* (London: ASI), 3; Plan Togo, *For the Price*, 23–26; ILO/IPEC, *Combating Trafficking*, 33–34, 67–68; UNICEF, *Traite d'Enfants*, 6.

96. HRW, *Borderline Slavery*, 1.

97. ASI, *Projet sous-régional*, 5.

98. ASI and ESAM, *Rapport sur les trafic des enfants entre le Bénin et le Gabon: Rapport de recherche* (London: ASI, 2000); ASI, *Projet sous-régional*; ASI, "The Cocoa Industry in West Africa: A History of Exploitation" (London: ASI, 2004); Kari H. Riisøen, Lise Bjerkan, and Anne Hatløy, *Travel to Uncertainty: A Study of Child Relocation in Burkina Faso, Ghana, and Mali* (Oslo: Fafo, 2004).

99. ASI, *Projet sous-régional*, 6:

100. See Mark Duffield, Joanna Macrae, and Devon Curtis, "Politics and Humanitarian Aid," *Disasters* 25, no. 4 (2001): 269–74; Liisa Malkki, "Speechless Emissaries: Refugees, Humanitarianism, and Dehistoricization," *Cultural Anthropology* 11, no. 3 (1996): 377–404.

101. Ben White, "Shifting Positions on Child Labor: The Views and Practice of Intergovernmental Organizations," and L. S. Wiseberg, "Nongovernmental Organizations in the Struggle Against Child Labor," both in *Child Labor and Human Rights*, ed. Burns H. Weston (Boulder: Lynne Rienner, 2005), 319–76.

102. See Eric Edmonds, "Child Labor," in *Handbook of Development Economics*, vol. 4, ed. John Strauss and T. Paul Schultz (Amsterdam: North-Holland, 2007).

103. See Benjamin N. Lawrance, "From Child Labor 'Problem' to Human Trafficking 'Crisis': Child Advocacy and Anti-Trafficking Legislation in Ghana," *International Labor and Working-Class History* 78, no. 1 (2010): 63–88. See also, Sally E. Merry, *Human Rights and Gender Violence* (Chicago: University of Chicago Press, 2006).

104. Harri Englund, *Prisoners of Freedom: Human Rights and the African Poor* (Berkeley: University of California Press, 2006), 25–70.

105. Makau W. Mutua, "The Banjul Charter and the African Cultural Fingerprint: An Evaluation of the Language of Duties," *Virginia Journal of International Law* 35 (1995): 339–80.

106. Jens Andvig, "An Essay on Child Labour in Sub-Saharan Africa—A Bargaining Approach," Working Paper 613, Norwegian Institute of International Affairs, Oslo, 2000.

107. Giuseppe Nesi, Luca Nogler, and Marco Pertile, eds., *Child Labour in a Globalized World: A Legal Analysis of ILO Action* (Farnham: Ashgate, 2008).

108. See Kaushik Basu and Pham Hoang Van, "The Economics of Child Labor," *American Economic Review* 88, no. 3 (1998): 413–14.

109. Mike Dottridge and Olivier Feneyrol, "Action to Strengthen Indigenous Child Protection Mechanisms in West Africa to Prevent Migrant Children from Being Subjected to Abuse" (working paper in possession of author, May 2007), 14.

110. Gavin Hilson, "'A Load Too Heavy': Critical Reflections on the Child Labor Problem in Africa's Small-Scale Mining Sector," *Children and Youth Services Review* 30, no. 11 (2008): 1233–45.

111. Michael Bourdillon, "Children and Work: A Review of Current Literature and Debates," *Development and Change* 37, no. 6 (2006): 1201–26. Viviana Zelizer, *Pricing the Priceless Child: The Changing Social Value of Children* (Princeton: Basic Books, 1994).

112. William E. Myers, "The Right Rights? Child Labor in a Globalizing World," *Annals of the American Academy of Political and Social Science* 575, no. 1 (2001): 38–55; Hilson, "'Load Too Heavy,'" 1235.

113. Makau W. Mutua, "Human Rights in Africa: The Limited Promise of Liberalism," *African Studies Review* 51, no. 1 (2008): 17–39.

9 ↬ Child-Trafficking Policymaking between Africa and Europe

MARGARET AKULLO

TRAFFICKING IN human beings is a major problem in Europe and beyond, but estimates on the number of children who have been trafficked do not provide a comprehensive picture of the size of the problem.[1] Africa is a region of origin for trafficked women and children and also a region of destination.[2] Many African girls and women are trafficked to Europe: many of them are Nigerian.[3] There are approximately 270,000 victims of human trafficking in the European Union (EU), with 10 percent of victims recorded as minors.[4] In addition, there are extremely low numbers of convictions in child-trafficking cases in Europe.[5] Between 2000 and 2007, convictions for child trafficking have only taken place in four out of twenty-seven EU member states. Very limited data exist on the number of unaccompanied children passing through the EU, some of whom may be victims of trafficking.[6]

Unaccompanied minors make up a small percentage of the total population of adult migrants. The majority of unaccompanied minors who arrive in the United Kingdom seek asylum, but a small number of others have other reasons.[7] The size of passenger traffic at London Heathrow Airport makes it the largest and busiest airport in the EU.[8] In 2003 over sixty million passengers—five million passengers a month, on average—passed through Heathrow, usually as family groups, often with friends, while others arrived alone, including unaccompanied children.[9] Trafficked children enter the UK either unaccompanied or accompanied by an adult, and all entry points into the UK are used as potential routes by traffickers.[10] The exact number of children passing through Heathrow Airport is unknown.[11]

In 2003, New Scotland Yard, the UK's Metropolitan Police Service, conducted an exploratory study on child trafficking called Operation Paladin Child at Heathrow Airport.[12] Scotland Yard's Child Abuse Investigation Command, based in London, led the study, which aimed to assess the scale and problem of child trafficking in London. British nationals or residents were not part of the study and will not be discussed in this chapter. Data were collected over a three month period and they suggest that most of the children arriving via Heathrow were of African origin. Paladin Child tried to trace the whereabouts of the unaccompanied children. Twenty-eight children could not be located after arriving at Heathrow Airport. At the conclusion of the study, fourteen children were found to be safe; the remaining fourteen were classified as untraced because neither UK police investigations nor enquiries by immigration and social services could locate them. However, there was insufficient evidence to conclude that these fourteen children were trafficked.[13]

The most important findings from Operation Paladin Child highlight the lack of child-trafficking statistics recorded worldwide and the challenge of formulating child-trafficking policy in the absence of comprehensive statistics. Nonetheless, Operation Paladin Child raised a number of issues on law enforcement's response to child trafficking. Since 2006 the UK has established two national agencies to deal with trafficking: the UK Human Trafficking Centre (UKHTC), which deals broadly with human trafficking and is part of the Serious Organised Crime Agency (SOCA), and the Child Exploitation and Online Protection Centre (CEOP), which is affiliated with SOCA and deals specifically with formulating child-trafficking policy. However, a proposal in 2010 to amalgamate both UKHTC and CEOP, to operate under one agency—the National Crime Agency (NCA)—stimulated debate on what this merger would mean for trafficked children.

Since most of the trafficked children in the UK appear to be from Africa, the EU has gradually moved toward engaging in an ongoing political dialogue with the African Union, which began with the so-called Cairo process.[14] By the early 2000s, the human-trafficking problem had emerged as a major issue within international development and diplomatic circles. Formal discussions between the two continents' governing bodies have propelled the issue of human trafficking into the center of discussion. In 2006 further work between Africa and Europe resulted in the joint AU-EU Plan of Action to Combat Trafficking in Human Beings, Especially Women and Children.[15] To what extent have these discussions contributed to effective child-trafficking policymaking between Europe and Africa? For its part, the EU has paid particular attention to trafficking, notably through the Council of Europe Convention on Action against Trafficking in Human Beings.[16] In December 2008 the UK ratified the convention, which adopted the same definition for trafficking in human beings as the United Nations Protocol to Prevent, Suppress and Punish Trafficking in Persons, Especially Women and Children, Supplementing the UN

Convention against Transnational Organized Crime. In 2011 the UK endorsed a new European Union (EU) directive designed to coordinate European efforts to combat human trafficking.

Operation Paladin Child is an example from Europe to analyze policy-making in child trafficking. Jean Allain examines the dialogue by the African Union in its attempt to formulate effective policies on child trafficking with Europe (chapter 7, this volume). The efforts made toward implementing these initiatives have resulted in a series of dialogues, which in turn have culminated in a number of European and African regional and national action plans on trafficking. The underlying argument for the present chapter is that, though common definitions, standards, and international instruments on trafficking exist in Europe and Africa, collaborative efforts from governments of source, transit, and destination countries still need to be properly coordinated for any effective policymaking to be successful. On a broader level, the chapter touches on some elements required for a policy framework to work between Africa and Europe.

TRAFFICKING AS DEFINED BETWEEN AFRICA AND EUROPE

In 2000 trafficking became a part of international law for the first time, through the United Nations (UN) Protocol to Prevent, Suppress and Punish Trafficking in Persons, Especially Women and Children, also referred to as the Palermo Protocol. It is one of two "Palermo Protocols" to the Convention against Transnational Organised Crime, with the other one being the Protocol against the Smuggling of Migrants by Land, Sea and Air.[17] The purpose of the UN trafficking protocol is to prevent trafficking, protect, and assist victims, in addition to promoting international cooperation in order to support efforts on the investigation and prosecution of trafficking crimes. According to the UN definition, which has now been widely accepted as the standard definition among international standards on trafficking in human beings, trafficking is

> the recruitment, transportation, transfer, harbouring or receipt of persons, by means of the threat or use of force or other forms of co-ercion, of abduction, of fraud, of deception, of the abuse of power or of a position of vulnerability or of the giving or receiving of payments or benefits to achieve the consent of a person having control over another person, for the purpose of exploitation. Exploitation shall include, at a minimum, the exploitation of the prostitution of others or other forms of sexual exploitation, forced labour or services, slavery or practices similar to slavery, servitude or the removal of organs.[18]

The Convention on the Rights of the Child defines a child as "a person below the age of 18, unless the laws of a particular country set the legal age for adulthood younger."[19] The UN trafficking protocol defines trafficking in children as "the recruitment, transportation, transfer, harbouring or receipt of a child for the purpose of exploitation." The difference between the standard definitions of trafficking and trafficking in children is that no violence, deception, coercion, or other fraudulent means are required for a child to be considered a victim of trafficking.[20] Furthermore, in 1989 the UN Convention on the Rights of the Child became an important international landmark reflecting the changing image of the child; it grants all children and young people (ages eighteen and under) a comprehensive set of fifty-four rights.[21] From a UK legislative perspective, a range of documented material supported by different acts covers guidance relevant to trafficked and exploited children.[22]

Child trafficking can be considered from a range of different perspectives. The UN, EU, and UK legislative instruments all promote a victim-centered approach to trafficking, an approach that is key to tackling child trafficking.[23] As stated in the UN's convention, trafficking is often related to the violation of children's rights, including the right to be protected from all forms of child abuse, neglect, exploitation, and cruelty. A victim-centered approach improves the standard of care provided to victims by applying an integrated approach that places child's rights at the center of all efforts in addressing trafficking.

Operation Paladin Child

The highly publicized murder of eight-year-old Victoria Climbié, in February 2000, led to the creation of a Child Abuse Investigation Command within the London police headquarters at New Scotland Yard.[24] A detailed account into the background of Victoria's death and the significant changes in child protection policies in the UK can be found at the website for the UK Department for Children, Schools and Families.[25] Victoria was born in Côte d'Ivoire on 2 November 1991 and used a false passport to travel to France with her aunt in 1998 and to the UK in 1999. From the point of her arrival in the UK, her aunt and aunt's partner subjected Victoria to physical abuse so severe that it led to Victoria's death in February 2000. New Scotland Yard confronted two important questions: why was Victoria's abuse not discovered earlier by the existing police child protection team and was Victoria also a victim of trafficking?

Victoria Climbié's death was linked to immigration crime because she entered the UK on a false passport. She was also subsequently suspected of being a victim of trafficking for social benefit.[26] As a direct result of her death, New Scotland Yard created the Child Abuse Investigation Command in 2000, and Operation Paladin Child was inaugurated in 2003. The purpose of Paladin

Child was to identify child victims of trafficking migrating through London Heathrow Airport. The overarching aim of the operation was "to protect children from exploitation by identifying and targeting those who facilitate minors into Europe via Heathrow."[27] In addition, there were a set of five objectives focusing on child trafficking: to identify victims of child trafficking; to identify those responsible for child trafficking; to establish methods used by traffickers to facilitate children into the UK; to locate addresses and destinations for trafficked children; to work in partnership with child protection agencies to prevent and disrupt future child trafficking.[28]

The criteria set for the quantitative aspect of the study was that demographic information of children was gathered from 26 August to 23 November 2003. In addition, the child had to be a non-EU passport holder, be under eighteen years of age, and be unaccompanied (not traveling with a parent, legal guardian, or older sibling and not part of a visit by a school, church, or sporting group recognized as an educational institution in a register kept by UK Immigration Service, now UK Borders Agency). Of 1,738 children recorded as having arrived at London Heathrow Airport, UK Social Services interviewed 551 (32 percent) considered to be at risk of trafficking.[29] The majority of those at risk of being trafficked from Africa came from Nigeria (46), South Africa (38), Ghana (36) Zimbabwe (28), Zambia (12), and Malawi (9).[30] Contrary to media reports of numbers of trafficked children traveling illegally, the vast majority of children identified by the Paladin Child study were traveling legitimately.[31] However, at the conclusion of the data collection and analysis phase, fourteen children remained unaccounted for, as the addresses given to UK immigration services were found to be either false or belonged to business premises.

The Paladin Child study did not identify any specific child-trafficking networks, victims, or offenders. Thus the final report, published in May 2004, was appropriately titled A Partnership Study of Child Migration to the UK via London Heathrow Airport. Although the study was initially meant to identify trafficked children, the results appeared instead to profile non-EU child migrants to the UK. The methodology applied to the study placed a focus on migration patterns rather than on identifying any mechanisms for the trafficking of children. The findings and methodology thus lend themselves more to the arguments in favor of enhancing border controls rather than mechanisms that protect the interests of the child above all else.

Victims Trafficked from West Africa to the UK

According to the UN, there are at least three ways to enter a country if the intent is to migrate illegally: some migrants enter legally but intentionally overstay their visas; others enter through a legal checkpoint but use false documentation or other forms of fraud to gain entry; and some migrants enter the country clandestinely, avoiding official points of entry.[32] Victoria Climbié entered through a legal checkpoint but used false documentation to gain entry into the UK. Operation Paladin Child participants all entered legally, as there was no evidence to suggest that they entered UK illegally or overstayed their visa. The findings of the Paladin Child study found that of the 1,738 children, 696 (40 percent) had visitor immigration status and were allowed to stay for up to six months. No further enquiries were made of the children with visas of up to six months to establish if they had actually returned to their country of embarkation. Fifty-nine (3 percent) children needed a visa to transit through the UK on their way to a third country and 249 (14 percent) qualified as students, which meant they had been accepted into a course of study by an institution on the official register of education and training providers.[33]

On a general level, estimates by the International Organization for Migration suggest that about 3.4 million Africans live in Europe, with North Africans generally making up two-thirds of that total.[34] The largest sub-Saharan African populations in Europe are the Ghanaians, Senegalese, and Nigerians. In the Paladin Child study Africa accounted for the highest number of child arrivals at Heathrow, with 629 (36 percent), the United States was second with 452 (26 percent), followed by Europe 341 (20 percent), and Asia 232 (13 percent). African children came mostly from West, East, and southern Africa.[35] The analysis also found that the greatest number of Africans came from Nigeria (185, or 11 percent). South Africa had the second-highest number of children at 142 (8 percent) and Ghana had 89 (5 percent). IOM, CEOP, and UKHTC statistics support these findings.[36]

International organizations have acknowledged Africa as a place of origin for women and children trafficked to Europe. UNICEF best illustrates the enormous challenge that Africa faces in protecting children and their rights. An analysis of information from the fifty-three African countries found that child trafficking affects more countries in Africa than any other form of trafficking, and as a result, one in four African countries has implemented a national project targeting trafficking in human beings.[37] The literature available appears to provide information mainly from West and central Africa, although there has since been an increased focus on the implementation of national projects in southern and East Africa.[38] UNICEF suggests that little is known regarding trafficking in and from Africa, and this prevents the implementation of effective law and policy.[39] Despite this, the commitment to and attempts by African states to combat trafficking are demonstrated in a number of regional instruments.[40]

While Operation Paladin Child attempted to identify trafficked children arriving at London Heathrow Airport, the methodology more accurately profiled unaccompanied migrant children from non-EU countries. The data represented as close to an accurate picture as possible of migration of non-EU unaccompanied children traveling through the airport over a three-month period in 2003. It is by no means a reflection of the scale of child trafficking. The data analysis suggests that African nationals appear to be the highest group of unaccompanied children nationals coming to the UK. Despite the limited time scales of the data collection exercise, there are many possible explanations for the high number of African arrivals. These possibilities might easily be explored by turning to other theories, such as those emphasizing economic disparities between countries or social or even environmental reasons.

The current information on victims of trafficking to the UK from Africa is best captured by the data provided by a Child Exploitation and Online Protection (CEOP) study.[41] Their analysis suggests that the trafficking of African children is more opportunistic and differs greatly from the organized criminal networks that traffic for example Vietnamese and Chinese children.[42] The study also suggests that West African traffickers often accompany their children at border controls into the UK, whereby the victim poses as a family member of the trafficker. Similar to Operation Paladin Child, CEOP's recent study suggests that West African children from Nigeria may account for the highest number of victims trafficked into the UK.[43] UKHTC data on likely cases of trafficking is provided by the National Referral Mechanism (NRM), which was introduced in 2009 as part of the Council of Europe Convention on Action against Trafficking in Human Beings.[44] Trained experts decide whether cases referred to them should be considered to be victims of trafficking according to the definition in the Council of Europe Convention on Action against Trafficking in Human Beings.

Between April 2009 and September 2010, 1,048 potential cases of trafficking were referred to the UKHTC (for referrals by nationality, see table 9.1; only the fifteen highest nationalities are represented).[45] Overall, Nigerian cases accounted for the highest number of referrals, and that outcome is supported by results from studies by Operation Paladin Child in 2004, CEOP in 2010, and the UKTC in 2010, indicating that trafficking from Africa appears to flow mainly from West African communities and involve mainly Nigerian women and girls.[46] Liza Buchbinder examines in detail the progress of Nigerian antitrafficking campaigns (chapter 11, this volume). It is, however, worth noting that Nigerian's efforts against trafficking earned it a tier 1 status in the US Trafficking in Persons Report 2010, as fully compliant with the minimum standards for the elimination of trafficking.[47]

Research suggests that children from West African countries are regularly trafficked into Europe.[48] The volume of the problem of trafficking in West Africa is enormous, with clearly recognized routes that encompass Benin, Burkina Faso, Cameroon, Côte d'Ivoire, Gabon, Guinea, Mali, Niger, Nigeria, and

TABLE 9.1

UKHTC trafficking case referrals, by nationality

Nationality	Referrals as of 30/06/11	Positive RG decision[a]	Positive CG decision[b]
Nigeria	298	140	55
China	177	83	27
Vietnam	160	106	34
Romania	87	73	64
Czech Republic	74	63	56
Slovakia	71	62	51
UK	60	57	53
Uganda	58	35	16
India	44	30	6
Albania	38	20	13
Total	1,067	669	375

[a]Where there are reasonable grounds to believe that the person referred could be a victim of human trafficking (that is, when a positive reasonable-grounds decision has been made) the suspected victim could be given a place within a safe house. The potential victim will then enter a reflection period, which lasts for forty-five days. This allows the victim to begin to recover from their ordeal and to reflect on what they want to do next. The next steps could be to cooperate with police enquiries or to be returned home; however, this reflection period allows for these decisions to be made with consideration. It also allows the competent authority team to make a more conclusive decision on whether the referred person is truly a victim.

[b]Conclusive-grounds decisions are considered only when a positive reasonable-grounds decision has been made. In making the conclusive decision the competent authority will consider the information provided to them to make a full and conclusive decision on whether the person referred is a victim of human trafficking. The NRM is the mechanism that will enable the UKHTC to identify the number of victims of this crime and to build a clearer picture about the scale of the problem of human trafficking in the UK.

Source: "NRM Statistical Data April 2009 to June 2011," at http://www.soca.gov.uk/about-soca/about-the-ukhtc/national-referral-mechanism/statistics.

Togo.[49] Many of these countries are both suppliers and receivers of trafficked children. In 2001 the heads of states in the Economic Community of West African States adopted the ECOWAS Initial Plan of Action against Trafficking in Persons (2002–3) indicating that trafficking in persons had become a major concern for all countries of western Africa.[50] The plan of action directed the ECOWAS executive secretariat to prepare proposals for controlling trafficking in persons in the subregion, with special consideration for the situation of trafficked children and a focus on criminal justice responses.

In 2006 the UN Office on Drugs and Crime produced a training manual for ECOWAS, intended to strengthen the capacity of the ECOWAS secretariat and its member states in implementing the ECOWAS plan of action, particularly as it relates to assessment of existing national legislation and the drafting of new legislation in response to the UN trafficking protocol.[51] ECOWAS, like the EU, recognized the importance of international cooperation in preventing human trafficking and as a result, twelve of the sixteen states in the West African region passed national laws that recognize human trafficking as a crime.[52]

It is clear that the ECOWAS initiative against human trafficking has encouraged states to adopt the ECOWAS Initial Plan of Action against Trafficking in Persons 2002–3.[53] The plan has, however, confronted two serious barriers: the free movement of people between the ECOWAS states and the extensive territorial scale of many West African countries. The trafficking of persons between nations in West Africa is extensive and in addition, the ECOWAS protocol that allows free movement of persons between ECOWAS states has further encouraged the growth of transnational crimes, including trafficking.[54] However, these barriers are addressed by the presence of bilateral and multilateral programs in Africa, made possible through funding provided by the United States, for example, for projects aimed at the prevention of human trafficking.[55]

TRAFFICKING POLICY

Although the European Convention on Trafficking details provisions in the prosecution of trafficking offences, the numbers of child-trafficking convictions in the EU are extremely low.[56] In 2009 a European Union Agency for Fundamental Rights study highlighted deficiencies in EU law in addressing child-trafficking cases and securing convictions in court.[57] The UK secured its first conviction for trafficking for domestic servitude in 2011.[58] The case has similarities to the 2000 case of Victoria Climbié.

The European Commission in 2010 addressed the low levels of convictions and tabled a proposal for a new directive on trafficking in human beings that "aimed at further approximating legislation and penalties, ensuring successful prosecution, better protection of and assistance to victims, and prevention of trafficking."[59] The directive, if implemented, will mean that the definition of trafficking at the EU level, which is currently limited to sexual and labor exploitation, will include other forms of exploitation, like forced begging and illegal adoption. In addition, the new EU directive means that prosecutions can take place when trafficking occurs outside its borders.[60] It will be easier to convict offenders in the EU's twenty-seven member states and allow suspects to be prosecuted for offences in other EU countries.

Since Operation Paladin Child in 2003, a radical reform in policing is about to take place in the UK.[61] The reform is based on a proposal to create a National Crime Agency (NCA) to lead the fight against organized crime and to protect UK borders at a national level. This proposal recommends amalgamating the UKHTC, CEOP, SOCA, the UK Border Agency, and the National Policing Improvement Agency into one agency.[62] The NCA will focus on organized crime and border policing and will further build on the intelligence, analytical, and enforcement capabilities and expertise of SOCA and CEOP. This radical change lends itself to the debate on whether child protection cases should be viewed and dealt with as organized crime. Advocates of child protection state that law enforcement efforts in protecting victims of trafficking should arguably focus on the best interest of the child and should not be offender focused.[63] The rationale behind the NCA is that it is focused on offenders and on protecting borders and suits the merger between the UKHTC, the UKBA, and SOCA, and not CEOP. This is because in child protection issues, the interests of a child, not issues concerning offenders, should be central to any police investigative efforts.

The 2000 Cairo process represented the first policy dialogue between the EU and African nations and it also led to the formation of the African Union.[64] The development of a new pan-African level of governance created an opportunity for the European Union–African Union dialogue that would enable discussions on African issues with continental implications. The follow-up to the Cairo process took place in Ouagadougou, Burkina Faso, in 2002, where it was agreed that this dialogue would be the only forum where Africa and Europe would discuss issues with global continental implications.[65] Since then, the EU has regularly engaged with the African Union on the issue of trafficking in the course of its bilateral political dialogue through the Ouagadougou Action Plan.[66] The plan guides African Union member states to develop and reform their policies and laws on trafficking in persons.

The Ouagadougou Action Plan has been central to the implementation of the African Union Commission Initiative against Trafficking Campaign (AU.COMMIT), and reflects an attempt by African countries to develop and reform their policies and laws on trafficking in persons.[67] Countries have been encouraged to engage in a number of steps involving the development of systematic research and effective methodologies, and in particular, to bring together relevant ministries and agencies to formulate policy and take action against trafficking. The Ouagadougou Action Plan proposed a strategic approach based on three principles similar to that adopted at the EU level: prevention of trafficking, protection of victims of trafficking, and prosecution of those involved in the crime of trafficking and related forms of abuse.

The AU.COMMIT—examined in detail in this volume by Jean Allain (chapter 7)—has emerged as one of the major program activities in Africa for 2009–12.[68] At face value, the EU and African states appear to be reaffirming their earlier commitments to applying the relevant international and regional legal instruments. These instruments promote the implementation of prevention and awareness-raising campaigns, which are approaches geared toward emphasizing the protection and assistance of victims. The legislative framework provides the basic context for rules governing and regulating trafficking.

The introduction of action plans in Africa shows Africa's attempt to address the causes of child trafficking. Action plans are central to policy decisions for assistance to victims. But this can be a short-term solution without the long-term impact of bilateral or multilateral agreements between countries. The importance of comprehensive data to inform policymaking should not be ignored.

TOWARD A CHILD-TRAFFICKING POLICY FRAMEWORK

The rediscovery of human trafficking as an international policy issue occurred in the 1990s as a result of the reported increase in prostitution involving mainly women and girls from Eastern Europe and West Africa.[69] Child trafficking has been recognized through various initiatives because national and regional action plans are now becoming an important policy tool for the prevention of human trafficking and the protection of victims. In Europe, a majority of the countries have adopted national action plans to counter trafficking in human beings, with some of these plans still in force while others have been succeeded by new action plans for a future date.[70] National action plans are also beginning to emerge in African countries, but whilst policies are being formulated, work still needs to be done to disseminate and implement these policies in Africa.[71]

Different legal and policy frameworks have been developed to address child trafficking in Europe.[72] But they have been mainly in the broader context of organized crime, sexual exploitation, and migration, thus failing on the issue of children's rights.[73] EU child-trafficking policy should detail guiding principles that show a national and international declaration embracing children's basic human rights. Policy responses will differ depending on the status of the country, and so it is important to be clear on whether a country is a country of origin, transit, or destination.[74] For example, returning a victim to their country of origin requires that reintegration is easy and that the security of victims is guaranteed. However, monitoring organizations that ensure the safe return of the victim can be difficult and may result in victims being retrafficked. To prevent trafficking, governments need to promote education and a better standard of living within the country of origin. Most important, policies should be developed around the best interests of the child whereby rather than focusing upon the "trafficking issue," it may be time to rediscover the "trafficking victim."[75] The following section explores elements of a comprehensive policy to deal with child trafficking.

Protection, Prevention, and Prosecution for Trafficking Victims between Africa and the EU

The current system of protection and care of victims of child trafficking in Africa is generally inadequate in the face of the increase in child trafficking.[76] Some African countries have yet to establish effective child protection systems. Even in countries that do have them, such as Ghana, Burkina Faso, and

Senegal, the scale of the problem demands the reforming and strengthening of existing systems.[77] Child protection issues require measures that would provide for employment, education, and training opportunities, as well as other aspects of assistance.

Europe and Africa have begun to recognize child trafficking as a specific policy area in its own right, one that is firmly rooted in child's rights.[78] Generally speaking, policy formation has focused on migration and law enforcement and has not adopted a children's rights approach. Europe and Africa aim to formally approve and fully implement all international conventions and treaties designed to combat child trafficking, in addition to protecting the fundamental rights of the child through the application and implementation of the UN Convention on the Rights of the Child. For example, Articles 32, 34, 35 and 36 of the UN Convention on the Rights of the Child recognize that children are particularly vulnerable to exploitation and abuse and suggest that girls are particularly at risk of being trafficked. The convention also recognizes that a child can be retrafficked. Central to child trafficking are Articles 32 and 35.[79]

Recognizing trafficking within the national child protection policies enhances cooperation at national and international level in order to support organizations and countries, as they shape adequate responses to prevent, protect, and provide assistance to victims. While policies should reflect synergy in relation to child protection and welfare, and law enforcement on the other hand, child protection also requires the enforcement of relevant legislation. This approach gives recognition to child trafficking as a comprehensive child protection issue.

Prevention on a multiagency level operates most effectively when it addresses migration and trafficking within the context of overall national development policy.[80] Preventive approaches are most effective when they are uniform and move beyond simply awareness raising. The EU encourages the idea that human trafficking be addressed as part of larger organized crime policy and defined as a clear priority for law enforcement.[81] The EU recognizes that prevention of trafficking, protection of victims, and efficient prosecution and punishment of traffickers are the three major cornerstones of countertrafficking policy. Legislative and nonlegislative instruments must be used to that end.

Within this framework, border controls are important mechanisms to ensuring effective prevention. But it must also be recognized that policy responses in relation to immigration can be complex, particularly in ECOWAS region, which has largely uncontrolled borders. However, the response to child trafficking demands a duty to provide unconditional support and protection to all children regardless of their country of origin.[82]

Discussions on trafficking have taken place in the context of the UN Convention on Transnational Organized Crime and related UN protocols.

The UN trafficking protocol suggests that trafficking takes place within the context of organized crime, whereby trafficking in persons involves organized crime networks or syndicates.[83] The term *organized crime* implies that there is a group of criminally minded individuals managed in a systematic manner. While organized crime certainly has a stake in human trafficking, looser systems probably prevail. Is there a chain of command central to the trafficking process or are they loosely connected based on the opportunity to traffic when the situation presents itself? Is the trafficking network based in the country of origin or the destination country? Does the presence of organized crime acknowledge the existence of illegal markets in trafficking? The lack of data can mean a range of things—for example, that the structure may be fairly flexible, thereby giving the notion that it is not exactly an organized network.[84]

Although there is little evidence relating to characteristics of traffickers, traffickers may be of the same nationality or ethnic origin as the victim or even family members.[85] Family members have been implicated as traffickers but they may not necessarily be aware of the resultant exploitation. Such practices prevent detection of children who are trafficked as domestic servants or for labor.

Vulnerability and widespread poverty are major contributing factors to the growth of child trafficking. If trafficking is linked to poverty, then combating child trafficking certainly requires addressing poverty related issues. This function, however, cannot appropriately fall within the remit of the police. The police can be expected to react to the consequences of trafficking only when a victim or trafficking network has been identified, not when preexisting conditions have given rise to child trafficking. The UN trafficking protocol, for example, suggests that trafficking is part of organized crime and one effort to combat trafficking can be advanced through a law enforcement approach, as in the case of Operation Paladin Child and in the case of Nigeria described by Buchbinder in this volume. In the EU, child trafficking is a policy area under the Justice and Home Affairs department, suggesting that the focus is on law enforcement.[86] While law enforcement is part of a policy response that needs to be supported by severe penalties, effective antitrafficking needs to incorporate both prevention and protection policy areas.

National Action Plans

National action plans have emerged as an important policy tool for the prevention of trafficking and protection of victims. Most EU countries and some African countries have national action plans on human trafficking, but very few of the plans specifically address child trafficking. The large number of actors in governments, nongovernmental organizations, and UN agencies in Africa and Europe, coupled with the diversity and range of mandates and approaches, means that the coordination of antitrafficking activities at the national and international levels still remains a challenge. Coordination in child-trafficking policymaking remains a crucial area of concern, and the establishment of national executing agencies, such as CEOP in the UK, which takes the policy lead in child trafficking, represents an important new trend. This development certainly enhances interagency collaboration coupled with the benefits from the expertise of NGOs who are also key to shaping adequate policy between the EU and Africa.

National action plans are further informed by comprehensive data. One of the major obstacles to effective policy development and implementation with regard to child trafficking is the limited knowledge on its scope. Data collection challenges, however, can be blamed only partly on the concealed nature of trafficking crimes. Data on trafficking tend to come from anecdotal evidence rather than from empirical evidence. Nevertheless, child-trafficking research should have harmonized methodologies in order to build on current policy responses. The UN protocol on trafficking illustrates the fact that trafficking in children is often mentioned at the same time as trafficking in women, and as such, data on women and children has tended to elicit a general policy approach that applies to both vulnerable groups. Desegregating trafficking data to reflect children as a separate risk group allows for a targeted policy response specific to children.

⤶

I acknowledge that in implementing a coherent policy against child trafficking between Europe and Africa, it is necessary to have regular discussions and coordination that go beyond protecting borders. Policy responses tend to "place illegal immigration, human smuggling, and human trafficking together under the 'migration–crime–security' nexus."[87] However, the move toward prevention and protection approaches of child trafficking by the European and African Unions clearly indicates a victim-centered approach to trafficking. At this point, we can even conclude that the dialogue between the European and Africa Unions in recent years suggests that both continents have begun to place the child at the center of policy and practice.

The partnership agreements between the European Union and the African Union demonstrate that Europe shares a common interest with Africa in addressing child trafficking, and the two regions continue to work collaboratively to realize the benefits of their cooperation. Since the historic first African Union–European Union summit, in Cairo in 2000, the partnership has been strengthened with many initiatives being launched to address human trafficking in general. Although legislation, legal instruments and national plans on trafficking in children exist, there is little evidence of successful implementation.

For example, most of the West African countries in the US Trafficking in Persons Report are ranked in the tier 2 and tier 2 watch list, indicating that these countries require further improvement in their efforts to combat trafficking.[88] Nevertheless, what is important is not the series of dialogues that have taken place but how countries can translate the discussions into child-trafficking policy and eventually into practice.

Any policymaking related to child trafficking is best informed by linking existing data to more rigorous quantitative and qualitative research. Policymakers require good evidence to support the process of policy development, and when comprehensive data are provided, services for trafficked children are identifiable, and, when implemented, positively affect their lives. Law enforcement coupled with public awareness does not necessarily solve the problem of child trafficking. Effective policies to combat child trafficking between Europe and Africa require significant cooperation between origin, destination, and transit countries. That cooperation should include the exchange of information, joint criminal investigations, and especially, specific arrangements and agreements on the return of victims. Human trafficking has been high on the agenda of most African Union–European Union consultative processes, and though this is a good opportunity for formal and informal dialogue on policy development, a lot still remains to be done to see child-trafficking policy translated into practice. The discussions appear to be largely on a political level, maybe because children are key indicators of social policy and as such attract political interest.

Despite the number of African-European agreements, in Africa policy implementation problems and constraints still exist at both national and local levels that hamper the implementation of child protection policies and effective delivery of services. For example, incorporating a standard child protection framework within most African countries requires an overhaul of social services and health, legal, and government agencies. Awareness-raising activities may not work particularly well in countries with weak child protection institutions. The identification of the vulnerabilities of trafficked children are key to formulating any kind of policy response to trafficking.

The strategic partnership between the African Union and the European Union recognizes that Africa and Europe are bound together by history, culture, and geography.[89] The joint strategy between the AU and the EU suggests that Africa and Europe will take the partnership to a new strategic level, which would eventually strengthen not only the political partnership but enhanced cooperation at all levels. Even if we acknowledge that the implementation process of the AU-EU dialogue attempted to incorporate long- and short-term action plans in all areas of the partnership, challenges continue with regard to implementation and coordination, both across the EU and Africa and between the political leadership and civil society. It remains clear that the differences in the socioeconomic situations in Africa will continue to create a varying mix of policy responses to child trafficking. While socioeconomic situations may become central issues for policy development, these should not obfuscate the vulnerabilities that face the child victims of trafficking networks.

NOTES

Abbreviations

ECOWAS   Economic Community of West African States
EUAFR   EU Agency for Fundamental Rights
IOM   International Organization for Migration
UNODC   United Nations Office on Drugs and Crime
USDOS   US Department of State

1. EUAFR, *Child Trafficking in the European Union—Challenges, Perspectives and Good Practices* (Luxembourg: *Office for Official Publications of the European Communities*, 2009), http://fra.europa.eu/fraWebsite/attachments/Pub _Child_Trafficking_09_en.pdf, 7.

2. UNICEF, *Trafficking in Human Beings, Especially Women and Children, in Africa*, 2nd ed. (Florence: Innocenti Research Centre, 2005), 37.

3. BBC News, "Tracking Africa's Child Trafficking," 23 April 2004, http://news .bbc.co.uk/1/hi/3653737.stm.

4. UNODC, *Trafficking in Persons: Analysis on Europe* (Vienna: UNODC, 2009), 8.

5. Most European countries record national conviction rates for human trafficking below one convict per one hundred thousand people. UNODC, *Trafficking*, 8.

6. EUAFR, *Child Trafficking*.

7. IOM, *Trafficking in Unaccompanied Minors in EU Member States: UK Country Report* (London: IOM, 2003), 8.

8. Heathrow saw 67 million passengers in 2004. See Air Transport World, "Europe's Biggest Airports," http://www.atwonline.com/magazine/article.html ?articleID=1319.

9. IOM, *Trafficking*, 8. See also UK Civil Aviation Authority, "Air Passengers by Type and Nationality of Operator" (2003), http://www.caa.co.uk/docs/80/airport_ data/2003Annual/Table_08_Air_Passengers_by_Type_and_Nat_of_Operator.pdf.

10. Samantha Dowling, Karen Moreton, and Leila Wright, *Trafficking for the Purposes of Labour Exploitation* (London: Home Office, 2007), 14.

11. In 2008–09, Hillingdon Social Services provided service at Heathrow Airport to 364 unaccompanied children, 205 of whom claimed asylum. Hillingdon, "Media Fact Sheet: UASC and Trafficking," http://www.hillingdon.gov.uk /index.jsp?articleid=19075. See also London Borough of Hillingdon, "The Impact of Heathrow Airport on the Hillingdon Health & Social Care Economy" (2006), http://www.hillingdon.gov.uk/media/pdf/m/f/heathrow_impact.pdf; Select

Committee on Home Affairs, "Ninth supplementary memorandum submitted by the Immigration and Nationality Directorate, Home Office," http://www.publications .parliament.uk/pa/cm200506/cmselect/cmhaff/775/775awe54.htm.

12. Margaret Akullo and P. Spindler, "Paladin Child: A Partnership Study of Child Migration to the UK via London Heathrow," London: New Scotland Yard, unpublished confidential report, 2004, copy filed with author, summary in http:// www.mpa.gov.uk/downloads/committees/ppr/ppr-040712-14-appendix01.pdf, Metropolitan Police Authority, London.

13. The UK Immigration Service landed 1,738 unaccompanied minors in the three-month study period between late August and November 2003. During the study 551 unaccompanied minors were risk-assessed for potential vulnerability to trafficking. Follow-up enquiries that included locating and visiting the minors at their address were carried out by Social Services.

14. European Centre for Development Policy Management, "The EU-Africa Partnership in Historical Perspective," Issue Paper for Public Consultation, Maastricht, 2006.

15. African Union, "Ouagadougou Action Plan to Combat Trafficking in Human Beings, Especially Women and Children, As Adopted by the Ministerial Conference on Migration and Development, Tripoli," 22–23 November 2006, http://au.int/en/dp/sa/content/ouagadougou-action-plan-combat-trafficking -human-beings-especially-women-and-children-0.

16. Council of Europe, *Council of Europe Convention on Action against Trafficking in Human Beings and Its Explanatory Report*, Council of Europe Treaty Series no. 197 (Strasbourg: COE, 2005), Action against Trafficking in Human Beings, 16.V.2005.

17. UNODC, *United Nations Convention against Transnational Organized Crime and the Protocols Thereto* (New York: UNODC, 2004), 53.

18. Ibid., 42.

19. "Factsheet—A Summary of the Rights under the Convention on the Rights of the Child" (UNICEF), http://www.unicef.org/crc/files/Rights_overview.pdf.

20. UNICEF, *Child Trafficking in West Africa: Policy Responses* (Florence: Innocenti Research Centre, 2002).

21. UNICEF, "Convention on the Rights of the Child," http://www.unicef.org/crc/.

22. See, for example, Department for Children, Schools and Families, Nottingham, UK, "Safeguarding Children Who May Have Been Trafficked" (2007); "Working Together to Safeguard Children" (2010); "What to Do If You're Worried a Child Is Being Abused" (2006); "Safeguarding Children and Young People from Sexual Exploitation" (2009); "The UK Children's Act 1998/2004"; "The Sexual Offences Act 2003"; "The Asylum and Immigration (Treatment of Claimants, etc.) Act 2004." The Sexual Offences Act 2003 introduces a range of offences covering trafficking for any form of sexual offence and carries a fourteen-year maximum penalty. The offense of "trafficking for exploitation," which covers nonsexual exploitation such as trafficking for forced labor and the removal of organs, is described in the Asylum and Immigration (Treatment of Claimants, etc.) Act 2004.

23. Council of Europe, The Council of Europe Convention on Action against Trafficking in Human Beings, CETS no. 197; UN, the United Nations Convention against Transnational Organized Crime and the Protocols Thereto; Safeguarding Children Who May Have Been Trafficked (2007).

24. UK House of Commons Health Committee, *The Victoria Climbié Inquiry Report* (London: HMSO, 2003), http://www.nationalarchives.gov.uk/ERORecords/VC/2/2/finreport/vicstory.htm.

25. Ibid.

26. An example of such a benefit in the UK is the child benefit: a tax-free weekly payment of approximately GBP20 that can be claimed for a child. The child must not be subject to immigration control in order to qualify for this allowance.

27. Akullo and Spindler, "Paladin Child," 12.

28. Ibid., app. A: "Aims and Objectives."

29. Ibid., app. G: "'Risk Assessment': (i) Category A risk—An unaccompanied child arrived in the UK aged under 16 years and stated that their stay in the UK is in excess of 28 days; (ii) Category B risk—An unaccompanied child staying in the UK with no date of return declared to Immigration Officers; (iii) Category C risk—An unaccompanied child not fitting the above criteria where concerns as to the safety of that child have been identified through other means."

30. Akullo and Spindler, "Paladin Child." Total arrivals for a three-month period for countries in the top twenty for trafficking were 1,084. Of this total 54 percent (590) were female; 51 percent (302) of female arrivals were of African origin.

31. See, for example, "Alarm at Scale of Children Trafficking into UK," *Evening Standard*, 17 May 2004.

32. UNODC, *Organized Crime and Irregular Migration from Africa to Europe* (Vienna: UNODC, 2006).

33. On 31 March 2009 the register of sponsors replaced the register of education and training providers published by the Department for Innovation, Universities and Skills (and previously by the Department for Education and Skills). The register of sponsors lists all organizations that the UK Border Agency has approved to employ migrants or sponsor migrant students. Register of Education and Training Providers, as last maintained by the Department of Innovation, Universities and Skills, 30 March 2009.

34. UNODC, *Organized Crime*, 6.

35. Akullo and Spindler, "Paladin Child," 31.

36. IOM, *Managing Migration—Challenges and Responses for People on the Move* (Geneva: IOM, 2003).

37. UNICEF, *Trafficking in Human Beings*.

38. Ibid., 15.

39. Ibid., 1.

40. See, for example, the African Charter on the Rights and Welfare of the Child (1990); the Plan of Action adopted by the Economic Community of West African States (2001); the ECOWAS and Economic Community of Central African States Joint Action Plan; and the South-Africa/Mozambique MOU (Memorandum of

Understanding) for extradition of perpetrators, http://europafrica.files.wordpress
.com/2008/10/au-commit-campaign-on-combating-human-trafficking-2009-2012.pdf.

41. Child Exploitation and Online Protection Centre, *Strategic Threat Assessment: Child Trafficking in the UK* (London: CEOP, 2010).

42. Ibid., 29.

43. Ibid. From March 2009 through February 2010 children from the following countries were trafficked into the UK: Nigeria (40), Sierra Leone (7), Ghana (1), Côte d'Ivoire (1), Liberia (1), and Guinea (1).

44. The NRM is a framework within which public bodies such as the criminal justice agencies, UK Border Agency (UKBA), local authorities, and third-sector partners can work together to identify individuals who may be victims of trafficking and provide appropriate protection and support.

45. National Referral Mechanism Data (2011), http://www.soca.gov.uk/about-soca/about-the-ukhtc/national-referral-mechanism/statistics

46. UNODC, *Transnational Trafficking and the Rule of Law in West Africa: A Threat Assessment* (Vienna: UNODC, 2009). See also UNODC, *The Globalization of Crime: A Transnational Organized Crime Threat Assessment* (Vienna: UNODC, 2010).

47. USDOS, *Trafficking in Persons Report* (2010).

48. Mirjam van Reisen and Ana Stefanovic, *Lost Kids, Lost Futures: The European Union's Response to Child Trafficking* (Geneva: Terre des Hommes, 2004), 13.

49. Rima Salah, "Child Trafficking in West and Central Africa: An Overview,". Paper presented at the Pan African Conference on human trafficking, Abuja, 19–23 February 2001, p. 8.

50. Economic Community of West African States (hereafter ECOWAS), "Initial Plan of Action against Trafficking in Persons (2002–2003)," Dakar, 2001, http://www.unodc.org/pdf/crime/trafficking/Minimum_Plano_CEDEAO.pdf.

51. UNODC, "Assistance for the Implementation of the ECOWAS Plan of Action against Trafficking in Persons" (Vienna: UNODC, 2006).

52. "A Regional Response to Trafficking in West Africa," UN, Global Initiative to Fight Human Trafficking, http://www.ungift.org/ungift/en/stories/a-regional-response-to-trafficking-in-west-africa.html. See also UNICEF, *Child Trafficking*.

53. ECOWAS, "Declaration on the Fight against Trafficking in Persons," Dakar, 2001, http://www.unodc.org/pdf/crime/trafficking/Declarationr_CEDEAO.pdf.

54. Victoria I. Nwogu, "Nigeria: Human Trafficking and Migration" *Forced Migration Review* 25 (May 2006): 32; UNHCR, Protocol A/P.1/5/79, Relating to Free Movement of Persons, Residence and Establishment.

55. USDOS, US Funds for 2008 for TIP Projects.

56. Council of Europe Treaty Series, Council of Europe Convention on Action against Trafficking in Human Beings and Its Explanatory Report, no. 197 (2005), chap. 5.

57. EUAFR, "Child Trafficking."

58. See "Pastor Jailed for Trafficking African Child 'Slaves,'" BBC, http://www.bbc.co.uk/news/uk-england-london-12789690.

59. The directive, if approved, will replace current EU legislation dating from 2002 (Framework Decision 2002/629/JHA), Europa, Press Releases, http://europa.eu/rapid/pressReleasesAction.do?reference=MEMO/10/108.

60. For example, while the UK has the power to prosecute in cases where trafficking occurs into, within, or out of the country, it has no power to prosecute in cases involving British citizens where the trafficking occurs outside its borders.

61. Home Office, *Policing in the 21st Century: Reconnecting Police and the People* (London: Home Office, 2010).

62. In April 2006 the Serious Organised Crime Agency (SOCA) was formed by the merging of the National Crime Squad (NCS), the National Criminal Intelligence Service (NCIS), the part of HM Revenue and Customs (HMRC) dealing with drug trafficking and associated criminal finance, and a part of UK Immigration dealing with organized immigration crime (UKIS), now the UK Border Agency. NPIA is the National Policing Improvement Agency.

63. Among such advocates is UNICEF.

64. "EU-Africa Dialogue in Burkina Faso," http://www.eu-un.europa.eu /articles/fr/article_1797_fr.htm.

65. Africa-Europe Dialogue (follow-up to the Cairo Summit)—Second Ministerial Meeting, Ouagadougou, 28 November 2002; Council of the European Union, Africa-Europe Ministerial Meeting, Ouagadougou, 28 November 2002, Final Communiqué 15197/02, Brussels, http://www.fes.de/cotonou/downloads / official/ACPEU/EU-+AFRICAOUGADOUGOUNOV2002.PDF.

66. African Union, "Ouagadougou Action Plan to Combat Trafficking in Human Beings, Especially Women and Children," Ministerial Conference on Migration and Development, 22–23 November 2006, EX.Cl/313 (X), annex 4, 3.

67. See African Union, "Media Advisory: Launch of the AU Commission Initiative against Trafficking," AU.COMMIT Campaign, 16 June 2009; African Union, "African Union Commission Initiative against Trafficking," AU.COMMIT Campaign, Strategy Document 2009–12.

68. African Union, AU.COMMIT Campaign on Combating Human Trafficking 2009–2012, 2009, http://www.africaunion.org/root/UA/Conferences/2009/juin /SA/16juin/sa/AU.COMMIT%20Campaign%20Strategy%20June%2016.doc. See also African Union Commission, "Media Advisory: Launch of the AU Commission Initiative against Trafficking (AU.COMMIT Campaign) Let's Combat Trafficking in Human Beings, Especially Women and Children: 2009–2012," ILO, http://www.ilo .int/public/english/region/afpro/addisababa/pdf/advisoryaucommit.pdf.

69. Anne Daguerre, "Whose Problem? Addressing Child Trafficking in France and Britain," *e-migrinter* no. 2 (2008): 143.

70. EUAFR, *Child Trafficking*, 120.

71. Mehari Taddele, program coordinator for migration at the AU meeting in Ethiopia , has stated, "The AU has already formulated policies and is now working on disseminating the policies. But the implementation process rests highly on the commitment of African governments." "Ethiopia: AU Launches Initiative against Human Trafficking," *Ethiopian Review*, http://www.ethiopianreview.com/articles/10033.

72. EUAFR, "Child Trafficking," http://ec.europa.eu/home-affairs/policies /crime/crime_intro_en.htm.

73. "Framework Decision on Combating the Sexual Exploitation of Children and Child Pornography," *Official Journal* (2003): L 013, 20.01.2004, pp. 44–48, http:// eur-lex.europa.eu/LexUriServ/LexUriServ.do?uri=CELEX:32004F0068:EN:HTML.

74. UNICEF, *Trafficking in Human Beings*, 8.

75. Galma Jahic and James O. Finckenauer, "Representations and Misrepresentations of Human Trafficking," *Trends in Organized Crime* 8, no. 3 (2005): 38.

76. UNICEF, *Child Trafficking in West Africa*, 18.

77. UNICEF, *Strengthening Social Protection for Children: West and Central Africa* (Dakar: UNICEF Regional Office for West and Central Africa, 2009), 45.

78. Van Reisen and Stefanovic, "Lost Kids," 22, 40.

79. UN Convention on the Rights of the Child, Articles 32, 34, 35, 36.

80. Van Reisen and Stefanovic, "Lost Kids," 50, recommendation 4.

81. UK Home Office, "Tackling Human Trafficking: Policy and Best Practice in Europe" (London: Home Office, 2006)

82. According to van Reisen and Stefanovic, "The EU has mostly tended to focus on the link between trafficking in human beings and illegal immigration." Van Reisen and Stefanovic, "Lost Kids," 41.

83. UNDOC, *Convention against Transnational Organised Crime*, Article 2.

84. Trafficking networks are often informal and secretive. See Salah, "Child Trafficking," 3. The three levels are the mobilization and recruitment of migrants, their movement en route, and their insertion and integration into labor markets and destination countries. See John Salt and Jeremy Stein, "Migration as a Business: The Case of Trafficking," *International Migration* 35, no. 4 (1997): 467–94; Bridget Anderson and Julia O'Connell Davidson, *Trafficking—A Demand Led Problem? A Multi-country Pilot Study* (Stockholm: Save the Children Sweden, 2002); Davidson and Bridget Donelan, *Review of the Evidence and Debates on the Demand Side of Trafficking* (Stockholm: Save the Children Sweden, 2002).

85. Dowling, Moreton, and Wright, *Trafficking*, 14.

86. Van Reisen and Stefanovic, "Lost Kids," 22.

87. Jo Goodey, "Migration, Crime and Victimhood: Responses to Sex Trafficking in the EU," *Journal of Punishment and Society* 5, no. 4 (2003): 423.

88. USDOS, *TIP* (2010).

89. Council of the European Union, "The Africa-EU Strategic Partnership, A Joint Africa-EU Strategy," 2007, 16344/07 (Presse 291), http://register.consilium.europa.eu/pdf/en/07/st16/st16344.en07.pdf.

10 ∽ The Story of Elsie

A *Case Study of Trafficking in Contemporary South Africa*

SUSAN KRESTON

ELSIE WAS born in the Eastern Cape to a mother who did not want her. Elsie does not know her date of birth, so she's never celebrated a birthday. She never knew her father and was raised from infancy by her maternal grandmother, who took care of Elsie until her death, when Elsie was ten. Upon her grandmother's death, Elsie went to live with an aunt and uncle. Shortly thereafter, her trafficking saga began, when she was sold by them to a German man, who sexually exploited her as well as giving her drugs and alcohol. Elsie decided to run away.

She began to live on the streets. She became friends with a girl, Thandi, who told her that she could make money if she moved in with her and her Nigerian boyfriend, a trafficker named Hennie. Elsie stayed with them and got involved with drugs and was forced into prostitution to support Hennie. She would make about R4,500 a day, about R1,500 in the morning and R3,000 in the night. Her clientele was dangerous. Moreover, Hennie raped Elsie and threatened to kill her. He also began to beat her when she didn't want to work, so she ran away again. She then began to work for a third trafficker, who also raped her, so once again she ran away and was prostituted at the hands of a fourth trafficker. She continued to be sexually exploited, and she started stealing and robbing to make the money demanded of her by the trafficker. She did not want to work on the streets but was repeatedly beaten to make her continue. During this time, she was using drugs and the trafficker raped her on several occasions.

She made friends with one of the other girls, Zola, who also was exploited by the trafficker. One particular day, the trafficker made a call and the girls heard him discussing money. The girls were given some money to go away and buy themselves something nice. The girls became suspicious and started talking about running away. They were overheard, though, and as a punishment, they were locked in the flat where they lived. During that time they were given no food, but copious amounts of drugs.

At the end of the week, trafficker number five arrived at the flat, gave the girls new clothes and new phones and took them to the bus station, where he gave them round-trip tickets to Bloemfontein, the largest city in the Free State, in the center of South Africa. The girls were told that it would be nice there, that there wouldn't be any drugs, that they would not have to work on the streets anymore, and that they would be taken care of. When the girls arrived in Bloemfontein the return half of the ticket was destroyed and they were taken to trafficker number six.

The girls were forced to work on the streets. The trafficker told them that he had paid a lot of money for their new clothes and shoes and cell phones and that now they had to pay him back. The trafficker told them that it was their job to make him rich. This trafficker wanted to advertise Elsie's "services" in the newspaper and wanted her to work in strip shows. She refused and was beaten so badly she could not walk or wash herself for a week. The trafficker refused to take her to a hospital because he was afraid she would disclose her situation. Eventually it was arranged for a doctor to come to Elsie, and she survived. The doctor never reported her abuse to anyone.

Zola then fell in love with their trafficker, which upset Elsie very much. Because of this Elsie decided to report what was going on to the police. The police used her information to raid the place where the girls were held, but then simply gave Elsie a bus ticket back to the Eastern Cape, without involving social services in either Bloemfontein or the Eastern Cape. On returning to the Eastern Cape, Elsie moved in with trafficker number seven.

As with all the other traffickers, Elsie was forced to bring back a certain amount of money on a nightly basis or face the brutal consequences. One night Elsie got into a car with a john who took her out of town, and when they parked off the road, the john became violent. Elsie, desperate to escape from the car, managed to climb into the backseat of the car. When she fell onto the backseat, a blanket covered it, but she could feel that there was something underneath it. She drew back the blanket and discovered the body of a dead child. Frightened by the discovery, she flew out of the car and ran toward the road without looking where she was going. She ran onto the road and was hit by a bus. It was this that saved her. She was taken to the hospital, and there she told her story of the last three years of her life.

↩

Trafficking in human beings has been referred to as the twenty-first century's slavery. It has been asserted that such slavery is more common now than during the Roman Empire or the transatlantic slave trade.[1] While trafficking is an ancient practice, it is also a contemporary one, and one to which South Africa is now responding.[2] This chapter explores the current changes to South African legislation on trafficking, as well as the proposed Prevention and Combating of Trafficking in Persons Bill, first tabled in Parliament in 2010. It will conclude with the aftermath of the case study discussed above, which may highlight some of the challenges still facing both the victims of this crime and those who work to prevent and prosecute it.

RESEARCH ON CONTEMPORARY SOUTH AFRICAN TRAFFICKING PRACTICES

Recent research on trafficking in children in South Africa has been primarily carried out by three different organizations: Molo Songololo (Molo), the International Organization on Migration (IOM), and UNICEF. Molo Songololo, an NGO in Cape Town that works with sexually exploited youth, published the first study in 2000. It dealt specifically with trafficking in children for purposes of sexual exploitation in South Africa. The study reported that there are between twenty-eight and thirty-eight thousand prostituted children in South Africa. It also reported that children comprised 25 percent of the prostituted population in Cape Town. It found that parents, particularly mothers, are among the primary traffickers in children, and noted the close relationship between intrafamilial sexual abuse and exploitation.

In 2003 both UNICEF and the International Organization on Migration published studies on trafficking. The IOM study focused on trafficking in women and children for sexual exploitation in southern Africa and found that within that region, South Africa is a main destination.[3] The victims, both children and adults, are recruited by coercion, force, or deception, most often concerning employment, marriage, and education. Tellingly, it found that victims are afraid of law enforcement and do not trust the police to assist. It also found trafficking in women and children for sexual exploitation to be a significant problem in southern Africa.

The IOM study focused, in part, on child trafficking from Lesotho to the eastern Free State of South Africa. It found that the child victims were both male and female, with half the children abducted and half deceived. Major sources of vulnerability included physical and sexual abuse at home and the death of one or both parents from AIDS. It found that the abuse of these victims was not necessarily about sex or money but about power and control, and the desire to humiliate, punish, and exploit.

The UNICEF study dealt with trafficking throughout Africa and identified South Africa as a country of destination, transit, and origin for victims, as well as having trafficking within its borders.[4] It found that trafficking is a recognized problem in approximately half the countries in Africa, with children trafficked at twice the rate of women. Later studies of global patterns of trafficking confirmed that in Africa children make up the largest group of trafficking victims—almost 60 percent of all reported trafficking.[5] The UNICEF study found that not only might victims be sought out by traffickers, they might also seek out traffickers, in hopes of securing a better life elsewhere.

A 2008 IOM study on internal trafficking within South Africa set out to identify patterns and make recommendations.[6] The study found that victims were recruited from rural areas or informal settlements and transported to the urban centers of Johannesburg, Pretoria, Cape Town, Bloemfontein, and Durban. Most were black or Coloured and under the age of thirty. Adolescent girls and young women who leave exploitative situations as domestic servants are vulnerable to recruitment into the sex industry. With respect to commercial sexual exploitation, women were just as likely as men to be recruiters, and boys under the age of eighteen are increasingly lured into sexual exploitation, frequently for use in pornography.

The dynamics of recruitment were also examined. The report noted that West African organized crime syndicates operate heavily in Pretoria, Port Elizabeth, Johannesburg, and Bloemfontein and these syndicates traffic local black South African females into commercial sexual exploitation. Organized-crime syndicates operated by foreign nationals use local South Africans as recruiters. Men and boys are recruited to work on farms under false promises of pay and suitable accommodation. Boys who are not in school or are on school holiday are more frequently targeted. Finally, the study found that children who are most vulnerable to recruitment for trafficking are child-headed households due to losses from HIV and AIDS, unregistered children, and children living in impoverished rural areas and informal settlements

In 2010, partly as a prelude to the FIFA World Cup, the Human Sciences Research Council published the first baseline assessment of trafficking in South Africa.[7] Commissioned by the National Prosecuting Authority, among its key findings were: that there is no clear understanding of the scale of the problem; that there were identified "trafficking streams," or patterns of movement; that victims were primarily women; that there were many types of exploitation, including trafficking for prostitution, pornography, forced marriage, domestic servitude, forced labor, begging, and criminal activity, including drug trafficking. Child-sex tourism was also noted, with Cape Town, Durban, Johannesburg, and Port Elizabeth believed to be primary destinations for underage sex tourism, involving children between ten and fourteen years of age. Other findings included profiling of who the traffickers were and how trafficking was linked to other illicit activities, such as narcotics trafficking. The report also addressed enabling factors, vulnerabilities, and cultural practices that might

be implicated. Finally, challenges to both victim assistance services and fu
research projects were explored. The HSRC observed that the primary va
of this report was to assess available information on human trafficking, to identify gaps in knowledge of the practice, and to suggest ways in which knowledge
and understanding can be improved. Much of the data gathered supports the
findings of previous studies.

In response to the HSRC study, the Institute for Security Studies identified
two fundamental problems with the report. First, the HSRC report provided
little information on its methodology or on the accuracy of its data. Second,
within a context of increasing xenophobia, the report presented trafficking as
a well-organized activity run by outside criminal groups. The ISS condemned
the report as "scare mongering" and as thereby preventing a more thorough
and meaningful discussion about trafficking in South Africa.[8]

In 2010 an additional study on trafficking in persons and smuggling of
migrants was commissioned by the UN Office on Drugs and Crime, with a
focus on the role of criminal organizations in these crimes. With a land border
of 4,862 kilometers, which it shares with six neighboring countries, its ten
international airports, and eight international seaports, coupled with excellent
regional and international flight connections, organized criminal networks
use South Africa as an important transit route and embarkation point when
trafficking persons or smuggling migrants from southern Africa to countries
around the world. South Africa is also a country of final destination for countless smuggled migrants and trafficked persons from the region and beyond.

With the research surrounding trafficking as a backdrop, this chapter will
now provide a critique of legislation on trafficking. This overview comple-
ments Liza Buchbinder's discussion of Nigeria and Togo (chapter 11, this volume), and Allain's discussion of international legislative responses (chapter 7).

SOUTH AFRICAN ANTITRAFFICKING LEGISLATION

Three major pieces of legislation are present in South Africa that concern
trafficking: the Children's Act of 2005, the Sexual Offences Act of 2007,[9] and
the Prevention and Combating of Trafficking in Persons Bill, tabled in Parliament in 2010.

The Children's Act, 2005

The Children's Act addresses trafficking in children as part of its larger focus,
both civil and criminal, on child welfare law generally. The act's overarching
purpose is to consolidate the currently fragmented child welfare law in South
Africa. The stated purpose of the trafficking chapter of this bill is to give effect
to the UN Protocol to Prevent Trafficking in Persons and generally to combat
trafficking in children.[10]

In relation to children, the act states that trafficking

> (a) means the recruitment, sale, supply, transportation, transfer, harbouring or receipt of children, within or across the borders of the Republic — (i) by any means including the use of threat force, or other forms of coercion, abduction, fraud, deception, abuse of power or the giving or receiving of payments or benefits to achieve the consent of a person having control over the child; or (ii) due to a position of vulnerability, for the purpose of exploitation; and
> (b) includes the adoption of a child facilitated or secured through illegal means.

This act specifically prohibits any person, natural or juristic, or a partnership to traffic a child or to allow a child to be trafficked.[11] It further prohibits the defenses of consent of the child or those in loco parentis, or both, as well as failure to complete the underlying criminal act (e.g., sexual exploitation, labor exploitation, or illegal adoption).[12] Behavior facilitating trafficking in children is also prohibited.[13] The sanctions provided in the act call for imprisonment not exceeding twenty years, a fine, or both.[14]

Though limited by its very mandate to protect children only, the Children's Act has many positive attributes. The definition of *trafficking* in relation to children is substantially based on the 2000 Palermo Protocol definition and criminalizes conduct, such as facilitation, related to the crime. In keeping with the South African constitution and international instruments to which South Africa is signatory, the act defines *child* as any person under the age of eighteen. The inclusion of the phrase "by any means including" in the definition of *how* the trafficking of the child is achieved, serves two purposes: first, it underscores that illicit means (fraud or coercion) are not required for trafficking when the offense involves a child; second, it allows for inclusion of new means into the existing definition, should new means come to light.

The act completely rejects consent as a defense for child trafficking, whether given by the child or the person having control over the child. This provision emphasizes that neither a child, nor parent or guardian can consent to the child's abuse or exploitation. This is particularly important in cases where the parent, guardian, or other person having "control" over the child is involved in the trafficking or exploitation of the child. Furthermore, the act includes the words "child labour" and "removal of body parts" (as opposed to only organs) in the definition of *exploitation*. It also specifically defines "practices similar to slavery" as including debt bondage and forced marriage.

Substantively, a major shortcoming of the act is that there is no prevention provision whatsoever. In contrast to international human rights provisions, the act does not prohibit the prosecution of the child victim of trafficking should that victim have engaged in criminal activity as a trafficked person. Moreover, the provision fails anywhere to provide for either education and consciousness-raising, or strategies and programs for eliminating the causes and risk factors in this crime.

Victim services are overwhelmingly dedicated to issues of repatriation of victim children to their country of origin. In the case of South African children found abroad, the provision is also made for their referral to a dedicated social worker for investigation. Immigration officials, police officials, social workers, social service professionals, medical practitioners and registered nurses are required to report a child victim of trafficking. They must refer that child to a designated social worker for investigation. There is, however, no requirement for anyone else to report such a trafficked child.

The act also provides mechanisms for the child to remain in South Africa if it is not in the child's best interest to return to their country of citizenship. This decision is made in conjunction with the availability of care arrangements in the country to which the child is to be returned, the safety of the child in the country to which the child is to be returned, and the possibility that the child might be trafficked again, harmed, or killed. The act also provides for the application of the child for asylum under the South African Refugees Act of 1998.

Though prescribing many victim services, without a long-term reintegration process, including psychological or medical assistance, the unique needs of trafficked children cannot be properly met. By failing to have measures in place to identify trafficked children as victims of crime, and to preclude their being charged with any offenses they may have committed as a result of being trafficked, this act does not afford the full protection of trafficked children that it sets out to do, as mandated by the UN Convention on the Rights of the Child.

The Sexual Offences Act, 2007

The Sexual Offences Act came into force in December 2007 and amended the Sexual Offences Act of 1957. The 2007 act clearly states that its provisions dealing with trafficking are transitional until other legislation is passed, meaning the Prevention and Combating of Trafficking in Persons Bill. The Sexual Offences Act is limited by the substance of its subject matter to criminalizing only trafficking for purposes of sexual exploitation or abuse. Its definition of trafficking, more expansive than that of the Palermo Protocol, includes

> the supply, recruitment, procurement, capture, removal, transportation, transfer, harbouring, sale, disposal or receiving of a person, within or across the borders of the Republic, by means of—(i) a threat of harm; (ii) the threat or use of force, intimidation or other forms of

coercion; *(iii)* abduction; *(iv)* fraud; *(v)* deception or false pretences; *(vi)* the abuse of power or of a position of vulnerability, to the extent that the complainant is inhibited from indicating his or her unwillingness or resistance to being trafficked, or unwillingness to participate in such an act; or *(vii)* the giving or receiving of payments, compensation, rewards, benefits or any other advantage, for the purpose of any form or manner of exploitation, grooming or abuse of a sexual nature of such person, including the commission of any sexual offence or any offence of a sexual nature in any other law against such person or performing any sexual act with such person, whether committed in or outside the borders of the Republic.[15]

The Sexual Offences Act specifically criminalizes trafficking for sexual purposes: "A person ('A') who traffics any person ('B'), without the consent of B, is guilty of the offence of trafficking in persons for sexual purposes."[16] This crime carries up to life imprisonment.[17] The act goes on to state:

A person who—*(a)* orders, commands, organises, supervises, controls or directs trafficking; *(b)* performs any act which is aimed at committing, causing, bringing about, encouraging, promoting, contributing towards or participating in trafficking; or *(c)* incites, instigates, commands, aids, advises, recruits, encourages or procures any other person to commit, cause, bring about, promote, perform, contribute towards or participate in trafficking, is guilty of an offence of involvement in trafficking in persons for sexual purposes.[18]

Consent is defined as a voluntary or uncoerced agreement. Lack of consent is defined as including, but not being limited to the following circumstances: "*(a)* where B submits or is subjected to such an act as a result of any one or more of the means or circumstances contemplated in subparagraphs (i) to (vii) of the definition of trafficking having been used or being present; or *(b)* where B is incapable in law of appreciating the nature of the act, including where B is, at the time of the commission of such act—(i) asleep; (ii) unconscious; (iii) in an altered state of consciousness, including under the influence of any medicine, drug, alcohol or other substance, to the extent that B's consciousness or judgement is adversely affected; (iv) a child below the age of 12 years; or (v) a person who is mentally disabled."[19] A person who has been trafficked is not liable to stand trial for any criminal offence, including any migration-related offense, which was committed as a direct result of being trafficked.

While the act does adequately cover the crime of trafficking for sexual purposes, it fails to provide either specific assistance to victims of trafficking or prevention initiatives. Additionally, by assigning different protection to children under the age of twelve than to all children under eighteen, it leaves a gaping chasm for disparate treatment of exploitation victims between the ages of twelve and eighteen. The act categorically states that children under twelve years cannot consent to trafficking. By implication then, those between twelve and eighteen can. This not only fails to afford equal protection to all children but fails to recognize both the Palermo Protocol's and the South African constitution's definition of children as those under eighteen years of age. Teenagers are as vulnerable as younger children to exploitation by adults abusing positions of power over them. In artificially dividing the younger children, who are "deserving" of absolute protection, from the older "undeserving" children, it reinforces a cultural bias against adolescent victims of sex crimes and exploitation and undermines the principle that children can neither legally nor genuinely consent to their own violation.[20]

The Combating and Prevention of Trafficking in Persons Bill

This bill was first tabled in Parliament in 2010 and defines trafficking as including

> the delivery, recruitment, procurement, capture, removal, transportation, transfer, harbouring, sale, exchange, lease, disposal or receiving of a person, or the adoption of a child facilitated or secured through legal or illegal means, within or across the borders of the Republic, of a person trafficked or an immediate family member of the person trafficked, by means of—(a) a threat of harm; (b) the threat or use of force, intimidation or other forms of coercion; (c) the abuse of vulnerability; (d) fraud; (e) deception or false pretences; (f) debt bondage; (g) abduction; (h) kidnapping; (i) the abuse of power; (j) the giving or receiving of payments or benefits to obtain the consent of a person having control or authority over another person; or (k) the giving or receiving of payments, compensation, rewards, benefits or any other advantage, for the purpose of any form or manner of exploitation, sexual grooming or abuse of such person, including the commission of any sexual offence or any offence of a sexual nature in any other law against such person or performing any sexual act with such person, whether committed in or outside the borders of the Republic.[21]

The draft bill has a prevention component, insofar as it provides for mechanisms to inform and educate persons at risk of becoming victims of trafficking, as well as informing and educating victims of trafficking on their rights. It also calls for state action to discourage the demand that fosters the exploitation of victims of trafficking, especially women and children, though it does not identify the cause or causes of such demand.[22]

The bill specifically criminalizes trafficking and involvement in trafficking. It targets those using the services of a victim of trafficking. It affords a more detailed definition of trafficking than the Palermo Protocol, including circumstances such as debt bondage and the destruction or concealment of identification or travel documentation in its coverage. It provides sanctions of up to life imprisonment or a fine or both for trafficking, and allows for up to fifteen years for using the services of a victim.

Chapter four of the bill provides an array of victim identification and protection services, including immunity from prosecution. The bill mandates comprehensive reporting and referral of suspected child victims to the police and provides for good-faith immunity in cases of incorrect reporting and confidentiality of the identification of the reporter. Professionals are mandated to report suspected adult trafficking victims, though generally such reports require the victim's consent. All other persons may report their suspicions to the police. Child victims must be referred to social workers and all victims must be provided health care services. The draft bill is a major statement on the rights of trafficked children and affords them a range of protections. The bill provides protection from prosecution for child victims even if they contravene the Immigration Act, assist another person in contravening that act, possess fabricated or false documents, or were compelled to be involved in criminal acts as a condition of being victims of trafficking.[23] Chapter five deals with foreign victims and provides for a recovery and reflection period of ninety days. If after thirty days the victim is unwilling to assist in the investigation, an enquiry must begin relative to the potential return of the victim to his or her country of origin.

The legal status of the victim is specifically dealt with, suspending any summary deportation of a victim. Though the victim is accorded the same right to medical treatment as citizens, there is no provision for any specialized treatment for children, in stark contrast to the providing of entire centers for adult victims. Finally, the repatriation of victims is addressed, making provision for ascertaining whether the victim, child or adult, will be safe and cared for if returned to his or her country of origin, as well as if the victim is returned to an area within South Africa from where he or she has been trafficked.

PROTECTION, PREVENTION, AND PROSECUTION

The Prevention and Combating of Trafficking in Persons Bill has many strong points, including a targeted approach to education and awareness raising, as well as the dissemination of general information regarding trafficking in persons. Additionally, all information and prevention campaigns are to be in the languages used by the audience, all campaigns are to be targeted not simply at large population cities but also at the rural communities, and all measures are to be reviewed periodically for effectiveness. By including a monitoring and evaluation component in the legislation, allowances are incorporated for improving programs that might not be best serving the public.

The bill criminalizes trafficking, attempted trafficking, accomplice liability, conduct facilitating trafficking and organizing or directing others to commit trafficking—thereby fulfilling the requirements set out in Palermo. Consent is eradicated as a defense when children are the victims. The bill also directly addresses aggravating factors that must be considered at sentencing:

> (a) the significance of the role of the convicted person in the trafficking process; (b) previous convictions relating to the crime of trafficking in persons; (c) whether the convicted person caused the victim to become addicted to the use of a dependence-producing substance; (d) the conditions in which the victim was kept; (e) whether the victim was held captive for any period; (f) whether the victim suffered abuse and the physical and psychological effects the abuse had on the victim; (g) whether the offence formed part of organized crime; and (h) whether the victim was a child.[24]

This bill is a vast improvement, but it fails to require specialized personnel with specialized training to prosecute the crime of trafficking. The value of such expertise cannot be overstated. While recognizing that not all jurisdictions, particularly rural ones, will not be able to support personnel exclusively dedicated to pursuing traffickers, nevertheless, the need for specialist training in this newly recognized form of gender-based violence and child abuse is beyond question and has been recommended by NGOs worldwide.[25] Trafficking has unique crime dynamics and victim needs. These must be understood and responded to in a tailored fashion. Such improvements will allow for better investigation and more successful prosecution and adjudication and will lessen secondary trauma to the victims of trafficking, such as is often encountered where the victims are interviewed by those without specific forensic and/or sensitivity training.

However, by failing to acknowledge and detail the causes of trafficking, particularly trafficking in women and children, the bill fails to provide an all-encompassing plan for discouraging the demand for trafficking victims. By ignoring the part that systemic misogyny and patriarchal culture play in this crime, and in all crimes of violence against women and children, it misses a decisive opportunity to bring a crucial dynamic behind this crime into the open.

Finally, there is a disquieting disparity between the sanctions prescribed for those who supply the trafficking victim and the ultimate consumer of this criminal activity, those who use the services of the victim. The maximum punishment prescribed for those who intentionally and unlawfully benefit, financially or otherwise, from the services of a victim is fifteen years in prison, as opposed to a potential life sentence for others in the chain of trafficking. This disparity violates the principle of equal treatment for those supplying the trafficking victim and those using that same victim. Both supply and demand must be eradicated, with punishment meted out on both sides of the exploitation equation with equal severity.

Protection measures include the referral of a child victim to a designated social worker. If the victim is an illegal foreign child and is brought before the children's court, the court may order that the child be assisted in applying for asylum. A finding that an illegal foreign child who is a victim of trafficking is a child in need of care and protection serves as authorization for allowing the child to remain in the republic for the duration of the children's court order. Criminal prosecution of a victim of trafficking is prohibited for

> (a) entering or remaining in the Republic in contravention of the Immigration Act; (b) assisting another person to enter or remain in the Republic in contravention of the Immigration Act; (c) possessing any fabricated or falsified passport, identity document or other document used for the facilitation of movement across borders; or (d) being involved in an illegal activity to the extent that he or she has been compelled to do so, as a direct result of his or her situation as a victim of trafficking.

Foreign victims are provided a mandatory ninety-day nonrenewable period of recovery and reflection. If after thirty days the victim is unwilling to cooperate with law enforcement and prosecuting authorities in the investigation of and the prosecution of a trafficker, an investigation to determine whether it is safe to return the victim to the country of origin or the country from where he or she has been trafficked should begin. The granting of a nonrenewable recovery and reflection period does not depend on the willingness of a victim of trafficking to cooperate with law enforcement and prosecuting authorities. Temporary residence may be granted if the victim has agreed to help law enforcement or if it is not safe for the victim to return to their country of origin or country from which they have been trafficked. If granted temporary residence, the victim may conduct work or study in South Africa. The victim of trafficking is entitled to apply for a permanent residence permit after five years' continuous residence in the republic, upon proof that he or she may be harmed, killed, or trafficked again if he or she is returned to his or her country of origin. The return of an internal trafficking victim to his or her place of origin within the country is governed by the same principles.

The bill also addresses deportation and repatriation of victims. Victims of trafficking may not be summarily deported. An adult repatriation cannot occur without considering the safety of the person during the repatriation process; the safety of the person in the country to which the person is to be returned; and the possibility that the person might be harmed, killed, or trafficked again. Before repatriating a child, consideration must be given to the best interests of the child; safety of the child during repatriation; the availability and suitability of care arrangements and the safety of the child in the country to which the child is to be returned; and the possibility that the child might be harmed, killed, or trafficked again. Reasonable steps must be taken to find suitable family members or an institution or organization that renders assistance to victims of trafficking in the country to which a person is to be returned and that is willing to provide assistance to such a person. Finally, repatriation of a South African victim requires the assessment of the risks to the safety and life of a victim if he or she is returned to the republic and to facilitate the victim's return. Child victims entering the republic must be referred to a designated social worker for investigation, and an adult victim must be referred to an accredited organization or provincial department of social development for an assessment.

While the bill provides an impressive array of services, there is room for further improvement. For example, while extensive adult services are envisioned, there is no parallel for services to child victims. Here again, there are disparities among victim services, and children will need specialized assistance with their journey through the rehabilitation and reintegration process, as the case of Elsie demonstrates.

While investigators and prosecutors now have some legislative weapons in their arsenal, until a comprehensive antitrafficking law is enacted and implemented, the frontline criminal justice professionals are working without all the resources needed to deal most effectively with this crime. Comprehensive trafficking legislation, as well as concordant training for those who will implement it, is key to more effectively combating trafficking. Budgetary support and coordination between police, prosecution, and social services is also critical to effective implementation. The National Prosecuting Authority (NPA) and the Association of Regional Magistrates of South Africa (ARMSA) have already begun trainings on the trafficking components within the Children's Act and the Sexual Offences Act. Specialized units within prosecution and investigation have also begun to deal with these cases, staffed by personnel who have received specific education and training on trafficking and in working with its victims.

Better victim services within such legislation will assist in investigation and prosecution, as currently many cases fail to be prosecuted due to victims either being intimidated into silence or being generally fearful of the criminal justice system. While the NPA does have a Witness Protection Programme, it will need to be tailored to meet the specific needs of trafficking victims. Through the Court Preparation Programme, which NPA has recently implemented, the victims of trafficking should receive additional support in understanding the criminal justice process and preparing for trial. Psychosocial support for victims may also assist them in feeling empowered and capable of facing the trafficker in court. By providing better support and protection to victims, the prosecution of offenders will also be strengthened through improved victim participation in the investigation and trial process.

THE AFTERMATH OF ELSIE'S EXPLOITATION

Elsie has been impacted by the trauma of being trafficked. She has low self-esteem and self-mutilation issues and has attempted suicide. She has scars over her entire body; many are self-inflicted. In interviews she says:

> I am confused. Sometimes I think to kill myself. I am lost. I call myself useless. I am foolish. I see a child with a mother and father and I cry and cut myself. . . . Sometimes I try to kill myself. I cut myself. I tried to hang myself. I take tablets. . . . I wanted to kill myself. I feel sad. It feels like I must die not to think about it. Seeing people dying, full of blood. Just to stop thinking about it. I see that woman dying. I can't stop thinking. When I cut myself, I don't feel pain. I just want to die. Then I will rest.

She also has to deal with her feelings of violation at the hands of the johns: "I didn't enjoy going with clients. I 'went away' when I was with them. I just did it. I forced myself to do it." Her ability to trust others has also been seriously damaged. Every time she went to a new trafficker she believed, with a child's naïveté, that he would treat her better and everything would be good. She cannot remember the number of times she was raped by clients, but she can remember in detail every time she was raped by one of the traffickers.

Her sense of who she is has also been compromised by what happened to her: "I want to play with other children. But not children like me—real children. I want to be a different person." Elsie suffers from both insomnia and nightmares: "I dream about it. It's like someone comes and chokes me. I can't take it anymore. Inside I am scared. It's like all the people are talking in my ears. It's bad dreams. . . . I don't sleep in the night. When I put my head down and close my eyes, I see all these things. Sometimes I wee in my bed when I am scared." Elsie also experiences flashbacks, depression, and fear of being found by the traffickers. Her having no family exacerbates these feelings: "I don't want to sit down doing nothing. I hear all the girls screaming, being beaten. I hear my voice. When I close my eyes, I hear all those things. I get scared. . . . I'm lonely. I don't have anybody. I'm lonely. . . . Sometimes I think they [the traffickers] will catch me. I'm crying, crying. My heart is sore. . . . I can't go out and play with other children. I'm scared. I close my eyes and I see them [the traffickers] doing bad things to me. . . . I can't even go to the toilet. I'm scared. I put a bucket in my room."

Elsie, like many children who have been horribly exploited and abused, remains surprisingly resilient. While it is easy to see that much trauma was inflicted on her during her trafficking, Elsie refuses to be destroyed by events. When asked what she wants to do with the rest of her life, she says, "I want to go back to school and be a social worker. I will give all the children who did bad things hugs so that I can help them. I think I am the key." She has also chosen a birth date for herself.

⤙

While additional protection is now in place in the form of enacted and pending legislation specifically dealing with trafficking in South Africa, many of the gaps in the system that allowed Elsie to be trafficked remain. The protection often afforded by a functional adult-headed family is still sorely missing in many cases. Mandatory referral mechanisms from police to social services will have to be effectively implemented to keep cases like Elsie's from falling through the cracks. In a country that is economically underresourced and has a large number of orphans and child-headed households, the safety of all children is far from certain.

While large numbers of police and other criminal justice professionals have now received some training and education on trafficking, as well as best practices on how to deal with trafficking and its victims when they are uncovered, many remain without the necessary knowledge to best combat this crime. Finally, until more resources are allotted to both prevention of trafficking as well as survivor rehabilitation and reintegration programs, the most complete effort to eradicate trafficking has yet to be realized.

NOTES
Abbreviation

SOA   Sexual Offences Act

This case study is based on the experiences of one female child, a victim of trafficking. None of the names in this study are real. The interviews used as the basis for this case study were conducted by forensic interviewers, social workers, and professionals with The Institute for Child Witness Research and Training to whom the author is indebted for their invaluable contribution to this chapter.

1. Rika Snyman, "Victims of Human Trafficking," in *Victimology in South Africa*, ed. Linda Davis and Snyman (Pretoria: Van Schaik, 2005), 282, citing I. Burrell, *Slavery Still Common in the 21st Century* (2000).

2. For recent scholarship and media portrayals, see Zosa de Sas Kropiwnicki, "Strategic Agents: Adolescent Prostitutes in Cape Town, South Africa," in *Child*

Slaves in the Modern World, ed. Gwyn Campbell, Suzanne Miers, and Joseph C. Miller (Athens: Ohio University Press, 2011), 221–37.

3. Jonathan Martens, Maciej Pieczkowski, and Bernadette van Vuuren-Smyth, *Seduction, Sale and Slavery: Trafficking in Women and Children for Sexual Exploitation in Southern Africa,* 3rd ed. (Pretoria: IOM, 2003).

4. UNICEF, *Trafficking in Human Beings, Especially Women and Children, in Africa* (Florence: Innocenti Research Centre, 2003), 10–25.

5. Kristiina Kangaspunta, United Nations Office on Drugs and Crime, *Trafficking in Persons: Global Patterns* (Vienna: UNODC, 2006).

6. Laura G. Bermúdez, *"No Experience Necessary": The Internal Trafficking of Persons in South Africa* (Pretoria: IOM, 2008).

7. Carol Allais et al., *Tsireledzani: Understanding the Dimensions of Human Trafficking in Southern Africa* (Pretoria: NPA, 2010).

8. Chandre Gould, Marlise Richter, and Ingrid Palmery, *Of Nigerians, Albinos, Satanists and Anecdotes: A Critical Review of the HSRC Report on Human Trafficking* (Pretoria: Institute for Security Studies, 2010).

9. The Criminal Law (Sexual Offences and Related Matters) Amendment Act, no. 32 of 2007.

10. Republic of South Africa, Children's Act, no. 38/2005, §1.

11. Ibid., §284(1).

12. Ibid., §284(2).

13. Ibid., §285.

14. Ibid., §305(8).

15. Republic of South Africa, Criminal Law (Sexual Offences and Related Matters) Amendment Act no. 32/2007, §70(2)(b) (hereafter SOA).

16. SOA, §71(1).

17. Republic of South Africa, Criminal Law Amendment Act 105 of 1997, schedule 2, pt. 1.

18. SOA, §71(2).

19. SOA, §71(4).

20. Kenneth V. Lanning, "Compliant Child Victims: Confronting an Uncomfortable Reality," *APSAC Advisor* 14, no. 2 (2002): 7.

21. Republic of South Africa, Prevention and Combating of Trafficking in Persons Bill, 2010 (hereafter Draft Bill).

22. Bridget Anderson and Julia O'Connell Davidson), *Is Trafficking in Human Beings Demand Driven?* Migration Research Series, no. 15 (Geneva: IOM, 2003).

23. Draft Bill, cl. 16.

24. Ibid., cl. 11

25. Anderson and O'Connell, *Trafficking in Human Beings;* American Bar Association/Central and East European Law Initiative, *An Introduction to the Human Trafficking Assessment Tool* (Washington, DC: ABA/CEELI, 2005); International Association of Prosecutors' Model Guidelines of the Effective Prosecution of Crimes against Children (1999).

11 ⤳ Ranking States

Tracking the State Effect in West African
Antitrafficking Campaigns

LIZA STUART BUCHBINDER

THIRTY YEARS after human trafficking reemerged as an international policy agenda and a decade after the Palermo Protocol defined trafficking as a crime, a surge in reports of trafficking in West Africa has given rise to an antitrafficking industry. Well into this global "war against trafficking," the debate continues among policymakers and scholars about best practices.[1] Two West African antitrafficking umbrella organizations, Réseau de Lutte contre la Traite des Enfants au Togo (RELUTET) in Togo and the National Agency for the Prohibition of Traffic in Persons and Other Related Matters (NAPTIP) in Nigeria, provide a lens through which we can analyze the national campaigns of these two countries to eradicate child trafficking.[2] Their respective approaches reflect a constellation of local, regional, and global factors, specific to each nation, including preexisting security apparatuses, power relations with donor governments, and the individual actions of influential political figures. As an abstraction, the techniques of governance involved in antitrafficking practice contribute to a particular rendering of the state that is distinct from "the material world of society" akin to a process Timothy Mitchell describes as the "state effect."[3] In the case of antitrafficking, the implications of such an effect touches on international relations and development aid as the US Department of State (USDOS)—which spearheads the global campaign—ranks 184 countries based on their compliance with the "minimum standards" set forth in the US Victims of Trafficking and Violence Protection Act (VTVPA) of 2000.

Although the category of trafficking encompasses numerous variations, this chapter draws on data specific to the campaign against child trafficking in Togo and between Togo and Nigeria. While the migration of children between these two countries lends itself to a regional approach (e.g., national governments addressing the movement of Togolese laborers into Nigeria as an interdependent phenomenon), these two countries offer two distinct modes of intervention. In addition to information from legal documents, newsletters, and pamphlets, the present study was also based on forty-two interviews carried out in 2004 and 2009 that focused on the testimonies of representatives from antitrafficking NGOs, government agencies, and safe houses.[4]

The study shows that Nigeria's antitrafficking campaign is centralized, adopting a law-enforcement approach, with mandated reporting of all NGOs to NAPTIP—a federally legislated "multidimensional crime fighting agency."[5] In contrast, Togo's approach is centered on child development and harm reduction, with NGOs working towards prevention through long-term strategies, such as improved schooling opportunities and vocational training. RELUTET is not mandated to coordinate with the government. Instead, its mission is to promote the "development of children" by overseeing NGO efforts to fight "efficiently" against child slavery using strategies that do not aggressively pursue criminal convictions.[6]

These two intervention models also speak to qualities specific to what they call child trafficking as a human rights violation. In contrast to other human rights issues, such as the right to clean water or housing, child trafficking overtly encompasses both development and criminal justice. One strategy of deterrence seeks to improve the educational system and job opportunities to discourage out-migration, whereas another uses the strong arm of the law to apprehend and prosecute. The latter—a criminalizing approach—scrutinizes the legality of migration practices per international law and addresses impunity with an expanded enforcement apparatus, while also relying on statistics (which critics largely debunk as inaccurate) and sensationalized discourse to communicate the urgency of the epidemic.[7] As the object of intervention in a US-led global campaign against child trafficking, these micropractices of ritual and migration link to larger processes of state making. How this is accomplished, in part, stems from the effect of modern techniques of "arrangement, representation, and control" that contribute to a strong, concrete state abstracted from civil society.[8] As Mitchell argues, to truly understand the state one must abandon notions of a structured institution and look for the "powerful, metaphysical effect of practices arising from internally erected distinctions in both state and society."[9] Rather than abandon the state, as a generation of political scientists did in the 1970s, Mitchell suggests we shift our gaze toward the "techniques of organization and articulation" that create this rendering of the state.[10] Drawing on Michel Foucault, Mitchell also emphasizes the importance of attending to the "side effects" of the "effect."[11] He believes that the impact of unintended consequences warrants interrogation, regardless of the success or failure of various initiatives.

DIFFERENT APPROACHES TO THE
ERADICATION OF CHILD TRAFFICKING

Many of the calls for criminalization of trafficking have come from donor governments or private humanitarian organizations promoting a law enforcement paradigm.[12] The bible of the global campaign is the 2000 Palermo Protocol, which makes the criminalization of trafficking its central strategy of deterrence.[13] However, a few months before the passage of the UN protocol, the US Congress passed the VTVPA, which also uses a criminal justice framework. Despite being a domestic law, the VTVPA has global reach by allowing the US president to impose sanctions on noncompliant countries—a move that has drawn criticism for promoting US specific priorities under the pretense of UN sanctioned international norms of justice.[14] NGOs and human rights groups, such as Free the Slaves and Human Rights Watch, also emphasize the one-to-one relationship between the "cultures of impunity" of weak states and the unmitigated rise in trafficking, echoing the Department of Justice's stance that deterrence will be successful only through zero-tolerance laws and "aggressive enforcement efforts by the United States and its global partners."[15] This approach has sparked considerable controversy, with academics raising concerns about the efficacy of criminalization and the unintended consequences of policies that privilege a standardized human rights protocol over local knowledge and practice.[16] In contrast to criminalization, a child-centered approach against trafficking privileges the well-being of children over punishing traffickers.[17] While many argue that national campaigns can and should strike a balance between the two strategies, Togo's and Nigeria's campaigns tend toward one or the other camp. The child-centered approach, as practiced in Togo, focuses on protecting childhoods through village-level dialogues about the pitfalls of rural flight, through improved access to education, and through victims' social reintegration. It also recognizes underlying motivations on the part of victims who "choose" to leave their homes for work abroad.

Many Togolese children work in Nigeria to earn the accoutrements of marriage. While human rights groups describe an exchange of three years of service for wedding gifts as modern-day slavery, a child-centered approach contextualizes this exchange as a form of socialization emerging from long-standing fostering practices and a desire to reinforce kinship ties. Rights groups have largely debunked the socialization argument as inappropriate cultural relativism since minors, regardless of their intentions, cannot consent to exploitation.[18] While the practice of sending adolescent children outside the home to work remains deeply embedded in ritual, it has become increasingly motivated by profit and less bound by kinship obligations. Instead, adolescents enter the West African labor market with shifting conceptions of familial belonging and a desire for self-determination.[19] Rather than focus on the pursuit of traffickers, a child-centered response addresses the root causes of trafficking by addressing the "second-generation" social, economic, and cultural human rights. In practice, this involves preventive measures that substitute trafficking children for work with other incentives, such as vocational training or improved educational opportunities.[20]

This approach has also sparked considerable controversy. Legal scholars tied to government agencies tend toward a zero-tolerance enforcement approach, whereas anthropologist Jacqueline Berman and legal scholar Anne Gallagher argue that strategies emphasizing enforcement tend to reinforce state sovereignties at the expense of victims, and frequently conflate complex free-market migration practices with violent crimes against women and children.[21] Development economists Sylvain Dessy and Stéphane Pallage also caution against the law enforcement approach to combat child trafficking. While they support an outright ban in theory, they see eradication efforts as counterproductive in countries with corrupt or ineffective policing mechanisms.[22] Rather than reducing the number of child laborers, the increased enforcement efforts drive up profits and thus supply. In addition, harassment and extortion by authorities only exacerbate victims' suffering without addressing the larger structural forces that keep traffickers employed.

While there are distinct differences between the two country's campaigns, there are also significant commonalities that speak to a general trend in contemporary humanitarian advocacy that Benjamin Lawrance describes as "neo-abolitionism" (see chapter 8, this volume). In talking about neo-abolitionism, Lawrance speaks to the way in which antitrafficking campaigns in West Africa have become increasingly driven by statistics, personal narratives, and a sense of crisis. Both Togolese and Nigerian NGOs display these traits to varying degrees, and each country's NGO and IGO publications reflect this, as well as the research-based advocacy that is another key aspect of neo-abolitionism. While these points of commonality exist, there is an alternative explanation for the strategies of Nigeria's and Togo's antitrafficking campaigns; the production of statistics and sentiments of panic, for example, within the framework of criminalization, humanitarianism, and the state.

NIGERIA'S ANTITRAFFICKING CAMPAIGN

In the mid-1980s a growing trend of Edo State girls traveling to Italy to work as prostitutes caught the attention of Italian immigration officials and Nigerian development NGOs, a trend that parallels an earlier history of trafficking discussed by Carina Ray (chapter 5, this volume). Bisi Olateru Olagbegi, the executive director of the Women's Consortium of Nigeria, a grassroots women's organization, was involved early in the process and remembers the families' jubilation when their daughters left for Italy. "In the beginning, parents were happy that their daughters were leaving . . . everyone thought it was a good thing."[23] Yet pressure from Italian immigration authorities to stem the influx of Nigerian sex workers and rising international awareness of child trafficking as a human rights violation shifted the climate.[24]

During a 1997 pan-African conference in Uganda, Italy emerged as a new priority for the Nigerian human rights community and delegates designated the practice "trafficking"—a finding that was later confirmed by a 2001 UNICEF publication that reported twenty thousand Nigerian girls had been trafficked to Italy.[25] The first major step in the formation of Nigeria's campaign came with the government's ratification of the Palermo Protocol. Amina Titi Atiku Abubakar, the founder of the Women Trafficking and Child Labour Eradication Foundation (WOTCLEF) and the wife of the then vice president, was chosen to draft West Africa's first nationwide antitrafficking legislation.

Coming from a central figure of the antitrafficking community, Abubakar's story provides an important backdrop to the particularities of Nigeria's campaign. Before becoming Nigeria's second lady, Abubakar lectured at Kaduna Polytechnic in the Department of Catering and Hotel Management. She noticed that many of her female students would abandon school to travel to Italy. Initially, she assumed it was for religious pilgrimages to Rome, until she traveled to Italy and witnessed the number of Nigerians working as prostitutes. As she explains in her interview for NAPTIP's quarterly newsletter,

> Before I left Rome, I had a covenant with God that if one day, I am given the opportunity to help these victims who are the future mothers of the nation, I will not hesitate to do it. It happened that as soon as my husband was sworn in as the Vice President in 1999, I remembered the covenant I had with God and I said to myself, time has come for me to liberate these victims from the traffickers' bondage. I could no longer fold my hands and allow these children to wallow in bondage. The passion I had for these victims motivated me to start the fight.[26]

Mirroring the trope of human rights as religious salvation, Abubakar continued her personal crusade by galvanizing support among the nation's political elite.[27]

Abubakar's efforts culminated with the passage of the 2003 Trafficking in Persons (Prohibition) Law Enforcement and Administration Act, which created the National Agency for the Prohibition of Traffic in Persons and Other Related Matters (NAPTIP)—a "multidimensional crime fighting agency."[28] The law was dubbed the WOTCLEF law, in recognition of Abubakar's organization and its role in drafting. Carol Ndaguba, Nigeria's former director of public prosecution, was named NAPTIP's first executive secretary.

NAPTIP IN PRACTICE

Since NAPTIP's inauguration it has undergone significant changes. In particular, recommendations from a 2005 USAID assessment of Nigeria's anti-trafficking campaign set the tenor for the agency's present operations.[29] The report highlighted particular areas of weakness, including poor infrastructure, inadequate technology resources for monitoring, and poor coordination with the Nigeria Police Force and the Nigeria Immigration Service.[30] In addition, it faulted the federal government's decision to place NAPTIP under the authority of the Ministry of the Interior instead of the Ministry of Justice, where it would be better positioned to coordinate with the existing law enforcement agencies. The report emphasized that improvements in the agency's police work and criminal investigations took precedence over all other pursuits, including prevention.

Subsequent to the USAID assessment, NAPTIP has become Nigeria's ultimate antitrafficking authority and all other organizations, including WOTCLEF, fall under its jurisdiction. The primary groups funding NAPTIP include UNICEF, the United Nations Office on Drugs and Crime, the International Organization for Migration, the British High Commission, USAID, the American Bar Association, and the French and Swiss embassies. While providing critical financial support, these donors are careful to follow NAPTIP's lead and limit their engagement to consultancy. In one respect, this facilitates better cooperation among the various stakeholders and ensures that development "guests" recognize NAPTIP's authority. On the other hand, an unspoken requirement for registration has frustrated and stifled local Nigerian NGO workers.[31]

In addition to coordinating the activities of nongovernmental and bilateral aid organizations, NAPTIP also oversees all law enforcement agencies that police trafficking, including the national antitrafficking task force, the border patrols, the local police, and NAPTIP's own investigation and monitoring department. There had formerly been competition among the various agencies for possession of captured traffickers. However, a 2003 restructuring of reporting procedures across the departments has kept officers consistently cooperative in transferring traffickers to NAPTIP.

As an example of how Nigeria's antitrafficking efforts build on existing infrastructure, NAPTIP's centralized character operates through established tracks to coordinate all trafficking-related law enforcement. Those established tracks take the form of the Nigeria Police Force, which is the principal law enforcement organization in the country and "naturally positioned to intervene in issues of human trafficking."[32] The NPF has over 320,000 police. Former

President Olusegun Obasanjo promised to increase it by forty thousand personnel per year for five years.[33]

NAPTIP's mission is to "stamp out human trafficking and to liberate and uplift the vulnerable, especially women and children, from dehumanizing and exploitative employment and usage."[34] To accomplish its goal of eradication, the agency follows a multipronged approach with an emphasis on crime fighting. Echoing the USDOS model of "prevention, prosecution and protection," NAPTIP organizes its efforts around four Ps: prevention, public enlightenment, prosecution, and partnership.[35] While purporting to strike a balance between victim-centered and criminal justice approaches, thirteen of NAPTIP's fourteen responsibilities are law enforcement measures.

THE FACE OF NAPTIP

The practices accompanying a criminalization approach also facilitate ideological effects that create a diplomatic platform for relationship building at an international level. The federal government constructed a large complex in the capital, Abuja, to house the NAPTIP headquarters with meeting rooms for teleconferencing with partnering institutions. In line with USAID's recommendation for increased international cooperation, NAPTIP has also undertaken to communicate the federal government's political will, including memoranda of understanding with regional and international stakeholders, training antitrafficking task forces in Europe and Africa, and drafting protocols for large-scale, stadium-size public events.

Many of NAPTIP's activities focus on diplomacy, and the agency has successfully established relationships with law enforcement organizations from Chad to the Netherlands. Nigeria's specific strategy of criminalization further facilitates these diplomatic gestures since the micropractices of "crime fighting" (workshops, joint police trainings, interregional memoranda of understanding, and surveillance networks) demand a transcontinental network. Carol Ndaguba embodies this diplomatic role, with actions that emulate a secretary of state. During her five-year tenure, she attended state banquets, hosted international summits, spoke at interregional conferences, and accepted awards for her role.[36]

NAPTIP's infrastructure also consists of safe houses in Abuja and Lagos.[37] In contrast to the criminal justice aspect of the law, safe houses represent the law's softer side, which mandates the protection of trafficking victims, especially women and children. Residents' experiences are often publicized as a reminder of the campaign's targeted beneficiaries accompanied by statistics on the number of "saved" children. NAPTIP acquires these children through sting operations, hotline calls, and referrals from collaborating police officers. Yet, this nonspecific dragnet catches numerous other children who are not victims of trafficking. Instead, many suffer from parental neglect, abuse, and abandonment.[38]

Of the six children I interviewed at NAPTIP's Abuja safe house, four were girls from the ages of sixteen to nearly eighteen. All the girls had come from the same village in Togo and had traveled to Nigeria with their "uncle," an unrelated man from the village, who had placed them in separate homes to work as domestic servants. One month previously, NAPTIP's special investigative unit conducted a sting, arresting the uncle and placing the girls in the Abuja safe house for rehabilitation. All four wanted to return to their employers. The eldest, Marie, was worried because she had received a one-year pay advance from her employer and still owed four months of work. Another said she was wasting time learning to bead necklaces instead of earning money. Like Marie, her only request of me was to convince NAPTIP to liberate them. An eleven-year-old boy awaiting his mother seemed less anxious to leave. He came to NAPTIP when a woman found him wandering the streets of Abuja after sneaking into a small bus 480 kilometers away in a market in Port Harcourt. He said he ran away from his uncle's home in search of his mother, who had remarried after the boy's father died.[39]

WOTCLEF also operates a safe house in Abuja in collaboration with NAPTIP, and it was there that I came across my first clear-cut case of trafficking. Of the seven girls I interviewed, Mariama's story was the most harrowing. She was fourteen, and with unusual eloquence she recounted the horrific details of her uncle bringing her from Togo to hawk water in the streets of Libreville. Over a four-year period, he subjected her to repeated physical abuse and neglect, forcing her to sleep in the streets and scavenge for food in trash heaps. When she returned, he would frequently tie her down and beat her with kitchen pots for failing to earn enough money. Mariama said that many journalists for television and radio have interviewed her in the past. A quick search on the Internet revealed that Reuters, IRIN news, the BBC, and Nigeria's *Punch* newspaper had all profiled Mariama under different pseudonyms.[40]

While Mariama's case represents an unmistakable example of child trafficking and the abuse it entails, it also reveals the way in which publicists use narratives of suffering to further legitimatize campaign efforts and to disseminate in newsletters, newspapers, and television spots an image of the safe-house child as indisputable victim of trafficking. It also reinforces Lawrance's observations that a focus on personal narrative and "a fluid media-NGO relationship with respect to the circulation of knowledge" are defining characteristics of current trends in West African antitrafficking advocacy.[41] As a sanctuary for many and a holding cell for others, the safe house encompasses much that is murky about the category of trafficking in practice, as a number of forces, including a nonspecific legal net and a robust publicity industry, work to essentialize a diversity of scenarios under a single narrative.

TOGO'S ANTITRAFFICKING CAMPAIGN

In the case of Togo, the country's antitrafficking efforts follow a child-centered and ostensibly NGO-driven campaign, with the government's involvement largely limited to the drafting of legislation—in collaboration with UNICEF and the ILO—and sanctioning the efforts of "civil society."[42] The idea that Togo could be a source of trafficked children began with a World Association for Orphans-Afrique (WAO-Afrique) exploratory survey of thirty people in 1997. "Le trafic des enfants au Togo" concluded that Togolese were trafficking young girls, some as young as seven, to Nigeria, Ghana, and Gabon for domestic service.[43] While the data were not generalizable because of the small sample size, the report introduced the concept of trafficking to the Togolese development lexicon. Unlike Nigeria, where the campaign gained momentum through the personal quest of a politician's wife, Togo's initiative emerged from international pressure. In particular, there were a series of widely publicized trafficking incidents in the late 1990s and early 2000s that added evidence to Togo's fledgling humanitarian crisis—most notably when the Nigerian-registered ship, the *MV Etireno*, lay stranded off the coast of Benin, reportedly carrying hundreds of Togolese children headed toward Gabon.[44] Cléophas Mally of the WAO-Afrique recalls contacting the prime minister: "There was that boat off the shore of Benin and there were Togolese children in there . . . and I wrote to the prime minister and said that this was a problem and [asked] what will the government do to help these children?"[45]

Soon after, the attention from a 2003 Human Rights Watch report opened the floodgates for the subsequent workshops, public enlightenment events, and legislation that have come to characterize Togo's antitrafficking campaign. The Palermo Protocol recommended that humanitarian efforts be directed toward the eradication of *worst* forms of child labor. Thus, trafficking became an important distinction to validate that campaigns were addressing an intolerable labor practice.[46]

Until 2005 Togo had no antitrafficking law and used its Children's Code to pursue traffickers.[47] Despite concerted international pressure, the National Assembly was slow to pass a law. Outside observers attributed the stalemate to corruption, political wrangling, and the lack of state capacity.[48] The government's reluctance to pass a law, its poor record of prosecutions, and its general dependence on international NGOs and bilateral agencies contributed toward a reputation for being lax on trafficking.[49] Repeatedly USDOS reports stated that the government did not meet the VTVPA's "minimum standards."[50] While reports acknowledge Togo's "significant efforts" to support the campaign, they seem to scramble for evidence. For example, in the section on Togo's prevention measures, the 2009 report described President Faure Gnassingbé's presence in a "day-long program to promote the government's anti-trafficking strategy" as a central example of his work toward addressing trafficking.[51]

In contrast to the government's "minimal" but "significant" efforts, Togo runs a robust campaign through the country's small circle of NGOs, coordinated by RELUTET. RELUTET is an umbrella organization that began at a 2002 conference in Grand-Bassam, Côte d'Ivoire, where delegates called for the creation of a central coordinating body. At the time there was stifling competition among the local agencies, and RELUTET began actively coordinating the forty-four member agencies' antitrafficking efforts and presiding over a monthly assembly. At meetings delegates determined the general mission of the campaign. Major institutional players in attendance included Terre des Hommes, Plan Togo, CARE International, representatives from the Ministry of Social Affairs, as well as a long list of small NGOs that arose during Togo's era of "democracy."[52]

RELUTET's strategy "to support the development of the child" reflects a consensus among its forty-four members and the country's overarching approach, which advocates child protection while acknowledging the pressures on impoverished families.[53] In action, this translates into programs that emphasize public enlightenment, victim rights, and improving the overall environment of the child, including better funding for education, microcredit for parents, and public health measures to quell the motivations behind trafficking. In general, civil-society groups champion this approach, whereas criminal justice measures are relegated to the central government.

The mission statements of individual organizations reflect this sentiment. For example, Plan-Togo, one of the most entrenched agencies in Togo, operates in the Central Region, arguably an epicenter for child labor migrants leaving for Nigeria. Plan does not collaborate with the police. Instead, its motto is Promoting Child Rights to End Child Poverty. Terre des Hommes is also a central player. It runs the country's largest rehabilitation center for trafficked children, the Oasis Center, and uses the Convention on the Rights of the Child as its conceptual framework. CARE International has been working in Togo since 1986 and the US embassy chose it to manage a large anti–child trafficking grant. CARE's mission is to end child trafficking by "improving education and social support."[54] Thus, instead of a strong alliance or subordination to law enforcement, the Togolese NGOs universally focus on poverty alleviation.

The child-centered approach is also in line with the political economy of the campaign, where the central government and civil-society groups lack the resources necessary to adopt a prosecutorial approach. Following the "austerity measures" of four World Bank structural adjustment programs adopted by former president Gnassingbé Eyadéma, Togo experienced a sustained period of institutional collapse.[55] In addition, the repressive silencing of prodemocracy demonstrations in the early 1990s led to an exodus of foreign aid and an expansion of "civil-society" organizations. Much of RELUTET consists of mom-and-pop NGOs—small-scale operations in a specific region of the country. For example, only twenty-four of RELUTET's forty-four members have access to a vehicle and only sixteen have Internet connectivity.[56] In a climate with few paid civil service jobs for educated Togolese, employment as a salaried development worker is attractive. Unless *sociologues* land a job with an international NGO, one alternative is to establish a local NGO and apply for grants.

The United States remains the biggest provider of antitrafficking interventions despite the decline in its aid to Togo. The United States, like many other Western governments, had a greater diplomatic presence in Togo before widespread protests against the president in 1991. In line with the wave of prodemocracy social movements following the fall of the Berlin Wall, opposition factions in Togo began pressuring for a multiparty system. Despite what seemed like significant gains in the 1991 Sovereign National Conference, the military retaliated against dissidents.[57] Eyadéma's brutal repression foreclosed most international development assistance.[58] In 2011, US development presence in Togo was limited to the US Ambassador's Self-Help Fund, the Peace Corps, and ad hoc grants from the Departments of Defense and Labor.

The most recent US antitrafficking project is a $5 million Department of Labor grant to be administered by the International Labor Organization (ILO). Entitled Projet Rêve, the program is designed to focus more on prevention and awareness than the expansion of law enforcement measures. A similar $2 million grant in 2001, for Projet COMBAT, aimed to "combat" trafficking through education with school tuition grants and teacher training. In addition, the antitrafficking "awareness raising" component targeted information sessions to students, as well as general village populations.[59] The US embassy chose CARE International to distribute the funds. In turn, CARE chose the local NGO AHUEFA (Humanitarian Association for the Advancement of Women) to orchestrate trafficking committees and community liaisons to organize events and household surveys in the Central Region. Mismanagement and diversion of funds, however, left little money to pay school fees or operating costs.[60] Instead of universal coverage, rural parents received only partial tuition for a select number of students. Projet COMBAT is a telling case of US support for a humanitarian approach in Togo. It also illustrates the challenges for local actors—and a small embassy staff—to implement program agendas coming from Washington. However, since Togo recently gained a seat on the UN Security Council, it may attract more attention from the US State Department, as Hillary Rodham Clinton's recent visit to Lomé suggests.[61]

Despite Togo's child-centered approach, recent USDOS Trafficking in Persons (TIP) reports focus on the Togolese government's limited criminalizing efforts. This includes providing details such as the Ministry of Security's training of thirty police officers and how government employees staff UNICEF's antitrafficking hotline.[62] The report's recommendations also continue to pressure the government to establish a National Committee to Combat Trafficking, which would be the Togolese equivalent of NAPTIP.[63]

TRAFFICKING, POWER, AND THE STATE

While Togo and Nigeria have unique factors contributing to their campaigns, their antitrafficking laws share a legal definition that captures a range of conceptual frameworks, including human rights, criminal justice, labor migration, and development. The Palermo Protocol has garnered criticism for an ambiguity that leaves critical aspects of trafficking undefined, and for an emphasis on law enforcement with little reference to a rights-based approach.[64] Yet, this broadly interpreted protocol and the subsequent country-specific laws have authorized a cascade of enforcement practices in the name of trafficked children's rights. Different theorists have proposed reasons for the adoption of one approach over another.

Vanessa Munro's five-country survey found that the differences were shaped by each government's respective understandings of *trafficking* as it related to the criminalization of prostitution. In countries where prostitution is illegal, such as Australia and Italy, Munro found a strong-arm prosecutorial approach and long prison sentences. In the Netherlands, where prostitution is legal, she found a "humanitarian impulse," with a particular emphasis on housing and reintegration assistance to victims.[65] Ann Jordan suggests that many governments adopt criminalization because they are uninformed about the causes of trafficking or the ways to effectively use a "rights-based" approach.[66]

Nigeria's reasons for criminalizing trafficking are different. A particular constellation of factors influenced the government's response to the protocol, including global determinations, such as the emergence of trafficking as a donor country priority, and more situated elements specific to Nigeria. The functions of NAPTIP reflect this assemblage, which reaches beyond structural considerations, such as the country's extensive police apparatus, or the influence of local actors like Abubakar. For example, the country's oil boom, in the 1970s, prompted a massive demand for agricultural and domestic workers, with the subsequent unregulated influx of foreign nationals leading to increased policing and border patrols.[67] These enforcement measures contributed to a representation of the Nigerian state as strong, sovereign, and the protector of the "rule of law" through legitimate force.[68] In contrast to Togo, where antitrafficking law has had less impact on an NGO-driven, child-centered approach, Nigeria's law has transformed its campaign. Not only did the act establish NAPTIP, it also allowed the judicial system to prosecute traffickers, and these prosecutions serve as a critical measure of the campaign.

Jean and John Comaroff's insights into the "fetishization of the law" are particularly salient to the Nigerian case. The Comaroffs argue that neoliberalism and its restructuring of relations of governance usher in an era of unprecedented heterodoxy and heterogeneity as migrating workers balance their polymorphous identities with a tenuous allegiance to a single nation-state. Within this climate of uncertainty, there comes a preoccupation with criminality and a reified form of law where "legal instruments *appear* to offer a ready means of commensuration" despite their apparent impotence in maintaining order.[69] In the case of Nigeria's criminalizing approach, fetishization of the law prompts the need for an extensive network of judiciaries, checkpoints, police units, and immigration officials.[70] This trafficking discourse and the resulting cascade of micropractices reassert the role of the state as the singular authority in the security of its population and projects an image of Nigeria's campaign as independent and state run—even though NAPTIP's daily operations, for example, are largely reliant on foreign aid.[71]

The Comaroffs propose that within this "culture of legality" there is a reversion to public displays of state-sponsored punishment—widely publicized in the mass media—in the name of upholding the rule of law. They explain, "the drama that is so integral to policing the postcolony is evidence of a desire to condense dispersed power in order to make it visible, tangible, accountable, effective."[72] Within Nigeria's campaign, the "drama" of postcolonial policing takes on an exaggerated and macabre quality that promotes a trope of the sovereign "state" battling the formidable evils of trafficking. News articles and internet blogs describe the practice as the "worst crime against mankind," with traffickers going into "every nook and cranny of the country [to] lure vulnerable children," and taking to "breeding slave children" in "baby farms."[73] Meanwhile, the NAPTIP website describes traffickers as protected by "voodoo men" and using "juju" shrines to further their operations, while *NAPTIP News* satisfies public curiosity over perpetrators' identities by providing detailed personal histories of convicted traffickers.[74] The newsletter frequently publishes dramatic reenactments, akin to children's comics, of hapless traffickers' failed attempts to evade the NAPTIP dragnet.[75]

The Comaroffs explicitly connect these popular obsessions with law and order and the modern nation-state, because discourses about criminalization produce particular imaginings of modern state power that "summon" the state into being. This is especially so when governance is restricted and law enforcement becomes a vehicle to "render [the state] perceptible to the public eye, to produce both rulers and subjects who recognize its legitimacy."[76] Mitchell also privileges the law's role in "state" formation and links it to the relationship between sovereign and disciplinary modes of power, where sovereign power makes an "appearance" in the legal code, creating an "ideological screen" that masks underlying "micropowers of discipline."[77] This ideological masking plays a central role in the larger political and economic ordering of society.

Within the human rights arena, the consequence of this masking is to shift the object of intervention from situated, historically specific understandings of rights to abstracted empty illusions, be it "the state," "the law," or "freedom."[78] Harri Englund notes how the universalism of rights discourse deflects attention from the perpetuating structural conditions of suffering and makes the assumption that each individual possesses equal rights and responsibilities, thereby denying "real-life" power relations that perpetuate "unfreedom."[79] James Ferguson observes a similar process of depoliticization with respect to development discourse on poverty in "real" nation-states versus "non-state" territories. The development discourse specific to Lesotho succeeded in depoliticizing the country's problems and confining responsibility to national terms.[80] Using Mitchell's terms, the "state effect" effectively depoliticized Lesotho's poverty.

With respect to antitrafficking, the techniques of organization tied to criminalization contribute to the illusion of a sovereign state and subsume a complex migrant labor system under the depoliticized legal discourse of trafficking.

～

The concept of trafficking easily straddles the institutions of development and criminal justice. Ferguson uses a globalized frame of reference to explain how international agencies, particularly financial donors, act more like policemen than benefactors.[81] While he was referring to structural adjustment, the same may be said for other reforms sought by powerful international interests. In particular, the USDOS's role in managing trafficking interventions is coercive since qualification for USAID programs is influenced by a recipient country's ranking in TIP reports, and the African Growth and Opportunity Act.[82] The USDOS began publishing the TIP report in 2001 and assigns a tier according to a government's compliance with VTVPA antitrafficking protocols. The VTVPA authorizes the president to impose sanctions on noncompliant "states."[83] And the importance of the rankings is not lost on antitrafficking officials.[84]

The entire TIP ranking system requires discrete, abstracted states to compare on a standardized rubric, and the state effect allows for this by producing flattened representations for univariate analysis. It also recapitulates regional relations between a behemoth, such as Nigeria, and a small state like Togo—allowing for comparison across incomparable political economic systems. Instead of attending to the forces driving trafficking, the focus becomes a technical one of perfecting law enforcement measures, with funds poured into police trainings, border patrols, and streamlining convictions within the judicial system. Nigeria's criminalizing approach is quantifiable and contributes to a representation of the state that is favorable for assessment, although it is unclear how much trafficked children benefit.[85] Instead, the process may have a greater impact reinforcing diplomatic relations among "state" representatives.

In contrast, the material practices of the Togolese approach do not contribute to an abstracted unit of analysis that is "TIP-intelligible." Togo's focus on life skills and supportive educational environments produces few statistics. Furthermore, Togo's poor crime-fighting performance projects an image of a government that cannot handle its trafficking problem, thereby perpetuating a failed state status. And while Togo's response to trafficking is a small contribution to the international disfavor its ruling dynasty has cultivated through nearly a half century of autocratic rule, the additional sanctions only exacerbate the population's "economic misery."[86] As Mally has repeatedly stated, the Togolese political leadership lacks the will to commit funds to antitrafficking initiatives. And yet the US government's queer mix of funding child-centered programs in Togo while sanctioning the government for its poor prosecution performance has helped shape a disfavored campaign that may silently be effective.

NOTES

Abbreviations

NAPTIP	National Agency for Prohibition of Traffic in Persons and Other Related Matters
RELUTET	Réseau de Lutte contre la Traite des Enfants au Togo
TIP	Trafficking in Persons report
USDOS	US Department of State

1. Dorothee Gimba, "War against Human Trafficking: The Journey So Far," in Policing Nigeria in the Twenty-first Century, ed. Solomon E. Arase and I. P. O. Iwuofor (Ibadan: Spectrum Books, 2007), 249; NAPTIP News, 1 (2005); "Doctors at War against Trafficking," http://doctorsatwar.org.

2. Nigeria's campaign addresses both internal and external trafficking issues. Togo focuses on child labor exploitation within and surrounding Togo. The term trafficking here refers to child trafficking, especially the illegal movement of child domestic servants, agricultural laborers, and sex workers.

3. Timothy Mitchell, "Society, Economy and the State Effect," in The Anthropology of the State, ed. Aradhana Sharma and Akhil Gupta (Oxford: Blackwell, 2006), 181.

4. Additional evidence comes from newspaper articles and NGO pamphlets and newsletters.

5. Bar A. O. Shuaibu, Director of Legal and Prosecution, NAPTIP's official website, "Legal and Prosecution Department," http://naptip.gov.ng/legal.html.

6. RELUTET, "Réseau de lutte contre la traite des enfants au Togo," "Missions," http://www.relutet.org/fr/reseau-lutte-traite-enfants-togo-page-libre.php?id_page=2.

7. Gail Kligman and Stephanie Limoncelli, *Trafficking Women after Socialism: From, to, and through Eastern Europe*, Social Politics: International Studies in Gender, State and Society vol. 12, no. 1 (Oxford: Oxford University Press, 2005): 118–40; Jo Doezuma, "'Loose Women or Lost Women?' The Re-emergence of the Myth of 'White Slavery' in Contemporary Discourses of 'Trafficking in Women,'" *Gender Issues* 18, no. 1 (2000): 23–50; Jacqueline Berman, "(Un)popular Strangers and Crises Unbounded: Discourses of Sex-Trafficking, the European Political Community and the Panicked State of the Modern State," *European Journal of International Relations* 9, no. 1 (2003): 37; Jean Comaroff and John L. Comaroff, "Criminal Obsessions, after Foucault: Postcoloniality, Policing, and the Metaphysics of Disorder," *Law and Disorder in the Postcolony*, ed. Comaroff and Comaroff (Chicago: University of Chicago Press, 2006), 273–99.

8. John Bendix, Bertell Ollman, Bartholomew Sparrow, and Timothy Mitchell, "Going beyond the State?" *American Political Science Review* 86, no. 4 (1992): 1020.

9. Ibid., 1007.

10. Timothy Mitchell, "The Limits of the State: Beyond Statist Approaches and Their Critics," *American Political Science Review* 85, no. 1 (1991): 77–96. See also Mitchell's account of political scientists "abandoning the state" in "Society, Economy and the State Effect."

11. Mitchell, "Society, Economy," 177.

12. Elizabeth Bruch, "Models Wanted: The Search for an Effective Response to Human Trafficking," *Stanford Journal of International Law* 40, no. 1 (2004): 6.

13. Ibid.

14. Janie Chuang, "The United States as Global Sheriff: Using Unilateral Sanctions to Combat Human Trafficking," *Michigan Journal of International Law* 27, no. 2 (2006): 437–94.

15. Sahara Group, "Best Practices on Rehabilitation and Reintegration of Trafficked Women and Girls," www.childtrafficking.com/Docs/sahara_jit_2004__best_pract.pdf; Cynthia S. Torg, "Human Trafficking Enforcement in the United States," *Tulane Journal of International and Comparative Law* 14, no. 2 (2006): 504; Kevin Bales, "Free the Slaves," 1 December 2009, http://www.freetheslaves.net/Page.aspx?pid=330.

16. Anne Gallagher, "Human Rights and Human Trafficking in Thailand: A Shadow TIP Report," in *Trafficking and the Global Sex Industry*, ed. Karen Beeks and Delila Amir (Lanham, MD: Lexington Books, 2006); Berman, "(Un)popular Strangers," 37. For commensurability, see Stacy L. Pigg, "Languages of Sex and AIDS in Nepal: Notes on the Social Production of Commensurability," *Cultural Anthropology* 16, no. 4 (2001): 481–541.

17. This approach is commonly referred to as the human rights approach. See Chuang, "United States," 447; Alexandra Amiel, "Integrating a Human Rights Perspective into the European Approach to Combating the Trafficking of Women for Sexual Exploitation," *Buffalo Human Rights Law Review* 5 (2006): 5–6; Niki Adams, "Anti-Trafficking Legislation: Protection or Deportation?" *Feminist Review* 73, no. 1 (2003): 135–39.

18. Jonathon Cohen, *Borderline Slavery: Child Trafficking in Togo* (New York: Human Rights Watch, 2003).

19. Liza Buchbinder, "Unraveling the Kinship Network: Child Labor and Migration in Togo" (master's thesis, University of California, Berkeley, 2006).

20. Amiel, "Integrating," 41.

21. For the enforcement approach, see Torg, "Human Trafficking"; Angela Giampolo, "Trafficking Victims Protection Reauthorization Act of 2005: The Latest Weapon in the Fight against Human Trafficking," *Temple Political and Civil Rights Law Review* 16, no. 1 (2006): 195–224; Mark Sidel, "Richard B. Lillich Memorial Lecture: New Directions in the Struggle against Human Trafficking," *Journal of Transnational Law and Policy* 17, no. 2 (2008): 187–216; Sara K. Andrews, "U.S. Domestic Prosecution of the American International Sex Tourist: Efforts to Protect Children from Sexual Exploitation," *Journal of Criminal Law and Criminology* 94, no. 2 (2004): 415–54. For noncriminalizing, see Gallagher, "Human Rights"; Berman, "(Un)Popular Strangers," 37–86.

22. Sylvane E. Dessy and Stéphane Pallage, "A Theory of the Worst Forms of Child Labor," *Economic Journal* 115, no. 1 (2005): 68–87; Dessy, Flaubert Mbiekop, and Pallage, "The Economics of Child Trafficking," Working Paper 0509, CIRPEE, 2005, http://ideas.repec.org/p/lvl/lacicr/0509.html.

23. Bisi Olateru Olagbegi (Coordinator, Women's Consortium of Nigeria), interview by author, Lagos, 8 February 2009.

24. For Nigerians in Italy, see Christiana Giordano, "Practices of Translation and the Making of Migrant Subjectivities in Contemporary Italy," *American Ethnologist* 35, no. 4 (2008): 588–606.

25. UNICEF, "Children's and Women's Rights in Nigeria: A Wake-Up Call," *Situation Assessment and Analyses*, 2001.

26. NAPTIP, "I Am Proud of NAPTIP's Successes," *NAPTIP News* 1, no. 1, 5 December 2005–6 March 2006, 13.

27. Talal Asad, "What Do Human Rights Do? An Anthropological Inquiry," *Theory and Event* 4, no. 4 (2000).

28. NAPTIP website, http://naptip.gov.ng/legal.html.

29. USAID, "Anti-Trafficking Technical Assistance: Nigeria Anti-Trafficking Assessment," 11–27 April 2005.

30. Nigeria's national monitoring system uses Italian software called SIDDA 2000, which was designed for the country's antimafia bureau; however, the USAID report found that NAPTIP lacked the training to use the program effectively.

31. Anonymous NGO worker, interview by author, Abuja, Nigeria, 15 February 2009.

32. Gimba, "Human Trafficking," 251.

33. S. G. Ehindero, "President Obasanjo's Reform Initiatives for the Nigeria Police," in Arase and Iwuofor, *Policing Nigeria*, xxiii.

34. NAPTIP, "Mission Statement," http://naptip.gov.ng/.

35. NAPTIP, "NAPTIP Is Now a Model for Other Countries," *NAPTIP News* 1, no. 4 (2007).

36. NAPTIP also promotes its success as a "model for other countries" by training police units in Europe and inspiring other countries, such as Malawi and Ghana, to create similar agencies.

37. The US government invested $1 million toward the establishment of a Lagos safe house. See USAID, "Nigeria Anti-Trafficking Assessment," 2005.

38. Godwin Morka, NAPTIP Lagos office, said non-trafficking-related cases of child neglect were the principal reason people called in to the hotline.

39. NAPTIP safe house, interviews by author, Abuja, Nigeria, 18 February 2009.

40. See Musikilu Mojeed, "Inside the Nigerian Transnational Human Trafficking Industry," 16 October 2008, http://archive.punchng.com/Articl.aspx?theartic =Art2008101523335195; "Nigeria: Stepping Up the Fight against Child-Trafficking," 10 December 2007, www.irinnews.org/report.aspx?reportid=75783; Andrew Walker, "Trafficked Children Tell Their Stories," *BBC News*, 5 February 2008, http://news. bbc.co.uk/2/hi/africa/7226411.stm.

41. See Lawrance, chap. 8, this volume.

42. USDOS, Trafficking in Persons report (hereafter TIP), 2001, www.state. gov/j/tip/rls/tiprpt/2001/index.htm.

43. Roger Kekeh, "Le trafic des enfants au Togo—Étude prospective a Lomé, Vogan et Cotonou," Lomé, Togo, WAO-Afrique, September 1997, 53 pp. and annexes.

44. *BBC News*, "The Slave Children," 5 October 2001, http://news.bbc.co.uk/2 /hi/programmes/correspondent/1519144.stm.

45. Cléophas Mally, WAO-Afrique, interview by author, Lomé, March 2004.

46. See Lawrance, chap. 8, this volume.

47. USDOS, TIP, 2005, www.state.gov/j/tip/rls/tiprpt/2005/index.htm.

48. Mally, interview; Essodina Abalo, International Labor Organization, interview by author, Lomé, 9 June 2004; USDOS, TIP, 2004; Cohen, *Borderline Slavery*.

49. Mally, interview, 2004.

50. For a critique of minimum standards, see Chuang, "United States," 349.

51. USDOS, TIP, 2009, 283, www.state.gov/j/tip/rls/tiprpt/2009/index.htm.

52. CIVICUS, "Étude diagnostique de la société civile togolaise," Lomé, Togo, 2006, http://doc-aea.aide-et-action.org/data/admin/societe_civile_togolaise.pdf.

53. For educational reform as antitrafficking, see RELUTET, "Missions," http:// www.relutet.org/fr/reseau-lutte-traite-enfants-togo-page-libre.php?id_page=2.

54. Plan International, "Where We Work," http://plan-international.org/where -we-work; Terre des Hommes, "Our Mission," http://www.terredeshommes.org /index.php?lang=en&page=abo; CARE International, http://www.careinternational .org.uk/where-we-work/togo.

55. For child trafficking and economic adjustments, see Kathryn Nwajiaku, "The National Conferences in Benin and Togo Revisited," *Journal of Modern*

African Studies 32, no. 3 (1994): 429–47; Austin N. Isamah and Rasidi A. Okunola, "Family Life under Economic Adjustment: The Rise of the Child Breadwinners," in *Money Struggles and City Life*, ed. Jane I. Guyer, LaRay Denzer, and Adigun Agbaje (Ibadan: BookBuilders, 2003); Claude Meillassoux, "The Economy and Child Labour: An Overview," in *The Exploited Child*, ed. Bernard Schlemmer (New York: Zed Books, 2000).

56. A. Bonavita, "Étude diagnostique du travail en réseau dans la lutte contre la traite des enfants au Togo," RELUTET (June–September 2007): 22.

57. Dirk Kohnert, "Togo: Thorny Transition and Misguided Aid at the Roots of Economic Misery," MPRA Paper, GIGA Institute of African Affairs (Hamburg, 8 October 2007), 6.

58. As a concrete example, CARE International, a major recipient of USAID funds, went from 120 employees in early 1990s to seventeen employees in 2009.

59. CARE International, "Projet COMBAT: Combattre le trafic des enfants grace á l'éducation," 2001.

60. Mahassou Alessoun, former antitrafficking village liaison for Ahuefa, an international organization to support the well-being of migrants (Ahuefa is a Togolese name given to girls who come from families who have experienced hardship; see ahuefa.org/about), interview by author, Tchamba, Togo, 19 March 2009; Philippe Yodo, director of CARE International Togo, interview by author, Lomé, 1 April 2009.

61. ITN Source, "Togo: U.S. Secretary of State Hillary Clinton Pays a Two-Hour Visit in the Latest Leg of Her West Africa Tour," 18 January 2012, www.itnsource.com/shotlist/RTV/2012/01/18/RTV170212/.

62. USDOS, TIP, 2009, www.state.gov/j/tip/rls/tiprpt/2009/index.htm.

63. USDOS, TIP, 2010, www.state.gov/j/tip/rls/tiprpt/2010/index.htm.

64. Ann D. Jordan, "Human Rights or Wrongs? The Struggle for a Rights-Based Response to Trafficking in Human Beings," *Gender and Development* 10 (2002): 28–37; Kara Abramson, "Beyond Consent: Toward Safeguarding Human Rights: Implementing the United Nations Trafficking Protocol," *Harvard International Law Journal* 44, no. 2 (2003): 473–502; Liz Kelly, "The Wrong Debate: Reflections on Why Force is Not the Key Issue with Respect to Trafficking in Women for Sexual Exploitation," *Feminist Review* 73 (2003): 135–39; Kay Warren, "The 2000 UN Human Trafficking Protocol: Rights, Enforcement, Vulnerabilities," in *The Practice of Human Rights: Tracking Law between the Global and the Local*, ed. Mark Goodale and Sally Engle Merry (Cambridge: Cambridge University Press, 2007), 262.

65. Vanessa E. Munro, "Stopping Traffic? A Comparative Study of Responses to the Trafficking in Women for Prostitution," *British Journal of Criminology* 46, no. 2 (2006): 318–33.

66. Jordan, "Human Rights?" 28–37.

67. See Jane Guyer, *An African Niche Economy: Farming to Feed Ibadan, 1968–88* (Edinburgh: Edinburgh University Press, 1997), 96.

68. Bendix et al., "Limits," 1008.

69. Comaroff and Comaroff, "Criminal Obsessions," 32, emphasis in original.

70. *NAPTIP News* 1, no. 4 (2007).

71. Berman, "(Un)popular Strangers," 50.

72. Comaroff and Comaroff, "Criminal Obsessions," 276.

73. ECPAT International, "NAPTIP: Human Trafficking Worst Crime against Mankind," July 5, 2009, http://www.ecpat.net/EI/Resource_newsclippings.asp?id =747; Amanda Kloer, "Nigerian Baby Farms Breed Slaves from Slaves," 21 July 2009, http://humantrafficking.change.org/blog/view/nigerian_baby_farms_breed _slaves_from_slaves. An accompanying photograph shows the heads of baby dolls embedded in a cabbage patch.

74. NAPTIP, http://www.naptip.gov.ng/naptip/docs/babandedeindex(2).html.

75. I. Umar Gusau, "Nigeria: Human Traffickers Nabbed in Borno," allAfrica .com, January 27, 2009, http://allafrica.com/stories/200901270459.html.

76. Comaroff and Comaroff, "Criminal Obsessions," 280.

77. Mitchell, "Society, Economy," 179.

78. See Leslie Butt, "The Suffering Stranger: Medical Anthropology and International Morality," *Medical Anthropology* 21, no. 1 (2002): 1–24.

79. Harri Englund, *Prisoners of Freedom: Human Rights and the African Poor* (Berkeley: University of California Press, 2006), 10.

80. James Ferguson, *Global Shadows: Africa in the Neoliberal World Order* (Durham: Duke University Press, 2006), 61.

81. Ibid., 97.

82. Anonymous US embassy representative, interview by author, Lomé, Togo, March 2009.

83. Chuang, "United States," 439.

84. *NAPTIP News* 1, no.1 (2007).

85. Dessy and Pallage, "Worst Forms," 68–87; Chuang, "United States," 437–94.

86. Dirk Kohnert, "Togo: Failed Elections and Misguided Aid at the Roots of Economic Misery," MPRA Paper 5207, GIGA-Institute of African Affairs (Hamburg, 2007), 30.

The Paradox of Women, Children, and Slavery

KEVIN BALES AND JODY SARICH

WOMEN AND SLAVERY

There is nothing new about the enslavement of women. There have always been women slaves. Until the publication of this book, it might have been possible to say that there is equally nothing new about our understanding of women in slavery. This volume, however, illuminates areas of women's enslavement in Africa, opening us to more nuanced interpretations that are desperately needed both to help frame the academic dialogues that deepen our knowledge of this issue and to inform the minds and hearts of practitioners and activists who attempt to turn that understanding into meaningful social change. Women, in their millions, still suffer in slavery today, and what we do not know about the unique experience of women in slavery could fill many volumes. Our hope is that this admirable collection will be followed by many more.

We do know that slavery, as a human activity, is continual and varied throughout history. We also know that women's experience of slavery is not unique in every way, but in crucial ways. For men, women, and children, slavery means the complete control of their lives by another person, as illustrated by Elisabeth McMahon in this volume. Violence is used to maintain that control, and in virtually every case that control is aimed at economic exploitation. Free will is lost and profits are generated for the slaveholder—that is the fundamental theme of all slavery. But there is another parallel theme, one in which the slaveholders derive other forms of benefit. These benefits include the psychological enjoyment of power over others, the use of people as articles of conspicuous consumption, and the unbridled sexual use of slaves.

It is the sexual use of slaves, as highlighted by Carina Ray and Susan Kreston, that marks and typifies the enslavement of women. All slaves tend to be reduced to the status of other, virtually all slaves are worked to create economic wealth for their slaveholder, all slaves are denied free will and expect and experience violence, but slaves that are women experience added dimensions to their enslavement. While some male slaves are sexually abused, sexual assault is the norm for enslaved women. Whatever the nature of their recruitment or passage into slavery, whatever type of work they are forced to do for the economic benefit their slaveholder, women in slavery will be sexually assaulted. This is the rule, not the exception. It applies to the very young and the old, it applies in the field, factory, and house, and this sexual use often extends beyond the slaveholder to his sons, friends, relatives, and free workers as McMahon, Richard Roberts, and Bernard Freamon document here. It is rare to be able to make a definitive statement about any human activity, except in this: for women, slavery means rape.

Habitual sexual assault shapes the experience of women slaves, as is vividly on display in the chapters by Ray, Kreston, and Marie Rodet. The bodies of men are also controlled in slavery, but it is primarily their ability to work that interests the slaveholder. Women do all the types of work that male slaves do, but they are also viewed as permanently available for sexual use. It is an appropriation and control of the interior as well as the exterior of their physical beings. If slavery transforms work from vocation to suffering, for women it also transforms an act of potential pleasure, love, and procreation into torture. The psychological impact of this assault is profound but little studied. This assault also points to the second key way that the experience of slavery for women differs from that of men.

Throughout history, slaveholders have been driven in ways that are both biological and cultural to impregnate their women slaves. The feminist writer Andrea Dworkin coined the term *phallic imperialism* in the late 1970s in a discussion of women's economic prospects. This term encapsulates the use of the bodies of women slaves for the production of new slaves. Not only does the slaveholder use an enslaved woman for pleasure, but he can also create in her body an extension of himself that will exploit her being from within. Upon birth, that child can be claimed as progeny, sold, or retained as a slave. For the woman slave, it is a kind of thievery of life itself transcending the loss of her own productive capacity.

This appropriation of reproductive capacity has a profound psychological impact. Although the reproductive capacity of all slaves can be used to a slaveholder's economic advantage, the reproductive exploitation of women slaves has no exact parallel in male enslavement. The types of violence imposed on male slaves, even when sexual, are almost always about power and punishment, only tangentially related to their economic worth in the sense that work should be performed harder and more obediently. For women, sexual violence in particular becomes a profit-making endeavor. Throughout most of human history, the acquisition cost of slaves has been high, normally thought of as a major capital investment. For that reason, the infants produced by raped women slaves, though useless for immediate labor, were considered worthwhile investments. This is not always the case today. In the last fifty years, due in large part to the unprecedented increase in the human population, a glut of potential slaves exists. This surplus in vulnerable human labor potential means that the cost of slaves has fallen to an all-time low and that slave infants are often viewed as simply not worth their upkeep. So while the rape of women slaves today may result in a child from her womb whom she will watch grow into another commodity belonging to her master, rape may also result in a child whom she will be forced to watch be malnourished, abandoned, or destroyed before her eyes.

The fact of the relative worthlessness of slave infants opens the third determining factor of women's experience in slavery. With the exception of male slaves once used as eunuchs, male slaves tend to retain control of all of their biological functions in slavery, though their access to sexual interaction may be restricted. For female slaves, the slaveholder regularly manipulates their reproductive biology. Abortion, sterilization, hysterectomy, female genital cutting, and the sewing up or other surgical alteration of the vagina, are all potentially part of enslavement. The violations of the human body on display in Kreston's and Rodet's chapters are unique to the experience of women slaves, and are in addition to other heinous forms of physical maiming or harvesting, historically inflicted on slaves of both genders, such as cutting or removal of the ears, mouth, nose, or other organs.

The point is that male slaves are primarily seen as beings of labor potential, as Jelmer Vos makes clear, but female slaves are seen in this way *and* as bodies that can be used in other ways: as sexual outlets, for their reproductive potential, and as items of conspicuous consumption. This leads to a paradox: while enslavement is the total control of one person by another, the enslavement of women achieves a totality exceeding that of men. All the chapters in this book address this difference in some way.

CHILDREN AND SLAVERY

There has not been a day in human history without the enslavement of children. In the past, the accepted and permissible control of children within most cultures included their exploitation extending into slavery. The "discovery" of childhood in the eighteenth century, combined with concepts of innocence and vulnerability, began to extend to children an interesting set of paradoxical rights. On the one hand, what would be called today "the worst forms of child labor" began to be regulated in law, if not in practice. At the same time, parental and governmental controls over children's lives were extended. In the past and today, parental controls, especially, often come into conflict with both national and international norms and laws. The result is a little talked about but profound tension that is both conceptual and practical. The protection of children assumed in law requires vigilance, physical protection extending to physical domination, de facto and de jure controls, the rights of children regularly suborned by the rights of adults, and, in many cultures, the expectation that adults have rights and children have few or none. International norms, such as those stated in the UN's Universal Declaration of Human Rights, may assign rights to children, but these continue to be controversial. Continuing the contestation outlined by Jean Allain, many norms are not just ignored, they are effectively rejected by many governments as well as individuals. One of the strongest arguments in the United States against ratification of the UN Convention on the Rights of the Child was that it would remove the right of parents and others to employ corporal punishment on children. Whatever the state of international conventions, socially and culturally there is no agreement on the rights adhering to children, nor policy, as Margaret Akullo's chapter demonstrates. This is in contrast to the wide consensus rejecting all forms of slavery.

This paradoxical situation exists within a larger context of trends that confound the application of rights to children, as Akullo makes clear. All forms of enslavement are supported by two key factors: economic and social vulnerability, and a lack of protection by the rule of law. It is not too great a generalization to say that, with very few exceptions among human cultures, women are more vulnerable than men, children are more vulnerable than adults, and girls tend to be the most vulnerable of all, as Liza Buchbinder, Ray, and Kreston demonstrate. Because the internal dynamics and power relations of families are seen as outside the regulation of law except in the most egregious circumstances, the rule of law often fails to reach to minors. This pattern is typically embedded deeply within culture and reinforced by religious dogma. Indeed, all social institutions in most societies tend to assume the complete control of children by older family members. The result is that children not only face possible enslavement within their family but are less likely to be protected from enslavement outside the family.

This concept of the "right" to control and dispose of children extends beyond private family arrangements to community-sanctioned religious practice. Two examples from West Africa demonstrate this clearly. The first is the use of children by religious guardians in Qur'anic *daraa* schools. Children—from a very young age—are handed over to such schools by their fathers. Ostensibly, this is an act of piety, but it is also used both as a means to discipline a child's mother and as a demonstration by the father of his complete control over the family. At the schools, the children are expected to receive theological training and memorize the Qur'an. They are also expected to support the imams or marabouts that teach them. The reality is that in many schools, the children, known as *talibés*, spend their days begging in the streets and are punished if they fail to bring in enough money. Their situation is one of complete control coupled with economic exploitation and little or no religious, or other, education. A 2010 Human Rights Watch report suggests that fifty thousand children are "forced to endure often extreme forms of abuse, neglect, and exploitation" in Senegal alone.[1] In a second example, girls and young women in other parts of West Africa are given as *vodounsi* or *trokosi* to priests as an act of atonement for sins committed by relatives. The priests use the girls as servants, to grow food and earn money, and for sex. All free will is lost. The enslavement may continue until the girl-child, as a woman, is incapable of further work due to illness, injury, or death. She may then be disposed of, and another girl is requested from her family to take her place. Any of her offspring remain the property of the priest.

The enslavement of children within families is also demonstrated in the ubiquitous practice of forced marriage of minors, as illustrated by Rodet and Roberts for West Africa. But even when forced marriage or enslavement through religious practice is not a threat, patterns of discrimination and prejudice are compounded for children. The lack of access to education, health services, adequate nutrition, and legal protection are exacerbated for children who are members of a group suffering discrimination, and leave them at a significant disadvantage. As Claire Cody has argued, nearly two-thirds of all births in Africa and South Asia go unregistered, and the impact of this lack of registration falls most severely on the poorest families or members of marginalized ethnic communities.[2] Without a birth certificate, a child is a nonperson, unable to prove identity and easily dismissed as ineligible for support programs. If a child is caught up in human trafficking and taken to another country, it becomes very difficult to repatriate them upon rescue, as their home country will reject them at the border. Recent policies enacted by the United States tie birth registration to aid, but the establishment of an open and comprehensive system will take time.

THE AFRICAN CONTEXT

It is right that a volume on women and children in slavery locates itself in Africa, a continent whose history is as rich in ecological beauty and human potential as it is in its subjection to the ecological and human weaknesses that predict vulnerability and exploitation. As mentioned above, statistical analyses confirm that the most powerful predictors of slavery in any country are an absence of the rule of law, usually seen as corruption, but sometimes as the

...nd lawlessness of a civil war, combined with the markers of social vulnerability, such as poverty, lack of education, and lack of health care. Other predictors include a context of environmental destruction or deterioration, civil unrest, and a general lack of state protection of human rights. Examining most of the world's countries in a systematic way shows a strong relationship between slavery and corruption. The levels of poverty and the amount of slavery in 193 countries provide a clear correlation. The poorest countries have the highest levels of slavery. (See tables 12.1 and 12.2, in appendix.)

In the context of Africa, poverty has another dimension. The United Nations has classified thirty-eight countries of the world as being "high-debt countries," which means that these countries are carrying a crippling load of debt owed to international lenders. A high-debt country has to use what little income or taxes it can gather to service debt rather than to invest in its own people. This is often called a *debt overhang.* Debt from the past bears down on a country, paralyzing it and preventing any growth in the future.[3] The types of investments a high-debt country is *not* able to make—schools, law enforcement, economic growth, and so on—are exactly the ones that are most likely to reduce the amount of slavery. Countries with the largest amount of debt overhang also have some of the highest levels of slavery (see table 12.3, in appendix). Clearly these three measures and relationships reflect the African reality in general.

The impact of slavery on women within such an economic and development context also extends to women who are not enslaved. Work by Robert Smith and by the antislavery organization Free the Slaves has demonstrated that slavery depresses economies and the development of human potential that benefits women.[4] At the same time, liberation from slavery generates a "freedom dividend" of increased economic activity, educational participation, and civic engagement that benefits women disproportionately. The study of women in slavery in Africa, both in the past and today, is so important because the continent has contained and continues to contain slavery in many forms, and understanding these forms will increase the likelihood of their abolition.

IMPORTING AFRICAN WOMEN SLAVES

Akullo, Buchbinder, Kreston, and Benjamin Lawrance do an excellent job of illuminating the processes of and reactions to human trafficking from Africa. If there is anything to add it is the example of the remarkable support for human trafficking inadvertently built into the system of visas for entering the United States. There are three types of visas for workers from overseas that are the locus of many cases of domestic slavery. The A-3 visa is for household employees of diplomats; the G-5 visa is given for domestic workers attached to the households of employees of international agencies such as the United Nations, World Bank, and the International Monetary Fund (IMF). The B-1 visa services a larger group, since it covers the "personal or domestic servants" who accompany businesspeople, foreign nationals, and American citizens with permanent residency abroad. All three visas cover such household workers as housekeepers, nannies, cooks, drivers, and gardeners. These servants are linked to named individuals and are clearly in a situation of control and dependence, yet once they have passed through border control they are normally lost to official view. No records are kept of the whereabouts of B-1 workers, and while an address is requested on the A-3 and G-5 application forms, there is typically no follow-up. Nearly four thousand A-3 and G-5 visas are handed out each year; about a thousand are G-5s, for the servants of UN, World Bank, and IMF employees. A significant number of these visas are issued to African women.

To get the visa, the employer simply has to state that he or she will provide "reasonable living and working conditions." Whatever paperwork is filed to get the visa can be disregarded as soon as the worker walks out of the airport; follow-up is rare. If a domestic worker ends up abused and enslaved, there are several possible outcomes, most of them bad. If she has an A-3 visa, her diplomat "employer" often cannot be arrested or prosecuted because claims of diplomatic immunity will delay arrest until they flee. If she has a B-1 visa, her location will not be recorded or checked, so her best chance is to try to escape; but if she does, she is officially defined as "out of status" and may be deported if found. With a G-5 visa, escape can also mean deportation, and while her employer does not have immunity, she or he can simply leave the country if it looks as if she might be caught. The US visa system, far from being an advantageous program, places exploited household workers at an extreme disadvantage. The irony of this situation is that the US government has a visa system in place that resolves most of these problems.

If you are fortunate enough to have the requisite education, financial resources for application fees, and interest in "educational and cultural exchange," you can come to the United States via a federally regulated au pair agency, and do the same type of nanny job some enslaved domestics were promised, but with a system of protections in place. Unlike the ignored servants receiving B-1 visas, these young women, typically educated, middle-class, and European, will be granted a J-1 visa, which is a ticket to safe and protected household work. With a J-1 visa, each au pair, or nanny, attends an orientation session and is introduced to a group of other nannies working in the same geographical area. In this way, they can form a network of friendships and also have contacts from their own country that they can call if they want to. After joining her host family, the nanny attends another orientation program to learn about educational opportunities, community resources, and contacts for a local support network. The nanny and her employers are required to discuss their situation with a counselor every month to report any problems and resolve disputes. The law stipulates that the host family has to pay the au pair a weekly stipend of at least the minimum wage, supplemented with another $500 for academic expenses. US State Department rules state that the au pair is not allowed to work more than forty-five hours a week and must have a private bedroom. Another rule requires a $500 fee to be paid by employers to cover inspection and enforcement costs. There is also a review of the suitability of the employers and their families and a requirement that "all adults living in the host family must pass a background investigation, including employment and personal character references." There is no limit imposed on the number of J-1 visas that can be granted each year. For the US government to operate these two systems in parallel is at best puzzling and at worst callous and exploitative. But the result is that underprivileged women, including many women from African nations, are easily enslaved after entering the United States legally, while privileged, mostly European au pairs are carefully protected.

There has been some progress under the Obama administration on visa abuse. In a diplomatic note to all foreign embassies, Secretary of State Hillary Clinton issued two new requirements governing the employment of domestic workers. First, all embassies are required to notify the State Department before they hire a domestic and apply for her visa. This provides the government with the opportunity to examine the potential employee and ensure that the diplomat is ready to meet the second requirement—providing a safe and legal job. An important point of the new policy is the State Department's assumption that diplomats will not be able to provide the legally required wages and working conditions unless and until they provide evidence to the contrary. To meet the requirements, the diplomat must guarantee that there will be a contract stating hours and wages; a separate and independent bank account controlled by the worker where the wages will be deposited; overtime payments; travel provided to and from the United States; and the assurance that all relevant federal, state, and local laws will be obeyed. If diplomats violate these guarantees, their embassy will be denied visas for workers. And if there is serious abuse of workers, diplomats will be placed on notice that their immunity can be revoked, making them susceptible to prosecution.

THE POWER OF CULTURE AND THE NEW SCHOLARSHIP

But the economic and political conditions contributing to and resulting from slavery are, of course, only one part of the larger picture. Culture, in all its forms, guides human behavior, legitimating and supporting some actions and proscribing others, as Ray, Vos, and Freamon demonstrate. This is especially the case with slavery, since the reduction of another being to an inferior status, often equal to that of an animal or other p. requires the formation of complex processes of rationalization, sometimes within a culture and always within the individual human mind that seeks to perpetrate this crime. These rationalizations are extensive constructions of myth, morals, and mindset, built from interlocking constructs — that women are inferior to men, that culture has the power to trump basic human rights, that social powerlessness of individuals or groups can justify violence against them, and so on. The power of these interlocking constructs is perhaps most evident in their support for slavery that occurs within the construct of marriage — the most common and the least understood form of the modern enslavement of women in Africa today. Despite advances in the historiography of African women's experiences as enslaved brides — stolen in armed conflict, traded for political favor, as members of harems — the contemporary trafficking of women in marriage within Africa (and elsewhere) is little understood and less studied.[5] This is a form of slavery almost entirely feminized and yet, unlike other forms of slavery, it has not been the target of the same legal and cultural responses and prohibitions afforded forms of enslavement that affect men. This is true even in those places where national laws appear to positively address slavery, trafficking, and the constituent crimes that add up to enslavement.

There is no reliable estimate of the number of adult women or children enslaved in forced marriages. Indeed, in many cultures forced marriages are not defined as such, in spite of clearly violating the criteria in, for example, the 1956 UN Supplementary Convention on the Abolition of Slavery. The minimum legal age required for marriage varies from country to country and is often ignored. Subgroups within many societies jealously guard the "right" to marry off minor girls despite their protests against it, and governments often overlook this practice as an "ethnic" or "cultural" practice. This relativistic approach opens the door to the commoditization of children. Mike Dottridge notes,

 In some cultures it is still common for girls to be abducted by the bridegroom or his relatives, for example in parts of Bénin and Ethiopia. In others, notably in China, it is common for an intermediary to be involved in the abduction, in order to make a profit by delivering a young woman to her prospective husband: in this case it qualifies as trafficking. In addition to abducting women for marriage, however, marriage agents play a role in many societies in negotiating marriages and are remunerated for their efforts. On the whole this traditional role is regarded as perfectly acceptable.[6]

The widespread combination of religion and government in the regulation of marriage speaks to this extension of control. It is hard to measure the extent of the importance of this control in any particular culture or society, but it is difficult to discover societies where any alteration or questioning of accepted forms of marriage does not elicit an extreme reaction. Even a number of those contemporary nation-states that purport to most deeply value individual human rights and choice are, at the time of writing, caught up in controversy over the control of marriage. Many citizens of Western European and North American countries known for their breadth of civil liberties are denied the right to legal marriage because of their choice of spouse. In these countries, legal challenges have been met with popular and electoral outrage, communities have been polarized, and conflict has resulted.

In many African contexts, the act of questioning accepted forms of marriage may generate even stronger reactions, as Rodet and Roberts show, and actions and opinions not in line with cultural norms are criminalized. All this points to the extreme sensitivity in all cultures when forms of marriage are questioned. There is an ideological undercurrent within most societies as powerful as the one that once guarded the legality of chattel slavery that insists that while many aspects of social life might change, marriage is untouchable. In the African context, often marked by interlocking systems of state, customary, and indigenous law, traditional forms of marriage have even greater insulation against change. This means that cases of enslavement by way of marriage are concealed behind more than just a veneer of normative cultural practice—they are hidden behind the force of law itself.

Behind that veil is the need for a clear understanding of how marriage, particularly forced marriage, is an identity and status externally fixed on an individual. Whether through codified or customary law, the extensive social and legal controls over marriage mean that it is a status rigidly fixed and guarded. For the woman who has been forced into marriage, her treatment is concealed by both her legal status as a wife and by a great fog of cultural practice and pronouncement describing this subjugation as normal, legal, and right. It is very much in the interest of those who are supportive of and benefit from forced marriage to present it simply as a form of cultural expression, just one more legitimate custom within the great diversity of human activity. To focus any consideration of forced marriage, first on the idea that discussion of marriage is an untouchable topic, and second on the rationale that it is simply a form of marriage reflecting valid cultural norms, diverts attention from the key point—that it is an imposition of status, culturally sanctioned and legally defined. Put simply, given that customary law is binding in many countries, forced marriage is the last legal slavery.

In Africa this can be demonstrated in the past and in the present. In the period immediately before and after the end of legal slavery in Africa, as illustrated by Roberts, McMahon, Vos, and Freamon, the effective difference between purchase and the payment of bridewealth was often fraught with ambiguity.[7] Former male masters, eager to retain the labor potential and sexual availability of their former female slaves, were clever enough to understand that by reframing their previous labor and sexual relations within the institution of customary marriage, they would legally retain the same levels of control they had always enjoyed. It would not have surprised those present at the time that the payment of bridewealth to secure an unwilling former slave "bride" was an attempt to repurchase within the new framework of marriage what had always been his property under the framework of legal slavery. The woman herself was most aware that this was not a marriage at all but rather a thinly veiled ruse to newly legitimize her enslavement within a different, legally binding social institution. Roberts has shown evidence that some of these unconsenting "brides" were able to secure divorces in court. Surely though others were less able. And it is to those others, those who were prevented through violence or its threat from walking away from the marriage that enslaved them, that our attention should be most closely drawn. It is virtually impossible to find these women's voices in the historical record.

However, the voices of women today who share similar stories are perhaps our truest guides for how to use the momentum gained through the insights present in this volume on the past and present enslavement and trafficking of women and children in Africa to combat the enslavement and trafficking of women and children in marriage in Africa today. Take, for example, a modern-day parallel to Bessey Assor, as described by Ray: the well-documented case of "Evie" from Nigeria, whose father promised her to be the youngest bride to a village elder in exchange for money and political power.[8] The first time she met the man, she begged him to reconsider—after all, the ceremony had not yet taken place. He raped her to demonstrate the certainty of his purchase. When she told her parents, her shame was met by her father's bitter warning that if she continued to resist, then the village elders would bury her alive. Neither her father nor the elders would suffer any consequences for her murder, since they were simply upholding his honor within the community. Her father made it very clear to Evie that there was no escape from this marriage. The transaction took place when she was a very young child. The bride-price was paid.

The difference between the legal purchase of an unwilling slave and the legally enforceable payment of bride-price to gain an unconsenting bride is no less ambiguous today than it was then. The only difference is the relative distance from the time when slavery was legal. It is our memory that has failed us. It is this volume that drives us forward.

TABLE 12.1

2009 levels of corruption and slavery for 177 countries

Level of slavery in country (%)

	NONE	RARE OR VERY LITTLE	PERSISTENT LOW LEVEL	REGULAR SLAVERY IN A FEW SECTORS	IN MANY SECTORS	TOTAL % (NO. OF NATIONS)
Low corruption	47.3%	52.7%	0	0	0	100.0% (29)
Moderate corruption	32.8%	34.4%	21.8%	6.3%	4.7%	100.0% (64)
High corruption	3.6%	19.0%	44.0%	19.1%	14.3%	99.9% (84)

Note: An annual report by Transparency International scores most of the countries in the world on their level of corruption. The relationship between corruption and slavery is statistically significant at greater than the .001 level (chi-square = 66.68, df = 8), and the Spearman's correlation coefficient is .589, also significant at greater than the .001 level.

TABLE 12.2

Current levels of poverty and slavery for 193 countries

Level of slavery in country (%)

	NONE	RARE OR VERY LITTLE	PERSISTENT LOW LEVEL	REGULAR SLAVERY IN A FEW SECTORS	IN MANY SECTORS	TOTAL % (NO. OF NATIONS)
Extreme poverty	0%	3.2%	48.4%	32.3%	16.1%	100.0% (31)
Moderate poverty	13.8%	17.2%	24.2%	17.2%	27.6%	100.0% (29)
Low income	21.2%	33.3%	39.4%	1.6%	4.5%	100.0% (66)
Middle income	30.0%	55.0%	10.0%	5.0%	0%	100.0% (47)
Rich nations	20.2%	30.1%	30.0%	10.9%	8.8%	100.0% (20)

Note: Poverty is measured by a country's gross domestic product. The relationship between poverty and slavery is statistically significant at greater than the .001 level (chi-square = 76.44, df = 16), and the Spearman's correlation coefficient is –.496, also significant at greater than the .001 level.

TABLE 12.3

Current levels of debt and slavery for 204 countries

Level of slavery in country (%)

	NONE	RARE OR VERY LITTLE	PERSISTENT LOW LEVEL	REGULAR SLAVERY IN A FEW SECTORS	IN MANY SECTORS	TOTAL % (NO. OF NATIONS)
High-debt countries	2.6%	5.3%	42.1%	26.3%	23.7%	100.0% (38)
All other countries	25.3%	36.2%	25.9%	7.8%	4.8%	100.00% (166)

Note: The relationship between debt and slavery is statistically significant at greater than the .001 level (chi-square = 42.62, df = 4), and the Spearman's correlation coefficient is .433, also significant at greater than the .001 level.

NOTES

1. Human Rights Watch, *Off the Backs of Children: Forced Begging and Other Abuses against Talibés in Senegal* (New York: Human Rights Watch, 2010), 2.

2. Claire Cody, "Birth Registration: A Tool for Prevention, Protection and Prosecution," in *Child Slavery Now: A Contemporary Reader*, ed. Gary Craig (Bristol: Policy Press, 2010), 175–88.

3. For a further discussion of debt overhang, see Jeffrey Sachs, *The End of Poverty: Economic Possibilities for Our Time* (New York: Penguin, 2005).

4. Robert B. Smith, "Global Human Development: Accounting for Its Regional Disparities," *Quality and Quantity*, 43, no. 1 (2009): 1–34.

5. Gwyn Campbell, Suzanne Miers, and Joseph C. Miller, eds., *Women and Slavery*, vol. 1, *Africa, the Indian Ocean World, and the Medieval North Atlantic* (Athens: Ohio University Press, 2007).

6. Mike Dottridge, *Kids as Commodities? Child Trafficking and What to Do about It* (Lausanne: International Federation Terre des Hommes, 2004), 20.

7. See Catherine Coquery-Vidrovitch, "Women, Marriage, and Slavery in Sub-Saharan Africa in the Nineteenth Century," in Campbell, Miers, and Miller, *Women and Slavery*, 48. For examples within colonial French West Africa, see Richard L. Roberts, "Voices of Slavery in the Colonial Courts of French West Africa in the Aftermath of Slavery," paper presented at the Tales of Slavery: Narratives of Slavery, the Slave Trade, and Enslavement in Africa Conference, University of Toronto, 23 May 2009.

8. Jody Sarich and Kevin Bales, "Gaining Freedom through a 'Well-Founded Fear': Uncovering the Voices of Modern Slaves in Asylum Applications in the United States," paper presented at the Tales of Slavery conference, University of Toronto, 21 May 2009.

Selected Bibiliography

This bibliography is in no way an exhaustive list of the sources consulted for this book. Rather, we invited the contributors to submit their recommendations for the most important publications pertaining to their respective areas.

Akullo, Margaret, and Peter Spindler. "Paladin Child: A Partnership Study of Child Migration to the UK via London Heathrow." London: New Scotland Yard. Unpublished, 2004. Copy filed with authors.

Allais, Carol, et al. *Tsireledzani: Understanding the Dimensions of Human Trafficking in Southern Africa.* Pretoria: National Prosecuting Authority of South Africa, 2010.

Argenti, Nicolas. "Things That Don't Come by the Road: Folktales, Fosterage, and Memories of Slavery in the Cameroon Grassfields." *Comparative Studies in Society and History* 52, no. 2 (2010): 224–54.

Bermúdez, Laura Gauer. "*No Experience Necessary*": *The Internal Trafficking of Persons in South Africa.* Pretoria: International Organization for Migration, 2008.

Brunschvig, R., "Abd," H. A. R. Gibb, et al., eds. *Encyclopaedia of Islam,* new ed., 1:24–41. Leiden: Brill, 1960.

Burrill, Emily S. "'Wives of Circumstance': Gender and Slave Emancipation in Late Nineteenth-century Senegal," *Slavery and Abolition* 29, no. 1 (2008): 49–64.

Burrill, Emily S., Richard Roberts, and Elizabeth Thornberry, eds. *Domestic Violence and the Law in Africa: Historical and Contemporary Perspectives.* Athens: Ohio University Press, 2010.

Campbell, Gwyn. ed. *Abolition and Its Aftermath in Indian Ocean Africa and Asia.* New York: Routledge, 2005.

———, ed. *The Structure of Slavery in Indian Ocean Africa and Asia.* London: Frank Cass, 2004.

Campbell, Gwyn, Suzanne Miers, and Joseph C. Miller, eds. *Women and Slavery.* Vol.1, *Africa, the Indian Ocean World, and the Medieval North Atlantic.* Athens: Ohio University Press, 2007.

Child Exploitation and Online Protection Centre. "A Scoping Project on Child Trafficking in the UK." London: CEOP, 2007.

———. "Strategic Threat Assessment: Child Trafficking in the UK." London: CEOP, 2010.

Clarence-Smith, W. G. *Islam and the Abolition of Slavery.* London: Hurst, 2006.

Coe, Cati. "Domestic Violence and Child Circulation in the Southeastern Gold Coast, 1905–28." In Burrill, Roberts, and Thornberry, *Domestic Violence.*

Diouf, Sylviane A., ed. *Fighting the Slave Trade: West African Strategies.* Athens: Ohio University Press, 2003.

Eltis, David. *Economic Growth and the Ending of the Transatlantic Slave Trade.* Oxford: Oxford University Press, 1987.

Eltis, David, and Stanley L. Engerman. "Fluctuations in Sex and Age Ratios in the Transatlantic Slave Trade, 1663–1864." *Economic History Review* 46, no. 2 (1993): 308–23.

European Union Agency for Fundamental Rights. *Child Trafficking in the EU: Challenges, Perspectives and Good Practices.* Luxembourg: Office for Official Publications of the European Communities, 2009.

Falola, Toyin, and Paul E. Lovejoy, eds. *Pawnship in Africa: Debt Bondage in Historical Perspective.* Boulder: Westview, 1994.

Ferreira, Roquinaldo. "The Suppression of the Slave Trade and Slave Departures from Angola, 1830s–1860s." In *Extending the Frontiers: Essays on the New Transatlantic Slave Trade Database,* ed. David Eltis and David Richardson. New Haven: Yale University Press, 2008.

Freamon, Bernard K. "Slavery, Freedom, and the Doctrine of Consensus in Islamic Jurisprudence." *Harvard Human Rights Journal* 11, no. 1 (1998): 1–64.

Gallagher, Anne T. *The International Law of Human Trafficking.* Cambridge: Cambridge University Press, 2010.

Glassman, Jonathon. *Feasts and Riot: Revelry, Rebellion, and Popular Consciousness on the Swahili Coast, 1856–1888.* Portsmouth, NH: Heinemann, 1995.

Hair, P. E. H. "The Enslavement of Koelle's Informants." *Journal of African History* 6, no. 2 (1965): 193–203.

Harris, David, Ralph Sandland, and Margaret Akullo. *Thematic Study on Child Trafficking: United Kingdom.* Brussels: European Fundamental Rights Agency, 2009.

Herlin, Susan J. "Brazil and the Commercialization of Kongo, 1840–1870." In *Enslaving Connections: Changing Cultures of Africa and Brazil during the Era of Slavery,* ed. José Curto and Paul Lovejoy. Amherst, NY: Humanity Books, 2004.

Hunwick, John. "Black Africans in the Mediterranean World: Introduction to a Neglected Aspect of the African Diaspora." In *The Human Commodity: Perspectives on the Trans-Saharan Slave Trade,* ed. Elizabeth Savage. London: Frank Cass, 1992.

Jayasuriya, Shihan, and Richard Pankhurst, eds. *The African Diaspora in the Indian Ocean.* Trenton: Africa World Press, 2003.

Klein, Herbert. "African Women in the Atlantic Slave Trade." In Robertson and Klein, *Women and Slavery,* 29–38.

Klein, Martin A. *Slavery and Colonial Rule in French West Africa.* Cambridge: Cambridge University Press, 1998.

Klein, Martin A., and Richard L. Roberts. "The Resurgence of Pawning in French West Africa during the Depression of the 1930s." In Falola and Lovejoy, *Pawnship in Africa,* 303–20.

MacGaffey, Wyatt. "Kongo Slavery Remembered by Themselves: Texts from 1915." *International Journal of African Historical Studies* 41, no. 1 (2008): 55–76.

Martens, Jonathan, Maciej Pieczkowski, and Bernadette van Vuuren-Smyth. *Seduction, Sale, and Slavery: Trafficking in Women and Children for Sexual*

Exploitation in Southern Africa. 3rd ed. PDF version. Pretoria: International Organization for Migration, 2003.

Médard, Henri, and Shane Doyle, eds. *Slavery in the Great Lakes Region of East Africa.* Athens: Ohio University Press, 2007.

Miers, Suzanne. "Contemporary Forms of Slavery." In "On Slavery and Islam in African History: A Tribute to Martin Klein," special issue, *Canadian Journal of African Studies / Revue canadienne des études africaines* 34, no. 3 (2000): 714–47.

Miers, Suzanne, and Igor Kopytoff, eds. *Slavery in Africa: Historical and Anthropological Perspectives.* Madison: University of Wisconsin Press, 1977.

Naanan, Benedict. "'Itinerant Gold Mines': Prostitution in the Cross River Basin of Nigeria, 1930–1950." *African Studies Review* 34, no. 2 (1991): 57–79.

Northrup, David. *Indentured Labor in the Age of Imperialism, 1834–1922.* Cambridge: Cambridge University Press, 1995.

Renault, François. *Libération d'esclaves et nouvelle servitude: Les rachats de captifs africains pour le compte des colonies françaises après l'abolition de l'esclavage.* Abidjan: Nouvelles Éditions Africaines, 1976.

Roberts, Richard. "The End of Slavery, Colonial Courts, and Social Conflicts in Gumbu, 1908–1911." In "On Slavery and Islam in African History: A Tribute to Martin Klein," special issue, *Canadian Journal of African Studies / Revue canadienne des études africaines* 34, no. 3 (2000): 684–713.

Robertson Claire C., and Martin A. Klein, eds. *Women and Slavery in Africa.* (Portsmouth, NH: Heinemann, 1983).

Rodet, Marie. "Continuum of Gendered Violence: The Colonial Invention of Female Desertion as a Customary Criminal Offense, French Soudan, 1900–1949." In Burrill, Roberts, and Thornberry, *Domestic Violence,* 74–93.

———. *Les migrantes ignorées du Haut-Sénégal, 1900–1946.* Paris: Karthala, 2009.

Romero, Patricia W. *Lamu: History, Society, and Family in an East African Port City.* Princeton: Markus Wiener, 1997.

Sheriff, Abdul. *Slaves, Spices and Ivory in Zanzibar.* London: James Currey, 1987.

Songololo, Molo. *The Trafficking of Children for Purposes of Sexual Exploitation—South Africa.* Cape Town: Molo Songololo, 2000.

Strobel, Margaret. *Muslim Women in Mombasa, 1890–1975.* New Haven: Yale University Press, 1979.

United Nations Children's Fund. *Child Trafficking in Europe: A Broad Vision to Put Children First, 2007.* Florence: UNICEF, Innocenti Research Centre, 2008.

———. *Trafficking in Human Beings, Especially Women and Children, in Africa.* Florence: UNICEF, Innocenti Research Centre, 2003.

United Nations Office on Drugs and Crime. *The Globalization of Crime: A Transnational Organized Crime Threat Assessment.* Vienna: UNODC, 2010.

———. *Global Report on Trafficking in Persons.* Vienna: UNODC, 2009.

———. *Trafficking in Persons: Global Patterns.* Vienna: UNODC, 2006.

Vos, Jelmer. "Child Slaves and Freemen at the Spiritan Mission in Soyo, 1880–1885." *Journal of Family History* 35, no. 1 (2010): 71–90.

Wright, Marcia. *Strategies of Slaves and Women: Life-Stories from East/Central Africa.* London: James Currey, 1993.

Contributors

MARGARET AKULLO is the regional project coordinator for a child sex tourism and child-trafficking initiative with the UN Office on Drugs and Crime, Regional Centre for East Asia and the Pacific, and a PhD student at Loughborough University. She is the coauthor, with David Harris and Ralph Sandland, of FRA *Thematic Study on Child Trafficking (United Kingdom)* (2009) and author of "Child Trafficking: A Metropolitan Police Perspective," *Siak-Journal: Zeitschrift für Polizeiwissenschaft und polizeiliche Praxis.* Akullo was a contributor to the recent publication by UNICEF, *Child Safety Online: Global Challenges and Strategies* (2011). E-mail: margaret.akullo@unodc.org.

JEAN ALLAIN is professor of law and director of the Human Rights Center, Queen's University, Belfast, and Extraordinary Professor, Centre for Human Rights, Faculty of Law, University of Pretoria. He is the author of several monographs, including *The Slavery Conventions* (2008) and *Slavery in International Law* (2012), and has published in the leading international law journals on issues of slavery and human exploitation. Allain was a Leverhulme Research Fellow (2010–11), researching the law of slavery in domestic jurisdictions and headed a research network funded by the British Arts and Humanities Research Council network setting out the parameters of the 1926 definition of slavery (2009–11). E-mail: j.allain@qub.ac.uk.

KEVIN BALES is professor at the Wilberforce Institute for the Study of Slavery and Emancipation and president of Free the Slaves. His book, *Disposable People: New Slavery in the Global Economy*, was nominated for a Pulitzer Prize and has been published in eleven languages. Desmond Tutu called it "a well researched, scholarly and deeply disturbing exposé of modern slavery." Dr. Bales served as a consultant to the UN Global Program on Human Trafficking and has advised the US, British, Irish, Norwegian, and Nepali governments, as well as the ECOWAS Community, on slavery and human trafficking policy. The film based on his book, which he co-wrote, won a Peabody Award and two Emmy Awards. He was awarded the Premio Viareggio for services to humanity in 2000. In 2005, he published *Understanding Global Slavery*. His work on slavery was named one of the "100 World-Changing Discoveries" by the Association of British Universities in 2006. His book *Ending Slavery:*

How We Free Today's Slaves was published in September 2007. In 2008, he published *To Plead Our Own Cause: Personal Stories by Today's Slaves* with Zoe Trodd, and *Documenting Disposable People: Contemporary Global Slavery* with seven Magnum photographers. In 2009, he published *The Slave Next Door: Modern Slavery in the United States* with Ron Soodalter, and *Modern Slavery: The Secret World of 27 Million People* with Zoe Trodd and Alex Kent Williamson. Dr. Bales presented on modern slavery at the 2010 TED Conference. He received the $100,000 University of Louisville Grawemeyer Award for "Ideas Improving World Order" in 2011. He is currently writing a book on the relationship of slavery and environmental destruction and, with Jody Sarich, a book exploring forced marriage worldwide.

LIZA BUCHBINDER recently completed her doctorate in medical anthropology in a joint PhD program at the University of California, San Francisco (UCSF) and UC Berkeley, and will be returning to her medical studies at UCSF. Her dissertation focused on the limits of naming violence against adolescent domestic servants through the rights discourse on child trafficking and called for alternative frameworks to address child labor exploitation in West Africa. E-mail: liza@berkeley.edu.

BERNARD K. FREAMON is professor of law and director of the Zanzibar Program on Modern Day Slavery and Human Trafficking at Seton Hall Law School. He teaches courses on Islamic jurisprudence, evidence, civil rights, and slavery. He is currently pursuing a major research and writing project on the abolition of slavery in the Islamic world. His forthcoming book, *Islam, Slavery, and Empire in the Indian Ocean World*, is the first installment in that effort. A member of the American Law Institute, Freamon has been a fellow at the Gilder Lehrman Center for the Study of Slavery, Resistance, and Abolition, Yale University. E-mail: Bernard.Freamon@shu.edu.

SUSAN KRESTON is a legal consultant to the UN, US, and foreign governmental departments, and to NGOs on trafficking in persons and violence against women and children. She was Fulbright Professor of Law and Psychology in South Africa (2005–8). She continues her work in southern Africa as a research fellow at the University of KwaZulu-Natal. Kreston has served as deputy director of the US National Center for Prosecution of Child Abuse. She began her career as a sex crimes prosecutor and then moved to England, where she taught human rights law at the University of Sussex. E-mail: susankreston@gmail.com.

BENJAMIN N. LAWRANCE holds the Barber B. Conable, Jr. Endowed Chair in International Studies at the Rochester Institute of Technology. His interests include comparative and contemporary slavery, child trafficking, and asylum claims. He is currently writing a history of nineteenth- and twentieth-century West African child trafficking with the support of a faculty fellowship from the National Endowment for the Humanities. He is the author of *Locality, Mobility, and "Nation"* (2007), editor of *The Ewe of Togo and Benin* (2005), and coeditor, with Emily Osborn and Richard Roberts, of *Intermediaries, Interpreters, and Clerks* (2006). Recent essays have appeared in *International Labor and Working-Class History* (2010), *Food and Foodways* (2011), and the *Seattle Journal for Social Justice* (2011). Lawrance is a consultant on contemporary politics and society in West Africa. He has served as an expert witness for over one hundred and forty asylum claims of West Africans in North American and European courts, and his opinions feature in appellate rulings in the United States and the UK. The recipient of several awards—including fellowships at Yale's Gilder Lehrman Center for the Study of Slavery, Resistance, and Abolition, Harvard's W. E. B. DuBois Institute for African and African American Research, and the Joan B. Kroc Center for International Studies at the University of Notre Dame—Lawrance was a Rotary Foundation International Ambassadorial Scholar and a University of California President's Fellow in the Humanities. He supervises PhD students in history, anthropology, political science, and cultural studies. E-mail: BNL@rit.edu.

ELISABETH MCMAHON is assistant professor of history at Tulane University with a PhD in African history from Indiana University. She taught at various schools, including the Behrend College of Penn State and the University of Illinois, Urbana-Champaign, before coming to Tulane in 2007. Her research, funded by a Fulbright IIE Fellowship and Indiana and Tulane Universities, focuses on the gendered social dynamics of the abolition of slavery for all strata of society living on Pemba Island, in Tanzania. She has published articles in the *International Journal of African Historical Studies*, the *Journal of Women's History*, *Quaker History*, and the *Women's History Review*. E-mail: emcmahon@tulane.edu.

CARINA RAY is assistant professor of African history at Fordham University. She is the coeditor, with Salah Hassan, of *Darfur and the Crisis of Governance in Sudan* (2009) and, with Jeremy Rich, of *Navigating African Maritime History* (2010) and is the author of "The 'White Wife Problem': Sex, Race, and the Contested Politics of Repatriation to Interwar British West Africa" (2009). Her forthcoming book is *Crossing the Color Line: Interracial Sex and the Contested Politics of Colonial Rule in Ghana*. E-mail: caray@fordham.edu.

RICHARD L. ROBERTS is the Frances and Charles Field Professor in History, professor of African history, and director of the Center for African

Studies, Stanford University. He has published numerous articles and ten books, including, *Domestic Violence and the Law in Colonial and Postcolonial Africa* (with Emily Burrill and Liz Thornberry, 2010); *Intermediaries, Interpreters and Clerks* (with Emily Osborn and Benjamin N. Lawrance, 2006); *Litigants and Households: African Disputes and Colonial Courts in the French Soudan, 1895–1912* (2005); *Two Worlds of Cotton* (1996); *Cotton, Colonialism, and Social History in Sub-Saharan Africa* (with Allen Isaacman, 1995); *Law in Colonial Africa* (with Kristin Mann, 1991); *The End of Slavery in Africa*, with Suzanne Miers (1988); *Warriors, Merchants, and Slaves: The State and the Economy of the Middle Niger Valley, 1700–1914* (1987). He has supervised over thirty PhD students, has served on the board of the African Studies Association, and has held fellowships from the NEH, the SSRC, the Stanford Humanities Center, and the École des Hauts Études en Sciences Sociales, Paris. E-mail: rroberts@stanford.edu.

MARIE RODET is lecturer in African history at the School of Oriental and African Studies, University of London. Her principal research interests lie in migration history, gender studies, and the history of slavery in West Africa in the nineteenth and twentieth centuries. Her most recent publications include *Les migrantes ignorées du Haut-Sénégal* (2009) and "Mémoires de l'esclavage dans la région de Kayes: Histoire d'une disparition," in *Cahiers d'études africaines* (2010). E-mail: mr28@soas.ac.uk

JODY SARICH is currently the Director of Research at Free the Slaves, a nonprofit organization whose mission is to end all forms of human slavery. She has thirteen years of experience in antislavery research and advocacy, as an educator, academic, and legal advocate. Focusing on slavery and servitude in sub-Saharan Africa, she received her MA in African History from the School of Oriental and African Studies in 1999. She received her JD, with a concentration in International and Comparative Law, from DePaul University School of Law in 2010. She has represented women seeking asylum in the United States under the Convention Against Torture and has served as an expert witness for women who sought asylum in the United States after having fled forced marriages in their home countries. Ms. Sarich is currently completing her PhD thesis on slavery in South Africa and writing a book, with Kevin Bales, exploring forced marriage worldwide.

JELMER VOS is assistant professor in the Department of History at Old Dominion University. He received his PhD from the School of Oriental and African Studies and was a postdoctoral fellow at Emory University and the Universidade Nova de Lisboa. He is currently preparing a manuscript on the history of the Kongo kingdom, northern Angola, under early colonial rule. Another part of his research concentrates on the eighteenth-century slave trade from Liberia and Côte d'Ivoire. His recent publications include "Child Slaves and Freemen at the Spiritan Mission in Soyo, 1880–1885," *Journal of Family History* (2010), and "Of Stocks and Barter: John Hold and the Kongo Rubber Trade, 1906–10," *Portuguese Studies Review* (2011). E-mail: jvos@odu.edu.

Index